FOREIGN POLICY MAKING AND
THE AMERICAN POLITICAL SYSTEM

———————

Foreign Policy Making and the American Political System

THIRD EDITION

James A. Nathan
and James K. Oliver

THE JOHNS HOPKINS UNIVERSITY PRESS
BALTIMORE AND LONDON

To Lisa, Alex, and Michael
And to Carol

© 1983, 1987, 1994 The Johns Hopkins University Press
All rights reserved
Printed in the United States of America on acid-free paper

First edition published 1983, Little, Brown & Co.
Second edition published 1987, Harper Collins, Inc.
Third edition published 1994, The Johns Hopkins University Press
05 04 03 02 01 00 99 98 97 96   6 5 4 3 2

The Johns Hopkins University Press
2715 North Charles Street
Baltimore, Maryland 21218-4319
The Johns Hopkins University Press Ltd., London

ISBN 0-8018-4771-0
ISBN 0-8018-4772-9 (pbk.)

Library of Congress Cataloging-in-Publication Data
will be found at the end of this book.
A catalog entry for this book is available from the British Library.

CONTENTS

PREFACE

IN A RUSH of remarkable events between February 1989 and August 1991 the cold war ended. The world looked on in amazement and wonder as the people of Central Europe resolutely, and for the most part peacefully, brought down the Stalinist regimes that had dominated the region for forty-five years. When, in the fall of 1989, Germans by the hundreds of thousands quite literally began pulling the Berlin Wall apart piece by piece and moved freely through the Brandenburg Gate, even the most cynical and jaded observers were forced to concede that profound changes were coursing through the international system.

But there were more amazing events yet. In the summer of 1991 the Soviet Union itself vanished—again peacefully—as Communist party hardliners, confronted by peaceful mass demonstrations in Moscow, Leningrad (soon to be renamed St. Petersburg), and elsewhere, failed in an attempt to overthrow Mikhail Gorbachev. By year's end Gorbachev had resigned as president, for the Soviet Union itself was voted out of existence by the Soviet parliament, to be replaced by a weak Commonwealth of Independent States wherein each of the constituent republics of the old Soviet Union became fully independent. In due course, Russia, the largest of the successor states, negotiated with the United States major reductions in strategic forces and haltingly began a process of restructuring its domestic political economy.

Although almost hyperactive in its global engagement throughout the cold war, the American foreign policy elite seemed stunned and paralyzed by its sudden end. First the Reagan administration and then the Bush administration reacted with deep suspicion and even disbelief as Mikhail Gorbachev called for a restructuring of Soviet society and East-West relations; began the drawing down of Soviet power in Central Europe; and then refused to intervene as Poland, Czechoslovakia, Hungary, Rumania, Bulgaria, and, what was most stunning, East Germany succumbed to the revolutions of 1989–90. Only after Gorbachev was himself being pulled under by revolution did Reagan and Bush become enthusiasts of the failing Soviet president.

Subsequently, Bush proclaimed a "new world order," but American policy lacked a focus comparable to the great effort mounted in the wake of World War II. Then, the architects of American foreign policy formulated the concepts of containment and extended deterrence that defined American policy for the duration of the cold war. Moreover, they modified the institutions and processes of foreign policy making in order to strengthen the hand of the president in the executive-legislative relationship and enhance the executive establishment. At the end of the cold war, however, its curators seemed unable to call forth anything other than the old routines. The war in the Persian Gulf was an impressive display of coalition building and application of firepower. Its outcome clarified little in the new world taking shape in the 1990s.

Notwithstanding the evanescence of the cold war, President Bush insisted that the baseline of military and intelligence capabilities accumulated during the exertions of the preceding forty-five years should not be significantly altered. The uncertainties of the new order required, it was argued, the continued application of the repertories of the past, including, it seemed, the exclusion of Congress from meaningful participation in the great questions of peace and war. Thus when George Bush committed American forces to the Gulf for Operations Desert Shield and Desert Storm, the largest and most complex campaigns since Vietnam, he insisted that he needed no congressional authorization. Congress was granted an eleventh-hour opportunity for an anguished debate and votes, but by that time the president had created facts that made anything other than congressional approbation unlikely.

For their part, the American people were hopeful observers of the drama in Central Europe and the Soviet Union. The Gulf War, fought as it was by large numbers of reservists, including women, and intensively covered by television, albeit under highly restrictive official observation and regulation, was even more commanding of public attention. In the aftermath of the Gulf War, the public's preoccupations turned to what many feared was a diminished American society facing an uncertain future constrained by debt and a deteriorating national infrastructure.

Not a few in the public and among the opinion leaders and the policy elite saw the problematic future resulting from the burdens of American foreign engagement during the cold war. People seemed to understand the inevitability of U.S. global involvement in the post–cold war world. Their judgments concerning that involvement were not yet formed, however, and they were not inclined to turn enthusiastically to a distant national leadership calling for yet more unexplained global activism. In fact, there was no coherent discussion of American foreign interests and policy by any candidate during the first post–cold war presidential election, in 1992.

The political leadership of the United States has therefore been presented with numerous opportunities to define and pursue a new course for American foreign policy, but a less than clear vision has been forthcoming. Instead, concerns about the deadlock affecting the American system abound. Skepticism concerning the creativity and competence of the American system at this critical juncture is therefore understandable. However, these have long been matters of concern to observers of American society and politics. Thus, early in the nineteenth century Alexis de Tocqueville concluded that American democracy, with its institutional fragmentation and increasingly democratized politics, constituted a "decidedly inferior" system for making and carrying out foreign policy.

This book seeks to examine these concerns by examining the relationship between foreign policy making and the American political system at the end of the cold war. Readers of our earlier assessments of foreign policy making and the American political system will recognize the debt this book owes to those analyses. This, however, is a different book. Some of the earlier historical material is incorporated, but the analysis of the executive establishment, the executive-legislative relationship, and the legal framework of the foreign policy process have been thoroughly reworked and emphasize the situation at the end of the cold war. Similarly, the treatment of public opinion, foreign policy lobbying, and the exercise of private power represents new material. The analysis of the relationships between the media, the president, and the people have been recast to reflect the situation at the onset of the post–cold war era.

As in the past, we have been encouraged by our many colleagues and students. The "IR Group" at the University of Delaware—Kurt Burch, Ken Campbell, Bob Denemark, and Bill Meyer—have been especially generous with their time and professional judgments. Moreover, in preparing this book, we have had the pleasure of working with a most supportive editorial group at the Johns Hopkins University Press. Most notable in this regard, Henry Tom and his assistant, Gregg Wilhelm, have been patient overseers of the project. We are deeply appreciative of their interest and assistance. We are also grateful for the support of the Eminent Scholar's Chair at Auburn University, Montgomery. We are, of course, solely responsible for the outcome.

FOREIGN POLICY MAKING AND
THE AMERICAN POLITICAL SYSTEM

CHAPTER I

Introduction

THIS BOOK IS an examination of the American foreign-policy-making process at the end of the cold war. In much of American foreign policy making there is a tension between "inefficiencies" imposed by the constitutional framework and the imperatives imposed by a globalist foreign policy. The routines and institutions developed in the last half-century were to meet persistent challenges abroad. Most policymakers realized that in confronting a threat of apocalyptic proportions America might lose the freedoms it sought to protect. By and large, however, most officials felt there was little choice but to adopt, from time-to-time, some of the expediencies of America's rivals.[1] A cumbersome eighteenth-century design was modified under the press of constant cold war into something that policymakers hoped would be more efficient. At the end of the cold war the system's efficiency remains in doubt; its relevance to the future, problematical; and the state of the democracy whose values the foreign-policy-making system is to protect and advance, uncertain.

THE DOMESTIC CONTEXT
OF FOREIGN POLICY MAKING

In comparison with other political systems the American constitutional framework has proved remarkably stable and resilient. Yet observers tend to concur with Alexis de Tocqueville's judgment that in matters pertaining to the conduct of foreign affairs, American democracy—indeed, all democracies—constituted a "decidedly inferior" form of government.[2] This classic concern about American democracy, reiterated by American textbook writers during the cold war,[3] has focused on three elements of the policy-making process:

I

1. The constitutional and institutional framework of American government, what James Madison termed the "partial mixture of powers" between Congress and the president
2. The foreign- and national-security-policy bureaucracy that developed as a corollary to America's expanding world role in the post–World War II era
3. The character and role of public opinion in American society

The Constitutional and Institutional Framework

The men who drafted the U.S. Constitution were not insensitive to the complexities and dangers of international relations. They understood that, as Alexander Hamilton put it, "the causes of hostility among nations are innumerable."[4] With the exception of Thomas Jefferson, few of the Founding Fathers experienced what Hamilton called those "reveries which would seduce us into an expectation of peace and cordiality." National security, what John Jay and others called our national "safety,"[5] required a chief executive able to respond to security threats and conduct diplomacy with dispatch. In sum, most of the Founding Fathers were pragmatists.

The institutional design problem was to establish a framework that was stronger than the Articles of Confederation, that is, one that provided for greater capacity in the national government, but not so strong as to threaten liberty. The framers of the Constitution responded by establishing a fragmented national government. Thus Congress and the president shared the most important roles in the formulation and conduct of foreign affairs.

Although the president was given the authority and responsibility to conduct war and diplomacy, the authority to commence war and commit the nation to significant foreign undertakings was reserved to Congress. The president was the commander in chief and responsible for the negotiation of treaties and the day-to-day conduct of diplomacy, but Congress tendered its advice and consent to treaties before they became the law of the land. Moreover, Congress maintained the Army and the Navy, declared war, and authorized limited, or in the argot of eighteenth-century international law, "imperfect," wars.[6]

The system was understood to be cumbersome, even inefficient, but as Madison argued when he spoke of the separation of the various branches in *The Federalist,* "Unless these departments be so far connected and blended as to give to each a constitutional control over the others, the degree of separation . . . essential to a free government, can never in practice be duly maintained."[7] The framers of the Constitution were not, therefore, unaware of the problems posed by the institutional structure they had created. But they hoped that America's geographic isolation, combined with a concentration on what was assumed to be the greatest American international asset, namely, fruitful commercial relations with the rest of the world, would save the new republic from the endemic international suspicions and wars of the Old World. The European system required military preparedness. The threat and use of military force rewarded strong monarchs and ministers who were capable of annulling individual liberty, if they allowed it at all. The European systems were, in short, the very forms of government Americans had rebelled against and abandoned.

The hopes that America would be utterly different were frustrated from the outset. Commercial relations required open seas; and the new leadership of America soon discovered that the safe conduct of commerce could be secured only by force, often at considerable distance from American waters. Although Americans wished to escape from the taint of Europe, Europe would not leave North America alone. The international politics of the Napoleonic era reached across the Atlantic. In the early nineteenth century the acquisition and opening up of the remainder of the continent itself led to conflicting American and European interests. As a result, war became a part of the new republic's experience almost from the beginning. And at every turn of foreign and military relations for the next 150 years, Americans found their fragmented executive-legislative relations a source of difficulty.

Bureaucratic Power and Politics

Within the executive itself, the pursuit of an internationalist foreign policy led to major institutional change. By 1947 President Truman had asked Congress to reorganize the executive branch. The National Security Act of 1947 established a new Department of Defense (DOD), a centralized intelligence establishment under a new Central Intelligence Agency (CIA), and a new National Security Council (NSC) to serve as a means for facilitating the integration of American foreign and defense policy.

Throughout the succeeding decades the executive national-security-policy establishment grew as the American world role expanded. An enlarged bureaucratic architecture augments the capacity of the president to conduct American foreign policy. At the same time, however, tens of thousands of people organized within scores of departments are an important constraint on the policy-making process.

The sheer number of departments inevitably means that many perspectives must somehow coexist. Thus, for example, early in the Reagan administration the secretaries of defense (Caspar Weinberger) and state (George Shultz) disputed the idea of arms-control negotiations with the Soviet Union, the substance of arms-control talks, and even whether existing arms-control treaties and understandings should be maintained. Secretary of State Shultz urged caution in renouncing any arms agreement, given the sensitivities of America's European associates to the appearance of a recrudescent cold war.[8] In contrast, Secretary of Defense Weinberger argued that U.S. defense required immediate deployment of almost any weapon the United States designed or developed and that U.S. decision making should not be influenced unduly by the Europeans.

Predictable, if not inevitable, personal rivalries and ambitions compound the problem of organizational fragmentation.[9] Substantive policy disputes sometimes become indistinguishable from individual attempts to control the flow of information to the president or to control the implementation of presidential decisions. Bureaucratic perception of American interests is also colored by the desire to protect the organization in which one works. Threats or opportunities tend to be defined, therefore, in a manner that can be most effectively dealt with by one's own agency, thereby enhancing the organization's budget and personnel. To the extent that the national security establishment responds to organizational and personal interests, the president faces significant obstacles in making coherent policy.[10]

The problem has at least two dimensions. First, the president must draw out analysis that will inevitably be influenced in some measure by organizational interests. Then, he must fashion and implement a policy with the help of his closest advisers, who in some measure always reflect the perspective of their respective organizations—State, Defense, the CIA, and others. In sum, even if the struggle between the president and Congress for control of the policy-making process were resolved, the constraints of bureaucratic power would remain.[11]

Democracy and the Policy-Making Process

One of the distinguishing characteristics of democratic government is the presumption that those who rule should be accountable to those who are ruled; moreover, people are assumed to have a right to participate, either directly or through representatives, in decisions that affect their lives. Clearly, decisions concerning foreign and national security policy affect the lives of Americans. Yet in perhaps no other area of public policy has the realization of democratic ideals proved more troublesome.

Democratic norms of accountability, participation, and representation do not mean that the people are omniscient. Rather, the presumption is that through the course of open and public debate facilitated by an unencumbered press a more or less wise and prudent course of action can be set. In a nuclear age, however, the domain of international politics has been commonly viewed as uniquely dangerous. Moreover, the sheer quantity of information, the subtlety of the judgments that must be made, and the delicacy of the relationships in this singularly threatening arena are frequently viewed as beyond the capacities of ordinary people. Foreign policy is thus seen as necessarily devolving to a specialized establishment with the necessary training, experience, and wisdom.

But if the exigencies of international politics are acutely demanding, should not policymakers be relieved of the constraints demanded by democratic theory? Is it not the case that full and open debate endanger the country? Do the demands of periodic elections not prove disruptive and debilitating and contribute to gross inconsistencies in policy? These disturbing questions are made all the more difficult by the apparent ignorance of the American people about public affairs in general and foreign affairs in particular. Policymakers fear that this ignorance may lead to volatility, which can put at risk laboriously constructed and delicately balanced international relations.[12] To be sure, some students of American public opinion have concluded that levels of public information about foreign affairs have increased during the last decades. Moreover, the public seems to have a reasonably sophisticated understanding of the problems confronting the United States in its foreign relations. Above all, more professional analysts of the American public are coming to support the view that the people are capable of forming coherent and generally prudent judgments about frustratingly complex questions when they are provided information and a full public debate.[13]

Whatever the arguments of social scientists and philosophers, to the extent that policymakers *believe* that the people are ignorant, even dangerous, the relationship between leadership and the people is problematical. If presidents, for example, believe that policy departures must be sold to an ignorant, uncomprehending, and resistant populace, the danger exists that threats will be overstated and dangers magnified in order to mobilize popular support. The reverse may also prove to be true: if one believes that the public is convinced of the necessity for confrontation with the Soviet Union, then efforts to improve relations must be similarly oversold. Thus, John Kennedy's test ban treaty in 1963 and détente and the Strategic Arms Limitation Talks (SALT) in the early 1970s were accompanied by massive public relations campaigns. Finally, there is also the risk that if the public comes to view debate as demagogic manipulation, the result may well be public cynicism and even indifference not only to the issue at hand but to the entire policy-making process.[14]

Finally, in the last decade and a half there has been the globalization of jobs, markets, interest rates, social problems, and even medical ills. The new circumstances surrounding economic interdependence seem likely to result in more public demands on public officials. Indeed, a kind of "distemper of democracy" threatens any coherent American international role.[15] Furthermore, to the extent the management of the international economy is a matter of institutionalized cooperation among many states, some decision making and administration may move to an *international* bureaucracy. The upshot may be an aggravation of the problem of democratic accountability.

Disparate claims for resources and attention jostle one another now, at the end of the cold war, with no self-evident criteria for establishing policy priority. The reduced salience of strategic military issues undercuts the central argument for a national security state. The cold war provided a kind of cement that held together the otherwise fragmented and fissiparous foreign-policy-making process. With the demise of the threat, not only international interests but domestic interests as well are undergoing redefinition. Any battle over resources is messy; without a Soviet menace, new claims on national resources will surely be accompanied by all the discord and acrimony that the Founding Fathers ensured as democracy's lot.

POLICY-MAKING DILEMMAS AND APPROACHES TO ANALYSIS

Understanding policy-making institutions is facilitated by the use of analytical frameworks. In addition to suggesting a set of questions to guide one's analysis, frameworks also suggest relationships, perhaps causal, between subsets of a phenomenon. In this sense, some political scientists have maintained that analytical frameworks hold out the hope of a comprehensive theory of policy making that would explain and perhaps predict policymakers' behavior.

This book does not aspire to the development of a comprehensive theoretical framework. However, the survey that follows developed as a response to a set of substantive and normative concerns. Our inquiry proceeds from Tocqueville's concern about the adequacy of the American system for sustaining a cogent foreign policy while serving the ideals of a democratic republic. Our central concern implies corollary issues: (1) the fragmentation of foreign policy making in the American constitutional design and (2) the demands of democratic theory for accountability to the people.

In much of this book, in one way or the other, we explore the nature and effects of institutional fragmentation. We start with an assumption that the growth of presidential power is an administrative reaction to both institutional fragmentation and the increased American role in the world.[16] But institutional fragmentation is compounded by a large executive branch establishment. Thus, ironically, the vast executive machinery dedicated wholly or in part to foreign policy constrains both the chief executive officer and the policy process.

Next, we turn our attention to the executive-legislative relationship. We trace the decline of Congress as a locus of policy making after World War II as well as its renascence in the wake of the "Vietnam Revolution" in the early and mid-1970s. We give special attention to the prospects for developing a new executive-legislative relationship built around congressional capability in two areas: (1) oversight of the military budget, foreign assistance programs, and the intelligence establishment; and (2) gaining a policy role by means of the War Powers Resolution.

Another level of analysis focuses on the relationship between foreign policy and the demands of democratic accountability. Thus we examine the character of public opinion and the images of the public held by policymakers. We also devote attention to the operation of private power in American foreign policy. We survey the activities of interest groups and examine the close relationship between the government and the arms industry. By considering multinational corporations, we are able to examine a form of private power that can act somewhat independently of any one government and thereby can take on some attributes of a private government.

In sum, this book seeks an overview of the performance, strengths, and weaknesses of the American political system in foreign policy making. The approach taken here relates the operation of foreign policy making to the normative demands of democratic governance. We recognize that any chronicle of the interplay between constitutional demands and the striving for efficient policy cannot be understood without reference to the larger context of fifty years of American policy.[17] But our analysis turns our attention inward to the contemporary balance between institutional capacity for policy making and the demands of democratic accountability.

CHAPTER 2

The Foreign Policy Presidency: Power and Problems

APPROBATION OF presidential power seems to have its own cycle. Harry Truman observed that the president had powers that "would have made Caesar, Genghis Khan or Napoleon bite his nails with envy."[1] In the wake of Vietnam and Watergate there was great concern about executive excess. But by the end of the 1970s, commentators had ceased to write of an "imperial" presidency; instead, they began to fret over the "imperiled" presidency.[2] By the middle of Ronald Reagan's second term the pendulum had swung again, this time toward an expansive vision of the presidency. Journalists again began to refer reverently to the majesty of the office.[3]

President Reagan's coefficient of friction was negligible. Michael Deaver, Reagan's first-term deputy chief of staff, wrote that up until the time that the Iran-Contra scandal materialized, "Ronald Reagan enjoyed the most generous treatment by the press of any President in the postwar era."[4] The Iran-Contra scandal was perhaps as profound an assault on the constitutional framework as the republic had ever suffered. Reagan aides had broken laws, committed acts of war, lied to Congress under oath, and lied to each other.[5] But there was no electoral retribution. Indeed, George Bush, as vice president a key participant in the Iran-Contra scandal, later became president himself and rode to the highest levels of public support in the history of public opinion polling in the wake of the Gulf War in 1991. Later, that support for President Bush faded, and his critics faulted him for his passivity and lack of leadership as the domestic economy slid into recession and the cold war ended.

The cold war presidency has, therefore, always been caught in a paradox. As political scientist Thomas Cronin notes, the presidency is "always too powerful because it is contrary to our ideals of a 'government by the people' . . . yet always inadequate because it seldom achieves our

9

highest hopes."[6] Now that the immediacy of nuclear menace has passed, presidents must make and administer policies in a more complex international environment that is perhaps less responsive to both American power and American interests.[7] The paradox of a powerful and yet constrained foreign policy presidency will therefore persist.

In the chapters that follow we examine the domestic constraints that contribute to the paradox of the foreign policy presidency. The most fundamental constraint of all, of course, is the Constitution's mandate to share foreign policy making with Congress (see chaps. 5–8). But the executive branch itself has proved to be no less a problem. On the one hand, there has been concern about the policy-making and operational capacity of the system. The cold war remedy lay in an expansion of the size and diversity of the bureaucracy under presidential executive authority as the scope and depth of American global involvement increased. At the same time, however, presidents have fretted about the responsiveness of the now larger foreign policy bureaucracy. Thus, between the 1960s and the early 1990s both Democratic and Republican presidents encouraged the development of powerful and virtually autonomous national security advisers and their staffs within the White House. Ostensibly these officials were to aid the president in defining policy options and overseeing policy coordination and implementation. However, during the thirty years between Kennedy and Reagan, roles as policymaker, independent diplomatic agent, and public spokesperson were added to the security advisers' portfolios as presidents sought independent and responsive foreign policy agents. Finally, during the Reagan years this process climaxed in the Iran-Contra scandal, with security advisers and their staffs undertaking covert operations while claiming that they were not bound by constitutional and congressional constraints. Ironically, therefore, the perceived need for presidential control had culminated in a presidency (yet again, as with Vietnam and Watergate) on the verge of going out of constitutional control.

THE POSTWAR FOREIGN POLICY BUREAUCRACY

The close of hostilities following World War II initiated a period of unparalleled U.S. world involvement. At the center of this activity was the Soviet-American relationship, in which military force became the most salient instrument of American foreign policy. The emergence and expansion of powerful new bureaucratic actors, such as the CIA, side by side with the traditional foreign policy units, such as the Department of State, contributed to new policy-making capacity—and problems.

The Cold War Foreign Affairs Machinery

The expansion of the foreign affairs bureaucracy after World War II had two manifestations: a much larger number of people involved in policy; and the organization of these people into an expanded number of departments, agencies, and bureaus charged with separate but often overlapping responsibilities. Before World War II there were fewer than 1,000 people on the rolls of the Department of State, with perhaps another 2,000–3,000 employees serving overseas. Immediately after the war, State added some 7,000 new employees, many from the ranks of the temporary bureaucrats who were employed during the wartime emergency, for example, in the Office of War Information and the Office of Strategic Services.[8] Embassy staffs grew, even though there were fewer embassies, delegations, and consulates after the war. By the end of the 1970s, though it was staffing fewer diplomatic posts, the State Department had grown to more than 23,000.

In 1938 the staff of the secretary's office numbered 21; in the 1970s it exceeded 350. Below the top level, the department has become a mix of geographic and functional bureaus, each headed by an assistant secretary of state. The five geographic bureaus—African, Inter-American, East Asian and Pacific, European, and Near Eastern and South Asian—are made up of scores of country desks, responsible for the daily monitoring of events around the world. The functional bureaus, which deal with congressional relations, intelligence and research, scientific and technological affairs, international organizations, drugs, human rights, and politico-military affairs, are responsible for policies that stretch across not only countries and regions but also other U.S. departments and agencies involved in foreign policy.

Even as President Truman was announcing the global mission of the United States in his Truman Doctrine speech, legislation was submitted to Congress for the National Security Act of 1947, establishing a Department of Defense under civilian leadership and a new intelligence establishment. By the 1980s these intelligence agencies employed eleven times as many people as the State Department employed and had a combined budget at least fourteen times the State Department's. By the 1990s the total intelligence budget (including budgets for the CIA, the National Security Agency (NSA), the National Reconnaissance Office, and the

Defense Intelligence Agency) was reported to be around $28 billion. Breakouts of the overall intelligence budgets are still classified. However, the CIA's budget was said to represent perhaps 15 percent of the overall intelligence funding, and its work force probably numbered 20,000 employees, fewer than half of whom are said to work in the Operations Directorate.[9] The annual cost of the NSA, the nation's code-breaking service, exceeds $4 billion; according to some estimates, it could be as much as $10 billion.[10] But the largest user of intelligence community funds is the Defense Department.[11] During the Reagan years the Pentagon's National Reconnaissance Office spent between $2 billion and $4 billion a year on intelligence satellites, and the Defense Intelligence Agency costs over $1 billion to run.

American activism involved much more than military and intelligence operations. There were, for example, large economic- and food-assistance programs. The economic-assistance program went through several bureaucratic incarnations but emerged in its present form, the Agency for International Development (AID), in the early 1960s. By the 1980s, AID employed more than 15,000 people, more than half of whom were aliens. AID's Washington staff numbered well over 3,000 people, and the more than 5,200 Americans AID posted overseas constituted a foreign representation larger than that of the Department of State.

Information programs are conducted by the United States Information Agency, employing more than 10,000 people, with representation in each American embassy. The Arms Control and Disarmament Agency, established in the early 1960s, has had some arms-control responsibilities, although its putative role as an arms-control advocate left it vulnerable to criticism during the early Reagan years that it was a remnant of détente and now, after the cold war, that it is superfluous. The Peace Corps has been responsible for sending thousands of Americans abroad to represent the United States. For much of the cold war, Peace Corps activity focussed on the Third World; with the end of the cold war, Peace Corps volunteers are being placed in the poorer countries of the former Soviet Union.

Finally, more than a half-dozen other departments and agencies maintain significant overseas representation, including the Departments of Agriculture, Energy, Interior, Health and Human Resources, Labor, Transportation, Commerce, Justice, and Treasury and the National Science Foundation. The intrusion of economic issues during the last decade has meant that the Treasury, Commerce, and Agriculture departments have developed powerful foreign policy bureaucracies. Indeed, the negotiations involving senior officials of these departments have assumed an importance equal to those of other representatives of the U.S. government.

The Problem of Coordination

Presumably—and since a 1961 directive signed by President Kennedy—all of this foreign activity and representation is coordinated by the Department of State. Ideally, effective use of the department's institutional position would ensure that the foreign policy establishment is operating within some consistent policy framework. However, so vast a government establishment has proved to be beyond the control of the secretary of state.

State's inability to serve as the agent of policy coordination results from more than a mismatch between its size and that of the foreign affairs bureaucracy to be coordinated. After all, the institutional focus of foreign policy coordination during most of the cold war years—the National Security Council and the national security adviser—never approached the size of the Department of State. Before the modern NSC took shape, at the start of the Eisenhower administration, the Department of State had lost its historic role as the primary agent of American international relations.

State was eclipsed because, simply put, its first function—diplomacy, the negotiation and resolution of disputes by means of treaties and other agreements—fell from consistent use. The increasing emphasis on the use or threat of force in American foreign policy meant that those agencies responsible for the overt or clandestine uses of force grew in importance. By the time of the Eisenhower administration the upheavals that had marked the formation of the Department of Defense had begun to subside. In the late 1950s, administrative and management control of the Department of Defense was increasingly centralized in the Office of the Secretary of Defense (OSD) and the chairman of the Joint Chiefs of Staff (JCS).[12] Simultaneously, the CIA emerged not only as an intelligence-gathering agency but also as an operational unit and began to regularly involve itself in clandestine undertakings throughout the world.

The remobilization required by the Korean War, the adoption of a defense posture based on the threat of massive nuclear retaliation, the extension of the American alliance system, the embrace of clandestine operations, and, of course, the absorption of the major portions of the budget by the Defense Department all pointed to the new salience of agencies that commanded coercion. Thus, it was probably inevitable that the relative weight of DOD and the CIA would increase. It did not necessarily follow, however, that the State Department would enter into the kind of precipitate decline that in fact occurred.

The Decline of the Department of State

During the earliest decades of the cold war, the Department of State underwent rapid expansion that left it, not stronger, but internally incoherent and demoralized. There were too many people for too little substantive work in a bureaucracy that demanded advancement or obliged retirement. Many in the department tried to resist the growth. In 1958 the ambassador to Brazil, Ellis Briggs, learning that he was about to be the recipient of a new science attaché, cabled the State Department that "the American embassy in Rio de Janeiro needs a science attache the way a cigar store Indian needs a brassiere."[13] Briggs's response was to no avail; within ten years the embassy had two science attachés.

Up to the early 1950s the State Department was also plagued by two personnel systems. Overseas, an elite officer corps, the Foreign Service officers (FSOs), represented policy. Typically, FSOs dealt with the traditional diplomatic tasks of reporting and representing official policy. At the same time, the State Department relied on a substantial number of civil service employees, who were responsible for administration, economic aid, and some intelligence work. By and large, FSOs staffed the policy-making positions, and civil service employees were seen as support for the FSOs. Much tension and not a little administrative confusion marked the relationship and pointed to a merger of the two personnel systems.[14]

In the end, however, merger probably did more harm than good.[15] Career civil servants who had never had any desire for foreign service were sent to remote outposts. Career diplomats—"generalists" by training and disposition—were shifted to technical jobs for which they were frequently ill-prepared. Since most technical and administrative positions were in Washington, FSOs lost overseas allowances and the opportunity to prove they had political skills that still constituted the essential criteria of promotion.

The personnel problems of the 1950s undercut the effectiveness of the State Department. First, the glut of FSOs watered down the esprit de corps of the original officer group, who considered themselves, with some justification, a part of a last great aristocracy. Second, promotions jammed up. Since the Foreign Service emphasized promotion or resignation after a few years in each grade, the pressure for good jobs (and good reports from one's superiors) became excruciating. Perversely, recruitment actually accelerated in the mid-1960s and again in the mid-1980s. Thus, there were even more people chasing fewer good jobs than ever.

A catalyst for even more change was the case of a competent and likable FSO named Charles Thomas. Forty-five years old, Thomas had spent nineteen years in the Foreign Service. A few months before the end of his "up or out period," he failed to receive his needed promotion, and thus he was "selected out." Thomas spent years trying for a review. But he was given a Kafkaesque runaround. Unable to collect a pension or to get another job, Thomas took his own life in order to make it possible for his wife and children to collect a government annuity. His wife sued the State Department and won. The perverse culmination of this tragedy became the subsequent "reforms" of the Foreign Service Act of 1980.

The 1980 Foreign Service Act revised promotion and retention standards based on "performance." But there still were not enough jobs in which one could achieve performance for a raise to the next level. So the key to better jobs and survival itself became an assignment that would lead to management positions in the newly created Senior Foreign Service. According to the 1980 reform, Foreign Service officers had twenty years to ascend the ladder to the final rungs. If they did not, they were retired. For all intents and purposes, diplomacy in America was rapidly becoming a twenty-year terminal career. The country's patrimony of area expertise, built up painfully over forty years, began to collapse. George Lamberty, head of the American Foreign Service Association, observed, "No one is willing to spend 2 or 3 years learning Chinese or Japanese. The word in the corridors now is get a job managing something and forget everything else or you're dead." As the under secretary for management, Ronald Spiers, put it, FSOs were facing "sudden death, overtime."[16]

Fear became the reigning mood in the Foreign Service of the 1980s. Since the job of a veteran FSO has almost no civilian counterpart, people in their middle or late forties were at a real disadvantage when they contemplated any job market. Skills such as bureaucratic survival and a diminishing grasp of perhaps a half-dozen foreign languages did not seem to be fungible assets in the private sector. Pensions and salary after twenty years in the Foreign Service were less than a military officer might make. The thirty-five-year "crisis at State" had lingered like a long summer's cold. In the mid-1980s the condition transmogrified into a kind of corporate stroke. Paralysis was one possible outcome, panic another. In any case, even if State recovered, prospects seemed bleak that it would ever be as good as new.[17]

The McCarthy Era and the Department of State

The debilitating effects of its internal environment were never the Department of State's only affliction. Starting in the late 1940s, it endured a series of savage attacks on the integrity and loyalty of its officers by members of Congress and Republican candidates for president. As the Soviet Union consolidated control in Eastern Europe and China was "lost" to Mao Zedong in 1949, popular frustrations with American foreign policy focused on the Department of State. Millions of Americans came to accept the explanation advanced by many conservative Republicans that America's policy failures were not the result of developments beyond its control; rather, they were the result of communist influence within the Democratic administrations stretching back to Franklin Roosevelt's New Deal.

In January 1950 Alger Hiss, a former high-level member of the Department of State, was convicted of perjury in a case involving the passing of State Department papers to the Communists. Three weeks later, Senator Joseph McCarthy (R.-Wis.), then a little-known first-term senator, charged that "the State Department . . . is thoroughly infested with Communists." Senator McCarthy went on specifically to indict the Foreign Service for its "traitorous actions."[18] McCarthy's charges subsequently extended across the whole policy-making establishment. The fear of a pervasive conspiracy grew to hysterical proportions. President Truman and Secretary of State Dean Acheson reacted to the senator's charges with denials and a defense of the State Department and the Democratic foreign policy. The Republicans, on the other hand, played on the anxiety and rode the resulting wave of fear and frustration over Korea into the White House.

President Eisenhower's reaction to McCarthyism was ambivalent. He needed the support of conservative Republicans, but it was not his administration that was being implicated in McCarthy's attacks. Eisenhower did not take McCarthy on frontally; he seemed to hope that McCarthy would defeat himself by overextending his charges and claims. Eisenhower may have been following a strategy of passivity in dealing with McCarthy, refusing "to get into the gutter with that guy."[19]

McCarthy's charges became more extravagant. He took on the Army in public hearings, where he was viewed (by an entirely new kind of mass audience, television) as a hectoring bully. McCarthy's drive was spent. A year later the Senate censured him. But as Emmet Hughes has observed, President Eisenhower's "strategy [of refusing to engage McCarthy], for all its sensible elements, could hardly be swift, and its slow working exacted a high price in the mutilation of reputations and careers."[20] Nowhere was this more evident than in the Department of State, where a group of ex-diplomats warned that "a premium has been put upon reporting and upon recommendations which are ambiguously stated or so cautiously set forth as to be deceiving. . . . The ultimate result is a threat to national security."[21]

FSOs who saw their colleagues coming under attack for their policy advice during the late 1940s and early 1950s instinctively pulled back from a forceful and forthright presentation of their views. Even in the best of times, challenging the prevailing orthodoxy was not easy; now it was a proven course of career disaster. A State Department shibboleth was repeated to each freshman class of entering FSOs: "There are old Foreign Service Officers, and there are bold Foreign Service Officers, but there are no old, bold Foreign Service Officers." McCarthy had a kind of eidetic effect on the collective mind of the State Department; he was like a flashbulb witnessed up close, seen much later when one's eyes were closed. And the terrible damage his name came to symbolize haunts the State Department's institutional memory. Of course, State did not slide beneath the waters of the Potomac. FSOs continued to hold diplomatic posts, serve on interdepartmental groups, and carry out their traditional functions. But the department was increasingly viewed as a problem as well as a part of the policy-making process.

COMPETING CENTERS OF BUREAUCRATIC POWER

Compounding the diminished position of the Department of State was the emergence of new and powerful bureaucratic actors. The responsibilities of the CIA and the Defense Department were closely associated with the Eisenhower administration's militarized variant of containment. By the mid-1950s, they had captured not only the budgetary resources but the bureaucratic center of power and policy as well.

THE DEPARTMENT OF DEFENSE

The evolution of the Department of Defense was marked by conflict.[22] A residue of strife lay in the bifurcation of the department between its civilian and military officials: tension remained between the Departments of the Navy, the Army, and the Air Force, on the one side, and the OSD and its attendant cadre of assistant secretaries, on the other. Complicating the picture was the ambiguous position of the Joint Chiefs, who were responsible to the various service interests as well as to the president, with no special reporting relation to the secretary of defense.

The first secretary of defense, James Forrestal, found that he could do little more than serve as a concierge for service needs and a mediator in negotiating interservice consensus. Forrestal, who as secretary of the navy had been in some measure responsible for the decentralized structure set forth in the National Security Act of 1947, with rather autonomous Departments of the Army, the Navy, and the Air Force, set about changing the situation once he was secretary of defense by establishing the Office of the Secretary of Defense and the position of assistant secretary of defense. Forrestal thus took the first step in the development of a centralized civilian counterweight to the military service departments and the JCS.

In 1953 Eisenhower tried to strengthen the hand of the secretary of defense by expanding his control over the uniformed services. At the heart of this effort was concentration of management and budgetary control in the hands of the civilian assistant secretaries. At the same time, however, this increase in the management capability of the secretary of defense did not result in expanded control over military planning. The Joint Chiefs served in large measure as advocates of their respective service departments. They remained outside the orbit of the OSD by retaining their exclusive hold on defense plans, which perforce included determining the resources needed for achieving political objectives with coercive means. The Joint Chiefs behaved in this regard very much as they had during the Truman years, as a kind of trading post at which their respective service interests were bargained, protected, and, where possible, advanced.[23]

In another reorganization, in 1958, the Joint Chiefs were made directly responsible to the secretary of defense. Eisenhower thus sought to break the linkage between the Joint Chiefs and the services. The secretary's personal role was extended to include the redefinition of service missions and roles, control over production, procurement, operational control of new weapons systems, and finally, increased direct authority over the activities of the service secretaries and their departments.[24] Command responsibilities for the Joint Chiefs were redefined in terms of a hierarchy of unified geographic and special functional commands (e.g., Europe, the Pacific, or the Strategic Air Command) rather in terms of the commanders' respective services. But the Joint Chiefs remained as spokesmen of the Army, the Navy, and the Air Force, respectively, and this retained identity complicated joint operations.

The decentralization of the department throughout the late 1940s and 1950s may have mitigated somewhat its bureaucratic preponderance. Nonetheless, it was the beneficiary of a foreign policy that emphasized the threat of force, the department's raison d'être. The Defense Department was therefore a growing, if troubled, institution rising to ascendancy within the executive policy-making establishment. Once the OSD gained added power and status, the department would become *primus inter pares* among the foreign affairs bureaucracies.

The McNamara Defense Department

With the arrival of the Kennedy administration, perhaps the most assertive secretary of defense assumed direction of the department. Robert McNamara propelled the Defense Department to the forefront of the Kennedy administration. But the department's prominence and that of McNamara himself were ultimately tied to the Kennedy administration's dependence on the instrumentalities of force.

McNamara moved quickly and without congressional consultation to consolidate his personal position. He did so by surrounding himself with acerbic, even arrogant, analytically brilliant men, most of whom had made their mark in business or academic life. The upshot was the establishment of vastly augmented programmatic and budgetary control in the hands of the administrative activist, McNamara, and his personal staff.[25] The OSD was soon involved at virtually every level of national security management and military planning. Commanders in the Pacific and Europe were given less autonomy, and McNamara's centralized budgeting procedures led to his staff's preempting most traditional military planning.[26]

Much of the interservice barter and compromise that had undermined previous reform efforts in the 1950s was confronted and bridged in less than a year. McNamara and his staff's assertiveness threatened many in his department, but his method ensured his prominence in the White House. Kennedy and his most intimate advisers admired cold, even ruthless, activism that resulted in greater presidential control of the instruments of policy. McNamara's vigor ensured the dominance of the man and his bureaucracy almost to the end of his tenure, when he at last resigned, broken by the Vietnam debacle he had done so much to shape.

As the Vietnam War lumbered on, the services struggled to ensure their resource base. McNamara's authority diminished. Many of his reforms proved illusive as McNamara himself devoted less attention to management questions and more to policy. Frustrated by what he was to describe in the 1980s as his role as covert advocate of a diplomatic solution to Vietnam (McNamara claims that he came to the conclusion that the war could not be won militarily in the fall of 1965), McNamara started to come undone emotionally. A victim of public weeping and shakiness, he was removed by President Johnson at the start of 1968.[27]

Vietnam and the Defense Establishment

If McNamara's administrative aggressiveness moved the Defense Department to the very center of American foreign policy formulation, it ensured that when the resulting policies met with disaster in Vietnam, the military establishment itself would suffer. What has come to be called the Vietnam syndrome was nowhere more manifest than within the professional military establishment.

Kenneth Campbell, a veteran of the Vietnam War and now a close student of the military establishment, described the post–cold war Vietnam syndrome as "a strong aversion to the use of military force—based on fears of another Vietnam—unless certain conditions are first met." He added that "the present military leadership is committed to avoiding any new Vietnams at almost any price."[28] Within the professional military, the "lessons of Vietnam" fermented for a decade and emerged in explicit form midway through the Reagan administration. Reagan's first secretary of defense, Caspar Weinberger, articulated the operational essence of this position in what came to be known during the 1980s as the Weinberger Doctrine. In the future, Weinberger insisted, force must not be used unless six tests were met: (1) vital U.S. interests must be at stake; (2) a clear and solid commitment to victory existed; (3) political and military objectives were clear; (4) the forces committed had to be of a size sufficient to achieve the objective; (5) public and congressional support had to be mobilized; and (6) the resort to force was to be a last resort.[29]

Throughout the 1980s and into the Gulf War, during 1990–91, therefore, the professional military constrained the commitment of U.S. military forces.[30] During the Reagan years, this pragmatism on the part of the military frustrated the most hawkish of the president's advisers, who came to view the military as virtual "wimps-in-uniform, so traumatized by their Vietnam experience that they are too timid to use force in all but the most easily-won conflicts."[31]

This latter characterization is clearly an overstatement. Throughout the 1980s and early 1990s the military option was turned to frequently: Grenada, Lebanon, raids on Libya, the Philippines, Persian Gulf escort operations at the end of the Reagan administration, the Panama intervention, and of course Operation Desert Shield/Storm in 1990–91. At the same time, however, none of these operations proved to be as all-consuming as Vietnam, and when they threatened to become so—for example, Lebanon—withdrawal followed. Moreover, in the runup to Desert Storm, President Bush went to great lengths to insist repeatedly that the Gulf War would not be another Vietnam. And as the early accounts of the war make clear, the military insisted upon, and received from the administration, satisfaction of each of Weinberger's tests as Desert Shield/Storm unfolded.[32] Finally, and notwithstanding President Bush's declamation at the end of the Persian Gulf war that "by God, we've kicked the Vietnam syndrome once and for all,"[33] when the prospect of military intervention in the ghastly Bosnian conflict emerged in mid-1992, it was the club of Vietnam with which skeptics cudgeled proponents of intervention.[34]

The Defense Department after Vietnam

In the late 1970s and during the early Reagan administration, as defense budgets expanded once again, the services saw their resources grow significantly. The post-Vietnam secretaries of defense were, in contrast to McNamara, solicitous of a professional military seeking to rebuild morale and combat effectiveness.[35] Even Henry Kissinger, President Nixon's omnipresent national security adviser, famous for his quest for control of the national security bureaucracy, avoided Department of Defense management issues. President Jimmy Carter briefly sought to crack the services' reassertion of control by imposing his own priorities, but the services maintained their lines of communication with Congress and used them to engage in guerrilla warfare with the White House. Thus, when the Carter administration denied the Navy a new nuclear aircraft carrier, Congress put it back into the Navy's budget, and Carter was forced to take the unprecedented step of vetoing a defense authorization bill.[36]

In the last year of his administration, Carter himself became a convert to the idea of defense expansion, and his last budget called for the largest single budget increase to date in U.S. peacetime, $70 billion. During the 1980s, Reagan Defense Secretary Caspar Weinberger represented a president largely ignorant of weapons technology and strategic doctrine. The White House priority in the early years of the Reagan administration was the largest buildup in defense spending since the early 1960s. As one high

DOD civilian told James Nathan in 1985, the Reagan team's "plan" was to "spend the Soviet Union into the ground." Weinberger's role was twofold: first, he was the dogged defender of the DOD requests before Congress and the press; second, he was the arbitrator of the internal DOD agreements regarding division of the lavish budgets of the decade. While huge resources were being handed to Defense, literally doubling the real budget in less than five years, the reform efforts of the late 1950s and early 1960s were smothered.[37]

Meanwhile, the sheer mass of Reagan defense budgets and concomitant defense procurement scandals, combined with cuts in domestic spending, fed a congressional movement for defense reform. David Packard, a former deputy secretary of defense, issued a report emphasizing the importance of greater unification of command and centralization of administrative control in the Joint Chiefs and a more rationalized procurement and financial-management system.[38] Significantly, some staunch conservatives in Congress aligned themselves with this reform effort. Thus in the House Armed Services Committee conservative Democratic Congressman Bill Nichols of Alabama worked with Senators Barry Goldwater (R.-Ariz.) and Sam Nunn (D.-Ga.), the chair and senior Democrat, respectively, on the Senate Armed Services Committee, to produce the Goldwater-Nichols Reorganization Act in October 1986.[39] Goldwater-Nichols advanced significantly increased unity of command. The chairman of the JCS and the Chiefs were taken out of the chain of command, which now runs from the president to the secretary of defense to the various war-fighting commands. With the 1986 reform, the chairman of the JCS himself became the principal military adviser to the president. The chairman also became responsible for preparing budget estimates consistent with the guidance for war plans prepared by the ten regional and functional commands. The general officers heading the commands, in turn, were given full operational control over the units and resources assigned to their command.[40]

The chairman's role, to supervise joint plans and advise the president, was supplemented by an understanding signed by President Reagan on January 14, 1987, which placed the chairman in the line of communications to the commands, transmitting direction from the president and the secretary of defense. But the sum of the chairman's job—advice, planning, and communication—could be pretty thin gruel, as reporter Bob Woodward noted, when "real commands" and real resources are the name of the game in Washington.[41] In the future, much of the chairman's power would depend on his relationship to the president and the secretary. If the chairman was not on intimate terms with the his superiors, the system could break down.

In fact, the services seemed to function better under the new "jointness" the reforms had mandated. Even though the reforms served to integrate the various combat arms, while taking power away from each service chief, the JCS actually supported the Goldwater-Nichols reforms, perhaps because they were alive to the implication of service rivalries in bollixed operations in Lebanon in 1982 and Grenada in 1983. In turn, the Goldwater-Nichols reforms themselves, as well as the competence of the chairman, General Colin Powell, in planning operations and advising the president, were widely credited for the military success of the largest joint operation since World War II, Operation Desert Storm.

But even one of the most successful tests at arms since Agincourt has not made the transition to the post–cold war world, with its pressures for major reductions in the budgetary base of the Pentagon, any easier. It is not easy to determine, therefore, whether the new willingness to cooperate among the services is driven more by a reformed internal administration than by a radically changed budgetary environment. In any event, apart from the White House itself, the Defense Department remains the single most important bureaucratic actor in the national-security-policy machinery. Absent an alternative foreign-policy consensus as well defined as that which came out of the early cold war, the bureaucratic weight of the Defense Department, by dent of its resources, will retain its centrality.

The CIA and the Intelligence Establishment

An intelligence function has long been a part of the American foreign affairs experience.[42] The self-sacrificing figure of the Revolutionary War spy Nathan Hale is quite literally kept in view for those who perform the intelligence function today in the form of a statue at the CIA building. Intelligence gathering was very much a part of the experience of the Civil War, during which the Pinkerton Agency was employed by the Union. At the same time, Robert E. Lee found that, in addition to espionage undertaken by Confederate sympathizers, there was also the simple expedient of reading the Northern newspapers for information concerning Union troop strengths, movements, and assessments of Confederate capabilities and intentions.

Lee's success at using what today would be called "open sources" raises the deeper question of the relationship between the intelligence function and American society. Specifically, the practice of espionage and the protection of society from the activities of those who conduct espionage against it pose some burden on a free society. Resolution of this tension has always been imperfect. Espionage has tended to be compartmentalized with defense and therefore has been rationalized as a necessary evil in connection with war. The situation changed dramatically in World War II and with the onset of the cold war. Intelligence and espionage were, of course, critical to the Allied victory in World War II. So, too, were covert operations. The military services conducted their own intelligence operations, but the Office of Strategic Services (OSS) was created to centralize strategic intelligence analysis and covert operations.

The OSS became the basis of the CIA, created in the National Security Act of 1947. The administrative structure of the CIA was built around four operating divisions, or "directorates." The administrative division was most peripheral, but the remaining divisions were, and remain, central to the bureaucratic power and problems encountered by the CIA. The Science and Technology Directorate monitors foreign broadcasts and other electronic intelligence but also operates the agency's substantial intelligence-gathering operations based on aircraft and satellites. The Intelligence Directorate and the National Intelligence Council are at the core of the analytical functions of the CIA, producing finished CIA "products," or analyses, for the executive branch. Many of the analysts in the Intelligence Directorate and the National Intelligence Council hold doctorates and are specialists in various regions or functional problems of foreign and national security policy. The Operations Directorate is the center for covert operations. It produces "raw" intelligence from clandestine sources that is screened for reliability before it is disseminated to the intelligence analysts. Operations Directorate personnel are proud of their ability to conduct operations under difficult circumstances. Their capabilities have been, in turn, the source of the agency's many covert successes but also the locus of many of its notorious shortcomings.

Within the CIA there has been a history of tension and conflict growing out of the more open analytical functions and the covert function built into the agency. In addition, there have been recurring debates concerning reliance upon technical means for gathering intelligence, that is, satellites and electronic devices, instead of upon agents operating covertly abroad. The analytical "product" itself has also been the focus of controversy. The mandate of the CIA to serve as the central coordinating point for the U.S. government's National Intelligence Estimate, or NIE, has produced perhaps some of the greatest controversies in foreign policy making. An intelligence estimate, after all, represents an image of reality and even the definition of a national security problem itself. The definition of a problem implies which agencies are most relevant to the situation. Thus, intelligence is seldom "neutral" in a bureaucratic sense, and the shaping of intelligence estimates can become intensely political.

The Federal Bureau of Investigation (FBI), the NSA, the Drug Enforcement Agency, the Treasury, the various Defense intelligence missions around the world, and still more agencies and bureaus overseas all gather raw and processed information. The extent to which the CIA represents an unbiased coordinator can be colored by its own covert operations. Analyses can reflect a bureaucratic desire to place one's own operations, intelligence gathering, or interpretation in the most favorable light possible. At this point, therefore, analysis is subject to the same bureaucratic politics that one would find in any other agency. The intelligence product that results from this process often represents a "negotiated" consensus position embracing multiple agency perspectives. Consequently, many top policymakers have criticized the CIA's estimates as being too unfocused and untimely to be of much operational use at the highest levels of the government.

From time to time during the cold war the CIA's intelligence product has also attracted criticism for being consciously skewed to suit and support a prevailing policy thrust of the White House. The problem is not that an intelligence estimate is watered down in pursuit of inter-bureaucratic agreement but that the intelligence estimate is "politicized" and "intelligence to please." During the 1970s, for example, the argument from the political right was that intelligence estimates concerning the strategic balance were overly optimistic and tended to stress an interpretation of Soviet behavior supportive of arms-control agreements. In order that domestic political support for the SALT talks would be sustained, it was charged, evidence of Soviet cheating on agreements was suppressed, and the unfavorable shift in the balance of forces was explained away. In contrast, during the Reagan years, "worst-case" analysis concerning the Soviet threat was supposedly the norm. Moreover, analysis of the balance of political forces within Iran was claimed to have been biased in support of the president's desire to pursue an arms-for-hostages swap. Some analysts in the CIA were persuaded to discover "Iranian moderates" where previously there were only fanatical followers of the Ayatollah Khomeini.

During the early years of the cold war, the CIA's operational role increased at the expense of the State Department, a development from which State has never fully recovered. But in the wake of the Vietnam disaster and a succession of revelations concerning the CIA's cold war involvement in covert operations and assassinations (both successful and unsuccessful), the agency underwent a wrenching process of internal "reform" that proved to be as demoralizing and disruptive as that experienced by the rest of the foreign policy establishment. During the latter 1970s in particular, large numbers of CIA analysts and operational specialists associated with the early cold war years were purged from the agency by a Carter administration that, initially at least, sought to move away from the cold war view of the world and the instrumentalities appropriate to that perspective.

Subsequently, as détente collapsed and the cold war returned with even greater intensity, the CIA's operational role received new emphasis. With the Reagan administration's ascendancy, the old cold war modalities reigned supreme as William Casey, himself a former operative with the wartime OSS, was made head of the CIA. Casey's commitment to a Manichean view of the East-West conflict and the international system and to the centrality of covert operations, as well as his contempt for Congress, oversight, and accountability of the intelligence function, placed the agency once again at the forefront of the foreign policy establishment.[43] But the agency's central position in the Reagan administration's foreign policy operations meant that when some of those operations failed spectacularly, the CIA was inevitably the recipient of much of the political fallout.

As the convoluted catastrophe of the Iran-Contra scandal began to unfold, both the CIA and those professionals who ran it during the Casey years found themselves confronted with political embarrassment and, in some cases, legal liabilities. No less troublesome for the CIA, however, has been the end of the cold war itself. Not only did the agency—along with virtually the entire U.S. government—find itself surprised by the dramatic Soviet retrenchment and then collapse, it now had to recreate itself in an international and intergovernmental context in which incremental shifts from a cold war norm are no longer sufficient. As the "new world order" began to take shape in the early 1990s, the CIA found itself with new leadership beset with questions concerning its future role in the intelligence function and, for that matter, what the focus of that function should be in a world politics that seemed likely to be dominated as much by economics, trade, international finance, drug trafficking, and the immigration of masses of people displaced by wars of nationalism as by the traditional security concerns of the preceding era.

New Complexities and Old Problems

This new agenda confronting the intelligence establishment carries implications for U.S. foreign policy beyond the interplay of the three centers of bureaucratic power—State, Defense, and CIA—that have largely defined the policy process during the cold war years. It seems inevitable that as the new agenda takes shape, new centers of bureaucratic expertise and power will emerge. The old centers and concerns will not vanish, but the policy process will become more complex.

Thus, as the 1990s opened, the policy-making establishment had to deal simultaneously with traditional security issues, such as a major war in the Persian Gulf, as well as the implications of the breakup of the Soviet Union. Strategic arms control remained crucial in U.S.-Russian relations, but negotiations were complicated by at least three new nuclear powers—Belarus, the Ukraine, and Kazakhstan—who inherited significant portions of the old Soviet strategic arsenal. At the same time, however, the negotiation of a free trade area for North America, along with a major global conference on the environment,[44] signaled that the Office of Trade representative and the head of the Environmental Protection Agency would become, at least from time to time, key foreign policy actors. The Treasury and Commerce departments, moreover, assumed a foreign policy weight at least as great as that of the Defense Department in planning for the future of U.S. relations with the successor states to the Soviet Union. Whereas for forty years force and the threat of force drove the policy agenda, now debate over the most efficient form of aid to a former adversary consumed policymakers. Even the Peace Corps became a relevant foreign policy instrument in the future of U.S. relations with the old Soviet empire.

It is conceivable that in this new policy-making environment the State Department could reemerge as the dominant player. Certainly during the Bush administration, Secretary of State James Baker established a policy-making position that recalled those assumed by the strongest secretaries of state of the cold war era. However, Baker's personal stature did not translate into a stronger State Department. Moreover, when President Bush's reelection prospects declined dramatically in the summer of 1992, Baker was summoned from the State Department to the White House to assume direction of the Bush campaign. Left behind was an "acting" secretary of state, Lawrence Eagleburger. A few weeks after the November election, an ailing, emphysemic Eagleburger was made secretary, but neither the time nor the energy remained for Eagleburger to exert leadership. A further proliferation of policy-making players as the policy agenda expanded and became more fragmented was the most likely prospect. The established bureaucratic centers of policy making seemed likely to try to claim portions of the new agenda.

Our brief survey of the major centers of bureaucratic power within the foreign policy establishment points to major problems of coordination and implementation. The president does not sit atop the bureaucracy as if it were a pyramid of power, commanding bureaucratic units to do his bidding. Rather, the president is confronted with well-established institutions and an ongoing stream of foreign policy. Much of the context and direction of policy is provided by the members of the foreign policy bureaucracy who have careers and perspectives that inevitably reflect more than the most recent presidential electoral returns. Of course, presidents come to office with their own priorities, their own vision of international reality, and their own sense of American interests. Presidential appointments to key policy-making positions within the bureaucracy are designed to implant their priorities. Nonetheless, it is rare that presidents—or their appointees—bring to their tasks the kind of accumulated experience that is represented by the foreign affairs bureaucracy.

For most of the cold war, the approaches adopted by presidents in managing the foreign policy process have differed only in detail. However, presidents, whether Democrat or Republican and whatever their initial administrative inclinations, have come to rely more and more on the special assistant for national security affairs and the staff of the National Security Council for getting on top of the national security establishment. Indeed, Ronald Reagan went a step beyond his predecessors in that his National Security Council staff became a means, not merely for managing the foreign policy bureaucracy, but, rather, for circumventing it. In the Iran-Contra fiasco, then, the ultimate response to the dilemmas of bureaucratic politics was: if the extant bureaucracy is deemed unresponsive, then create a new one whose loyalties run only to the president. Moreover, the resulting government within the government acknowledged no constitutional limits.

CHAPTER 3

The Development of the National Security Council System

THE NATIONAL SECURITY ACT of 1947, the same act that initiated the expansion of the national security establishment, also provided for the National Security Council (NSC). The NSC was to be the president's means for coordinating foreign policy. It was to comprise the president, the vice president, the secretaries of state and defense, the chairman of the Joint Chiefs of Staff, and the director of the Office of Emergency Preparedness. The president could invite any other officials whom he desired to participate, and since the early 1950s such officials as the director of the Central Intelligence Agency, the directors of the various foreign aid agencies, and officials from the Treasury Department and the Bureau of the Budget (renamed the Office of Management and Budget during the Nixon administration) have been invited to participate.

The ostensible purpose of the NSC was the coordination and integration of the foreign and defense policy of the United States. Other unarticulated but just as real functions were twofold: first, to assist Harry Truman, a man widely disdained as a novice in the postwar Congress, in informing himself on foreign affairs; second, to give the military a formal voice in the diplomatic process.[1] In point of fact, however, the actual use of the NSC has been left up to the president.

THE FORMATION OF THE NSC SYSTEM: THE EARLY YEARS

Truman used the NSC sparingly. His own view was that foreign policy could not be shared with a cabinetlike institution such as the NSC. Truman emphasized this point in his memoirs: "In some ways a Cabinet government is more efficient—but under the British system there is a group responsibility. Under our system the responsibility rests with one man—the President."[2] Moreover, Truman resented the assertion by his congressional and bureaucratic critics that he was somehow too amateurish to make decisions on his own. As if to underscore his primacy in policy, Truman did not use the NSC until the outbreak of the Korean War.[3] Instead, Truman relied on the Department of State and Secretaries of State George Marshall and Dean Acheson to effect the policy-making control he desired.

Eisenhower's decisional style called for comprehensive and extensive staff work.[4] He preferred full representation of all points of view, but he did not want to become overly involved in lower-level bureaucratic squabbling. This view of policy making was reflected in an enlarged NSC system. Frequent and expanded meetings of the NSC were held (sometimes there were forty to fifty people in attendance), with the president a regular participant. Position papers were developed at the departmental and agency level and passed on to the NSC through a planning board whose responsibility was the coordinating and, in many instances, compromising of divergent positions. Particularly during Eisenhower's first administration, the NSC met quite frequently and dealt with a broad range of policy questions.[5]

Eisenhower's security advisers have testified to Eisenhower's active participation in NSC meetings, even to the point of resolving some questions during the meetings themselves. In other instances he apparently deferred decision until later or after a series of meetings.[6] But other observers, some of them intimate associates of Eisenhower's, emphasize his relationship with John Foster Dulles. Sherman Adams refers, for example, to Eisenhower as giving Dulles "the responsibility for initiating foreign policy." But Emmet Hughes recalls that Eisenhower always qualified such a grant of authority; he quotes Eisenhower as saying, "I'm supposed to have left too much to Dulles. Well . . . he has never done a thing that I did not approve beforehand."[7]

In short, the president established an elaborate complex of committees and subcommittees and embedded them in a set of procedures that would guarantee that position papers would touch all bureaucratic bases. It would be a mistake to view this structure as the crux of the policy-making process, however. Eisenhower undoubtedly relied on thorough staff work and orderly follow-up to coordinate the activities of the bureaucracy. On the other hand, it appears that the parameters of policy were developed through the interaction of Eisenhower and his secretary of state.[8]

THE KENNEDY AND JOHNSON ADMINISTRATIONS

The administrations of John F. Kennedy and his successor, Lyndon B. Johnson, confirmed the trend toward centralization of the decision-making processes in the White House.

The Kennedy Years

Kennedy, as his biographer and aide Theodore Sorensen noted, "abandoned the notion of a collective, institutionalized presidency." Instead, Kennedy "relied . . . on informal meetings and on a personal White House staff, the Budget Bureau and ad hoc task forces to probe and define issues for his decisions—on special Presidential emissaries and constant Presidential phone calls and memoranda—on placing Kennedy men in each strategic spot."[9] Kennedy therefore heeded the criticism of the Eisenhower NSC system, with its interlocking committees that led to countless "coordinated" position papers but little policy.[10] Kennedy wanted control of the national security process in his hands in the White House.

The result was the dismantling of the huge Eisenhower NSC structure. Kennedy also discontinued the regular and extended meetings of the cabinet and the NSC and even discontinued regular White House staff meetings.[11] He turned instead to a small foreign policy staff under Special Assistant for National Security McGeorge Bundy, which would operate out of the White House. The NSC as a statutorily established and defined body remained, but the decision-making and coordinating roles found a home in the ad hoc dynamics of the Kennedy White House.[12]

The Kennedy administration's attitude toward the Department of State was ambivalent. Arthur Schlesinger, Jr., a Kennedy staffer and chronicler, reports that Kennedy's personal opinion of the department was split between his "sympathy for the diplomatic enterprise"—his admiration for men such as Charles Bohlen, Llewellyn Thompson, and Averell Harriman—and his despair over bureaucratic layering, institutional conservatism, convoluted rhetoric, and other institutional pathologies that infected the department.[13] Kennedy apparently thought the department could be resuscitated, and he attempted to move it toward a role of leadership in policy coordination. In a letter to all chiefs of mission in May 1961 the president sought to underscore the U.S. ambassador's primacy, who was "to oversee and coordinate all the activities of the United States Government" in the country in question.[14] But a letter to chiefs of mission could never be sufficient, and one suspects that

Kennedy knew it. For what the Kennedy and subsequent administrations were working against was a deeply embedded organizational culture biased toward caution and even inaction. McCarthy's ghost undoubtedly sat in numerous offices in Foggy Bottom, and compounding this was Kennedy himself. In Kennedy's view, the secretary of state was to take care of the management of the department and operation of ongoing policy, while high-level politics, diplomacy, and crisis management were the business of the president.

By establishing a separate White House staff under Bundy and then using it as an aggressive extension of the president, Kennedy was conforming to the image of the presidency described by Richard Neustadt in 1963: "A President, these days, is virtually compelled to reach for information and to seek control over details of operation deep inside executive departments."[15] In effect, the president became his own secretary of state, and his staff became a small surrogate State Department.

Kennedy's relationship with his secretary of state compounded the problems at State. Dean Rusk came to be secretary of state after a long apprenticeship in foreign affairs. Rusk was hired on the basis of an article in 1960 in which he advised any new secretary to be responsive to White House direction.[16] But Rusk fared poorly in an environment dominated by the president's brother and attorney general, Robert, an aggressive White House staff under Bundy, and the vigorous advocacy of Secretary of Defense Robert McNamara. Rusk, like his department, was shoved aside in the clash of more assertive men and departments.

Indeed, Rusk suffered endless humiliations for his bland, "Buddha-like" calm and his meticulous care with detail. Arthur Schlesinger describes Rusk as "a man bred in the large organizations of mid-century . . . his organizational instinct was for service, not for mastery."[17] Rusk's own model of selfless service was his personal hero and mentor, General (and Secretary of Defense and State) George Marshall. Rusk believed in keeping his personal counsel private; it was only years later, perhaps goaded too long by charges that he was everything from a nervous wreck to negligent in the Cuban missile crisis, that Rusk revealed to a collection of his tormentors his central role in boldly resolving the crisis. His aging antagonists, however, refused to apologize or retract anything.[18]

The Johnson Years

Lyndon Johnson's administration began in the shock of John Kennedy's assassination in 1963. For his first few months in office, Johnson relied heavily on former Kennedy men, many of whom held him in contempt as something of a buffoon and boor. Most notably, McGeorge Bundy remained as Johnson's special assistant for national security affairs until late 1965. The demands of Vietnam, however, inevitably dominated policy and policy making.

Johnson, who desired personal control of the myriad details of policy making and demanded absolute loyalty, stood astride almost every element of policy. The prior steady accretion of power in the White House was stepped up dramatically during the Johnson years, while the relationship between the president and the secretary of state changed significantly. The same characteristics of Rusk's personality and administrative style that had so baffled the Kennedy men suited him well in the Johnson administration. Rusk's dogged loyalty to the president's objectives was perfectly matched to a president slogging ever deeper into the mire of Vietnam. As criticism, raised in many instances by Kennedy men who were now out of power, became more shrill, Rusk became even firmer.

A symbolic effort was made in 1965 and 1966, before all was sucked into the vortex of Vietnam, to reinforce the position of the Department of State. A series of institutional changes designed to reinvigorate the interdepartmental coordination role of the department were made.[19] The focal point of this change was to be a new Senior Interdepartmental Group (SIG) comprising the deputy secretary of defense, the administrator of AID, the director of the CIA, the chairman of the Joint Chiefs of Staff, the director of the United States Information Agency (USIA), and the special assistant for national security affairs. Since the under secretary of state was at the head of the SIG, the State Department apparently had "full powers of decision."[20]

The State Department's position was to be further augmented by the establishment of a planning-programming-budgeting system (PPBS). The concept of the PPBS had been taken from the Department of Defense, where Robert McNamara had used it with some success in his strengthening of the Office of the Secretary of Defense. The idea was to provide the Department of State with a means of overseeing the budgets of the various agencies involved in foreign affairs. It was reasoned that if budgetary decisions were in fact decisions about how resources are to be allocated, then State Department budgetary oversight would provide the department with the most fundamental means for coordinating interdepartmental activity.[21]

The Johnson policy-making system was stillborn. Difficulties emerged with respect to several elements of the structure. The SIG was ineffective.

Disputes that found their way to the SIG tended to be of such import as to be irresolvable without White House intervention. In any event, participants in the process have indicated that the SIG was often bypassed.[22] Moreover, the department was thrust into a role for which it was ill-prepared.

First, PPBS was found to be inapplicable to foreign affairs. It was never apparent to trained diplomats how to quantify "policy" and "interest" or how to record the amount of time it took to write one kind of report or another. Organizational inertia of the department contributed to the failure. But the notion that policy innovation and control could be supervised using the same management techniques that worked for the Department of Defense under McNamara was probably a defective idea in the first place.

Second, the Johnson approach to interdepartmental coordination envisioned the department's taking the initiative in an intensely conflictual milieu of multiagency policy making. But as Nicholas Katzenbach, the under secretary of state for administration, observed in 1967, "Administration has often been regarded as rather unfashionable, smacking vaguely of filing cabinets, travel allowances, or paper flow. It has also been thought of as only marginally relevant to the actual making of foreign policy."[23]

But day-to-day foreign policy making was increasingly an exercise in interagency coordination. The demands of policy making required, therefore, the marriage of "substance" and "administration," as well as a certain aggressiveness, in short, precisely the kind of behavior the State Department was incapable of without strong departmental leadership and presidential support. And neither of these was forthcoming because of the most important foreign policy concern during the Johnson administration—Vietnam.

The impact of Vietnam on the policy-making processes of the Johnson administration cannot be overstated. The prosecution of the war became all-consuming. Consequently, resources were absorbed at an astonishing rate: literally millions of dollars a day and comparable hours of labor and time. Clearly, nurturing nascent structural reforms of policy processes was not a high-priority item. Similarly, the Department of Defense, the CIA, and those elements of the Department of State most deeply involved with the war became the institutional focus of policy and policy making. In this environment SIG and PPBS at State were decidedly less important than other acronyms that pervaded presidential briefing papers and American households: VC, ARVN, KIA, MIA, POW.

The president's personal domination of the policy process proceeded with even greater urgency as he sought to absorb and stay on top of every detail of the war effort. Yet, paradoxically, the dynamic also pulled Johnson toward an ever-smaller group of decision makers—McNamara at Defense, Richard Helms of the CIA, General Earl Wheeler, chairman of the Joint Chiefs of Staff, Rusk at State, and, always, W. W. Rostow, his special assistant for national security affairs. These advisers and the president constituted the so-called Tuesday Luncheon Group. But as the group of top decision makers grew smaller, their proceedings more informal, and the focus of the president more myopic, Johnson's relations and communications with the remainder of the bureaucracy became so tenuous that he lost control. Access to information and political insight that he so vitally needed during Vietnam escaped his grasp.[24]

Perhaps the most obvious development of this period was a movement away from the hierarchically structured NSC of the Eisenhower years. The centralization of policy making growing out of the Vietnam War undoubtedly heightens this impression. Nevertheless, both Kennedy and Johnson were presidents who sought personal control of policy and policy making. The 1960s also marked the continued decline of the Department of State as a policy-making institution and the continued rise of the Department of Defense, particularly under the aggressive leadership of McNamara. Both Kennedy and Johnson made gestures toward reinvigoration of the State Department, but in the end the department's own organizational culture, the resource demands and policy-making weight of DOD, and the underlying desire of both Kennedy and Johnson to be their own secretary of state prevailed. The department reaction was characteristic: another study of what was wrong with the department amidst signs of further deterioration of department morale bordering on open rebellion among some younger FSOs.

A corollary of these developments was the emergence of the special assistant for national security affairs as a key foreign and national security policymaker. Under both Truman and Eisenhower the position was not a major one in that their special assistants did not undertake the active roles in both policy making and coordination of departmental and agency positions that Bundy and Rostow did. Under Bundy and Rostow, the position evolved somewhat informally and was not characterized by extensive institutionalization during the 1960s. Rather, the special assistant and his staff inherited and then assumed an expanded role in response to the perceived needs of two presidents who sought the expansion of presidential power and influence over the foreign and defense policy establishments.

The collapsing of the functions of the NSC system into the White House staff, the policy-making salience of the special assistant for national security affairs, and the parallel deterioration of State's position were all part of a general and ongoing consolidation of power in the White House. The span and depth of White House control over DOD and the CIA are less clear, but the thrust of developments with respect to the bureaucratic system is apparent by the end of the 1960s.

THE SYSTEM OF NATIONAL SECURITY POLICY MAKING IN THE 1970S

In February 1970 Richard Nixon issued a statement concerning his perceptions of the problems of policy making. He observed that "efficient procedure does not insure wisdom. But . . . adequate procedures are an indispensable component of the act of judgment."[25] President Nixon had some definite ideas concerning his predecessors. He saw the ad hoc approaches of the 1960s as having "the advantages which come with informality—speed, frankness, and so forth." But, he said, they "often ran the risk that relevant points of view were not heard, that systematic treatment of issues did not take place at the highest level." He also found the processes of the 1950s inadequate, but for different reasons: "The machinery gave too much emphasis to consensus and too little to the presentation of alternatives."[26] It was not with a little irony that in substance Nixon and his chief foreign-policy architect, Special Assistant for National Security Affairs Henry Kissinger, violated every one of the strictures of the president's own analysis.

The Nixon Administration

Just before the election, on October 24, 1968, candidate Nixon told a radio audience that many of the ills of policy making could be traced to the abandonment of the NSC under previous Democratic administrations. It was Nixon's intention to "restore [it] to its preeminent role."[27] Notwithstanding Nixon's claim that he had "intend[ed] to have a strong Secretary of State,"[28] he relied heavily on a system firmly anchored in the White House under the control of his special assistant for national security affairs. William Rogers, a close friend of Nixon's, and Melvin Laird, the defense secretary, were skilled administrators with a reputation for honesty and probity. They were chosen not as policymakers but as competent administrators.[29]

At the hub of an interlocking system of review groups, ad hoc groups, and formal committees was the Senior Review Group, chaired by Henry Kissinger. The Review Group was responsible for preparing papers for consideration by the NSC and the president. In this capacity it served as a gatekeeper to monitor the flow of paper from six interdepartmental groups. Committee representation ran across the major foreign policy departments and agencies, but Kissinger or his representatives chaired the Senior Review Group and the ad hoc committees attached to it. The pivotal point of institutional power in the operation was not necessarily the Senior Review Group itself but rather Kissinger's staff of over 100 and his budget of $2 million (two and a half times the size of Bundy's and three times Rostow's). The magnitude of this operation suggested that Nixon had developed nothing less than a personal foreign ministry within the White House.

Foreign policy "action" was clearly in Kissinger's hands: his daily personal contact with the president and the drop in the number of NSC meetings from thirty-seven in 1969 to ten in 1971 are indicative. More important was the simple fact that on almost every issue of significance Kissinger was Nixon's primary adviser, negotiator, and contact point with the bureaucracy and in many instances with the press and the public. The only important exception to this pattern was international economic affairs.[30]

This personalized operation was a reflection of the president's own overriding interest in foreign policy. Unlike in the 1960s, however, Nixon made not even a gesture toward the Department of State until he virtually colonized it by moving Kissinger to the secretary's position. Public statements reemphasizing the secretary's position did not obscure the fact that in vast areas of foreign policy planning and operations the Department of State had been relegated to a staff-support role for the president's personal superagency in the White House. Thus, in a sense, Nixon dealt with the ongoing "problem at State" by simply ignoring it and building another agency in its place.

In his truncated second term Nixon retained the arrangement with the figurehead at State removed. Kissinger replaced Rogers as secretary of state. Moving Kissinger to State, even as he retained his position of national security adviser, however, did not mean that the centralization of presidential authority had ended. Rather, with Kissinger physically located in Foggy Bottom, there was an opportunity to mobilize the staff resources of the State Department and to append them to the NSC structure. A revealing illustration of the relationship between the Department of State and the White House occurred during Kissinger's October 12, 1973, press conference during the Yom Kippur War. To the question, "As Presidential National Security Adviser, how do you evaluate the handling of this crisis by the State Department?" Kissinger answered, "Well, . . . we are very impressed, in the White House, by the leadership that the State Department has received."[31]

The prospect that the Department of State itself would see any rejuvenation during Kissinger's stewardship was not bright. Kissinger's disdain for the foreign affairs bureaucracy preceded his entering the Nixon administration. He wrote in 1968 that bureaucracy produces policy that merely "emerges from compromise which produces the least common denominator and is implemented by individuals whose reputation is made by administering the status quo."[32] As Kissinger moved to State, there was little promise that those whom he considered but sorry administrators of the "least common denominator" would have much of a role in policy formulation or execution. Moreover, the personal style of the new secretary, deeply suspicious and secretive, and not just a bit contemptuous of what he called the "intellectual squalor" at State,[33] could hardly be regarded as encouraging.

Further, Nixon himself had a long history of deep, indeed nearly pathological, suspicion of the State Department. Nixon had begun his career, after all, in exposing a putative communist, Alger Hiss, a high-ranking State Department economics officer who had been at the Yalta conference. In the 1950s Nixon had called Acheson the "Red Dean" of the "Cowardly College of Communism"; and once, in the spring of 1969, Nixon began a NSC meeting by complaining to the assembled about those "impossible fags" at the State Department, oblivious to the fact that most in the room were FSOs on detail to the NSC from the Department of State.[34]

The strength and weakness of the Nixon/Ford system was clearly Kissinger.[35] In the first place, neither Kissinger nor his NSC staff was able to get on top of international economic problems in the same way they did political and strategic issues. In fairness, we should recall that issues of "high politics," such as Vietnam and SALT, certainly commanded the most attention when Nixon entered office. But the series of international monetary crises that crashed in on the White House between 1970 and 1973 soon forced the president into the scrambling reactive posture he so deplored. Many years later, Nixon himself would reflect: "I did not really want to make Henry secretary of state. . . . I felt what we needed was somebody with economic expertise though Henry had absolutely no competitors when it came to geopolitics, but economics was not his area of expertise."[36]

A second area of concern was the coordination of the activities of the intelligence community. Kissinger is said to have found the estimates produced by the intelligence community difficult to use in anticipating future crises. These "Talmudic" documents, as Kissinger disdainfully called them, were so abstract and so qualified that they were nearly useless to policymakers, unless one waded through the footnotes and backtracked to the individual analysts and, in turn, the analyst's sources.[37] But one cannot help wondering whether the establishment of the National Assessments Group was not a reflection of Nixon and Kissinger's desire to reduce the independence of the intelligence agencies and whether it did not mask a White House effort to whip into line a CIA that had been so uncooperative in some of the domestic areas elements of the Nixon White House wished the CIA to pursue.[38]

Third, Kissinger's reach was impressive, but his grasp did not seem to extend to such matters as the budgetary operations of key agencies. Perhaps the most significant case in point here was DOD. In 1970 a Defense Program Review Committee (DPRC) was established as Kissinger's means for infiltrating and then controlling DOD's budgetary process. The White House succeeded in imposing a bit more control on the Defense Department, but Kissinger found himself deflected by Secretary of Defense Melvin Laird. Unlike Robert McNamara, who saw his role as one of imposing White House priorities, Laird adopted the posture of a broker between Defense and the White House. Thus, Laird was opposed to extensive White House intervention and successfully stymied White House input in the bargaining between service branches.

To a certain extent, these problems were a reflection of Henry Kissinger's conception of the conduct of foreign policy, namely, that the conduct of foreign policy is a hard, one-man job: "I've always acted alone. Americans admire that enormously. Americans admire the cowboy leading the caravan alone astride his horse, the cowboy entering a village or city alone. . . . This romantic, surprising character suits me."[39] The foreign policy establishment was, however, just too big for any person to manage from policy conception through implementation, no matter how determined, energetic, or devious that person might be. In any event, Nixon's obsession with White House control required that

Kissinger try to be at the head of all caravans simultaneously, whether they were headed for the Middle East, the Paris Peace Conference, the SALT talks, Moscow, or Peking.

As the Nixon administration lost its authority over Watergate, foreign policy became nearly the sole province of Henry Kissinger. Kissinger used his numerically shrinking NSC staff mainly to circumvent his colleagues at the Department of State, of whom he grew ever more distrustful. During the Yom Kippur War in 1973, for instance, Kissinger, in order to avoid informing the Middle East and other relevant bureaus, sent messages to the Middle Eastern heads of state using White House–based CIA communications facilities. The messages were drafted by the NSC staff, and high State Department officials were unaware that they had even been sent.[40] Similarly, Kissinger visited Moscow without telling U.S. Ambassador Jacob Beam that he was in town, and American State Department officials involved in the U.S.-Soviet relationship commonly found themselves in the embarrassing position of having to ask Soviet diplomats what the official U.S. position was.[41] And after the Greek coup in July 1974, Kissinger invited the new premier, Constantine Karamanlis, to visit the United States and discuss the Turkish invasion of Cyprus. He did not, however, inform the U.S. embassy in Athens or consult the State Department desk.[42]

Since Gerald Ford was, at best, a novice in foreign affairs, Kissinger's accountability diminished even more after Nixon's departure in August of 1974. However, Kissinger's management of foreign policy ironically conformed to his assessment of the nineteenth-century German chancellor Bismarck: "Institutions are rarely able to accommodate genius or demoniac power. . . . Statesmen who build lastingly transform institutions that can be maintained by an average standard of performance. This Bismarck proved incapable of doing. His very success committed Germany to a permanent tour de force."[43]

The Carter National Security Establishment

"Every time we've made a serious mistake in foreign affairs," Jimmy Carter told President Ford in their second debate during the 1976 campaign, "it's been because the American people were excluded from the process."[44] Predictably, Carter took office vowing to change all of this—to reduce the visibility of the NSC, narrow its functions, and reduce the rivalry between the president's national security adviser and the secretary of state. No longer would the special assistant for national security affairs be, as he was in Nixon's time, a first among equals; instead, he would work in a "collegial" atmosphere.[45]

The new special assistant for national security affairs was a forty-eight-year-old former Columbia University professor, Zbigniew Brzezinski. Comparisons between Kissinger and Brzezinski were almost inevitable. Both were quick, acerbic immigrants with apparently boundless energy and ambition. Both had the ear of the president. And both, in their role as national security assistant, faced rivalries with secretaries of state who were uncomfortable with bureaucratic brawling. Cyrus Vance was chosen by Carter because he was perceived to be an experienced and articulate representative of the "Eastern establishment." Carter had run for office on a platform that was critical of the traditional foreign and national security establishment, but now that he was in office, he felt the need to reassert policy continuity in a post-Vietnam era of conspicuously fragmented consensus.

At his first meeting with his other statutorily designated cabinet officer, President Carter conferred "cabinet rank" on his NSC adviser.[46] With an initial brief to determine the agenda for NSC meetings, Brzezinski was to be in charge of "ideas" and to make sure that policy papers flowed regularly; he was also to ensure that memoranda received by the president fairly represented every agency position. Brzezinski was also charged with overseeing policy follow-through. Cyrus Vance, too, was to have an independent role, with coequal access to the president by means of a four- or five-page "Secretary's evening report." The president was to return the secretary's paper by noon the next day with marginal notes. But Brzezinski, whose office was literally down the hall from the president's, who managed paper flow, and who was the president's jogging and tennis partner, enjoyed almost unfettered access to the president.[47] For these reasons, plus Brzezinski's captivating method of describing events, the special assistant ascended over potential bureaucratic competitors.[48]

At the outset, great emphasis was placed on the close interpersonal relationship between Brzezinski and Vance.[49] There were, as well, formal procedures designed to strengthen the coequal roles of the Departments of State and Defense, on the one hand, and the NSC, on the other. The day he entered office, Carter issued a directive intended to reduce the dominance of the NSC and "place more responsibility in the departments and agencies while ensuring that the NSC continues to integrate and facilitate foreign and defense policy decisions."[50]

By this directive, NSC-2, the number of special NSC staff committees was reduced from seven to two. The two remaining committees were the Policy Review Committee (PRC) and the Special Coordinating Committee (SCC). The PRC, to be chaired by the secretary of state, was to develop policies where basic responsibility for conceptualizing or implementing policy might fall in one agency, say, Treasury, but would touch on other agencies as well. The SCC, chaired by Brzezinski, was essentially the replacement for the crisis management operations developed by Kissinger.[51] In addition, there were to be ad hoc NSC groups chaired by Brzezinski when "particular policy, including those which transcended departmental boundaries," arose.[52]

At first glance, it appeared that the NSC's role as an action unit was being replaced by a kind of organizational gatekeeping and "think tank" function. Instead of seven nearly all-embracing committees, all chaired by the special assistant, there were to be only two principal committees, only one of which was chaired by Brzezinski. In fact, however, much of the foreign policy action remained where it had been located for the preceding fifteen years—in the NSC.

The Limits of the Carter System of National Security Policy

Two sets of realities eroded the efficiency of this system. First, authority is not easily divisible. The introduction of the security adviser as a putative "coequal" to the secretary of state was not only at odds with the hierarchical nature of power and authority; it was confusing to foreign governments. Second, incoherence was fostered by the inherent conflict in the policy perspectives of the Vance State Department and the Brzezinski-led NSC. The secretary of state was predisposed to the exercise of diplomacy and reconstitution of détente, while Brzezinski focused on the necessity of confronting the Soviet Union. In the end, Brzezinski's perspective won out. But the victory was a long time coming: between Inauguration Day and the enunciation of the Carter Doctrine in early 1980 (marking the final and official embrace of Brzezinski's point of view) the tense interaction of the perspectives of Vance and Brzezinski only reinforced an appearance of policy incoherence and indecision.

The Problems of "Multiple Advocacy"

The argument for multiple advocacy was explained by the State Department's special adviser for Soviet affairs, Marshall Shulman, as follows: "It would be unfortunate if there were a single orthodoxy so that [the president] did not have to hear a range of possible assessments or speculation. A diversity of views enriches the menu of possible responses."[53] There is undoubtedly something to be said for such diversity within the context of internal debate over policy, but problems arise. As Philip Odeen, a management consultant called in by the Carter administration, put it, when "agencies have not adjusted to this informal approach and the White House has not developed means to ensure decisions are communicated clearly and promptly to the agencies . . . the perceptions of the results by the principals differ."[54]

In the end, the Carter system seemed to be, if anything, more controlled by the security adviser and NSC staff than even during Kissinger's incumbency in the first Nixon administration. Of the thirty important papers reaching Carter's desk between the end of 1979 and the last months of 1980, twenty-six were initiated and supervised by the NSC, while only three had come from State, and one came from Defense. But in spite of apparently rigid NSC control of significant policy issues, there never seemed to be an agenda or set of priorities in the Carter years. As one NSC staffer said, rolling his eyes, "We are living the agenda of United States foreign policy."[55]

Much of the Carter administration's foreign policy was hammered out in high-level meetings at which the president was not in attendance. The minutes of these meetings were forwarded (by Brzezinski) to Carter, who would indicate his preferred course in the margins of the case most convincingly presented. In the Carter administration, therefore, there were few hints of separate courses of action argued tenaciously through the bureaucracy. There was instead a top-level free-for-all guided mostly by instinct and wit.

Thus, in the end, multiple advocacy exacerbated uncertainty concerning who made foreign policy decisions. Multiple advocacy also compounded public and governmental apprehension about who was an authoritative public voice of American policy. When political leaders were confronted with the seemingly antithetical pronouncements of Andrew Young, Carter's sometimes heretical ambassador to the United Nations, and statements by Brzezinski or with the incongruous juxtaposition of the Vance and Brzezinski world-views in the same presidential address, friend and foe were confounded. A Washington press corps that thrives on interpersonal conflict and bureaucratic struggle could only amplify the cacophony. Perhaps the best face that could be put on the situation was that advanced by Anthony Lake, then the Department of State's director of policy planning: "Our approach is to make constant pragmatic, case-by-case decisions, seeking the most constructive balance among our interests and adjusting our tactics as circumstances change."[56]

Multiple advocacy might have been made to work if the president had invested considerable time and effort in the thankless and problematic task of cajoling and convincing the policy-making establishment to accept his priorities and perspectives. But such a possibility assumes that the president had an agenda and priorities, and Jimmy Carter never succeeded in articulating either, much less giving evidence of a willingness to wage bureaucratic political warfare personally.

Conflicting Policy Perspectives

The incoherence of the Carter administration's policy processes derived from a divergence of views concerning the substance of policy as well as the nature of the policy-making arrangements. There was, above all, disagreement about the character of the Soviet Union and the centrality of the Soviet-American relationship.[57] Moving the Soviets aside to make way for the Chinese, challenging them to "competition in places like Somalia," and changing the idiom of arms control, at least initially, to a public relations exercise were destructive of the legacy of détente bestowed by Kissinger.

Underlying the lurching process whereby this was done was irresolvable tension within the Carter administration between two views of international reality. On the one hand, there was the view of Secretary of State Vance, who seemed predisposed to recognize what was thought to be a new set of international conditions. The Soviet-American confrontation remained important, but it was only one of many. In contrast, Brzezinski represented a perspective that held that the Soviet-American relationship remained uppermost. Although new forces were certainly taking their place on the agenda, these new forces remained peripheral to the essence of America's position since World War II. Indeed, the new international relations had not supplanted the old; they constituted a more dangerous arena within which a much more capable Soviet Union battled an America more constrained by diminished economic wherewithal and the burdensome legacies of Vietnam.[58]

Carter tried to straddle both positions, but by late 1978 continuation of that posture had become ever more awkward. The fall of the shah of Iran and the hostage crisis, wherein Iranian radicals captured U.S. embassy personnel, pushed Carter further toward the conservatives. With the Soviet invasion of Afghanistan, Carter forswore any hint of a departure from militant containment and enunciated a doctrine no less open-ended and, in its details, more belligerent than that advanced by Truman in early 1947. As Brzezinski's world-view prevailed, a measure of policy coherence was achieved. But Carter's hesitant approach to the more traditional view of international reality merely confirmed that Carter himself was a Hamlet-like chief executive.

Brzezinski Ascendant

Edmund Muskie took over from Cyrus Vance after Vance resigned in April 1980 over the issue of using military force to rescue American hostages in Iran. Vance had promised the Europeans, apparently in good faith, that no such dramatic efforts would be undertaken. In fact, Vance learned that the hostage rescue plan—a plan in which the Joint Chiefs of Staff feared one-third of the hostages and probably thousands of Iranians would be killed—was to go forward only twenty-four hours before the ill-fated helicopters took off. Vance protested, but according to one of Vance's assistants, Carter overruled him, using Brzezinski's logic, that is, that the mission was essentially military and not political.[59] There was speculation that Vance's replacement, former senator Edmund Muskie, would have a political base as a result of his long years in the Senate and thus might be able to combat Brzezinski for primacy.[60]

Although Muskie professed to love his job, he was soon heard to complain that he had to contend with as many as twenty-five items on any one working agenda. As irritating as the number of issues tossed the way of the new secretary was the fact that the agenda was largely fixed at the NSC, leaving Muskie time for only hasty reaction.[61] There were substantive disputes as well. The State Department was initially cut out of development of major changes in U.S. strategic planning, which included shifts in nuclear targeting doctrine and nuclear war-fighting strategies, with important implications for relations with the North Atlantic Treaty Organization (NATO). Brzezinski explained that the reason State was not told of the study was that it concerned a narrow defense question. "We only got to physically see the [ongoing] study 24 or 48 hours before the first meeting," a former State Department official, Leslie Gelb, recalled. This was the last time the State Department was to hear about the study until it was about to be announced as policy in August 1980. Gelb complained that the whole issue was "preposterous" and "dangerous": "It's preposterous because the responsibility for framing nuclear war fighting strategy is the NSC's, not the National Security Council

Staff. And the Secretary of State is a member of the National Security Council. . . . it [is] dangerous because to think that you can separate defense policy from policy-decisions of nuclear war from foreign policy considerations shows a dangerously narrow view of war and diplomacy and of life."[62]

Only in January 1980, in the midst of the crisis in U.S.-Soviet relations resulting from the Soviet invasion of Afghanistan a month earlier, did the Carter system operate smoothly. One Carter administration official at the center of the policy process summed up the outcome when, for the first time since the early 1970s, there was talk of an armed conflict with the Soviet Union: "The policy machinery for the first time is working well. There have been no disputes of major substance, no cracks along the Soviet policy fault line as during the first three years of the administration." The bracing effect of a military crisis was captured by the official's observation that "Afghanistan was a godsend, . . . It gave point and opportunity for action."[63] And "action" had been the management style of U.S. foreign policy for thirty-five years.

Carter attempted to begin his administration as an agnostic on the place and character of Soviet-American relations. He subdivided issues in his cabinet, promoted interpersonal cordiality, and tried to ensure the presence of multiple perspectives on foreign policy in the policy process.[64] Without many preconceptions about foreign policy, for a while Carter was able to hold conflicting positions simultaneously. His was not the view of the diplomat attempting to mediate longstanding rivalries; rather, it was the view of the engineer trying, through experimentation, to reach solutions to dispose of problems. In the end, what "worked" were the old routines of the cold war, managed in much the way they had been managed by his predecessors.

During the Nixon and Carter administrations the security adviser, first Henry Kissinger and then Zbigniew Brzezinski, became the primary adviser to the president on decisions, and the overseer of policy once decisions had been taken. In fact, by the end of the Carter administration Brzezinski had all but replaced the secretary of state. On the threshold of the 1980s, however, serious questions were raised about the role and prominence of the security adviser. In addition, there were concerns about his lack of accountability. If the security adviser was to be regarded as an authoritative interpreter of foreign and national security policy, how was the role of the secretary of state to be understood? If the security adviser and the secretary of state disagreed, whose word was final? In sum, even as the position of the security adviser seemed to peak in the late 1970s, the old problems of coherence seemed paradoxically more intense, for not only did the old bureaucratic perspectives and interests persist but now there was a babble of authoritative voices at the top.

CHAPTER 4

The National Security Council System at the End of the Cold War

IF THE CARTER administration's disarray confirmed the necessity of coherence, the Reagan administration's policy-making travails suggested that ideological consistency in itself was insufficient insurance against policy incoherence. During his first term in office Ronald Reagan had to fire his first secretary of state (Alexander Haig) and his first national security adviser (Richard Allen) and then convince his second secretary of state (George Shultz) not to resign when he complained of being jostled or outmaneuvered by other official and unofficial contenders in the foreign policy arena. Secretary of State Shultz feuded privately and publicly with Secretary of Defense Caspar Weinberger. Weinberger, in turn, viewed the president's parade of national security advisers with contempt. And both Shultz and Weinberger found themselves circumvented by several of President Reagan's national security advisers and Director of the CIA William Casey.

It did not seem to matter that the public philosophies of those engaged in this bureaucratic warfare were usually distinguished from one another only by nuance. Major reorganizations were required throughout Reagan's tenure as his foreign policy personnel feuded, maneuvered, failed, and were replaced. By the end of his two terms, Reagan would have more security advisers than there had been in all the preceding years of the National Security Council combined and would see his administration nearly wrecked by the NSC staff, who had turned the NSC into a secret operational arm of the White House engaged in extensive illegal activities.

THE REAGAN ADMINISTRATION

It was widely assumed that in an administration little experienced in foreign affairs and preoccupied with domestic questions, Secretary of

State Alexander Haig would quickly dominate foreign policy making. Haig's experience as one of Henry Kissinger's top aides provided him with stature sufficient to reverse the decades-long decline of the secretary of state's position, especially in view of Reagan's intention to downgrade the position of the security adviser.

Haig started very early—indeed, before Inauguration Day—by claiming his preeminence as the "vicar" of foreign policy making. By and large, Haig had his way in placing hard-line but well-known and generally respected career FSOs and others familiar to the Washington establishment in the State Department. At the same time, however, Haig's claims to preeminence were clouded by his aggressiveness, which seemed to grate on the coterie of California insiders President Reagan brought to the White House.

The Vicar Exposed

It was not just Haig's rhetorical bombast that irritated the Californians. From the start, Haig was suspected of coveting the presidency. He had briefly pursued the nomination in 1980. Moreover, to many Reagan faithful, Haig seemed to represent an extension of Henry Kissinger's more moderate détente philosophy.[1] There was speculation that the appointment of William Clark, an old friend of Reagan but a man with embarrassingly little experience in foreign affairs, as under secretary of state was designed to constrain Haig. During his confirmation hearings, Clark was unable to identify the leader of South Africa and professed ignorance of the then substantial Western European antinuclear movement.[2] In Europe, the press characterized Clark as a policy "nitwit." Clark's task was never substantive; rather it was to serve as a dependable liaison between the White House and the State Department and its somewhat alien (to the Reagan intimates) secretary of state. In this capacity, by virtually all accounts, Clark was effective.[3]

At almost every turn, Haig's quest for bureaucratic supremacy was frustrated. Brought up short, early and in public, Haig did himself no great service with his startling performance before the national television audience that watched for word on Reagan's health after a would-be assassin pumped a bullet into the president's chest in March 1981. Flushed, with hands trembling, Haig proclaimed himself to be "in control." He might have been; but his tight-voiced intensity and inaccurate narration of the constitutionally mandated succession process (putting himself several rungs closer to the presidency than constitutionally warranted) gave impetus to open press speculation about the effects of Haig's triple-bypass heart operation of the previous year. Ambassadorial appointments, because of the need to pass White House ideological muster, proceeded at a maddeningly slow pace.[4] Malcolm Toon, a former ambassador, complained of the inordinate percentage of political appointees at the start of the Reagan years: "We have a man in London who owes his place in life to the fact that his parents founded a furniture polish dynasty. His only qualification for the job is that he speaks English." And when Reagan's old Hollywood friend John Gavin, the Spanish-speaking actor, was appointed to Mexico, an extremely sensitive post, some Mexicans were heard to complain that if the United States had to send them an actor, "why not Wonder Woman?"[5]

Haig and Secretary of Defense Caspar Weinberger were frequently at odds on issues that overlapped their respective domains. In some cases observers were impressed by what they took as conscious embarrassments of the secretary of state by the White House.[6] In trade policy, the White House stripped even more of the turf from State and assigned it to the Commerce Department and the office of the special trade representative. Haig's opposition to the sale of Airborne Warning and Command System (AWACS) and F-15 fighters to Saudi Arabia was noisily overruled. A grain embargo imposed against the Soviet Union at the time of the Afghanistan invasion was lifted, against State Department advice, even as the Soviets appeared on the verge of invading Poland.

Haig also displayed a substantial capacity for injuring himself. His most natural constituency in Congress should have been some of the moderate senior Senate Republican leadership. However, he was undermined by his own gaffes. One especially piquant tale recounted Haig sending a letter to Senator Howard Baker, the Republican majority leader, its typed salutation reading "Dear Senator Baker." Haig, seeking a personal touch, struck the formal opening and inked in "Dear Harold."[7]

The Reagan System: A Black Hole?

Reagan's first special assistant for national security affairs, Richard Allen, was never able to occupy the openings Haig left. Unlike most of his predecessors, Allen reported through a senior White House adviser: White House counselor Edwin Meese, another old California acquaintance of the president, who correctly admitted little knowledge of foreign and defense policy. In addition to his diminished institutional standing, Allen had been damaged before Inauguration Day by a story in the *Wall*

Street Journal noting that he seemed to have acted for private business interests while he was on the Kissinger White House staff in the early 1970s. And when, in the midst of increasingly bitter and public feuding between Allen and Haig over the control and direction of policy, it was revealed that Allen had received a thousand dollars and a gift of wristwatches from Japanese journalists to set up interviews with Nancy Reagan, Allen's credibility was at an end. Although he was subsequently cleared of any violation of law, Allen's resignation was requested, and he left in early 1982.

The NSC staff did not carry the weight it had carried in prior decades. They were isolated by presidential directive from speaking to the press, and in private some complained that they had been cut off from the traditional flow of information.[8] But if the Allen NSC was not much of a rival to Haig, and if Haig's influence was contained, observers were left to wonder where the locus of decision might, in fact, reside.

Initially, a set of informal policy groups were established, chaired, respectively, by the secretary of state, the secretary of defense, and the director of the CIA, William Casey.[9] Below this level were a series of interdepartmental groups chaired by State (in previous administrations such groups had been directed by the NSC staff). A more informal National Security Planning Group, comprising the vice president, the secretaries of state and defense, the CIA director, and Reagan's closest personal White House advisers, Meese, White House Chief of Staff James Baker, and Deputy Chief of Staff Michael Deaver, served as the inner circle of policy making. Within this group, Meese was to function as the coordinator and director. Allen, the security adviser, was to be a "note taker." After Allen's departure and some later reorganization, subsequent security advisers became full participants in this planning group.

The initial Reagan policy arrangements were no less chaotic than those of the Johnson and Carter administrations. The system's operations were marred by poor preparation, poorly delineated areas of responsibility, and few systematically prepared policy statements. In fact, after one year in office the Reagan administration failed to produce policy reviews and guidance on major areas of the world, including the Middle East and the Soviet Union and China. The central figures of the Reagan years differed with one another on most issues. Yet as meetings broke up, each participant was left to rely on his own notes and impressions. Lacking official minutes or memoranda on the content of discussions, the participants, especially Haig (and subsequently his successor, George Shultz) and Weinberger, were frequently at odds. Edwin Meese, erstwhile coordinator of the "system," tried to put it in the best light. "We have," Meese insisted, "a highly centralized but participatory decision-making system." But when it was suggested to him that many who participated in the system had taken to characterizing the system as a kind of "black hole," into which issues entered but policy never seemed to emerge, Meese responded: "Exactly; that's the way we like it. [I]t is important that decision-making doesn't get a great deal of public or even internal Government attention other than from those who are directly involved, until the President makes a decision."[10]

If, however, the "system" was dependent upon presidential activism, then much of the problem lay with Reagan himself. From the onset, Reagan's interests seemed to run to domestic and economic policy questions. His performance at press conferences was generally given high marks on the latter issues. On foreign policy questions, by comparison, he appeared to be inept and uninformed. In 1982, for example, he proposed major strategic arms reductions that were based upon his ignorance of the actual distribution of strategic warheads across the forces of the United States and the Soviet Union.[11]

Matters were not helped much by the president's lack of interest in current events. Press Secretary Larry Speakes recollected that "he read the comic pages first." Once in December 1982, while on tour in South America, Reagan raised his glass to his hosts in a toast to "the people of Bolivia," when actually he was in Brazil. Eventually, allegations emerged that there was not a functioning president at all. Both the president and his wife resorted to an assortment of astrologers for advice about auspicious dates for various presidential activities, including the signing of the intermediate-range nuclear forces (INF) agreements.[12] To the dismay of his advisers and of his wife, Reagan occasionally referenced Old Testament prophecy for strategic planning guidelines when speaking not only to religious groups but also to journalists.[13] Henry Kissinger confided to a small group of scholars, in front of an open microphone, "When you meet the President, you ask yourself . . . how he should be Governor much less President."[14]

Reagan was aware of the charges and resented them. At the height of the Iran-Contra scandal, he protested to a group of Florida high-school students, "I am not a potted plant president."[15] The president's staff and his wife were acutely aware of Reagan's limits and sought to protect him. His work schedule was kept light, often taking up only a few hours a day. But as Lou Cannon, Reagan's generally sympathetic biographer, has observed, "Ignorance has consequences. Reagan's lack of knowledge, or even interest, in the substance and processes of foreign policy and arms control gave an enormous advantage to those who made the last presentation to the president on any contested issue. Officials plotted among themselves for this opportunity."[16] Indeed, it appeared that the president seldom sought to involve himself in significant policy questions and that his top aides excluded him from them. Thus, when the Department of Defense confirmed a shift in nuclear war-fighting strategy, the president was not included in the decision-making process. "We don't get the President involved in that kind of stuff," said Meese.[17]

It appears that Reagan's major first-term national-security-policy initiative, the massive buildup of defense spending, lacked a clear strategy. Secretary of Defense Weinberger admitted that there had been no "combination of central objectives and a well-defined plan" for using the defense resources requested from Congress during the buildup.[18] David Stockman, Reagan's first budget director, confessed that he did not analyze the defense budget proposals. "And so defense, which was going to cost hundreds of billions more, had to be assigned huge, arbitrary out-year numbers without any debate or review." Stockman had hoped that Weinberger would impose a measure of fiscal responsibility on the services. Instead, Weinberger wanted more. Stockman, fatigued by a succession of endless work days, erred in projecting future costs. When he discovered the error weeks afterwards, he said, "I nearly had a heart attack. We had taken an already-raised defense budget and raised that by 7 percent. . . . and compounding it over five years—we had ended up increasing the real growth rate of the United States defense budget by *10 percent* per year between 1980 and 1986. . . . But by then the . . . budget was out and they were squealing with delight throughout the military-industrial complex."[19] There would be little "squealing with delight" by the end of the decade as the federal budget deficit accumulated aggregate deficits greater than any encountered by the U.S. government throughout its entire previous history.

The Vicar Defrocked

Allen's dismissal as security adviser gave the administration an early opportunity to remedy these sloppy managerial conditions. Clark was made security adviser, and the position was given new preeminence. There was speculation that Haig's influence would increase because he and Clark had developed a close working relationship during Clark's year at State. On the other hand, Clark noted: "The conflict [is] . . .

inherent in the system. . . . I now must view the area of national security from a Presidential perspective rather than from the State Department perspective."[20]

The remark proved prescient, for within months reports of increased tension between the White House and Haig reemerged. In mid-1982 Clark and Haig disagreed on the wisdom of placing an embargo on the sale of technology to the Soviet Union for a natural gas pipeline to Europe. Clark aligned himself with Reagan to deny the Russians American technology and to punish European subsidiaries of American firms if they went through with sales on their own. Haig maintained that the embargo could damage America's relations with its NATO allies. Haig, with great emotion, threatened to resign over the issue unless the sales went through. To Haig's surprise, the president abruptly accepted Haig's resignation and appointed in his place another former Nixon administration cabinet officer, George Shultz.[21]

In contrast with his first year in office, the president would now be briefed on a daily basis by Clark and by the secretaries of state and defense before each press conference. And Clark took steps to ensure that the president would become a more active participant in foreign policy. Judge Clark apparently resorted to films, documentaries, and even flip charts prepared by animators in order to help bring the president up to date on policy.[22] But apart from whether Clark, a man who a year before had admitted that his foreign policy experience consisted of "72 hours in Santiago,"[23] would be able to coordinate the policy process, there remained in place all the problems that demanded precisely such coordination. Notwithstanding a drop in the decibel level of bureaucratic conflict after Haig's dismissal, there persisted the longstanding institutional tensions between the State Department, Defense, and the CIA.

Shultz at State

The new secretary of state's relaxed style and his long and close personal relationships with members of Reagan's cabinet were assets. The president had reportedly been extremely impressed by Shultz's service on several transition task forces. Perhaps the policy-making machinery could work with less gear grinding than during Haig's tenure.

Shultz's views and style promised greater convergence between State and Defense. His views on arms negotiations at the strategic level and European weapons and forces seemed somewhat closer to Weinberger's than Haig's. But Shultz, like Haig, was reluctant to bully the Soviets with embargoes or rhetoric and was sensitive to economic issues that seemed to have escaped Secretary Weinberger. Moreover, the secretary of defense was deeply suspicious of most policy advice emerging from the Department of State or, for that matter, the NSC.[24] Thus, bureaucratic and interpersonal difficulties remained.[25] Perhaps they could have been overcome with presidential leadership, but it was not forthcoming.

At the end of July 1982, Shultz made it his first task to get a handle on the mundane: personnel and management. The new secretary staffed the State Department's senior management and personnel offices with seasoned authorities on East-West matters. By the beginning of 1983, Shultz had removed the director of the Arms Control and Disarmament Agency (ACDA), Eugene Rostow, who, as a neoconservative member of Reagan's original team, apparently did not believe that arms control should be part of Reagan's first-term agenda. Rostow's successor, Kenneth Adelman, although a protégé of the neoconservatives, was inexperienced, which gave some warrant for a belief that ACDA would be less of an obstruction to dealing with the Soviets on nuclear weapons issues.

The new secretary placed on the State Department's policy planning council senior academics and trusted senior FSOs to bring him up to speed on national security issues and to serve as advisers for long-range planning.[26] In mid-1984 the veteran cold war elder statesman Paul Nitze was brought to the department and made first among equals in matters relating to arms control. Nitze had languished as the INF negotiator in Geneva, where he had been forced to advance positions that Haig later confessed were not negotiable from the Soviet viewpoint.

By mid-December 1984 right-wing bells began to clang loudly over the changed character of the State Department. Meese, Clark, and Weinberger were all said to have protested Shultz's staffing arrangements at State.[27] Shultz went unchastised by the White House, however, perhaps because the pace of his appointments, as well as his own demeanor, was generally so relaxed. Some observers, especially in the press, bemoaned the apparent glacial pace of movement from the State Department or Shultz himself. But because he was persistent, steady, gray, and cautious, he was usually effective in dealing with the White House and gaining access to the president virtually at will, a capacity he appeared to consider a privilege and used with care and deference.

Shultz's public reticence was partly attributable to his temperament and partly, perhaps, good bureaucratic politics. By remaining unobtrusive during his first months in office, Shultz became better entrenched earlier and less of a target for the ever-watchful Reagan right. In his press relations, Shultz was considerate of the White House. Shultz made sure that the White House spokesperson routinely briefed reporters three hours before the State Department spokesperson appeared. Shultz conserved his own appearances before the press. When he did come forward, his statements were painfully elliptical, evasive, and without much substance. Since the president deferred to authority in foreign policy matters, Shultz usually got his way except on matters of force, on which Reagan apparently heeded the keepers of authority in these matters, the Pentagon and the CIA. In private, Shultz was willing to yield to Defense and the CIA virtually all of the Central American question, a kind of litmus test of "Reaganism" for the rest of the Reagan camp but an issue on which Shultz was said to be something of a moderate.[28]

All of this made Shultz more effective in confrontations with the secretary of defense. Shultz's moderate presentation of the issues was reassuring next to the apocalyptic rhetoric of Weinberger. When there developed an incessant and intense exchange of vitriol between Weinberger and Shultz, Chairman of the Joint Chiefs Adm. William Crowe recalled, "The President never arbitrated. He just let the water seek its own level, which seemed to me a funny way to run a railroad."[29]

The president's Strategic Arms Reduction Talks (START) initiative, for example, was the subject of confusion and conflict within the administration. There was little agreement concerning what was to be reduced and how. Moreover, participants in the debates note that the president was largely uninterested. The upshot, as one participant put it, was "wholly chaotic": "Reagan seldom said anything that wasn't written on [a] card. . . . He was very passive. He wanted a consensus, and when it wasn't forged he didn't lay down the law. Everyone went off in a different direction. We'd leave a meeting and have no idea of what, if anything, had been decided."[30]

Without leadership at the top, bureaucratic struggle and personal conflict were inevitable.[31] By the beginning of Reagan's second term, the NSC had lapsed into bureaucratic immobility and trench warfare as it tried to mediate the disputes, with a covert bias toward Shultz. Robert "Bud" McFarlane, Reagan's third national security adviser, later recalled Reagan's saying: "If I were to fire George and put Cap at State, I would get bad policy. So I'm not going to fire Cap." Reagan then looked at McFarlane and said that it was up to him to "make it work."[32] As a result of the president's attitude, one participant complained, the only thing "systematic about this is the president's aloofness, [and] his failure to give enough guidance and direction to the players on his team."[33]

The Iran-Contra Scandals

The Reagan foreign-policy-making style culminated in the Iran-Contra scandals. In addition, the Iran-Contra affair provides an important case study that illustrates the problems associated with the development of the NSC staff as a quasi-independent actor in the policy process. We will deal with the executive-legislative dimensions of the scandals in subsequent chapters; here we will focus on the decision-making processes within the Reagan administration.

Reagan evidenced unusual interest in matters relating to Iran and the Contras. Indeed, as Theodore Draper's exhaustive research suggests, Reagan was an active, informed participant in important elements of the Iran-Contra embarrassment. Specifically, Reagan signed at least three "findings"[34] authorizing the transfer of arms to Iran with the expectation that there would be a hostage release.[35] Reagan signed his second "finding" authorizing the deal on January 17, 1986. Draper reports that "it was his Finding, and he had plenty of time to know what he was doing. . . . since his secretary of state and secretary of defense had voiced their opposition, only his stubborn determination to continue dealing with Iran made all that followed possible."[36] Reagan may have been engaging in a massive exercise in self-deception. He denied that there was an arms-for-hostages deal, but none of the participants are in doubt that he was an active participant in the process.

Reagan was hardly attentive to the tedious details of negotiating the swap of arms for hostages. Nor were the principals involved in the process much better informed: Admiral Poindexter, Reagan's fourth national security adviser, consciously set about cutting out of the operation the Departments of State and Defense and the Joint Chiefs of Staff—all demonstrated skeptics—and turning the "enterprise" over to Poindexter's own NSC staff. An active-duty Marine, Lt. Col. Oliver North, on loan to the NSC, was charged by Poindexter with pushing the arms-for-hostages effort forward.

The Iran-Contra scandal was a virtual textbook case of bureaucratic politics and warfare at its most perverse. Moreover, the operation was all the more remarkable for the attitudes held by the major players— Poindexter and North—toward the rest of the U.S. government. Poindexter argued that the president totally controlled foreign policy and that "Congress could not use its powers over appropriations to limit the President in any way."[37] As Admiral Poindexter subsequently observed, "Now, because the cost of failure is very high, the bureaucracy is not willing to . . . endorse high-risk operations. . . . I think one of the roles of the NSC staff has got to be to push them vigorously, I feel that in the very real world that we live in, the NSC staff has got to be the catalyst that keeps the process moving forward and that often involves an operational role for the NSC staff. Their only loyalty is to the President."[38]

Poindexter set up a mechanism for circumventing the usual government departments. He required only one individual to do the job, his young and enthusiastic aide Lieutenant Colonel North. North's commitment to the president seemed unlimited. In testimony, North asserted that it was duty to his commander in chief that compelled him to lie to Congress and anyone else who stood in the way of what he understood to be the mission set by the president: "This lieutenant colonel is not going to challenge a decision of the Commander in Chief. . . . and if the Commander in Chief tells this lieutenant colonel to go stand in the corner and sit on his head, I will do so." "Every centurion," North maintained, "had a group of shields out in front of him, a hundred of 'em, to take the spear."[39] He was obviously proud to "take the spear" for his commander in chief/president/centurion—the differences were not always evident in Lieutenant Colonel North's theory of governance.[40]

For his part, Reagan, in trying to free U.S. hostages held by Iranian militants, acted in contradiction to his public pledges to the U.S. people and his stated policy, which he was trying to enforce with Operation Staunch, the multilateral effort to impede the sale or transfer of arms to Iran during the Iran-Iraq War of 1982–88 (even as the United States was giving covert aid to Iraq). Also, in arming the Contras with proceeds gleaned from the sale of arms to Iran, the president breached specific legislative proscriptions.

The Boland Amendments of September 19, 1983, and October 12, 1984, prohibited the use of funds to support activities designed to overthrow the Nicaraguan regime. The president's response to Congress's efforts to stop funding the Contras was to urge his NSC aide, Robert McFarlane, to find a way to keep the Contras together "body and soul." McFarlane and North came up with a scheme for establishing "institutes" and "trusts" in conjunction with "public diplomacy" programs set up by Congress and to be run by the State Department. Subsequently, they used third countries and wealthy individuals (who were rewarded with a presidential audience) to raise funds, which were then funneled to the Contras "covertly."

As in the case of the Iran arms affair, Shultz challenged the arrangement. Shultz especially objected to the use of third countries, but in a full National Security Planning Group meeting in June 1985 he was overridden. Again, Reagan was present; he was described by others in the meeting as attentive to the arguments. The president heard his chief of staff, James Baker, argue that the solicitation and use of third-country funds was of dubious legality. Shultz recalls that Baker characterized the activity as an "impeachable offense." Reagan, however, wanted to go ahead with arming men he felt were the functional equivalent of American heroes of 1776.[41] As a result of Reagan's apparent enthusiasm, efforts were made to solicit money and aid from Brunei, Taiwan, Korea, Israel, Saudi Arabia, Japan, Panama, Guatemala, Honduras, Costa Rica, El Salvador, and even drug cartels. It is uncertain whether Secretary of State Shultz was informed.[42]

The final element in the scandal was the "diversion" of "profits" from the sale of arms to Iran. The monies were passed to the Contras in April 1986. North has testified that this illegal activity was "neat." The evidence on whether Reagan knew anything about North's inspiration is murky. Reagan insists that he knew nothing about the diversion, which may be true, or he may have forgotten, as he seems to have forgotten other important details about the hydra-headed scandal. Indeed, his memory was so deficient about what he had done or not done that his own investigatory commission, under the direction of Senator John Tower, decided that it was useless to question him further.[43] Later, the president explained that he forgot what U.S. policy was or that he did not know or that he did not understand what his administration had been doing. Presidential Chief of Staff Donald T. Regan, said to be the most powerful chief of staff in the history of the presidency, blamed the NSC, claiming that it told so many "cover stories" that "it sort of confused the President's mind."[44]

Subsequent investigation by the Tower Commission and Congress focused on the diversion rather than on the constitutionally much more important issue of the illegal funding of the Contras. As one of the investigators, Congressional Research Service's Louis Fisher, wrote later:

Despite . . . long standing principles and precedent, Colonel Oliver North testified . . . that the President could authorize and conduct covert operations with non-appropriated funds. . . . Such conduct . . . risk[s] . . . [and] invite[s], and deserve[s] impeachment proceedings. [For the President] would have failed

to see the laws are faithfully executed and he would have precipitated a constitutional crisis by merging the power of the sword with the power of the
purse.[45]

When public disclosure burst upon them and the wheels finally fell off
the operations in November 1987, Poindexter and North sought to cover
it up. This reaction was consistent with earlier behavior on Poindexter's
part. When the CIA became involved in North's arms transfer in the
summer of 1985, the CIA demanded that there be a presidential finding,
as required by law, to cover their participation in the operation. Since
there never had been a signed finding, Poindexter drafted one authorizing
what had been done the preceding August and September and had Reagan sign it in December, over a year later. When the scandals finally
became public, Poindexter destroyed the finding.

One Reagan aide called the foreign policy process at this time, with
some generosity, an exercise in "decisional autonomy." In truth, it was
more akin to a sort of decisional autism. Presidential agents conducted a
privatized foreign policy, selling arms to Iran. Iran, however, was pro-
scribed by law as a recipient of U.S. weapons due to Iran's contributions
to a worldwide series of bombings, hijackings, and assassinations. At the
same time that new U.S. arms were showing up at the front in the Iran-
Iraq War, the State Department was trying to coordinate a European
arms embargo in order to isolate the radical Khomeini regime. Meanwhile, NSC staffers sojourned again to Khomeini's domain in order to
exchange U.S. arms for U.S. hostages held, not by Iranians, but by
Lebanese. Paying tribute to kidnappers was at odds with a U.S. policy
dating back to Jefferson and Barbary pirates. Indeed, the U.S. did not pay
ransom; the administration had publicly sniffed and scolded when the
French and Germans negotiated trades of prisoners for various forms of
lucre in order to release some of their captives.

The urge to make a deal with Iranian "moderates" continued. Even
after amazing peregrinations of NSC officials had been published in November 1986 by the Lebanese magazine *Al-Shiraa* (which, in turn, had
learned of the NSC comings and goings in Tehran via pro-Iranian broad-
sides literally lying in the streets of Beirut),[46] the NSC initiative lurched
on. Meanwhile, Secretary of State George Shultz confessed to a head-
shaking interviewer on "Face the Nation" that he could not exercise the
authority to stop it.[47]

Throughout the U.S. government, officials had come to act on what
they believed to be the operant assumptions of "Reaganism." If the

testimony of Poindexter can be believed, the national security assistant, along with his underlings, and Director of the CIA William Casey calculated what Reagan really intended in Latin America and Iran and then carried on—without burdening the president with the liability of either knowledge or an explicit decision on his part. In the end, how a serving, "by-the-book" vice admiral in the U.S. Navy, only two months into his job as national security assistant, could undertake on his own an initiative to bargain for hostages using U.S. arms sales to Iran and then "skim" the proceeds to fund a U.S.-backed insurgency seemed inexplicable. Attorney General Edwin Meese, subsequently alleged to have orchestrated the effort to keep the investigation away from the president, offered what he believed to be a compelling explanation, namely, that the president would have approved the scam had he been asked.[48]

Aftermath

Chief of Staff Donald Regan was apportioned "primary responsibility for the chaos that descended upon the White House" when public disclosure of the Iran-Contra affairs occurred. In the final analysis, however, responsibility for the disaster was placed on the president and his lax and detached administrative style. The Tower Commission, appointed by Reagan, noted that "President Reagan's personal management style places an especially heavy responsibility on his key advisors." Nonetheless, "the NSC system will not work unless the President makes it work. After all, this system was created to serve the President of the United States in ways of his choosing. . . . As it was, the most powerful features of the NSC system—providing comprehensive analysis, alternatives and follow-up—were not utilized."[49]

The "black hole" of Reagan's national security system had very nearly consumed his presidency. Late 1987 and early 1988 saw the near unraveling of the Reagan administration. There was a round of top-level resignations, extended televised congressional hearings, appointment of a special independent prosecutor, indictments, and trials, the latter extending into the early 1990s. Indeed, questions concerning then vice president Bush's involvement in the Iran-Contra affairs dogged him into the 1992 presidential campaign and may have contributed to his electoral defeat. Special Prosecutor Lawrence Walsh released some of former secretary Weinberger's notes that put the lie to Bush's prior contention that he had not been "in the loop."

As Iran-Contra threatened his administration, Reagan became "listless and dispirited" as a struggle developed for control of his policy-making structure.[50] A more pragmatic group of policymakers emerged. Frank Carlucci, a veteran of the Foreign Service as well as the Department of Defense and the CIA, took over the NSC, eliminated its covert operational arrangements, and "set out to restore its proper role as an interagency body. That is its honest broker role."[51] When Weinberger resigned, Carlucci moved to the Defense Department. He was succeeded at the NSC by his military aide, Lt. Gen. Colin Powell. A moderate outsider, Judge William Webster, was installed at the CIA after Casey's death. No less important, White House Chief of Staff Donald Regan was replaced by former senator Howard Baker, a man whose moderate, "inside Washington" credentials were beyond challenge. "More than any other single person," Lou Cannon reports, "it was Howard Baker who brought Reagan back."[52]

Under Howard Baker and Colin Powell, a much more orderly policy process was instituted within the White House. The pragmatic bent of the new members fit naturally with the survivors of the Iran-Contra debacle, George Shultz at State and James Baker at Treasury. Moreover, the postcrisis administration was the beneficiary of a dramatically improving foreign policy environment, as Mikhail Gorbachev seized the foreign policy initiative. Critics of Reagan's response to Gorbachev's diplomatic offensive blamed Reagan for losing the initiative. But diplomatic innovation is seldom an attribute of presidencies entering the twilight period imposed by the Twenty-second Amendment. To his credit, Reagan did become more focused, if not on the issues per se, then on the larger question of engaging Gorbachev in his quest to end the cold war.[53] The last months of the Reagan administration proceeded smoothly, absent the chaos and rancor that had afflicted the operation during the preceding seven years.

THE BUSH NSC SYSTEM

The pragmatic style of the last months of the Reagan administration carried over into the Bush administration. As has been the case throughout the history of the NSC, the style of the president drove the process. If Reagan was largely an innocent in foreign policy, a distracted and, at best, episodic foreign policy administrator, Bush seemed almost hyperactive and "hands-on."[54]

The most frequently noted manifestation of Bush's intense personal involvement was his tendency to converse frequently with other leaders on the telephone. In addition, until the political pressures of the 1992 campaign forced him to suppress his passion for personal diplomacy, the president's attention to face-to-face diplomacy with foreign leaders in Washington or abroad bordered on the obsessive. Early in his administration, for example, when he visited Japan for Emperor Hirohito's funeral, Bush arranged for eighteen meetings with other heads of government who were also in Tokyo at the time. During the runup to the Persian Gulf War, Bush was apparently in daily, sometimes hourly, telephonic contact with coalition leaders. And in those areas where Bush felt he had special expertise (he had been director of the CIA, U.S. ambassador to the United Nations, and U.S. representative in China), he exercised a high degree of personal control over policy.

The Bush Policy-Making System

This highly personalized style of foreign policy activism might imply a difficult relationship with the secretary of state. That this was not the case suggests the importance of another characteristic of the Bush foreign and national security apparatus: the president's close personal relationship with the top foreign policy and intelligence officials in his government—Secretary of State James Baker, National Security Adviser Brent Scowcroft, Secretary of Defense Richard Cheney, and Director of the Central Intelligence Agency Robert Gates. His closest relationship was with his secretary of state, who, because of his unrestricted access to a president who trusted him implicitly, proved to be extremely active and powerful. Baker had directed Bush's campaign for the presidency in 1980, and when the president's reelection campaign faltered in the fall of 1992, Baker reluctantly acceded to his old friend's importuning and left the Department of State to assume direction of the White House reelection effort.

Moreover, Bush's senior advisers had a similar background and style. All had had long Washington experience. Virtually all of Bush's closest advisers carried an air of conservative pragmatism that was the hallmark of the Republican presidencies of the 1950s and 1970s. Baker was trusted by the president; in turn, Baker's relationships with Scowcroft and Cheney were solid. Thus, the Bush administration was remarkably free of the interpersonal warfare that marred the Carter and Reagan administrations.

Baker's intimacy with Bush and his good working relationships with the security adviser and the secretary of defense did not mean that the

Department of State prospered under Baker.[55] Unlike Shultz, Baker relied on a very small circle of advisers who had worked with him in his prior positions as chief of staff and Treasury secretary under Reagan. However, few of these men and women were professional diplomats, and Baker did not bring many senior FSOs into his inner circle. When he returned to the White House in the second half of 1992, his Treasury and State Department coterie accompanied him. Although the State Department was put under the direction of Under Secretary of State Lawrence Eagleburger, a respected foreign service professional and one of the few old State Department hands to gain entry into Baker's group of confidants, there was little doubt that control of the broad framework of foreign policy was even more firmly in the White House.

Baker shared Bush's propensity for highly personalized diplomatic contact. Unlike Shultz, Baker severely reduced the amount of contact with the assistant-secretary level of the department, a level regarded by Shultz as crucial enough to report directly to him. Under Baker, the tendency was for these mostly career officials to report through a handful of the secretary's personal deputies, many of whom were junior in rank to the assistant secretaries.

Baker was also adept at maintaining contact with Congress. Indeed, one of his first initiatives as secretary of state was to work very carefully to hammer out a "cease-fire" with congressional Democrats on Central America. This allowed the Bush administration to quickly put behind it one of the poisonous issues that had infected Reagan's relations with Congress. Otherwise, Baker's style was to stake out a few major areas within which he personally dominated diplomacy except when the president chose to get directly involved, such as in negotiations with Gorbachev and, later, Boris Yeltsin. In the case of the Middle East after Desert Storm, Baker clearly took the lead within the administration.

The other key piece in this generally stable and smoothly functioning system was NSC adviser Lt. Gen. (ret.) Brent Scowcroft. Scowcroft fit the mold of the deeply experienced, pragmatic moderate that Bush seemed most comfortable with. He had served as Kissinger's military aide and then as security adviser after Kissinger went to the Department of State, and he was noted for running a low-profile, "honest broker" NSC.[56] During the late 1970s he worked for Kissinger Associates, where he was a colleague of Eagleburger's. When he had previously served as security adviser, he had had none of the empire-building propensities of his predecessors. Scowcroft's views of Reagan's administration of foreign and defense policy were a part of the Tower Commission report, and he was known to be a "scathing critic" of both the style and substance of Reagan's proposals. Thus he had termed Reagan's call to eliminate all nuclear weapons "insane" and Reagan's Strategic Defense Initiative (SDI) a "wild fantasy."[57]

The system of day-to-day coordination set up by Scowcroft was centered in the hands of his deputy, originally Robert Gates,[58] leaving Scowcroft free to serve as the president's personal adviser. Scowcroft would provide the president with a daily international briefing as well as a daily CIA briefing, information Reagan had seldom received. Scowcroft, in sum, conceived his role as coordinator, adviser, and policymaker *without* the impulse to dominate the process, a remarkable contrast to the power-seeking appetites of a Kissinger or a Brzezinski. He was, in short, "a model of the trustworthy, self-effacing staffer, . . . who avoided the Washington social scene, and had a priest-like dedication to his work. It was his one interest."[59]

In Secretary of Defense Richard Cheney, Bush once again had in a key position a man with White House administrative experience. Cheney had served as chief of staff in the Ford White House. In addition, he had served in Congress as part of the Republican leadership and had been a member of the House Select Committee that investigated the Iran-Contra affair. Because of his experience in the White House, Cheney was sensitive to his role as both an advocate of his department and the president's agent. Cheney evinced a greater skepticism about the changes under way in the Soviet Union, a position that sometimes drew criticism from Baker at State. This harder line on defense issues served him well, however, in his relations with the military establishment.

Cheney was clearly solicitous of the effects of the Vietnam syndrome on the professional military in that he was careful to include full JCS participation in any decisions to use force. Thus, Colin Powell, who had been a key member of the salvage operation at the end of the Reagan administration and was appointed chairman of the Joint Chiefs by Bush, was given full opportunity to voice reservations concerning the use of force in the preparation for the Persian Gulf War (something he was obliged to do, in any event, under the Goldwater-Nichols Act). Cheney was also responsive to Powell's insistence that should force be used, the military would have what it thought it needed and would be left largely alone with respect to planning and executing the war. Operation Desert Storm was, therefore, very much a DOD exercise. At the same time, the military was not given a veto. Notwithstanding Powell's reticence to fight, the final decision remained with the White House.

The Limits of the Bush System

Although the Bush foreign- and national-security-policy machinery came to be viewed by many observers as a model of smooth efficiency, it was not without its problems. The secretary of state, for instance, had a tendency, disconcerting to some, to disassociate himself from issues that might backfire. Baker distanced himself from Bush's overtures to China after the Tiananmen Square Massacre of 1989, leaving the matter to Scowcroft at the NSC; and, in the early part of the runup to war against Iraq, Baker seemed to test the winds before firmly placing himself behind the war with nearly frantic efforts to raise funds from allies, an effort some called despairingly his "Operation Tin Cup." At the same time, Baker found himself dealing with the disintegration of the Soviet bloc but made every effort to postpone any commitment of funds to Gorbachev's efforts until the Soviet prime minister was nearly in mortal peril.

In part, Baker's practice of choosing issues that seemed not so much "easy" as they were "manageable" was a function of the process he installed at the State Department. A close-knit team of six or seven advisers could only engage an issue or two at a time. The result, many of his critics felt, could be seen in the inattention given to Saddam Hussein's ambitions and, once the war had begun, the inattention to the results of American victory.

Baker and Bush were so busy keeping the anti-Saddam coalition together that there was virtually no postwar planning. After the war, not one professional in Southwest Asian politics was brought into the Bush inner circle.[60] Ambassador Thomas Pickering, the first member of the career Foreign Service to serve as U.N. ambassador (a cabinet-level post until the Reagan years) and by all accounts the most successful U.N. ambassador since Adlai Stevenson, was unceremoniously moved to India. Pickering's flaw, it was said, was that he had been "too visible," stealing the limelight from a jealous secretary of state who harbored ambitions for even higher office.

From the very outset, critics of the Bush administration viewed it as experienced but without any larger strategic vision. Without a vision of the "new world order" the president proclaimed as the cold war evanesced, the administration was largely at the mercy of events. The orderly professionalism of the policy-making system might impress, but good procedure could not guarantee imaginative foreign policy.

As Soviet power collapsed, the president seemed always to be behind the curve of change. Initially, Bush and his inner circle downplayed Mikhail Gorbachev's earnestness (he was termed a "drug-store cowboy" by presidential spokesman Marlin Fitzwater) in promoting an end to the cold war. Then, having belatedly embraced Gorbachev, the president and his administration proved reluctant to support those within the collapsing Soviet Union who were pushing for change as Gorbachev's grip on power began to slip. Finally, as the remnants of the old Soviet order fumbled their coup attempt in the late summer of 1991, the Bush administration seemed unable to decide whether it would support the new Russian leadership of Boris Yeltsin.

In fairness to the Bush team, few were able to anticipate the magnitude of what unfolded. In addition, the Bush administration was forced to carry the burden of the financial profligacy of the Reagan administration and therefore had little margin of resources. Nonetheless, German chancellor Helmut Kohl's aggressive political response to the collapse of the East German state stood in contrast to Bush's apparent passivity. On the other hand, Bush's management of the buildup to and prosecution of the war against Saddam Hussein was certainly impressive. But subsequent revelations about the administration's prewar policy of support for Saddam, including funneling aid to the Iraqis, left even the management of the war under a cloud.

The Bush administration's greatest strength—pragmatism—proved to be a source of weakness as well. Bush and his most intimate advisers seemed more comfortable as curators of the status quo than as breakers of new diplomatic ground. Notwithstanding James Baker's subsequent role as facilitator of Middle East peace talks, former White House communications director David Gergen, who worked under Baker while Baker was Reagan's chief of staff, has observed: "I don't think he would pretend to bring to the job of secretary of State initially the conceptual framework that Henry Kissinger did."[61] And Brent Scowcroft said of himself, "I don't have a quick, innovative mind. I don't automatically think of good new ideas. What I do better is pick out good ideas from bad ideas. But I don't have an original mind. You can't say I don't have an ego. It is comforting to be doing things that make a difference. In the end, it's the job that's more important."[62] In short, these were men who were extremely adept at driving the system, but they would not provide it with direction. For this they were dependent upon the president, and it was precisely George Bush's dubious ability to master what he once called, derisively, the "vision thing" that left a sense that his administration was but a bridge to something different. When Europeans spoke of a "new architecture," not only the language but the conception seemed alien to President Bush and those with whom he was comfortable.

Policies seemed to have almost a vaporous quality in the Bush years. Americans went to war to divest the drug lords of Panama, but post-Noriega drug exports burgeoned. There was to be an energy policy in the wake of the Gulf War. But Congress objected to a remedy that opened coasts off Florida, California, and the Arctic wilderness to drilling. There was to be a permanent U.S. presence in the Persian Gulf, but the Saudis lost interest. There was to be a program to "defang" Saddam Hussein, but the Saudis fretted that Saddam's undoing would be taken in the coin of regional "instability." There was to be arms control in the Middle East following the Gulf victory, a suppliers' agreement that might exercise, in Bush's words in May 1991, "collective self-restraint." But only a month later Cheney opined that limits on arms sales to Gulf associates would be "counterproductive."

Caution was so embedded that there was no certainty Secretary Baker would actually show up at the conference that inaugurated the historic Arab-Israeli peace conference. Indeed, the American delegation did not secure a hotel room until forty-eight hours before the meeting convened in Madrid. The professionals in the State Department and the CIA were frozen out of the great issue of the transformation of the Soviet empire. When Ambassador Robert Strauss issued anguished calls decrying the lack of White House attention to the imploding former Soviet Union—a "Goddamn outrage," he fumed—he was answered with a silence that bespoke the ultimate White House priority: the election looming on Tuesday, November 4, 1992.[63]

THE PAST AND FUTURE OF THE SYSTEM OF NATIONAL SECURITY POLICY MAKING

The U.S. system of national security policy making came about in response to a world-view that emphasized the necessity of American leadership of a global struggle against an implacable Communist foe. The need was to create and then orchestrate a broad range of instrumentalities in order to structure world order. Down through the Reagan and Bush administrations, the assumptions about American policy and policy making remained unchanged. During the cold war, policy became a global political and economic engagement of and preparation for combat with an unyielding Soviet Union. The compelling administrative need was for a reorganization of policy processes to strengthen the hand of the president. Thus began the strain toward efficiency, responsiveness, and centralization of policy making and administrative processes.

The United States viewed its national security as synonymous with its conception of international order; and American interests were viewed as nearly universal. A consequence of this definition of interests was to push the United States into a wide sphere of potential and actual interventions. A circular dynamic was thereby set in motion: the United States had to maintain a presence everywhere, because the ideological confrontation was potentially everywhere; to fail in one place was to endanger the entire structure. Peace and global order were indivisible. Disorder in one place therefore threatened order every place.

The thrust of policy and bureaucratic arrangements that followed a global definition of American interests reflects an approach that contrasts with classic diplomatic procedures. For diplomacy involves something quite different from the dogged commitment to global confrontation. The European diplomatic tradition is reflected, as Sir Harold Nicolson points out in his book *Diplomacy,* in the *Oxford English Dictionary* definition of *diplomacy:* "Diplomacy is the management of international relations by *negotiation;* the method by which these relations are adjusted and *managed* by ambassadors and envoys; the business or art of the diplomatist."[64] The spirit of the diplomatic enterprise is accommodation and compromise.

During the cold war these skills and approach were not very much in demand. Not surprisingly, the department responsible for developing and applying these skills, the Department of State, was pushed aside in the scramble for policy control by new bureaucratic actors with skills deemed more appropriate to presidents who had given up on persuasion and negotiation and now sought a capacity for "massive retaliation," "assured destruction," "counterinsurgency," "pacification," and all the accouterments of a diplomacy of violence.

It became commonplace during the 1970s to bemoan the institutional preeminence of the special assistant for national security affairs, the Defense Department, and the CIA and the diminished capacity and stature of the Department of State.[65] But the institutional structure of the national security system is largely a function of presidential need for centralizing management of a grand strategy predicated, for the most part, on the threat and use of force. Presidents have therefore sought to gather more power into the White House. Moreover, it has been the rare national security adviser who could delegate power without biting his nails in anxiety over the fate of policy consigned to the miasma of corridors that make up the foreign policy bureaucracy. It might be preferable to have a national security adviser who was, as Henry Kissinger put it in April 1980, "the orderer of options. He should make sure everybody gets a fair hearing. . . . He should not appear on television. He should not see foreign diplomats. If he does, he is conceived as the alternative to the Secretary of State. . . . When I was the Security Adviser, I violated every one of these rules except the one that I never went on television."[66]

In the end, the positions of the national security adviser and the NSC were dependent, not on the personnel of the NSC staff, but on the relationship of the staff to the president and the degree to which U.S. policy was specifically or potentially involved in a great test of arms. When the danger of nuclear Armageddon loomed, a reputation for speed, will, and determination, the presumed virtues of the NSC system, were at a premium. In recent years, however, the will to orchestrate force seem to have dissipated.

The American military, for instance, was content to leave events in the Balkans to run their course. It was feared that virtually any serious intervention in Yugoslavia would lead to a quagmire reminiscent of Vietnam or Lebanon. In the waning days of the Bush administration, General Scowcroft and Acting Secretary of State Lawrence Eagleburger, both genuine experts on Yugoslavia—Eagleburger had been a U.S. ambassador there, and Scowcroft spoke Serbo-Croatian—would not press President Bush to action. It was an election season, and Bush was not about to buck his JCS chairman or his defense secretary to make a grand gesture. A similar quandary faced Bill Clinton. Although he was disposed to action, the uniformed services were not, and Clinton, encumbered by his domestic priorities, his youthful resistance to Vietnam, and a draining fight with the Joint Chiefs over homosexuals in the services, could not bring himself to lead where his service chiefs, public opinion, and the European allies would not willingly go. Slaughter and mayhem threatened Europe once again. But without U.S. (or European) leadership, events were left to play themselves out.

Virtually the only foreign policy issue—apart from the lingering albatross of Iran-Contra—that achieved and sustained salience during the 1992 campaign was the North American Free Trade Agreement, or NAFTA. Moreover, as public debate over the merits of the agreement developed, primary public advocacy for the administration's trade policy was in the hands of Carla Hills, the head of the Office of the U.S. Trade Representative. Foreign economic policy issues had intruded into the center of foreign policy making before, but executive attention had been episodic.

At the end of the cold war, the possibility emerged of a refocused American foreign policy. Although some traditional security concerns remained, post–cold war national security expanded to include economic security. In response to the cold war, policy-making institutions and executive-legislative relations underwent more than forty years of transformation. The global changes of the late 1980s and early 1990s will likely compel no less far-reaching changes.

CHAPTER 5

Congress and Foreign Policy

CONGRESS IS THE constitutionally mandated partner of the president and has played an active role in U.S. foreign policy making for most of the history of the republic. But beginning in World War II, and for nearly two decades more, Congress largely acquiesced to presidential initiative. In part, Congress's cold war attitude can be traced to the Constitution's design. Throughout the period between the end of World War II and the onset of difficulties in Vietnam there was widespread agreement in Congress that constitutional checks and balances were inadequate to the tasks of world leadership. The constitutional framework was constructed for a small and geographically isolated America. But the threats to American and international security posed by a disorderly and dangerous postwar world seemed to demand greater efficiency than had been considered possible or desirable in the late eighteenth century.

It is important to underscore the underlying consensus that developed, albeit fitfully, during the late 1940s regarding presidential dominance in foreign policy. The consensus held firm until the late 1960s. Hence, it was possible to develop and sustain a system of bipartisan and executive-legislative relationships that circumvented the difficulties of the constitutional design.

But when there was no deep policy consensus concerning American objectives and means, as was the case in the Korean War, intense and bitter partisan debates complicated policy making. Indeed, executive-legislative wrangling in the early 1950s over symbolic and real issues, such as subversive infiltration of the government, loyalty oaths, the firing of the iconographic general Douglas MacArthur for insubordination, led to policy-making incoherence. Accordingly, much of Eisenhower's initial effort was directed at reestablishing the bipartisan consensus that Truman had developed between 1947 and 1949 when he proposed, and Congress accepted, the fundamentals of "containment": the Truman Doctrine, the Marshall Plan, and the North Atlantic Treaty Organization

(NATO). Insofar as Eisenhower succeeded in reestablishing consensus he was also able to institutionalize executive primacy.

By the late 1960s, however, consensus had begun to disintegrate under the burden of Vietnam. And as consensus gave way, executive-legislative understanding came undone. By the early 1970s, with consensus in ruin, Congress charged through the rubble, aiming not at bipartisanship but at codetermination.[1] By the onset of the 1980 campaign season, however, both Jimmy Carter and his Republican challenger, Ronald Reagan, were asserting a need for a return to the old verities of containment.

In the early 1990s, the brief Gulf War seemed to reestablish presidential primacy. But the effect was momentary: the collapse of the Soviet Union cut away the basis of American foreign policy for the preceding forty-five years. The Bush administration, led by cold war tacticians, asserted U.S. leadership in the creation of a "new world order," but they proved unable to define the substance of the order they had in mind; nor did they mobilize the means to build it.

Congress, constrained by the massive deficit piled up during the Reagan years, distracted by its own internal scandals and the largest turnover in membership in the post–World War II period, was certainly no seedbed of foreign policy leadership. Absent the exigencies of a compelling foreign crisis, the executive-legislative relationship inclined toward stasis.

THE RISE AND DECLINE OF BIPARTISANSHIP

President Truman's view of the presidency and Congress set the tone of virtually every American response to the early cold war. Truman's "passionately held conviction," as Secretary of State Dean Acheson put it, was that the president's position was supreme.[2] On the other hand, Republican Joe Martin, in his maiden address as Speaker of the House, had said, "Our American concept of government rests upon the idea of a dominant Congress."[3] Truman, himself a product of Congress, was quite conscious of institutional jealousies and a congressional reluctance for world involvement. Thus he carefully prepared the ground for the North Atlantic Treaty and the Marshall Plan by assiduously courting Speaker Martin and Senator Arthur Vandenberg, head of the then prestigious Senate Foreign Relations Committee.

Presidential Dominance of Bipartisanship

Truman's views have been held by his successors. With a ritual nod to Congress's constitutional grant of foreign policy power, postwar presidents have sought broad discretion. Truman's concern was the commitment and use of American military power. Indeed, Truman's perception and use of presidential foreign- and national-security-policy power is doubly important: first, the substance and parameters of American foreign policy were established in a manner that made security concerns paramount; and second, Truman's response to cold war events provided a lasting precedent. Presidential initiatives in Korea and Berlin and in covert activity (often without prior congressional consultation) became the pattern of Truman policy making.

Subsequent presidents continued the cursory or post hoc consultations with Congress, and as Congress yielded to this procedural shortcut, it became a custom the American people came to expect, even demand. Action was the defining characteristic of a worthy and strong president. Presidential government was even cast in terms of quasi-constitutional justification. By the mid-1960s, members of the executive branch spoke of "inherent" powers of the president. These "recognized powers" included the authority to initiate or continue military action without congressional approval. By the early 1970s, however, members of Congress had begun to ask whether the "dog of war"—as Jefferson and Franklin termed executive war—was not permanently off its leash.

Students of executive-legislative relations frequently point to the Korean War as the pivotal event in the postwar development of overriding presidential war powers.[4] The unilateral steps taken by Truman in late June 1950, at the onset of war, were breathtaking. Congressional and popular support for the president was high at the start (as was the case at the outset of the Formosan crisis in 1956, the Cuban missile crisis in 1962, and Vietnam in 1964). Burning throughout the early cold war period, however, was a sputtering fuse of constitutional crisis. As Senator Vandenberg noted: "The trouble is that these 'crises' never reach Congress until they have developed to a point where Congressional discretion is pathetically restricted. When things finally reach a point where a President asks us to 'declare war' there usually is nothing left except to 'declare war.'"[5]

Crises by definition are aberrations in the normal course of events that require unusual reactions. By the spring of 1950, the thinking within the Truman administration suggested that crises were a permanent part of

American policy requiring bold presidential action. By 1959 a new chairman of the Senate Foreign Relations Committee, J. William Fulbright, was summarizing the congressional mind: "So it is the President that must take the lead. . . . We would accede to his requests. If he puts it the other way around, it is going to fail. . . . I'm talking about political management . . . of the Congress. Our strong Presidents always have, if they are successful in this field, to counteract the parochial interests of our Congress."[6]

The forces set in motion in the late 1940s culminated in Vietnam. Senator Fulbright described the executive-legislative relationship as follows: "The circumstance has been crisis, an entire era of crisis in which urgent decisions have been required, decisions of a kind the Congress is ill-equipped to make with the requisite speed. The President has the means at his disposal for prompt action: the Congress does not. When the security of the country is endangered there is a powerful premium on prompt action, and that means executive action."[7]

The Tonkin Gulf Resolution and After

The scope of presidential activity authorized under the Tonkin Gulf Resolution in 1964, shepherded thorough the Senate by Senator Fulbright, was enormous. In part, however, the resolution was a piece of the larger bluff that accompanied presidential authorizations in smaller undertakings, such as the guarantees offered Taiwan in the mid-fifties and a promise tendered to Lebanon in 1957. Few in Congress believed that giving the president fulsome support in facing down Ho Chi Minh would mean that huge numbers of troops would actually be called to protracted battle. But as the succeeding years demonstrated, President Johnson was quite willing to exploit all the ambiguity of the resolution's language. Moreover, congressional testimony revealed that the purported attacks that prompted the submission of the Tonkin resolution may never have taken place, at least not in the form the administration suggested.[8]

Many in Congress came to associate themselves with the position held by Senator Fulbright after 1967, namely, that President Johnson's expansion of the war was not justified under the Tonkin Gulf Resolution. The strongest statement of this position was that Congress and the American people were deceived and that the resolution called for a limited commitment, not a "functional declaration of war," as the administration contended.[9]

Congressional action cannot be explained solely in terms of executive deception, however. From March 1961 on, the *New York Times, Time,*

Newsweek, and other newspapers and journals regularly, and for the most part accurately, reported events in Southeast Asia. In May 1961 the *New Republic* forecast: "If these Americans are under fire, they will shoot back; and once there are casualties, the prestige of the United States will be committed. . . . The choices will then be humiliating withdrawal or deeper involvement in a stalemate which may not admit of a 'victory' in anything less than a decade—some experts say even longer."[10] As Henry Fairlie notes, "There was always sufficient knowledge within the public realm to form a political judgment."[11]

The fact is that Congress did make a judgment. There was, of course, a good deal of institutional self-deception at the time of the Tonkin Gulf Resolution and later. In fact, Senator Fulbright accurately foresaw the implications of the resolution. Senator John Sherman Cooper asked Fulbright during the floor debate on the resolution, "Looking ahead, if the President decided that it was necessary to use such force as could lead into war, we will give that authority by this resolution?" The chairman of the Foreign Relations Committee replied, "That is the way I would interpret it." But, Fulbright added, he was under the impression "that the President will consult with Congress in case a major change in present policy becomes necessary."[12]

Misunderstandings and outright deceit notwithstanding, Senator Fulbright and most other members of the Senate were prepared to accept the resolution because it was, in Fulbright's words, "consistent with our existing mission and our understanding of what we have been doing in South Vietnam for the past 10 years." Furthermore, he asserted: "We are not giving the President any [extra] powers [that he does not have] under the Constitution as Commander in Chief. We are in effect approving the use of the powers that he has. That is the way I feel about it."[13]

Thus, overshadowing the entire debate was congressional predisposition toward both presidential initiative and the substance of Johnson's Vietnam policy. Lyndon Johnson maneuvered Congress into accepting a broad statement of presidential authority; but binding the president and Congress together in 1964 was the mutual conviction that Communist regimes ought to be opposed, even if this involved supporting a corrupt but "pro-American" regime in Saigon, or anywhere else.

Within two years, of course, Senator Fulbright and a small number of senators had concluded that, contrary to the rhetoric of almost a quarter-century, the meaning of the "national interest" was no longer self-evident and that the executive did not possess any special wisdom about the national purpose. Needless to say, Johnson and his successor, Nixon, disagreed. Both presidents agreed with Secretary of State Kissinger's assertion that foreign policy "is not a partisan matter."[14]

A few in Congress sought to reopen debate quieted for more than twenty years. They found, however, that Adlai Stevenson's fears in the mid-1950s were warranted. Stevenson had written that criticism "conjures up pictures of insidious radicals. It suggests nonconformity and nonconformity suggests disloyalty and disloyalty suggests treason, and before we know where we are, this process has all but identified the critic with the saboteur and turned political criticism into an un-American activity instead of democracy's greatest safeguard."[15]

A distaste for partisan debate was but an extension of the operational needs of the cold war presidency. From this perspective, the imperatives of American national security require flexibility, responsiveness, and even a measure of ambiguity. The logical extension of a call for closely held policy and tightly managed foreign policy is centralizing operations in the White House. Undoubtedly, however, another advantage suggested itself to many in Congress, namely, that if the president claimed the initiative in foreign policy, he could also be saddled with the responsibility for failure.

The atrophy of responsible debate quickly became apparent. The substantive issues were submerged by vilification. The president publicly impugned the patriotism of antiwar members of Congress, who, for their part, questioned the chief executive's sanity. At the same time, Johnson administration officials, as well as a number of academics, even some who were opposed to the war, reiterated the rationale for bipartisanship. Legislation that would limit a president's foreign policy powers, it was argued, was dangerous: world order demanded a nimble executive.[16]

Throughout the Nixon-Kissinger years the executive contended, as Kissinger told the Senate Foreign Relations Committee in 1973, that "the foreign policy of the United States transcends parties and Administrations."[17] But the proposition begs two issues: First, what is to be the exact content of that foreign policy? Second, how ought that foreign policy be derived and executed? The core of Kissinger and Nixon's argument with Congress was that the "national interest" and American foreign policy values were "continuing" and self-evident to thoughtful people of goodwill, hence partisan debate was not only unnecessary, it was a threat. In fact, however, the values and substance of American national security were no longer self-evident. The challenge of the late 1960s was to assumptions that had stood for more than twenty years.

THE VIETNAM REVOLUTION

From spring 1973 until well into 1976, Congress mounted an assault on the prerogatives of a presidency severely weakened by the twin failures in Southeast Asia and Watergate. January 1973 had seen the signing of the Paris peace accords, confirming the withdrawal of American troops from Vietnam. At the same time, Cambodia came under increasing pressure from the Khmer Rouge insurgents, and the Nixon administration resumed massive bombing there. The reaction in Congress was no less explosive.

Initial congressional attempts to cut off funding of the Cambodian bombing during February, March, and April 1973 were circumvented by the White House claim that it had the right to shift funds within the defense budget to pay for the bombing campaign whether Congress approved or not. Congress was hardly eager to dispute Nixon's assertion that the bombing was necessary to cover the last of the withdrawals of U.S. forces and to ensure that all prisoners of war were released or accounted for. But in May 1973 the Senate passed a supplemental appropriations bill stipulating that "none of the funds may be expended to support directly or indirectly combat activities in, over or from the shores of Cambodia or in or over Laos by United States forces."[18]

By early June the House of Representatives had agreed and the measure was sent to a Watergate-besieged President Nixon, who promptly vetoed the bill. A veto override failed, but the amendment to stop the bombing in Cambodia was soon attached to other legislation, such as a bill to raise the national debt ceiling, which the president could not veto if the government was to continue to operate. On June 29, 1973, therefore, Nixon accepted the inevitable end of the Cambodian bombing campaign.

Throughout the remainder of the Nixon presidency and the Ford presidency, Congress reduced executive requests for economic and military assistance to the faltering Vietnamese and Cambodian regimes. And as Saigon and Phnom Penh collapsed in the spring of 1975, Congress, notwithstanding administration attempts to lay the blame at its door, refused to extend to President Ford any emergency funds, even for refugee assistance.[19]

As the struggle over the Cambodian bombing cutoff was coming to a head, Congress approached a climax of its four-year effort to reclaim the right to participate in the decision to commit American troops. In 1973 both houses passed war powers legislation. The Senate legislation attempted to define in detail circumstances in which the president could use force without prior consultation. The House approach was even tougher, cutting off ongoing hostilities involving U.S. forces by means of a concurrent resolution. A concurrent resolution does not require a presidential signature to become law; its use in stopping a U.S. military operation in the field would constitute a legislative veto. Prior consultation was also called for in both bills.

In the final version of the War Powers Act, passed in October 1974 over a presidential veto, the president was required to report to Congress within forty-eight hours after the beginning of hostilities. The president could continue hostilities for a maximum of sixty days in the absence of congressional authorization and then could take thirty days more to complete a withdrawal of U.S. forces. The heart of the War Powers Act was the provision for concurrent resolution by both houses at any time requiring the earlier withdrawal of troops.[20] Other provisions included:

1. Limitation of the presidential commitment of troops to actual or imminent hostilities to declared wars, authorization by a specific act of Congress, or a national emergency created by attack
2. A requirement that the president consult with Congress "in every possible instance" before committing troops to actual or imminent hostilities
3. A reporting deadline of forty-eight hours when troops are committed without a declaration of war, the information to include whether troops are equipped for combat or in numbers sufficient to enlarge an existing combat presence
4. A stipulation that if any portion of the act was found invalid in court, the rest of the legislation would remain in force

Simply put, the War Powers Act of 1974 allowed Congress to stop a war at any time by passing a concurrent resolution. U.S. forces could be brought home from a war or any other circumstances involving "hostilities" by a simple majority vote of both the House and Senate.

With the evidence of nearly a quarter-century, it is clear that the effectiveness of the War Powers Act has been limited.[21] Presidents have refused to strictly comply with it. Congress has not been willing to take the responsibility for codetermination of some of the tougher calls about the use of force, even when the chance presented itself. Neither the public nor Congress has much interest in the question of who makes war when the horizon is placid. When Senator Joseph Biden (D.-Del.) called for hearings on the issue in 1989, the room was devoid of press and camera, and few fellow senators stayed for more than five minutes, and then, one felt, only because of Senator Biden's seniority and interest in the issue.[22] In addition, the legislative veto was called into question by a 1983 ruling in an obscure immigration case.[23]

The passage of the resolution over Nixon's veto, along with the Cambodian bombing cutoff, was the high point of the "Vietnam Revolution" in Congress. New restrictions were voted on U.S. military assistance; debate was initiated on increasing the role of Congress in controlling nuclear exports; and in the wake of Watergate-related exposés of abuses of power within the intelligence establishment House and Senate intelligence committees were established.

When Turkey invaded Cyprus in July 1974 in response to a Greek-backed coup, Congress immediately cut off military assistance to Turkey.[24] Notwithstanding Secretary Kissinger's fulminations over "the growing tendency of the Congress to legislate in detail the day-to-day or week-to-week conduct of our foreign affairs,"[25] the anti-Turkish coalition held well into the Carter administration. In 1975 and early 1976 Congress similarly restrained the president's attempts to intervene in the Angolan civil war. At the same time, Senator Henry Jackson mobilized sufficient forces in Congress to demand that strategic nuclear delivery vehicles in any future strategic arms limitations talks be of equal numbers on both sides.[26] Congress also imposed preconditions on trade agreements with the Soviet Union so stringent that the Soviets were never willing or able to meet them.

THE "NEW" CONGRESS

Clearly, the presidents of the 1970s confronted a different Congress. The institution changed as each election brought scores of new members. Thus, after the 1978 election more than 75 percent of the Democrats in the House had served six years or fewer, and about 50 percent had served four years or fewer. By the 1980s, sixty men and women who had served during 1969 had passed from the Senate scene. By the late 1980s a definable Vietnam generation of senators and congressmen and congresswomen were ensconced in Congress. In most instances, whether Democrats or Republicans, they agreed with these sentiments expressed by liberal Democratic senator John Kerry: "Whether or not people were for or against Vietnam, I'm sure we have very similar views about how America ought to make judgments about putting soldiers into places of risk. I think a universal theme for all of us would be: Don't ever put soldiers in that position again, asking them to make sacrifices without guaranteeing that you're going to follow through and give them the capacity to win."[27]

Not surprisingly, therefore, when the Reagan administration moved to put marines into Lebanon, most Vietnam veterans in Congress were opposed. Senator John McCain, a conservative Republican and former POW, protested: "I was so upset . . . and concerned. I think if I'd not had my Vietnam experience, I would have gone along. . . . But I knew that 1,500 marines . . . were not going to affect the outcome and unfortunately, that some young Americans were going to die needlessly."[28] These Vietnam veterans were by no means controlling Congress in the 1980s. However, there was greater skepticism about the use of force. Thus the changed executive-legislative relationship that grew out of the early 1970s was preserved in its essentials, leaving some observers predicting insoluble problems.[29]

Congressional institutional capacity was enhanced as well. When Congress established budget committees, it provided itself with the institutional capacity to compare the competing claims of the federal bureaucracy and restructure national priorities. Under the 1974 arrangement, the House and Senate budget committees were required to prepare a budget resolution that recommends target figures in major functional areas of the federal budget. In addition, these committees had to supply target figures for total federal expenditures, tax, and debt.

Initially the process seemed to work more or less as intended. The budget resolution, though largely advisory to other congressional committees, was nonetheless the focus of serious debate. During the early 1980s, for example, the Republican-led Senate Budget Committee "served as the focal point of President Reagan's fiscal revolution."[30] The Senate Committee was again central to the prolonged negotiations concerning deficit reductions completed in 1990. The 1990 agreement, a five-year accord, in fact, however, seriously limited congressional discretion. Thus, by the early 1990s there was a growing sense of frustration within Congress that the massive deficits so constrained the budgetary process as to reduce the budget committees to overseeing technical details.[31] In the end, congressional influence on the budget was lodged in the appropriations committees—where it had been before the Vietnam Revolution.[32]

The establishment of the Congressional Budget Office (CBO) in 1974 did not free Congress from its dependency on the executive any more than the new budget committees had. On the contrary, Congress's dependence upon the executive's information and analysis of policy options seemed to increase as the complexity of governance and the sheer weight of numbers—trillions of dollars of unexpected obligations—cascaded on Congress's collective consciousness. The initiative for providing the numbers and, indeed, for defining the problems lay with the executive, and the best that CBO could do was to say whether the data the executive provided were good or bad.

Congress also moved to increase the responsibilities of the General Accounting Office (GAO) and the Congressional Research Service (CRS) of the Library of Congress. During the 1970s GAO sought to shift from an essentially investigative arm of Congress. It was hoped that GAO would anticipate public policy issues and provide Congress with more timely analysis. By 1990 GAO had, in fact, been provisioned with a considerable analytic capability. Employing more than 5,000 people and operating with an annual budget of $364 million, GAO produced some 880 reports, more than 3,800 legal rulings, and undertook some 1,500 audits and investigations for Congress.[33] In the five years between 1985 and 1990 GAO saved the U.S. government some $79 billion.[34] Similarly, the CRS more than doubled in size during the 1970s and by the decade's end was able to provide 565 professional analysts, 50 of whom were assigned to the CRS's Foreign Affairs and National Defense divisions. For many in Congress, CRS reports provided indispensable analytic tools on everything from the efficacy of U.N. missions around the world to the historical meanings of the war powers.[35] Support staff for committees also expanded. To be sure, not all of the increased committee resources were devoted to foreign affairs. Nonetheless, staff available to the House Foreign Affairs Committee and the Senate Foreign Relations Committee tripled.

All this analytic capability did not make Congress more able to "co-determine policy." Perhaps the better budgetary information and investigative, research, and even staff capabilities that were at hand after the onset of the 1980s would have made a difference if there had not been the 1970s "reforms" of the committee and subcommittee system. Traditionally congressional committees had been controlled by a network of autocratic chairs. By the mid-1970s, the old baronial chairpersons could be removed by means of a simple majority vote. In addition, numerous subcommittees were established that assured that most members of the majority could, during their first term, chair their own subcommittee.

The resulting "balkanization" of committees and the expansion of committee staff ironically led to even less foreign policy coordination of the executive branch's appropriations requests. By 1992 a foreign aid bill might have to run a gauntlet of committees and some 148 subcommittees with overlapping jurisdiction.[36] The fractionation of Congress thus resulted in a lack of overall perspective. Institutional fragmentation probably precluded Congress from acting as a responsible counterweight in the budgetary process even had there been a larger consensus regarding either Congress's role or U.S. policy objectives.

Increasing Personal Resources

As members of the "new" Congress of the 1970s voted to increase the congressional bureaucracy, they also moved to increase their individual resources. Thus, the personal staff available to each senator increased from about 1,750 in 1967 to more than 3,200 by 1977. In the House, the increases were from just over 4,000 to almost 7,000. Much of the new staff assistance was committed to nonpolicy chores, such as answering constituent mail. Nevertheless, by the 1980s the membership of the House and Senate could count on the services of about 750 legislative aides in the House (7 times the number they had in the 1960s) and 350 policy-oriented legislative assistants in the Senate (4 times the number in the 1960s).[37] The increase in personal resources indicates deeper changes. The reforms of the 1970s were aimed not so much at increasing the power of Congress as they were at increasing the power of the individual members of Congress.

At the beginning of the 1990s the ironic, indeed Sisyphean, consequences of the reforms enervated the joy of service. For many in Congress, the fun was gone. And so had some tired, well-regarded veterans. "All reform movements," said Henry Hyde (R.-Ill.), one of the ninety-two original members of the House class of 1974, "end up as a struggle for power." "The purity of motive," Hyde continued, "somehow becomes diminished as the arena loads up with carcasses."[38] Republican Congressman William S. Broomfield, ranking Republican on the Foreign Affairs Committee, reflecting on his thirty-six years in the House, stated: "The partisanship is so bitter that it's difficult to get anything through. . . . Everyone is trying to get the political advantage and everyone is suffering. . . . I just felt I didn't want to continue."[39] Looking back, Timothy Wirth, departing senator from Colorado and member of the House class of 1974, waxed nostalgic: "It was glory time," he recalled. "You really had a sense of why you were there and what you were doing. Not at all like now." On his decision to leave the Senate, Wirth reflected: "I surprised myself with the clarity of my analysis. I saw myself about to go through seven months of horror—a negative campaign that would be hurtful to all concerned. And for what? To spend another six years in an institution that didn't work? To continue an insane life that required me to spend the vast percentage of my time doing things I didn't want to do?"[40]

Paralleling these developments have been changes contributing to a diminution of control by the traditional party leadership. In the Senate the changes can be traced to the style of the Senate majority leader when that post was held by Mike Mansfield (D.-Mont.) and his successor, Senator Robert Byrd (D.-W.Va.), throughout the 1960s and early 1970s. Mansfield fostered a concept of the leadership that encouraged individual members of the Senate to develop and pursue their own interests. These decentralizing and democratizing developments had their counterparts in the House, where Carl Albert (D.-Okla.) and Thomas O'Neill (D.-Mass.) proved unable or unwilling to assert the kind of control typical of the 1950s and 1960s. Indeed, when Speaker Jim Wright's (D.-Tex.) short but abrasive tenure, during which he sought to reestablish the prerogatives of the leadership, ended in scandal in 1989, the Democrats turned to Thomas Foley (D.-Wash.), perhaps the most deferential Speaker in decades.[41]

Other changes served to fragment Congress's collective attention. New voting practices of the full House, such as electronically recorded voting, meant that detailed voting records now were available to the hometown newspapers. The result was, in the words of one member, that "everyone scurries to vote on everything." Having lost anonymity, members tended even more than the leaders to vote with their eyes on their constituency. By the late 1970s, House proceedings were televised, making individual members more visible then ever. Members eagerly sought a limelight (cost-free to the taxpayers) that could reach into 435 separate constituencies. In 1986 the Senate consented to have its proceedings televised as well. Under the all-seeing eye of C-SPAN, conformity to the leadership's position risked political extinction if the leadership's position proved unacceptable back home. Throughout the 1980s, with an extremely popular Republican president occupying the White House, congressional Democrats seemed especially reluctant to follow their Capitol Hill leadership lest the "Great Communicator," President Reagan, speak directly to the people and thus expose members to the discipline of the ballot box. The result then was that for most of the 1980s the leadership had far less control over congressional outcomes.[42]

Indeed, the loss of control of congressional leadership became apparent as early as the mid- and late seventies. One study of amendments to legislation coming out of the House Foreign Affairs Committee noted that in the Ninety-first Congress (1969–70) only 39 amendments were offered on 30 bills. (Floor amendments to legislation proposed in committee are indications of dissatisfaction with the normal workings of Congress.) In contrast, during the Ninety-fourth Congress (1975–76), 112 amendments were offered to 42 bills and resolutions of the same committee. More than two-thirds of all amendments in the Ninety-first Congress were offered by members of the committee, but during the Ninety-fourth Congress, almost 75 percent were offered by nonmembers of the committee.[43]

The Aftermath of Reform

The results of these developments were summarized by Democratic whip David E. Price as lone-ranger ethics. The results of the "reforms" of the 1970s and the mutations of the modern intimacy with constituents achieved a kind of infamy, termed "gridlock." Congressman Price described it more fully as the tendency of members and their staffs to "latch onto a piece of policy turf, to gain control of a subcommittee, and to cultivate an image of policy leadership." The decline in "incentives to engage in the painstaking work of legislative craftsmanship, coalition building, and mobilization" resulted in a pandemic Hobbesian individualism that swept both chambers.[44]

The Panama Canal treaties ratification process, during 1977 and 1978, offered a dramatic example of how a single individual—in this case a junior senator, Democrat Dennis DeConcini of Arizona—nearly destroyed agreements that had taken thirteen years to negotiate. DeConcini attached a reservation to the treaties that provided for the use of American force in the event that the canal was closed. The Carter administration found itself involved in lengthy and frustrating negotiations with the freshman senator.

For much of the late 1970s and 1980s, the one-time center of foreign policy authority and debate, the Senate Foreign Relations Committee, appeared disabled. By the mid-1980s the turnover in this committee was greater than in virtually any other committee. It was a telltale sign of its diminished stature that at least one Democratic senator, Christopher Dodd of Connecticut, acknowledged that he obtained a seat on the committee in 1980 because no one else wanted it. Throughout the decade, Dodd, Joseph Biden, and Claiborne Pell (D.-R.I.), the senior members, were forced to recruit members to a committee that had once been regarded as the most desirable assignment in Congress.[45]

Assignment to the Senate Foreign Relations Committee had proven dangerous. The electoral rejection of past committee chairs William Fulbright (D.-Ark.) and Charles Percy (R.-Ill.) was widely attributed to their fascination with foreign affairs. Indeed, four out of five chairs in the late 1970s and early 1980s had lost reelection bids. Half the members of the committee in the mid-eighties had served four years or fewer, compared with the historical norm of eighteen years. Most of these electorally enforced retirements were seen as voter retribution for senators' inattention to their domestic base while concerning themselves with, and cavorting in, distant lands.[46]

Moreover, the Senate Foreign Relations Committee, like Congress as a whole, was becoming more partisan. The growing tendency to vote along ideological lines was mirrored by the decision, in the late 1970s, of the committee minority and majority leaders to have separate staffs. Staff reports ceased to be the starting point of debates and became a kind of political kabuki, a public jostling for position and advantage.[47] As in Congress as a whole, the number of subcommittees within the committee proliferated, each constituting a small, well-staffed fiefdom. The committee's power and influence were further eclipsed by new centers of Senate power. Other committees, such as the Armed Services, Finance, Agriculture, and Banking committees, gained prominence as these areas intruded into traditional Foreign Relations Committee preserves.

In the second term of the Reagan administration, a new chair of the Foreign Relations Committee, Senator Richard Lugar (R.-Ind.), reasserted some of the committee's previous authority. Lugar managed to steer the first foreign aid bill through the Senate since 1981. (For five years there had only been continuing resolutions.) Lugar, along with Congressman Stephen Solarz (D.-N.Y.) in the House, was instrumental in turning the administration away from Philippine president Marcos in time not to be caught on the wrong side of a revolution. Similarly, Lugar pressured the Reagan administration to move away from its policy of "constructive engagement" with South Africa as strong sentiment for economic sanctions against the racist regime grew in Congress. Lugar's Senate committee brokered resolution of stalemates with the House over arms sales to Jordan and the issue of aid to the Contras in Nicaragua.[48]

But the redemption of the Senate Foreign Relations Committee proved short-lived. The return of Democratic control of the Senate in 1986 saw

Claiborne Pell, a veteran of thirty years in the Senate, but a man little inclined to exercise forceful leadership, assume the chairmanship of the committee. Senator Pell, with a genteel, lackluster, cerebral, and laconic personal manner and a penchant for what his colleagues saw as tangents (e.g., an interest in extraterrestrials and extrasensory perception), shied away from an authoritative role as chair. Meanwhile, Senator Jesse Helms (R.-N.C.), an aggressive and talented exploiter of senatorial rules and procedures, asserted the prerogatives of seniority and claimed the minority leadership of the committee, displacing Senator Lugar in the process. Helms took advantage of Pell's refusal to assert control and used the committee to advance his own conservative agenda by holding diplomatic nominations hostage.

Other members of the committee soon lost interest in the often rancorous proceedings and attended to their other committees. A quorum proved rare, and thus the business of the committee languished. By the time the Bush administration arrived, there were indications that Helms had overplayed his hand. Democratic members of the committee outflanked Helms by decentralizing the committee's work. Skepticism remained, however, about whether strengthening the subcommittees would strengthen the committee.[49]

The House Foreign Affairs Committee gained somewhat greater visibility as the Senate Foreign Relations Committee declined. The House Foreign Affairs Committee and its chair, Dante Fascell (D.-Fla.), received mixed reviews. The committee was said to be the realm of "the House's most proficient high-wire artists and acrobats, jugglers and sword swallowers, backed up behind the scenes by a small team of skilled trainers and handlers. And though you don't always know what you'll see at Foreign Affairs, it's usually worth the price of admission."[50]

Membership on the House committee was more stable than on the Senate committee, so members on the House committee had more tenure. Perhaps because the House majority was secure, there was more room for members to acquaint themselves with substantive and difficult issues. Longtime committee chair Dante Fascell was very independent and often found himself at odds with the majority of Democrats on the committee. Fascell's support for the Reagan administration regarding the Contras was a special cause of consternation for most of the other committee members. The committee's second-ranking Democrat, Lee Hamilton of Indiana, gained wide respect in Congress for his substantive grasp and political skills. Hamilton, a not infrequent author of "think pieces" in elite journals such as *Foreign Affairs,* assumed leadership of the Iran-

Contra investigations in the House. With Fascell's retirement in 1992, Hamilton assumed leadership of the committee.[51]

Various of the House committee's subcommittee chairs were viewed as quite talented.[52] For example, the chair of the Subcommittee on Asian Affairs, Stephen Solarz, though widely perceived as abrasive and ambitious, was nonetheless regarded as enormously effective and "one of the few members of Congress who can command a one-on-one meeting with any foreign leader in the world."[53] Before the transformation of Congress in the 1970s—Solarz entered Congress in the immediate aftermath of Watergate—such clout usually belonged solely to the chair of the Senate Foreign Relations Committee. Public hearings such as those held by Solarz on the wealth of Philippine president Marcos at the moment the Philippines were going to the polls turned out to be a critical part of public and indeed executive-branch education. Similar challenges to the president were issued on everything from Central American policy to SDI.[54] But Solarz's visibility and expertise in foreign affairs were not sufficient to insulate him from the perils of redistricting and the scandal of his kiting of 700 checks on the House members' bank. (He was not the only one: scores of other House members also kited checks on the House bank.) Solarz was defeated in a Democratic primary in September 1992.

The expansion of resources available to the individual members of the House and Senate contributed to the denaturing of congressional power. A bright, photogenic, and articulate member—a Solarz, a Biden, or a Hamilton, say—might for a time be able to command the attention of the White House, the cognoscenti within the beltway, or even world leaders but could hardly command more than an episodic glance and nod from most in Congress, who had other interests and other agendas, not the least of which was, almost always, reelection.

THE 1980S — AND AFTER

With the 1980 election, for the first time since the onset of the cold war in the late 1940s the Republicans won control of the Senate, and they held that control until the 1986 election. Especially in the area of economic policy, the combination of a Republican-controlled Senate and the traditional alliance of Republicans and Southern Democrats in the House was sufficient to allow the passage of much of Reagan's economic agenda. Apart from increases in defense spending, however, the record on foreign affairs was more mixed. And by mid-decade, conservative power had begun to ebb. The Iran-Contra scandals further diminished Reagan's ability to dominate the congressional agenda.

The 1986 election returned Congress to Democratic control. The ideological center of gravity of Congress shifted somewhat to the left, especially in the Senate.[55] Southern Democrats, the linchpin of many conservative hopes, were gradually tending to vote like the rest of their party, that is, more liberal. The effects of the Voting Rights Act of 1965 were undeniable. In Congress, more African-Americans, Latinos, and white Southern moderates made an appearance. The South remained a key swing group in House voting, but the Southerners were somewhat less reliable partners for Republicans than in the past.

Democratic party liberalism receded only slightly after 1985, when the average Democrat was more liberal than 70 percent of the Senate. In one count conducted in 1987–88, the average Senate Democrat was still likely to vote a more liberal position than 64 percent of the Senate Republicans. In the House, Democrats were more liberal than they had been at the start of the 1980s. Thus, the decade of the 1980s saw the two parties more clearly define their respective ideological coherency and, consequently, pull further apart in voting across the board.[56]

The tendency to deadlock was exacerbated by the lack of any coherent consensus among the wider public or elites regarding foreign policy. Two prominent Congress watchers in the mid-1980s observed that "the current congressional stalemate is rooted in demographic characteristics of modern electoral politics, in the structure of Congress, and in the nation's search for a persuasive policy vision."[57] Although there was much talk of renewed bipartisanship with George Bush's ascendancy to the presidency, partisan divisions in Congress grew, if anything, sharper in the early 1990s.[58]

It was unclear whether congressional *immobilisme* was unavoidable. Certainly the end of the cold war did nothing to clarify American foreign policy goals. On the other hand, a series of developments in the early 1990s opened up the possibility of the largest turnover in congressional membership in modern history. Redistricting following the 1990 census provided an incentive for some members of the House who found themselves confronting new and less hospitable constituencies to retire. Moreover, members with large campaign war chests could, for the last time in 1992, take the monies for their own retirement.[59]

In 1989 a series of revelations concerning questionable financial practices resulted in the voluntary retirement of the Speaker, Jim Wright. In 1992 the new leadership was engulfed by yet another embarrassing series of disclosures: members of the House had routinely overdrawn their checking accounts in a special—and poorly administered—bank maintained for their convenience. Because the overdrafts were covered by the deposits of other members of the House, no public funds were involved. Nonetheless, the image of hundreds of members of Congress routinely bouncing checks—some twenty-two members kited hundreds of checks—reinforced a popular image of a Congress populated by arrogant elitists who perverted the institution in order to provide themselves with perquisites.

By the spring of 1992, more than seventy members of the House and six members of the Senate voluntarily opted out. Twenty-five percent of the House Foreign Affairs Committee left, including the chair, Dante Fascell. Fascell was untouched by scandal, but he was jeopardized by both redistricting and a new populism that rejected Fascell's favorable disposition toward foreign aid. Asking himself if, after thirty-eight years, "it wasn't time to do something else," Fascell succumbed to the logic of change and the appeal of $596,000 in campaign funds that could be converted to personal use.[60]

Some Democrats were also retired by the voters. As a result, there were more new faces in Congress in January 1993 than at any time since World War II. The Democrats retained control of the House and the Senate in the 1992 election; however, the future character of the House of Representatives in particular seemed less predictable than at any time since the Vietnam Revolution had worked its way through Congress in the early 1970s.

CHAPTER 6

The Constitutional Framework of Executive-Legislative Relations

THE ASSERTION OF congressional foreign policy prerogatives has invariably confronted the ambiguities of the constitutional language. The presidency has asserted that this very ambiguity perforce requires executive primacy, given the dangers of the world. The interplay of executive and legislative authority has therefore proceeded in an arena where the contestants—the president and Congress—operate from different conceptions of the rules and where the referee—the courts—has proven very reluctant to intervene. Moreover, when the courts have spoken, their judgments have sometimes been contradictory, or open to self-serving reading by the Congress and the president. On balance, presidents have gotten the best of these legal disputes, the judgments of numerous eminent legal scholars notwithstanding.[1] Therefore, before turning to a narrative of the executive-legislative relationship, we should give some attention to the constitutional ground over which Congress and the president have struggled.

TWO IMAGES OF THE CONSTITUTION

Constitutional commentary concerning foreign affairs is substantial.[2] Recent scholarship suggests that two landmark Supreme Court decisions— *United States v. Curtiss-Wright Export Corporation,* decided in 1936, and *Youngstown Sheet & Tube Co. v. Sawyer,* decided in 1952[3]—are useful frameworks within which the constitutional claims of the president and Congress may be understood.[4] The *Curtiss-Wright* decision has formed the basis for a sweeping definition of presidential power; in contrast, the *Youngstown* decision offers a much more circumscribed vision.

The Curtiss-Wright *Vision*

The *Curtiss-Wright* decision grew out of the Roosevelt administration's indictment of the Curtiss-Wright Company for conspiring to sell machine guns to Bolivia, then involved in a bloody dispute with Paraguay. Congress had passed a joint resolution prohibiting military aid to either country and had granted the president the authority to stop such sales. The Curtiss-Wright Company claimed that the resolution represented an unconstitutional delegation of congressional authority to the president. A U.S. district court agreed with Curtiss-Wright, and the government appealed to the Supreme Court. In an opinion written by Justice George Sutherland, the Supreme Court reversed the district court and ruled that the federal government possessed the authority to restrain and regulate the Curtiss-Wright Company's behavior outside the United States.

Justice Sutherland, who had previously served in the U.S. Senate as a member of the Senate Foreign Relations Committee, had written and spoken widely on the necessity for a strong presidency. Sutherland was an ardent nationalist and took the opportunity provided by *Curtiss-Wright* to write his own views of the nature of world politics into the constitutional canon. Subsequently, proponents of presidential power have seldom missed an opportunity to assert the vision advanced in *Curtiss-Wright* of the necessity for presidential primacy in foreign affairs.[5]

In Sutherland's view, power and authority in international affairs are not encumbered. The federal government gained extraordinary powers in the domain of foreign affairs from the fact that America is a sovereign state and, as such, must act effectively in the international community. The United States acquired its sovereignty, Sutherland argued, via England at the time of independence. The federal government thereby gained authority for action in foreign affairs from its position as an effective member of international society and not from its domestic system of law. Thus, in Sutherland's view, "the investment of the Federal government with the powers of external sovereignty did not depend upon the affirmative grants of the Constitution."[6] Rather, executive powers in foreign relations are "inherent" and derive from the fact that the U.S. government is a sovereign "subject" under international law.

While Sutherland's reasoning was predicated on a notion of sovereignty congruent with turn-of-the-century Anglo-American jurisprudence,[7] Sutherland also mustered a historical warrant for his views that the powers of the federal government in foreign affairs are inherent in the presidency. The concern of the framers of the Constitution, Sutherland argued, was that the republic could defend itself: "And in that context, those who drafted the Constitution were determined not to impede the government in its conduct of foreign affairs."[8]

Sutherland's view has been the subject of withering academic commentary. His argument that there was some kind of mystical transfer of power from the crown to the union is seen as problematical given that two governments existed before the Constitution was drafted—the Continental Congress and the Confederation—which complicates the seemingly direct transfer of sovereignty posited.[9] Furthermore, Sutherland's assertion of virtually unlimited governmental power in the hands of the national government deriving from some extraconstitutional source stands in direct contradiction to the fundamental principle of "constitutionalism" itself, namely, the notion of limited government with limited power, that is presumably at the heart of the American system. Louis Henkin bluntly dismisses the matter of the putative "rights" of a sovereign power passed to the United States from England. For the framers, Henkin argues, only citizens' "rights antedated any constitution, antedated society, antedated government."[10]

Sutherland's breathtaking claim was that extraordinary powers ultimately reside in the hands of and were to be exercised solely by the president.

Not only . . . is the federal power over external affairs in origin and essential character different from that over internal affairs, but participation in the exercise of the power is significantly limited. In this vast external realm, with its important, complicated, delicate and manifold problems, the President alone has the power to speak or listen as a representative of the nation. . . . As Marshall said in his great argument of March 7, 1800 in the House of Representatives, "The President is the sole organ of the nation in its external relations, and its sole representative with foreign nations."

Michael J. Glennon scathingly responds to this assertion: "Does Sutherland seriously mean to suggest that the President could have imposed criminal penalties on Curtiss-Wright without any statutory 'basis'?"[11] Glennon's point is that Sutherland is arguing for an executive authority vested in the president not by any exertion of legislative power, though Sutherland does argue that Roosevelt in fact acted within the context of a grant from Congress, but with such an authority plus the "very delicate, plenary and exclusive power of the President as the sole organ of the federal government in the field of international relations—*a power which does not require as a basis for its exercise an act of Congress*, but which, of course, like every other governmental power, must be exercised in subordination to the applicable provisions of the Constitution."[12]

Here then, is the basis of all subsequent claims for presidential primacy. The national government possesses extraordinary powers derived from the fact of its mere existence as the sovereign and not from the Constitution. "Participation" in the exercise of those powers is limited because, it is argued, the president is the "sole organ of the nation in its external relations." And finally, lest there be any doubts as to Sutherland's argument, the president's authority is *not* derived from Congress but is drawn from some reservoir of "plenary power" inherent in the president's function as the "sole organ of the federal government in the field of international relations."

Legal opinion has been skeptical of Sutherland's reasoning throughout the intervening half-century. In the first place, Sutherland's assertion that the president is the "sole organ" of the United States in international affairs rests ultimately on an appeal to the authority of Marshall, who in the passage quoted by Sutherland was speaking not as Chief Justice but as a member of the House of Representatives. But even if we are to grant Marshall's views unusual force, it is important to note that Marshall was merely asserting the unexceptional notion that the president was the sole organ with respect to diplomatic representation and negotiation. Sutherland grudgingly admits this important qualification in that after implying that "this vast external realm" requires extraordinary power, he appends, "the President alone has the power to speak as a representative of the nation."

From what is in fact a very limited claim of the president's authority as sole diplomatic representative Sutherland then advances a breathtaking claim, namely, that the president's powers are not derived from Congress. Whence are they derived? Presumably they stem from that reservoir of "very delicate, plenary and exclusive" inherent powers of the president that are derived from the president's unique role as "sole organ." But is the function of "sole organ" limited or not? It seems clear from Sutherland's opinion that he is not arguing for a view of presidential foreign policy power confined to that of chief diplomat. For there is a broader claim, namely, that when the president acts as the summation of federal power in international affairs, he is acting just as the British prime minister might act in the name of the British crown when pressing an international claim.

But what of the president's "plenary and exclusive" powers? Sutherland the judicial conservative reverts to a more constricted view, holding that the president must act "in subordination to the applicable provisions of the Constitution." Why, if the president's plenary and exclusive powers are a function of the president's role as sole organ "in the field of international relations"? And if the president's foreign policy powers derive from beyond the constitutional pale, why should the president's power "be exercised in subordination to the applicable provisions of the Constitution?"

As numerous students of the foreign affairs powers of the Constitution have pointed out, Sutherland was a nationalist, a proponent of a strong presidency in foreign affairs, but he was also a judicial conservative and ardent critic of a strong domestic national government. Hence, Sutherland wants it both ways. He must argue by means of dictums—that is, by assertion and not legal precedent—the existence of a "vast external realm" that is "different" and requires, therefore, a "different" president, a "sole organ" of national power that, it seems, operates beyond checks and balances. At home, however, Sutherland the judicial conservative draws back from the implication that the Constitution somehow does not apply to certain activities (but which ones?) and slides toward a more constrained view of the president as "sole organ" of representation, reintroducing "applicable provisions of the Constitution" (but here, too, which ones?).

The Youngstown Vision

Something approaching a presidential claim that tested the foggy edge of the permissible foreseen by Sutherland seems to have occurred in the midst of the Korean War. In 1952 President Truman ordered Secretary of Commerce Sawyer to seize and operate the nation's steel mills in order to neutralize a nationwide steelworkers' strike. Truman claimed the authority to do this based on "the aggregate of his constitutional powers" as chief executive and commander in chief: "the order (of Sawyer) was made on findings of the President that his action was necessary to avert a national catastrophe which would inevitably result from a stoppage of steel production" during the national emergency of the Korean War.[13] The steel companies sought an injunction against the U.S. government's action and appealed to the Supreme Court, which issued the landmark opinion in *Youngstown Sheet & Tube Co. v. Sawyer.*

The Supreme Court rebuffed the president. Justice Hugo Black's majority opinion sought to place presidential authority within the constitutional matrix: "The President's power, if any, to issue the order must stem either from an act of Congress or from the Constitution itself."

Black, speaking for the Court, could find no such congressional grant of authority; nor would he accept the notion that some set of unenumerated powers—though the Court did not deny their existence—were a sufficient basis for the presidential action. As Justice Felix Frankfurter argued in a concurring opinion, "Enumerated powers do not mean undefined powers."

To Justice William O. Douglas, the Korean War and the prospect of a steel strike clearly constituted an emergency,

but the emergency did not create power; it merely marked an occasion when power should be exercised. And the fact that it was necessary that measures be taken to keep steel in production does not mean that the President, rather than the Congress, had the constitutional authority to act. . . . The President can act more quickly than the Congress. . . . Legislative power, by contrast, is slower. . . . [But we] cannot decide this case by determining which branch of government can deal most expeditiously with the present crisis. The answer must depend on the allocation of powers under the Constitution.

The Court was not insensitive to the ambiguities of the constitutional framework, but in *Youngstown* it rejected any quick-fix assertion of some sort of cabalistic process whereby a reservoir of plenary extra-constitutional power existed upon which only the president could draw. Indeed, Justice Robert Jackson, in his landmark concurring opinion, sought to return matters to constitutional ground. Jackson's language is the basis of the alternative constitutional vision to that advanced in *Curtiss-Wright*. Diffused power, "the better to secure liberty," is, in Jackson's view, the central reality of the constitutional design. The framers assumed that the Constitution "enjoins upon its branches separateness but interdependence, autonomy but reciprocity. Presidential powers are not fixed but fluctuate, depending upon their disfunction or conjunction with those of Congress." Jackson then defined a framework for the operation of this interdependent executive and legislative power.

1. When the President acts pursuant to an express or implied authorization of Congress, his authority is at its maximum, . . .
2. When the President acts in absence of either a congressional grant or denial of authority, he can only rely upon his own independent powers, but there is a zone of twilight in which he and Congress may have concurrent authority. Therefore, congressional inertia, indifference or quiescence may sometimes, enable, if not invite, measures on independent presidential responsibility. . . .
3. When the President takes measures incompatible with the expressed or

implied will of Congress, his power is at its lowest ebb, Courts can sustain exclusive presidential control in such a case only by disabling the Congress. Presidential claim to a power at once so conclusive and preclusive must be scrutinized with caution, for what is at stake is the equilibrium established by our constitutional system. . . .

To Jackson, the stakes in the steel-seizure decision were not presidential power per se but the "equilibrium established by our constitutional system." Jackson was prepared to "indulge the widest latitude of interpretation to sustain [the president's] exclusive function to command the instruments of national force, at least when turned against the outside world for the security of our society." But Jackson did not feel that the command of the armed forces clearly granted to the president constituted "support for any presidential action, internal or external, involving use of force." Jackson continued: "No doctrine that the Court could promulgate would seem to me more sinister and alarming than that a President whose conduct of foreign affairs is so largely uncontrolled, and often even is unknown, can vastly enlarge his mastery over the internal affairs of the country by his own commitment of the Nation's armed forces to some foreign venture."

Some analysts suggest that since the *Youngstown* decision focuses on "internal affairs" stemming from claims based on national security powers, it is of limited importance in illuminating broader foreign affairs issues.[14] Others, however, see Jackson's concurrence as nothing less than "squarely reject[ing] the *Curtiss-Wright* vision."[15]

The *Youngstown* decision finds the practical operation of presidential power to be limited and defined through its interdependence and interaction with those powers possessed by Congress. None of the *Youngstown* decision is based on appeals to arguable legal theories or to problematic histories of "sovereignty," passing from the British crown to successor governments, or raw *dictums* about extraconstitutionally derived reservoirs of power.[16] Rather, *Youngstown* centers the source of foreign affairs powers *within* the Constitution.

But in rejecting *Curtiss-Wright*'s sweeping vision, the *Youngstown* decision by no means assumes that the great issue of institutional conflict over foreign policy is resolved. There is, after all, as Jackson argued, a "twilight zone" of concurrent power within which it was assumed that some sort of "struggle" would inevitably occur. That this indeterminacy limits the government's efficiency is clear; but the *Youngstown* case also holds that these limitations are a central value in the American system.

The *Youngstown* case makes it clear that disputes between Congress and the president should not be resolved through appeals for executive efficiency in the face of the exigencies of a dangerous world. Moreover, *Youngstown* implies that the courts would inevitably be called upon to scrutinize closely the twilight zone of institutional struggle of Congress and president, something recent courts have generally been reluctant to do.[17]

The Two Visions in the Post-Vietnam World

Whatever Jackson's expectations in the *Youngstown* case, executive-legislative-judicial interaction after Vietnam has seen the rise to primacy of Sutherland's *Curtiss-Wright* vision. In the wake of Vietnam, many academics have expressed dismay at the reluctance of the Court to become involved in foreign affairs issues. The Supreme Court, now dominated by appointees of presidents who saw their foreign policy powers under assault—Nixon, Ford, Reagan, and Bush[18]—turned, when it chose to intervene, as Harold Koh notes, to "muffling debate and uncritically supporting the executive."[19]

A post-Vietnam executive-legislative relationship has been established within Jackson's "twilight zone" of institutional struggle. But when the Court has seen fit to provide illumination, it has more often than not chosen the light cast by *Curtiss-Wright* rather than the more balanced conception of interdependent powers embodied in *Youngstown*. Thus, the Court's performance as a reluctant referee has little diminished the deadlock that many see as the dominant characteristic of government. Ironically, therefore, *Curtiss-Wright*'s primacy has not furthered another part of Jackson's *Youngstown* vision, namely, that "while the Constitution diffuses power the better to secure liberty, it also contemplates that practice will integrate the dispersed powers into a workable government."[20]

THE TRADITIONAL POWERS OF ADVICE AND CONSENT

Treaties

The Constitution provides in Article 2, Section 2, that the president "shall have power by and with the advice and consent of the Senate, to make treaties provided two-thirds of the Senators present concur." But the Constitution does not make it clear whether the Senate is to take part in the negotiation of a treaty or merely to deliberate on a treaty's merits after the executive has concluded the bargaining. Since Washington's painful experience at the hands of the Senate in 1789, when he was treated as an inferior party and asked to leave the Senate chamber while his diplomacy was being discussed, the executive has maintained its distance from Congress during the negotiation of treaties. Washington was heard to exclaim after storming from the Senate that "he would be damned if he ever went in there again,"[21] and no president did until Gerald Ford volunteered his testimony before the House Judiciary Committee on the pardon of Richard Nixon.

Only the lesson of Woodrow Wilson's failure to ram American participation in the League of Nations through the Senate in 1919 tempered presidential disdain of senatorial participation in the negotiation of treaties. But the fear that great issues settled at the conference table might come unstuck if the Senate refused to accept the result seems, until the 1970s at least, somewhat misplaced. For although the Senate can modify a treaty with amendments or reservations, as in the case of the Panama Canal treaties, senators have rarely availed themselves of the opportunity. The Senate, in fact, has seldom rejected or refused to act on treaties.[22]

Presidents, moreover, have developed and employed the executive agreement to circumvent Senate involvement in international agreements almost altogether. Arthur Schlesinger, Jr., notes in his study of the rise of the "imperial presidency" that "the executive agreement is one of the mysteries of the constitutional order. Gradually, in a way that neither historians nor legal scholars have made altogether clear, the executive agreement began to emerge in the early republic. The executive found this form of compact a practical convenience. The Senate accepted the device if only to spare itself the tedium of having to give formal consideration to a multitude of technical transactions."[23]

But what began as a convenience became, by the twentieth century, a potent device in the hands of activist presidents who sought means to further their conception of an energetic presidency. Between 1940 and 1970 about 95 percent of the formal understandings the United States undertook were in the form of executive agreements. Indeed, during a time when America's global involvement has been more intense than at any time in its history, some 5,653, or 83 percent of all the executive agreements up to that time, were made. Over the same years, in contrast, only 310, or about 28 percent of all America's treaties up to that time, were concluded. Moreover, as Allison Lippa recently noted, this count "only reflects the published statistics compiled from the Department of State's *List of Treaties and Other International Agreements*. Classified agreements, unavailable to the public and perhaps not even available to Congress, are not included."[24]

Some constitutional authorities have challenged the constitutional standing of the executive agreement. Raoul Berger, perhaps the most forceful proponent of a diminished executive, emphasizes the complete absence of any reference to such agreements in the Constitution and what is, in his view, the extremely specious reasoning of *Curtiss-Wright,* which also confirmed the constitutionality of executive agreements as well as proposed an expanded view of the inherent power of the presidency.[25] Nonetheless, executive agreements have assumed the same force and validity as treaties.[26] They bind succeeding administrations to their provisions. They become part of the international law binding the United States and hence, under the Constitution, of equal force with domestic law. Although an executive agreement has been described by the Supreme Court as lacking the "dignity" of a treaty, its effect is the same.[27]

There have been attempts by Congress to abridge the executive's ability to make such agreements.[28] Nonetheless, the habit of negotiating agreements and neglecting to inform Congress continued in spite of debate, disclosure, and legislation.[29] No law yet compels the president to reveal all aspects of relations with other governments; so far, the procedures in place seem to bind only the State Department, and not, for instance, the NSC, the CIA, or even the secretary of defense, from reporting certain dealings that might be the functional equivalent of an executive agreement.[30] Raoul Berger has argued that it was the intent of the framers of the Constitution that virtually no international business be conducted by the president without Congress: inasmuch as treaties are the law of the land, their consequences are simply too important to be entered into without senatorial "advice."[31]

In some respects, the treaty has become an instrument whereby presidents have tried to build legitimacy for their actions by implicating Congress in the undertaking. If an agreement is controversial or if the executive feels that it might later need to extract domestic legislation or funding from Congress in order to execute the document, then the formal machinery of a treaty is sometimes sought. Thus the Nuclear Test Ban Treaty was signed in 1963 with the Soviet Union only after substantial congressional support was enlisted. Similarly, the Nixon administration submitted the "Interim Agreement" on strategic offensive weapons (SALT I) to the Senate for review and approval along with the Antiballistic Missile (ABM) Treaty. The latter required advice and consent, of course, but the Interim Agreement did not. Nevertheless, the administration sought to anticipate any objections to so fundamental a policy departure by allowing hearings and a vote on the agreement, accompanied by a round of "in-depth" briefings and full-scale lobbying directed at those hawks who might disagree with the agreement. At the same time, the administration anticipated the argument of those who might demand cuts in the defense budget because of the agreement by allowing Secretary of Defense Laird to threaten ostentatiously that he would not support the treaty unless full defense appropriations were forthcoming.[32]

A similar attempt by the Carter administration to build support for the SALT II agreement with the Soviet Union proved less successful. Carter, anticipating strong opposition to the treaty from Senate Republicans and conservative Democrats under the leadership of Senator Henry Jackson, sought to preserve the option of presenting the agreement much as the Nixon administration had done. By 1978 it was apparent, however, that such a ploy would be resented even by supporters of the agreement.[33] In the meantime, the Carter administration had allowed a number of senators and congressmen and women to serve as observers to the negotiations process. With the exception of driving home to the Russians the importance of the verification dimensions of the agreement to ratification, these members of Congress could not be said to have actually participated in the substantive negotiations themselves. Nonetheless, the Carter administration hoped that their presence would ease what everyone in the administration had come to realize would be a brutal test of the president's leadership.

As the negotiations dragged on through the late 1970s, however, it became apparent that no amount of briefing of Senate committees, no number of congressional observers in Geneva, and, ultimately, no defense-spending concessions to Senate hawks could guarantee passage of the treaty. Indeed, the treaty, like so much else in the new Congress, had become a lightning rod for congressional activism, individualism, and opposition to Carter foreign policy itself.[34]

The SALT II treaty was not voted on; the Soviet invasion of Afghanistan in December 1979 led the Carter administration to withdraw the agreement. It seems unlikely that the treaty would have been treated any less roughly than the Panama Canal accords had been before it. In both cases it was apparent that the ratification process had become something other than a debate on the substantive merits of a particular agreement. Rather, the treaties had become symbols of an administration's foreign policy as a whole and tests of strength between the administration and Congress, which could claim (with justification) that it had not been consulted but merely "informed" and then required to "consent."

Just as SALT became hostage to Congress in the late 1970s, arms control was transformed into Congress's godchild in the mid-1980s. In 1984 the GOP-controlled Senate voted 77 to 22 urging a resumption of a comprehensive nuclear test ban treaty. In late February 1986 the House passed a nonbinding resolution supporting the resumption of negotiations for a test ban treaty. The White House opposed both measures, claiming that a test ban should come only after an arms-control formula had been worked out. Otherwise, the White House claimed, the United States would be unable to modernize its weapons stocks. The process took on the attributes of one of those Indonesian shadow puppet shows in which jealousies and passions play far into the night but are not resolved.

In the Reagan years, treaties were given novel interpretations in an effort to defeat arms control. Just before the Geneva summit meeting in the winter of 1985, the Reagan administration hardliners argued that the ABM Treaty actually permitted the testing of elements of the new SDI. According to American negotiators explaining the ABM Treaty in testimony to the Senate in July 1972, Article 5, Section 1, of the treaty banned space-based testing of ABM "components." Nonetheless, just before President Reagan was to meet President Mikhail Gorbachev for the first time, the State Department's legal adviser, apparently to the mortification of the secretary of state, issued a report indicating that antimissile space components, could, after all, be tested. The new interpretation so disrupted Congress, as well as moderate elements in the State Department, that the administration retreated.[35] In 1988 the Senate amended the INF Treaty to say that it was to be understood "in accordance with the common understanding of the Treaty shared by the president and the Senate at the time the Senate gave its advice and consent to ratification." The amendment was adopted 72 to 27.[36] Thus by the end of the decade it seemed understood that neither the president nor the Senate could unilaterally change the meaning of an agreement by means other than mutual consent.

Although presidents have been frustrated in their efforts to change treaties, they have not been constrained from unilaterally terminating agreements. In a landmark case in 1979, *Goldwater v. Carter,* the Court held that a president could abrogate a treaty—in this case breaking diplomatic relations with Taiwan (in order to establish relations with mainland China). Congress, the Court said, could have confronted the president on the issue but chose not to; hence the Court felt no reason to intervene.[37] After *Goldwater,* President Reagan terminated on his own the bilateral treaty of "Friendship, Commerce, and Navigation" with Nicaragua, as well as U.S. membership in UNESCO.

Along with termination there has evolved, by use of executive agreements, what Harold Koh calls "Swiss cheese ratification," wherein a president submits a treaty negotiated with virtually the whole international community but then, in a unilateral executive agreement, undertakes to undercut the same agreement. This was the case in an arrangement negotiated by a Reagan-era secretary of commerce—as a "side deal"—that allowed the Japanese to harvest whales under a treaty the United States had just negotiated for a Japanese "zero quota."[38] The practice continued into the Clinton administration as international trade agreements were abridged by "voluntary unilateral restraints" and, similarly, an asylum treaty was voided by the U.S. Coast Guard's involuntary return of Haitian refugees. Both stratagems, perhaps legal under U.S. law, were generally forbidden by a normal reading of U.S. treaty commitments.[39]

Appointments

Another aspect of advice and consent has to do with presidential appointments. Here again, however, the efficacy of the constitutional grant has become questionable. In early American history Senate confirmation was a serious exercise, sometimes affecting the establishment of diplomatic relations. But as executive agreements circumvent treaties, the use of personal representatives of the president circumvents the power to supervise appointments.[40] Major foreign policy officers such as national security advisers are rarely seen on Capitol Hill. White House staff, some of whom serve regularly as presidential envoys, are not subject to Senate confirmation, although it was the clear intent of the framers of the Constitution that all presidential envoys be confirmed. The questions of who voted for Kissinger, Brzezinski, McFarlane, Poindexter, and Scowcroft (and their senior staffs), who confirmed them, and to whom they are responsible are answerable only by the names Nixon, Carter, Reagan, and Bush.

The appointment process mandated by the Constitution is, then, vitiated by the use of executive agents. On the other hand, Congress has not always treated diplomatic appointments in a serious fashion. Congressional committees have spent enormous energies on the scrutiny of FSOs, the rank-and-file diplomats of the Department of State, while high- and low-ranking intelligence or military personnel go unexamined.[41] Then, too, congressional scrutiny has been inordinately applied to ambassadors, who are almost universally considered competent.[42] In contrast, questionable designees are routinely approved. Thus, when defeated Republican senator Chic Hecht of Nevada came before the Senate for consideration as the Bush administration's ambassador to the Bahamas, he observed he would "feel at home in the Bahamas" because "I've been involved in gambling in Nevada and I've been involved in banking for 25 years. . . . Also I understand it is a nice lifestyle. I love golf and they have a lot of nice golf courses and good fishing."[43]

Men and women who have made large contributions to a president's campaign treasury but have no conception of the problems of the countries to which they are appointed are routinely approved by the Senate, with a sigh of resignation from dissenters.[44] Moreover, political costs inflate more rapidly than the rest of the economy. Whereas in 1956 a $22,000 contribution brought one an ambassadorship to Sri Lanka, the Nixon appointee to Luxembourg, Ambassador Ruth Farkas, reportedly gave more than $300,000 to Nixon's 1972 campaign.[45] Indeed, Nixon is reported to have been forthright about the sale of posts. Investigative reporter Seymour Hersh paraphrased some still unreleased White House tapes that capture Nixon insisting "that those who wanted to serve in the more desirable foreign posts [were] told that initial contribution guaranteed them the assignment of only one year: to stay longer would require more cash."[46]

The Reagan administration sent political appointees to every country in southern Africa, traditionally a careerist preserve.[47] Theodore C. Maino, a St. Louis building contractor, became the ambassador to Botswana. As he told the Senate Foreign Relations Committee, his qualifications were evidenced by a "commitment to public service, having a lifetime association with the Boy Scouts of America." Robert Phinney, an executive of the Gerber baby food company, went to another African country. He testified that his qualifications for the job were "a commitment to public service, having been involved with the Public Library Foundation, the Boy Scouts of America, the Rotary Club, and the local Chamber of Commerce."[48] Many of President Reagan's supporters felt, however, that the number of political appointees was not large enough. The State Department's claim to professionalism was, they claimed, only a "protective mythology," designed for self-protection and self-promotion.[49]

It is conceivable that campaign finance laws for presidential elections that limit the amount of money that can be contributed and provide for public financing of presidential races could, in time, eliminate much of this custom. There were, for example, fewer examples of blatant ambassadorial payoffs in the Carter administration following the 1976 election, the first election administered under the new finance law. On the other hand, in the Reagan administration the number of ambassadorial posts given to political supporters was at the highest level since World War II.

The basis of episodic congressional scrutiny of appointments is often a mix of political and personal concerns. For example, the nomination of Theodore Sorensen, former presidential assistant to President Kennedy and Carter's designee to head the CIA, was withdrawn. Ostensibly, the source of opposition stemmed from revelations of Sorensen's use of classified materials in the preparation of his memoir of the Kennedy years. In fact, however, many of Sorensen's congressional opponents were skeptical of his dovish views during the Vietnam War and feared that he would not be tough enough toward the Soviet Union. Similarly, the nomination of Paul Warnke, a strong proponent of arms-control measures, as head of the Arms Control and Disarmament Agency and chief SALT negotiator was greeted with dismay by those skeptical of the SALT process. Warnke was eventually approved, but the attendant fight was a harbinger of the Carter administration's subsequent difficulties with SALT itself.[50]

In the case of the Senate rejection of President Bush's appointee former senator John Tower to be secretary of defense a range of motives seems to have been at work. Tower had not been liked during his twenty-four years in the Senate. Thus, for some, rejection of him as defense secretary represented a way to settle old scores. In addition, however, some observers felt that Tower's rejection based on his purported abuse of alcohol and harassment of women and his profiteering from his Senate service as a defense consultant after leaving the Senate also reflected a change in the Senate itself. The behavior for which former senator Tower was attacked might have been ignored in the past; but a newer generation of senators, it was said, was more sensitive to ethical issues, changing public attitudes toward alcohol abuse, and the role of women in society and was therefore applying a different and higher standard.[51]

The lack of amity between Congress and the executive has meant that substantive consultation between them has truncated the process of advice and consent. Under present circumstances, Congress's recourse has been to use the consent function to force congressional views into the process. Consequently, laboriously crafted agreements often confront a politically volatile mix of honest policy disagreement and resentment at having been excluded from a serious partnership.[52]

Advice and consent to treaties and appointments therefore have not proved to be effective means for sustained and systematic congressional participation in foreign policy formulation. But even if agreements were always subject to some sort of congressional review, questions would remain about the utility of such a process. Congress might not take the exercise any more seriously, for instance, than it takes the appointment process. Similarly, even if there were a congressional review of special assistants to the president, Congress's overall participation in policy making would remain indirect. Furthermore, congressional capacities in the appointment process are badly polluted by the pro forma handling of incompetent nominees and, on other occasions, zealous inquisitions of political targets of opportunity. Congress's advice function has been further tainted by the requirement of great sums of money, an issue that cuts equally across the White House and Congress.

There is merit, nonetheless, in the notion that if executive officials knew that congressional review of any agreements they negotiated remained a possibility, a more meaningful concern for congressional opinion might be forthcoming. Similarly, if appointees were assured that their probity and qualifications were an issue, perhaps better-qualified individuals would materialize.

There are, of course, negative consequences of congressional review. Congressional review of treaties opens the possibility of capricious and disruptive interference with often delicate diplomatic activity. Executive review of appointees also opens up the possibility that perfectly good candidates will not want to risk having their finances, ancient personal liaisons, and lapses of judgment dredged up and exposed for partisan amusement. The drafters of the Constitution were willing to take both these chances, however, for to do otherwise left the executive less than accountable. And, in the final analysis, accountability was essential to the constitutional framework within which executive-legislative relations were to be played out.

CHAPTER 7

The Power of the Purse and Congressional Oversight

IF THE POWER to raise taxes and appropriate funds had been given to Congress, the framers' intentions about a distinct congressional imprint on policy would be clear. It is in the budgetary process that a nation makes fundamental choices. The decision to appropriate or not appropriate funds is critical, for at that juncture resources and rhetoric are married. Without that union no programs can exist, no services can be provided, and no policies have substance. Thus, institutions that stand astride the budgetary process have access to the most important processes in modern government.

The founders envisioned this power of the purse residing in the legislature. They had had bitter experience with arbitrary and high taxation, and they felt that representatives would be more responsive to the people, and the legislature more rational, than a potentially arbitrary and capricious executive.[1] In addition, they understood that control of the appropriations process and close monitoring of expenditures provided the legislature with powerful means for overseeing the executive. However, the push during the twentieth century for efficient executive power has undermined the "original intent" of the founders.[2]

THE BUDGETARY PROCESS AND EXECUTIVE-LEGISLATIVE RELATIONS

The Budget and Accounting Act of 1921 required that the president prepare a federal budget. Subsequently, Roosevelt and Truman developed large and complex White House budgetary bureaucracies, which over time succeeded in gathering increasing initiative in the budgetary process. Congress's constitutional powers to raise, audit, and spend have remained intact. During the course of the cold war, however, presidents succeeded in circumventing much real congressional control of the budgetary process.

Presidential Budgetary Discretionary Power

First, presidents arrogated to themselves the authority not to spend money appropriated by Congress. This process of impoundment came under periodic attack from Congress; and it was brought under some measure of control by court actions and the Budget and Impoundment Act of 1974.[3] Presidents, however, can still seek the same end by what is called recision (from *rescind*, i.e., "to cancel"), and they can defer expenditure of appropriated monies. One chamber of Congress can disapprove a recision; deferrals, however, are a much more open instrument of executive power, since they place the onerous trial of relegislating monies for a program on Congress. Hence, under present law, if the president defers spending authority from one year to another, the issue cannot be acted upon again unless both the Senate and the House pass a law demanding that the funds be spent. Of course, if the action is relegislated, it can be either deferred yet again or simply vetoed.[4]

More important during the cold war period was the exploitation of discretionary powers extended to the president by Congress. The early practice of Congress was to specify what funds were to be spent for what purposes. Although there were earlier instances of "discretionary funds," the demands for and routine granting of enormous discretionary amounts grew exponentially with the onset of Soviet-American hostility.[5] The result was to leave Congress's power of the purse in some doubt, for if the president could spend money that was not specifically authorized and not spend money that was authorized, Congress had become but an ornament on the presidential juggernaut.

Some of the transfer of power to the president to allocate funds proceeded from the ostensibly pragmatic and realistic premise that neither Congress nor the president can foresee all the conceivable circumstances that might arise in a given fiscal year. Consequently, it has been felt, the president should have available a variety of funds to meet unusual situations as they arise. *Contingency funds* have been set aside for emergencies affecting the national security and defense. *Transfer authority* allows a department or agency head to shift specific amounts (specified by Congress) from one category to another within an agency. *Reprogramming* allows for the rearrangement of funds for specified categories of items within a departmental budget. *Excess stocks* involve discretionary disposal, either through sale or transfer to another agency, of new or little-used equipment. And finally, *pipeline funds* are funds that are authorized in one year but not expended and are then carried over to the following year.

In fact, however, presidents have employed funds for activities only marginally related to emergencies.[6] Moreover, they have had little apparent accountability concerning how they spend these funds. To no small extent, therefore, contingency funds, transferred funds, reprogrammed funds, "excess stocks," and "pipeline" monies have become a kind of private presidential treasury independent of Congress. Billions of dollars were thus available to presidents throughout the 1960s and 1970s; and with the huge defense outlays of the 1980s, the situation assumed almost unimaginable proportions.

In 1985, for example, more than $60 billion was available in unobligated but unexpended balances as a cushion in case Congress decided on deficit reductions. Another "excess" $37 billion was discovered in 1985 in Defense Department monies budgeted for an inflation rate that never materialized. Senator Alfonse D'Amato (R.-N.Y.) noted that this $37 billion windfall amounted to more than all the cuts that Congress had made in the hefty 1985 Defense Department budget. During the Reagan years the median amount of unobligated and unexpended balances each year was about $45 billion. Indeed, unspent funds were piling up so fast by the mid-1980s that even if the budget were frozen on the spot, the outlays would grow by 8.4 percent through 1990.[7]

So flush was the Defense Department in the Reagan years that it seemed able to create money. Thus, in 1985 Defense Secretary Caspar Weinberger notified the Senate Armed Services Committee that he had "found" an "extra" $4 billion in accounts that he intended to apply to the 1986 budget. Coincidentally, the committee was about to cut $4 billion from the budget request of the president in order to "restrict" the increase to the level of inflation. The money Weinberger found was described as $1.6 billion for inflation that had not occurred, $1.5 billion for monies set aside but not paid to contractors, $1 billion in research, and $900 million in excess cash on hand. Senator Allan Dixon (D.-Ill.) took the floor and spoke so loudly he could be heard down the hall: "Whatever money the Pentagon wants is apparently squirrelled away over there somewhere. And they'll spend it the way they want, no matter what the elected representatives of the people say."[8]

In the Bush years, the Agriculture Department replaced military-assistance sales programs as a means of financing programs without congressional concurrence or, at times, even knowledge. There were suspicions, for instance, that $5 billion from the commodity credit program was diverted to Iraq so that Iraq could arm itself with a vast panoply of modern weapons.[9] Indeed, three days before Iraq's invasion of Kuwait in August 1990, Secretary of State James Baker lobbied successfully to stop the congressionally mandated cutoff of agricultural credits in furtherance of an ill-conceived plan to moderate Iraqi dictator Saddam Hussein.[10]

Once the war with Iraq began in February 1991, Agriculture Secretary Clayton Yeutter approved U.S. aid to a Turkish-owned tobacco monopoly as a way of funding the operation of Turkish bases hosting American planes that were, at the time, attacking Iraqi troops. This "under the table foreign-aid," as Senator Patrick Leahy (D.-Vt.) termed it, was apparently useful in reversing Turkey's ban on the use of their bases for offensive operations, even though, as one unnamed official confessed later, it "no doubt violated our own regulations [that] . . . are based both on the law and the legislative history [of the program]."[11]

Another source of under-the-table foreign aid developed in the Bush years was the sale of U.S. treasury bonds at a discount to their market value. U.S. bonds were sold to the Mexican government at a rate that in effect was a $192 million subsidy to the Mexican government so that it could cut its debt payments and restructure its debts. GAO argued that although the action was "neither appropriate, nor good public policy," it was technically legal. But Henry Gonzales, chairman of the House Banking Committee, complained that the practice undermined "the constitutional prerogative and responsibility" of Congress for appropriating and allocating monies. However, similar debt-reduction packages were funded in other Latin American countries in the early Bush years, apparently without much congressional notice or complaint.[12]

The end of the cold war held some prospect for a reduction of discretionary funds. Thus, in 1990, hearings were held on the persistence of large balances of unexpended funds estimated in excess of $100 billion, with DOD controlling more than $50 billion; AID, in excess of $11 billion; and the Executive Office of the President, at least $4.3 billion. Senator William Roth (R.-Del.) characterized the funds as "sort of like having a checking account with automatic overdraft protection, except the bills get paid by increasing the federal deficit." Congressman John Dingell (D.-Mich.) commented on one instance in which DOD had used the funds to undertake an unauthorized $1 billion fix on faulty electronic gear on the B-1 bomber.[13]

Other observers noted that Congress had "discovered" a well-known situation. In 1990, as a former congressional aide who had looked into the issue of unobligated funds eighteen years earlier noted: "Congress' nose isn't clean on this. It comes up every four or five years, and it looks like a new problem."[14] From the Pentagon's perspective, with unobligated balances in the defense budget standing at more than $35 billion in 1992, the issue was largely a public relations problem.[15] Congress moved somewhat beyond posturing, however, and passed legislation in 1990 that terminated one of the accounts into which DOD had for thirty years been dumping unexpended funds for subsequent, and largely unmonitored, spending. Thus, as of November 1990, DOD had five years to cancel its so-called "M Accounts," from which, for example, as much as 30 percent of Air Force investment had been funded during the 1980s.[16]

Who Pays for War?

In the 1980s and early 1990s the Reagan-Bush policymakers discovered a novel way to find monies Congress had never appropriated in order to conduct policy and even to wage war. To arm the Contras, Reagan's State Department and NSC petitioned monies and assistance from potentates, satrapies, and allies. The sultan of Brunei gave money. The Taiwanese and the Koreans apparently anted up. Taiwan, Chile, Guatemala, El Salvador, and Honduras contributed some combination of weapons, logistic support, and money to the "Enterprise," as it became known. According to a January 5, 1985, entry in Lt. Col. Oliver North's notebooks, the South Africans delivered two hundred tons of arms to the Contras via Costa Rica.[17] The Saudis, it turns out, had been giving monies for U.S. projects in Latin American since 1981; by 1985 the Saudi contribution to the Contras was estimated by NSC Adviser McFarlane to have exceeded $31 million. According to McFarlane, the Saudis had magnanimously insisted that their help to the Contras "was only a gift."[18]

An Israeli team apparently lifted the Contras' supplies into Honduras from Israeli stocks (which were then replenished by the United States under normal bilateral aid arrangements). The Israelis had huge stocks of weapons, and their military prowess, intelligence service, and ability to keep secrets were greatly admired by the CIA and the NSC. At one point, virtually the whole resupply operation was being run by Israelis.[19] Cocaine was said to have been ferried to the U.S. market on the return leg of the supply operations.[20] A point man in Central America in this two-way guns and cocaine traffic was, apparently, Panama's General Manuel Noriega. Supervising the American interest in supplying the Contras in this phase of the "Enterprise" was Felix Rodriguez. Rodriguez, sometimes called Max Gomez, is said to have reported to Vice President George Bush.[21]

None of this is anticipated in the Constitution. There was no exception among the framers to Hamilton's rigorous insistence that "money only can be expended . . . for an object to an *extent* and *out of funds* which the laws have prescribed."[22] Moreover, in this instance the Boland Amendment prohibited the CIA, Defense, and all other agencies from expending any funds to aid the Contras.[23] It is unlikely, therefore, that Congress anticipated that the NSC would ferret monies from "private" and foreign sources.

So successful had been the "out-sourcing" of funds for the Contra war against the Nicaraguan government that the Bush administration employed it again in funding the war against Iraq in 1991, albeit this time with congressional encouragement. The White House established "Desert Shield Working Capital Account," into which cash contributions were accepted from Germany, Japan, South Korea, Kuwait, Saudi Arabia, and the United Arab Emirates.[24] Operation Tin Cup, as Secretary of State James Baker's fundraising was privately called by senior FSOs, was undertaken so that the president and Congress would not be inconvenienced by the Constitution. The effort amounted to nearly $80 billion, an amount so large that at the end of the war, all expenses included, the United States still had money left over.[25]

The Legislative Veto

In the 1970s, Congress sought to use a legislative veto to constrain presidential budgetary autonomy and to enhance its own capacity to monitor foreign policy more closely. One of the most important of these efforts was in the area of military assistance.[26] The Foreign Assistance Act of 1974 required that any proposed sale of more than $25 million be submitted to Congress for review. Congress then had up to twenty days to halt the sale by a concurrent resolution passed by both houses. The action could not be vetoed. Subsequently, the Arms Export Control Act of 1976 extended the waiting period to thirty days and included a requirement that any transfer of major defense equipment in excess of $7 million be reviewed. Other amendments were added that required the president to report to Congress quarterly on prospective and anticipated sales and transfers.

There have been a number of instances in which Congress challenged proposed arms transfers under the Arms Export Control Act. In no case were legislative vetoes actually voted, but the mere introduction of concurrent resolutions proved sufficient to force presidents to negotiate with Congress and in some cases actually to change the terms of the sale.[27] In the area of arms sales and transfers, therefore, the existence of the legislative veto may have increased congressional leverage.

On June 23, 1983, however, the Supreme Court, in *Immigration and Naturalization Service v. Chadha,* held that a one-house veto circumvented the constitutional method of passing laws by a "legislative shortcut." The Court said that any bill that called for a vote of disapproval had not been properly "presented" to the president for signature or veto in accord with constitutional procedure.[28] The sweeping breadth of the Court's opinion seemed to invalidate both one-house and two-house vetoes,[29] but in 1987 the Court ruled that the striking of the legislative veto did not invalidate laws of which the veto was a part unless the veto was critical to the passage of the law in the first place.[30]

In order to get around the veto aspect of the *Chadha* decision, Congress began passing legislation requiring a vote of approval (instead of disapproval) by one or both chambers or by the relevant committees.[31] As Louis Fisher, of the Congressional Research Service, has pointed out, hundreds of laws requiring a vote of approval were passed in the years following the *Chadha* decision.[32] The new wording of most legislation would read: "Failure of either House to act by the end of 90 days shall be the same as a veto of disapproval."[33]

The Reagan administration's encouragement of large arms sales abroad was slowed because of the new stipulations. Thus, a two-house vote of approval was used to monitor funding of the Contras in Nicaragua. Funds would cease after February 1985 unless Congress passed a joint resolution of approval. The approval of "nonlethal" aid just squeaked by, and the president had to search for other means to pass funds for "lethal" purposes to the Contras (see above). Congress has also required the use of two-house votes of approval for continuing resolutions to the foreign aid legislation. In addition, the 1984 foreign aid authorization stated that funds should not exceed the previous year's amount unless appropriations requests were submitted through the regular procedures of the House and Senate committees on appropriations.[34] Finally, resolutions of approval were required for other Reagan defense spending programs. For example, the controversial and hugely expensive MX strategic missile was subject to the approval of both houses in a concurrent resolution before funds could be used for its construction.

Thus, the result of the twenty-year argument over the legislative veto may be ironic in terms of the apparent intent of the Court to vest more authority in the executive. It could be argued that the mere existence of the veto brought increased attention to the institutional and policy views of Congress.[35] There were, however, only two cases when one house passed a resolution of disapproval; in both cases the Senate refused to go along with the House vote of disapproval. It should be recalled that the Tonkin Gulf Resolution was repealed by the enactment of a new law, not a concurrent resolution. Moreover, the Nixon administration's prosecution of the Vietnam War was not ended by a legislative veto, but by Congress's use of its most fundamental authority: it simply refused to appropriate further funds to continue the war. The loss of the legislative veto need not, then, redound all that favorably for executive power.

OVERSIGHT AND PROGRAMMATIC CONTROL: DEFENSE BUDGETING

There is no more important domain of congressional oversight than the defense budget. Congress must oversee the administration of tens of billions of dollars for personnel, operations, maintenance, procurement, and the development of new weapons. In the early 1990s the end of the cold war led Congress to an unparalleled examination of the assumptions underlying the military establishment. Decisions concerning weapons procurement and military bases have formed the core of this new consideration of the defense budget.[36]

But a substantial body of opinion suggests that, as in the past, it is unlikely that Congress will be a central player in reformulating defense. The essence of this wisdom is that "members of Congress examine the defense budget in terms of how it promotes their own electoral prospects rather than how it promotes the national interest. As a result, 'grandstanding' and 'pork barreling' abound on Capitol Hill, but relatively little reasoned consideration of American defense needs takes place. The lesson typically drawn from this is that Congress contributes little to America's national security debate."[37]

Bases, Budgets, and Defense Policy

Congressional behavior reflects a mix of motives embracing both parochialism and policy concerns.[38] The political economics underlying this rationale are not very complicated. The presence and level of operations of a military base in a congressional district tend to have more important consequences for the local economy than any particular weapons contract. An obvious exception is a small state, such as Connecticut, where much manufacturing is linked to defense contracts rather than to bases.[39] Thus, for example, Fort Ord in California, England Air Force Base in Louisiana, Eaker Air Force Base and Fort Chafee in Arkansas, and Fort Benjamin Harrison and Grissom Air Force Base in Indiana were all targeted for closure by the Defense Department in 1991. The effects on employment were dramatic: some 17.5 percent of jobs in host communities were affected.[40]

Not surprisingly, earlier proposals for base closings during the 1960s and 1970s were met by a strong protective response on the part of Congress. By the mid-1980s, congressional restrictions on the Defense Department were such that Secretary of Defense Weinberger observed: "The restrictions that are presently on the books for closing bases mean that practically speaking we cannot close any facility, no matter how much we want to or how little need there is for it."[41] By the end of the 1980s, however, the political pressure surrounding the question of base closings had become especially intense. On the one hand, the federal deficit focused attention on military spending; on the other, the justification for the defense budgets of the preceding forty years evaporated.

In 1988, Congress and the president had sought to cut through this politically snarled question with passage of the Base Closure and Realignment Act. The act established the Base Closure Commission, made up of retired members of Congress and the military and people drawn from the private sector. The Base Closure Commission was to review the Pentagon list of suggested base closings and then prepare its own list; the commission would not necessarily be restricted to the list prepared by the Pentagon. Congress and the president then could either accept or reject the commission's proposed closures, but it could not amend the list. In 1991 some eighty-six bases were to be closed as the result of this process.[42] By 1993 the process had begun to target some of the largest and economically most important bases in the United States. When, for example, Charleston, South Carolina's many installations were targeted for closing, up to one-third of the area's employment and half of the region's real estate value were put at risk.[43] The upshot was a "frenzy" of political activity within Congress that threatened the very process that had been designed to preclude such parochialism.[44]

As with bases and base operations, Congress's potential role in the development and procurement of new weapons systems can be undermined by interrelated political and economic dependence. In states such as Washington, Missouri, California, Texas, and Georgia 10–40 percent of the labor force is involved in the production of weapons systems. Total defense spending in California, including salaries for active and retired service personnel, amounted to $41 billion a year by the mid-1980s.[45] According to one Department of Commerce analysis, perhaps 70 percent of all manufacturing jobs in Connecticut in the late 1980s were related in some way to defense contracts.[46] Under these circumstances, senators and congressmen and women from these states find it difficult to credit analysis implying a reduction in production and procurement of weapons from their district or state.

Members of the armed services or appropriations committees, however, find themselves caught between conflicting sets of expectations. On one side, there is the pull of constituency and electoral needs, which implies an uncritical attitude if military appropriations benefit their districts. On the other, there is the tug of Congress's own norms, which, in the case of the appropriations committees, demands a scrutiny of executive requests. Indeed, most close analysis of congressional behavior indicates that parochial porkbarreling and logrolling cannot be demonstrated conclusively with respect to conventional and many strategic weapons. Rather, ideology seems a better predictor of decision making concerning these and many strategic weapons such as the ABM system, the B-1 bomber, the MX strategic missile, and SDI.[47] Robert Art notes that each house now changes as much as 60 percent of the "line items," or some twelve hundred "budget lines," on an average per year.[48] Perhaps 80 percent of the line-item changes are the result of fiscal or management concerns rather than policy disagreements.[49] Furthermore, during the late 1980s both the House and Senate Armed Services committees came under the leadership of men—Senator Sam Nunn (D.-Ga.) and Congressman Les Aspin (D.-Wis.)—who tended to move oversight in the direction of policy and missions.[50]

James Lindsay reviewed the extensive literature on congressional behavior concerning defense budgeting and oversight and concluded that Congress's behavior no longer conforms to the typically unflattering portrait. But as Lindsay notes, "Now, no serious observer of congressional behavior can quibble with the claim that legislators generally are neither altruistic nor disinterested. Yet recognizing this political reality does not warrant the conclusion that oversight was not conducted."[51] On the other hand, the handling of the perennially contentious issue of base closings can be viewed as less than satisfactory. Creating a commission to assume the initiative and take the political heat defuses the issue somewhat. On the other hand, handing the issue to the commission also represents an evasion of constitutional responsibility for oversight. Moreover, the political upheaval accompanying the 1991–93 base-closing proposals makes clear that deferring to a commission in no way "depoliticizes" the issue. Similarly, the enormous federal budget deficit piled up during the 1980s led Congress to devise methods for cutting popular programs that might have reduced the immediate political pressure but do not enhance congressional oversight capacity.

The Politics of Budget Cutting

By 1985 it was clear that the combination of tax cuts, massive increases in defense spending, and the growth of domestic social entitlement programs would result in an aggregate deficit during the Reagan administration larger than any accumulated during the preceding two hundred years of the republic. During 1985 Congress passed, and the president signed into law, a radical revision of the budgetary process designed to impose automatic across-the-board spending cuts should normal budget procedures fail to produce cuts. Central to the formula for reductions was the provision that one-half of reductions were to come from defense, and one-half from domestic programs, except social security and most other major social welfare programs. Under the law—known as Gramm-Rudman-Hollings, after its three authors (hereafter "Gramm-Rudman")—the automatic cuts were to be worked out via a complex procedure involving the Office of Management and Budget (OMB), CBO, and GAO.[52]

The automatic cuts, or "sequestrations," were quickly challenged in the courts and found unconstitutional in July 1987 on the grounds that the role assigned to GAO, a congressional agency, in the final determination of the cuts constituted a violation of the principle of separation of powers. Subsequently, Congress changed the legislation to give OMB, an executive agency, the final authority in determining the magnitude of cuts necessary to achieve congressionally mandated targets.[53]

In 1990, as Gramm-Rudman expired, the budget process was again subject to an extraordinary executive-legislative agreement. In the 1990 agreement the budget was divided into three components—defense, domestic, and foreign aid—with targets set in each area. Unlike in the Gramm-Rudman process, however, sequestrations in the event of overruns could only be imposed within each category where a breach of ceilings occurred. Thus overruns in domestic spending could not be met with cuts in defense. OMB was given the authority to decide in questionable cases.

Overruns in, for instance, the research costs of nuclear power or the cleanup costs at reactor sites in the Department of Energy might be either domestic or defense. It would be up to OMB, and not Congress, to decide which overruns would be assigned to the defense or the domestic programs category. In sum, the response to the fiscal crisis presented by the federal budget deficit undercut the budget process reforms of the 1970s and the oversight position of Congress. "I don't think people realize just how much power has been shifted from one end of Pennsylvania Avenue to the other," one experienced congressional aide warned.[54]

The magnitude of the budget deficits of the 1980s forced the two branches into a series of ad hoc "summits" and "agreements" ceding ever more control of the budget process to the president. At the same time, however, the end of the cold war weakened the president's position. For even as the Pentagon brought forward proposals for a 25 percent reduction in the military establishment based on the withdrawal of the Soviet presence from Central Europe, the Soviet Union itself collapsed. All Bush administration assumptions underlying the new, base defense force of 1.6 million evaporated. Indeed, the nearly half-century "emergency" undergirding so much of the president's position vis-à-vis Congress was gone.

Thus, while events may have worked to enhance Congress's leverage on defense issues in the 1990s, much constitutional ground remained to be retaken by Congress. Nowhere were the uncertainties more evident than with respect to oversight of the intelligence establishment.

OVERSIGHT OF THE INTELLIGENCE ESTABLISHMENT

Congressional oversight of the intelligence establishment during the cold war traversed a long road. Until the early 1970s there was hardly any oversight at all. But as the Democratic party's most influential cold war insider, Clark Clifford, remembered, "Congress chose not to be involved and preferred to be uninformed."[55] During the last years of the Vietnam War there was a great spurt of activism regarding intelligence oversight, followed by years of cordial inattention. The end of the cold war has brought calls for a major restructuring of U.S. intelligence efforts.[56] Nonetheless, the substance of intelligence oversight in the early 1990s was little changed from the patterned caution of the post-Vietnam years.

At the outset of the cold war, congressional oversight of the intelligence establishment was severely circumscribed. In part, Congress gave away its right to oversight, and in part it let the right go by default during this early period. In any event, there was no congressional oversight of the CIA budget, personnel, organization, or operations.[57]

Ritualistic oversight continued into the early 1970s. The Senate Armed Services subcommittee that was charged with oversight responsibility rarely met, allowed no staff to be present when rare meetings did eventuate, and kept no records.[58] Senator Fulbright complained that the committee seemed to be "more interested in shielding CIA from its critics than in anything else."[59] In a November 23, 1971, debate Senator John Stennis (D.-Miss.), chair of one of the four congressional oversight subcommittees, argued: "You have to make up your mind that you are going to have an intelligence agency and protect it as such and shut your eyes and take what is coming." For most in Congress, self-imposed ignorance was the very definition of responsible oversight.[60]

Congressional inaction was caused by something more fundamental than structural inadequacies in the oversight process. Congress acted to support, even strengthen, an institutional relationship that guaranteed that the CIA would retain a great deal of autonomy and ensured that the policies the CIA served would remain intact. Once the congressional consensus behind America's global role began to crack under the press of Vietnam and the weight of disturbing revelations that the CIA had been employed against domestic dissent, Congress moved to investigate not only the CIA but the previously sacrosanct FBI and the NSA as well.[61] Investigative committees were set up in both the Senate and the House.[62] The House committee "self-destructed" in a swirl of controversy surrounding its chair's prior relations with the CIA, staff divisions, and lax internal security.[63] However, Senator Frank Church's (D.-Idaho) Senate Select Committee to Study Governmental Operations (Intelligence Activities) provided a more thorough and disturbing assessment of intelligence activities over the previous twenty years.

The Church Committee documented a series of illegal and questionable activities of the CIA, the FBI, and the NSA. These included the CIA's assassination attempts directed at Fidel Castro and covert operations against national leaders in the Dominican Republic, Chile, and South Vietnam. Congressional investigations verified that the CIA and the NSA had routinely conducted mail surveillance programs and monitored the international telephone and telegraphic communications of American citizens for thirty years.[64] Antiwar activists and civil rights leaders, especially Dr. Martin Luther King, Jr., were favored targets for surveillance.[65]

Other areas of operations were deleted from the final Senate report in order to protect intelligence sources and methods, including budgetary oversight, relations with American academic institutions and religious groups, and the use of the Department of State's diplomatic corps as a cover for espionage. Subsequent revelations documented research on mind-control drugs and experimentation on unsuspecting subjects in the United States and Canada, where the mentally ill were given LSD and sensory-deprivation "treatments." In major cities, passers-by in subways were sprayed with mind-bending chemicals. Suicides, psychotic breakdowns, lingering mental illness, and the inevitable lawsuits plagued the program for years.[66]

The Senate committee's extensive recommendations included new statutory authority, or "charter reform," designed to clarify the purposes of various elements of the intelligence establishment, lines of responsibility, as well as recommendations concerning the quality of the intelligence product. The committee's final report recommended tighter restrictions on intelligence activities, especially covert operations, and outright prohibition of political assassinations and subversion of democratic governments. The report also recommended that the CIA not support governments that systematically violate human rights and suggested a prohibition of the use of academics, journalists, or religious leaders for covert operations. The Church Committee recommended an expansion of congressional oversight arrangements, including creation of a permanent Select Committee on Intelligence, which would have responsibility for (1) receiving prior notification of all covert operations, (2) authorizing the national intelligence budget annually, and (3) preparing the new charter for the intelligence establishment.

By mid-1976 the Select Committee was in place, and review of the intelligence budget and covert operations was under way. However, as congressional opinion drifted toward a harder line on foreign and national security issues in the late 1970s, charter reform attracted the criticism of those who were now advocating a more activist American posture with an attendant unleashing of the intelligence establishment. Ultimately, the reform process came to a virtual halt, and budgetary oversight began to attract criticism as well.

Most in Congress agreed with Senator William Hathaway (R.-Maine), who argued in 1978, "Once we've opened the door and given them a little peek, the demands will grow. . . . And quite frankly, gentlemen, I don't know if we'll ever be able to slam the door shut."[67] Not until May 1980 did a new CIA charter proposal emerge from the Senate Intelligence Committee, a drastically scaled-down, 4-page version of a comprehensive 132-page proposal developed in the committee over the preceding three years.[68] But this, too, was considered overly ambitious by hawks in Congress and the guardians of national security within the administration. The charter died a quiet death in the spring of 1980.

A compromise was reached in the form of the Intelligence Oversight Act of 1980, which reduced the reporting requirements established in the mid-1970s. The eight committees with responsibility for intelligence oversight were reduced to two. Notification of a planned intelligence activity was to be given in a "timely" fashion. In cases where extreme discretion and speed were in order, information could be restricted to the notification of a group of eight: the chairs and ranking minority members of the intelligence committees, as well as the Speaker and minority leader of the House and the majority and minority leaders of the Senate. This slimmed-down coterie of overseers was to be "fully and currently informed of all intelligence activities," including "any anticipated intelligence activity." But the president could act "consistent with due regard for the protection of unauthorized disclosure."[69]

From the perspective of those in Congress who were interested in meaningful intelligence oversight, the real message in the failure to pass an intelligence charter, as well as in the subtext of the intelligence act of 1980, was that Congress was not willing to take on an issue that had little electoral sympathy and no real constituency. Nor were the committees enabled to oversee the monies spent for these activities. Although Congress successfully asserted its right to be informed, it was not willing to assert any further right to impede activities. The CIA could merely dip into its contingency funds to support the ever-increasing pace of covert activities that marked the 1980s.

The American Bar Association stated in 1985 that the language of the proposed 1980 intelligence "charter . . . clearly contemplated . . . a basis for withholding information from Congress entirely."[70] The only recourse Congress would have under the Intelligence Act of 1980 would be to take the issue to the public and thus scuttle or delay the operation by subjecting it to publicity; or it could go one step further and pass legislation that specifically forbade the activity about which the committees had been informed. "Going public" would be a breach of specific pledges to keep operational security about ongoing activities. As a result, for most of the first Reagan years, Congress found itself nearly paralyzed by partisanship in dealing with one of the most activist directors of intelligence in the history of the agency, William Casey.

The American Bar Association found that the aggressive partisanship of the mid-1980s signaled that the whole process was "breaking down . . . that the intelligence product [was] being politicized," and that there was "a trend toward partisanship in the actions of the oversight committees," especially in the House.[71] The caution of the Democratic leadership and the partisan conception of the committee on the part of the Republicans led the most senior and aggressive investigative analysts on the staff, Loch Johnson and Diane La Voy, to quit.[72] But the politicization of intelligence appeared to be a two-way street. According to a House Intelligence Committee report and the testimony of dissatisfied senior CIA analysts, intelligence reporting, especially on Central American issues, was tailored to suit the administration.[73]

Acrimony spread from the House committee to the Senate committee in mid-1984 when it was revealed that the CIA had covertly mined Nicaraguan harbors. CIA director Casey had exploited his penchant for mumbling and verbally garbling portions of his testimony to obscure the operation from the Senate committee. The result was a cascade of bitter recriminations, including the temporary resignation of Senator Daniel Patrick Moynihan, the ranking Democratic minority member, from the Senate Intelligence Committee. In the wake of the mining disclosure, the committee extracted from Casey a written promise that it would be kept informed of all covert operations for which presidential approval would be required. In June 1986 Casey signed an amended version of the agreement covering presidentially approved covert operations in which "significant military equipment actually is to be supplied for the first time in an ongoing operation."[74]

At the same time, however, the CIA was deeply involved in the Reagan administration's arms-for-hostages deal with Iran, none of which was reported to the committee. Casey would subsequently argue that he felt obligated to withhold the information from Congress because the "finding" signed by Reagan approving the arms transfer included a provision that Congress not be informed of the operation. What Casey did not reveal was that the finding was retroactively prepared. In fact, the only reason that there was a finding at all was because the CIA general counsel insisted on a legal cover for what would otherwise have been an illegal transfer of arms to Iran. The finding was never made public because

Security Adviser John Poindexter, concerned about a public airing of the backdated document, destroyed it.[75]

What should not be lost sight of, however, is that the executive-legislative relationship had deteriorated before Iran-Contra. The harsh character of the debate over Central American policy and leaks emanating from the committees in the 1980s were, in part, a function of the vast increase in the scale of CIA global operations.[76] There were, for example, operations in southern Africa and Afghanistan, attempts to overthrow Libyan leader Qaddafi, and "black" activities by special Army units and the Air Force whose existence had not even been disclosed to Congress.[77] The ensuing breakdown in comity and trust between the two intelligence committees and the administration was partly due to these vastly augmented covert actions, as well as policy disagreements within the committees about proper intelligence objectives and methods.

Thus in the wake of the Iran-Contra scandal, the new CIA director, William Webster, saw his task as primarily one of reconstructing the executive-legislative relationship with respect to intelligence oversight. Indeed, in an interview a year after his reappointment by President Bush, Webster felt compelled to respond to charges that he had become overly solicitous of congressional opinion.[78] Webster's success was measured by the chair of the Senate Intelligence Committee, David Boren: "Mr. Casey had left the agency embroiled in the Iran-Contra controversy, a situation where there could have been a real reaction against it. Webster came in and restored public confidence in the agency. No one, not his harshest critics, would question his personal integrity or devotion to the rule of law."[79]

But if Webster succeeded in rebuilding comity between the CIA and Congress, little else seemed to have changed in the relationship. Secretary of State George Shultz told the Iran-Contra committees that he had "grave doubts about the objectivity and reliability" of CIA reporting and that the State Department's Bureau of Intelligence and Research refused to compromise its own reporting with CIA's *National Intelligence Daily*.[80] Senate Intelligence Committee member Patrick Leahy quipped that the biggest difference between the information contained in the *National Intelligence Daily* and the coverage in the *New York Times* was the crossword puzzle. A former Senate Intelligence Committee Republican staffer, Angelo Codevilla, wrote that the CIA had "too much money, with too little payoff,"[81] and former CIA veteran John A. Gentry wrote, "The agency's reputation [raised] . . . serious concerns about its ability to produce convincing warning messages about a genuine threat. I believe the debilitating effects of a lack of confidence by policy makers in the integrity of and relevance of the CIA are hard to over-emphasize."[82]

Post-Iran-Contra reform proposals touched other areas: (1) strengthening the reporting requirements of the president regarding covert operations, (2) making more independent the CIA inspector general, (3) reorganizing congressional oversight by creating a joint intelligence committee, and (4) creating a separate head of all intelligence operations within the government. Only the inspector general's office, which is subject to Senate confirmation and reports to Congress as well as to the director of the CIA, had been strengthened by the early 1990s.[83]

The proposal to establish a joint intelligence committee was rejected as reflecting a desire to restrict congressional oversight by further reducing the number of people to whom the CIA would have to report.[84] The CIA itself managed to successfully resist the idea of an intelligence "czar" as reducing the control of the director of the CIA.[85] The proposed strengthening of the reporting requirements elicited the most intense bargaining but ultimately went nowhere, as President Bush insisted that he reserved the option of not telling Congress anything at all.[86]

Reform seemed, therefore, increasingly problematical. First the Gulf War and then the collapse of the Soviet Union distracted Washington. The next opportunity for change arose with the replacement of Webster with Robert Gates as director in 1992. Gates, a career CIA officer and the number-two man at the agency during the Iran-Contra scandal, had been Reagan's initial choice to replace Casey, but the appointment had been withdrawn because of Gates's inability to defend convincingly his behavior concerning Iran-Contra.

Gates's Senate approval in 1992 demonstrated that he could survive Iran-Contra, but the fate of the postscandal reform movement—like that of the reform effort fifteen years earlier—was less certain. Not only did President Bush resist more strict reporting requirements on CIA's activities and budget, he asserted an even more expansive claim of executive prerogatives. Thus, for a number of months after President Bush vetoed the 1991 intelligence authorization, funds were spent for ongoing operations even though Congress had taken no action as required by the National Security Act of 1947. To be sure, the administration did not officially claim that it had the right to spend monies not appropriated; and the Senate Intelligence Committee was careful not to officially denounce the practice. The result, a disturbing precedent for constitutional forms, continued an overall inclination of Congress to yield to the president in covert matters without much struggle.[87]

The new director of the CIA, Gates, reported to Congress in April 1992 that any changes in the intelligence establishment should be "evolutionary, conforming to the reality of an unstable, unpredictable, dangerously overarmed and still transforming world." Furthermore, congressional guidance and participation in the process was deemed neither necessary nor welcome: "The Administration believes legislation is unnecessary," said Gates. "Indeed, in a fast-changing world I believe legislation would be unwise."[88]

Although the president had wanted the intelligence budget "immunized,"[89] in Bush's final year the CIA found itself faced with the same budget exigencies as the rest of the government faced. Gates had listed some 176 intelligence activities that the agency would now concern itself with, from weapons proliferation to environmental health. Asked what information no longer needed to be gathered, Gates confessed that "not one" item had been identified.[90] But by the end of 1992 the days of CIA's budgetary carte blanche seemed to be ending.

Although the final budget figures were still classified, the total figure the intelligence community received was said to be some 8 percent less than in the administration's request. The total reduction scheduled for fiscal year 1994–95, amounted to the most draconian cuts since Congress's oversight review procedure had begun. According to outgoing director Robert Gates, intelligence manpower was to decline dramatically by 1997. Early retirements, hiring freezes, and a diminished satellite capability all seemed inevitable parts of the worldwide drawdown in U.S. competence at arms.[91]

The oversight capacities of Congress remain a matter of intense debate. Is Congress overly deferential to the executive? Could such a fractious body, representing so many interests, ever have a considered judgment about policy? Is Congress responsible? Or, as the executive frequently complains, is Congress prone to "micromanagement"? Congress hardly seems above reproach when a Speaker of the House undertakes his own negotiations on a Central American peace settlement;[92] or when members of Congress behave parochially, as in the issue of base closings; or when Congress inserts unwanted weapons systems in the defense budget.

In fact, in the mid-1980s Congress seemed on occasion to have saved the administration from itself. Congress took the lead in pushing for reform in South Africa and the Philippines, areas in which the administration favored an untenable status quo.[93] At the end of the Bush years, Congress stepped forward and prodded a curiously cautious president to offer the Russians the wherewithal to dismantle their nuclear weapons and resettle their returning soldiers expelled from the former Soviet satellites in Eastern Europe. In the case of Central America, Congress provided the elements of caution to the Reagan administration's obsession with the region. It would be hard to argue that the Reagan administration's circumvention of congressional restrictions and oversight efforts made for better policy in the Iran-Contra affair.

To be sure, partisan division, with a Congress controlled for the most part by the Democratic party and the presidency in the hands of the Republicans, exacerbated the endemic institutional fragmentation of power in the American system. After all, divided power is not just an artifact left behind by the founders; it is deliberately devised and central to the entire constitutional design. As a result, confused decisional processes are the hallmarks of every administration and Congress. It is little wonder, then, that in the wake of Iran-Contra and the passing of the cold war consensus the executive-legislative relationship would seem even more abrasive.

Yet before attempting to reach definitive conclusions concerning executive-legislative relations, we should look to the question of war and peace. In no area of the constitutional design is the fragmentation of power more explicit. And in no area of the executive-legislative relationship since the Vietnam War has the "invitation to struggle" been more readily accepted by Congress, and the outcome so mixed.

CHAPTER 8

The War Powers and Executive-
Legislative Relations

AT THE HEART of the Vietnam Revolution in executive-legislative relations was the War Powers Resolution.[1] Congress was deeply implicated
in the origins of the Vietnam War, but as the years wore on, many in the
legislature felt that they had been duped. A generation later, we know
their concerns were well founded. In the fall of 1965, for instance, after
nineteen thousand U.S. battlefield deaths, it was Robert McNamara's "private belief" that the Vietnam War could "not be militarily won."[2] Yet for
the next two years, in public and in closed testimony, McNamara persisted in ardently defending the war. In those two years there were over
forty thousand battlefield deaths. Congress felt itself to have been especially misled as to the circumstances surrounding the Gulf of Tonkin
incident and the putative "enabling grant" of authority to the president,
the Tonkin Gulf Resolution.[3]

By 1969 the country had no more belly for war, but the conflict
lumbered on, each folly compounding the next. Neither Lyndon Johnson
nor Richard Nixon wanted to "lose" Vietnam. In this sense, the war
continued not because it was in the national interest but because it was
simply not in the interest of the incumbent to be saddled with the results
of an inevitable failure. Congress repealed the Gulf of Tonkin Resolution, but the war persisted. Congress cut off monies, but more monies
materialized—from contingency funds, from carryover funds, from reprogrammed funds, from a Feed and Forage Act that had not been used
since the Civil War. Congress restricted the war, but the war expanded to
Laos and Cambodia. At long last, language was passed over a presidential veto that unarguably ended funding for the war.[4] In this context,
after three years of hearings, Congress delivered the War Powers Act.

The passage of the War Powers Act over a presidential veto on November 7, 1973, was hailed by many as a historic breakthrough for Con-

gress. Senator Jacob Javits (R.-N.Y.) declared, "Never in the history of this country has an effort been made to restrain the war powers in the hands of the President. . . . [This bill] will make history in this country such as has never been made before."[5] In contrast, there were a few skeptics who, like Senator Barry Goldwater (R.-Ariz.), complained that under the language of the act, "the President is no longer prohibited from initiating original actions. He needs only to report during the first 60 days. . . . This language puts into law language that is not contained in the Constitution." Senator Thomas Eagleton (D.-Mo.), one of the originators of the War Powers Act, also felt that the final product was simply a license to make war and voted against it.[6]

Not surprisingly, Goldwater and Eagleton's interpretation of the war powers bill was accepted by several in the executive.[7] It was obvious, however, that Congress intended something quite different. The passage of the War Powers Act rested on three political assumptions that, at the time and for a time thereafter, formed something of a national consensus: (1) that U.S. armed forces should not enter hostilities without adequate domestic support; (2) that only a compelling national interest should dictate a commitment of troops; and (3) that Congress should provide a kind of "reality test" for the president in these matters.

As late as 1984, Secretary of Defense Caspar Weinberger echoed the first two of these assumptions when he insisted that there be a clear expression of the national interest and objectives in committing U.S. forces. Concerning the first of these assumptions he argued: "Before the U.S. commits . . . forces abroad there must be . . . assurances we have the support of the people and the Congress." This support, he added, "cannot be sustained without continuing and close consultation with the Congress."[8]

Congress concurred. The legislative purpose of the War Powers Act was to ensure that commitments were vetted before they acquired an independent life of their own. Congress saw itself not as some kind of institutional loose screw, rattling around the machinery of state, but as assisting the president in fitting interests to national security policy. In this regard, the War Powers Act was seen as an institutional mechanism for "codetermining," with the executive, policies that fall well within a constitutional sphere of overlapping responsibilities.[9]

Finally, Congress viewed itself as a natural check to the possibility that the president might proceed in his determination of the national interests in isolation, without the benefit of independent political judgment. Congress did not want the president to decide issues of war and peace in any state of grand isolation. Then, too, Congress wanted to avoid the darker prospect that a president alone might attempt to calculate the national interests with deficient faculties.

The intent of the War Powers Act is, therefore, reasonably clear. In this chapter we will turn to an examination of the actual development of executive-legislative relations regarding the use of force after its passage.

EXECUTIVE-LEGISLATIVE RELATIONS UNDER THE WAR POWERS ACT

In the 1970s there were few opportunities for U.S. commitments to become, to paraphrase Clausewitz, "things unto themselves." Nonetheless, in a series of actions presidents ignored the spirit of the War Powers Act. What was more important, Congress proved unable or unwilling to challenge the executive. In the 1980s, on several occasions, U.S. presidents courted military disaster with alarming brio. Yet Congress continued to show but faint resistance.

Uncertain Beginnings

In four instances during the 1970s in which American military personnel were committed by the president—the transport of refugees from Da Nang, Vietnam, in April 1975; the evacuation of American nationals from Cambodia as well as Vietnam in April 1975; and the evacuation of Americans and others from Lebanon in 1976—presidential reports were filed with Congress, but in a perfunctory manner.[10] In a fifth case, involving the transport by American aircraft of European and African troops into Shaba Province, Zaire, in 1978, President Carter refused to file a report, contending that the fact that the aircraft landed to the rear of combat operations exempted the airlift from the War Powers Act's reporting requirements.[11]

Perhaps more than any other incident, the Ford administration's response to the capture of the American freighter *Mayaguez* by Cambodia was a harbinger of what was to come in the 1980s. In mid-May 1975 President Ford did not consult Congress, though the act enjoins the president to consult "in every possible instance . . . before introducing United States armed forces into hostilities or into situations where imminent involvement is clearly indicated by the circumstances."[12] Rather, Ford informed a select congressional group two hours after he ordered

American warplanes to fire on Cambodian gunboats presumed to be involved in the *Mayaguez* incident and U.S. Marines to invade Koh Tang Island, where the ship was moored.

Just twenty minutes after the crew of the *Mayaguez*, aboard a fishing boat flying a flag of truce, had been seen by an American destroyer, the *Wilson,* and four hours after the Marine assault on Tang Island had begun to rescue this same *Mayaguez* crew, which Cambodian radio already had reported as released, U.S. warplanes struck the Cambodian mainland to "protect the marines" on Tang Island from the ragtag Cambodian "Air Force."[13]

It was apparent that the United States wanted to unfurl completely its display of firepower so that American arms could be seen to awe what the chairman of the Joint Chiefs of Staff had termed the "little revolutionaries" of Asia. Three weeks before the *Mayaguez* incident began, President Ford grumbled that the American setback in Indochina was causing him to look "indecisive." "I have to show some strength, . . . in order to help us . . . with our credibility abroad."[14] A few hours before the incident, Secretary Kissinger told a St. Louis audience, "Given our central role, a loss in our credibility invites chaos."[15] And the day after the incident, "high ranking sources" told a *New York Times* reporter "that the seizure of the vessel might provide the test of American determination in Southeast Asia . . . the United States has been seeking since the collapse of allied governments in South Vietnam and Cambodia."[16]

The rescue of the *Mayaguez* was therefore an exercise to show that America was still a global cop and that a mighty stick could still be brandished. The administration had attempted for weeks to shift the blame for failure in Southeast Asia to the Ninety-fourth Congress. Now the Ford administration could claim that if only given a free hand—as he had usurped for himself in the *Mayaguez* case—American arms could, after all, secure American interests.

If Congress had wanted to apply the War Powers Act, it would have been forced into the impossible post hoc proof that success might have been achieved by patient and quiet undertakings to release the sailors of the *Mayaguez*. But even if the route of patience had not been tried, threats seemed to yield the required result before the bombing and invasion of Tang Island began. And with the actual use of force, there was no doubt that proper consultation was required. In any event, once it was plain that action was about to proceed, Congress failed to demand real consultations as the War Powers Act requires. The prohibitions of the War Powers Act (and the four other specific legislative acts that forbid military "activities in or over or off Cambodia, or North Vietnam or South Vietnam" financed from "past, present, or future appropriations") were ignored.[17] Harvard legal historian Raoul Berger wrote heatedly two weeks after the chorus of congressional yahoos began to subside: "It is a reproach to Congress that it once more gives its sanction to yet another dismal 'precedent' that future Presidents will not be slow to invoke against Congress."[18]

President Carter did not consider the War Powers Act when American forces were committed in Zaire, nor did he heed the act later, in Iran in the abortive rescue attempt of April 1980. In both instances the commitments were simply defined as falling outside the scope of the War Powers Act. In the Iranian case, the Carter administration asserted that because the mission was a rescue attempt, it was humanitarian and thus beyond the scope of a War Powers Act. It is important to note, however, that this rescue attempt involved the insertion of more than a hundred heavily armed men aboard more than ten military aircraft hundreds of miles inside the territory of a presumably hostile foreign power. Moreover, there were implications far beyond Iran.

The United States could have found itself in a hair-raising facedown with the Russians over the fate of Iran.[19] The only organized opposition to the Khomeini clique at the time was the Tudeh (i.e., Communist) party. Had the mission succeeded with perhaps heavy Iranian casualties by dint of the covering fire that was planned for the mission, the Ayatollah's regime could have lost credibility and opened the way to conflict within Iran. Iran could have become so chaotic in the wake of a "successful" rescue mission that, whether the Tudeh or some other group came to power, the sclerotic leadership in Moscow, having misjudged the West once in Southwest Asia, at the time of the Afghanistan invasion, might have misjudged the United States again. The Russians might well have found reason to repeat an intervention in an area they had last occupied by force as recently as the late 1940s. The potential for wider war suggests that far more was involved than a mere "humanitarian rescue." Once again, however, the war powers question was pushed aside. Congress was ignored.

Politics, Pragmatism, and Principles

Because of President Reagan's immense popularity, one might think that congressional opposition to his military initiatives would be unlikely. By mid-1986, however, congressional dissatisfaction with the president's belligerent actions in Central America was sharper and better defined than would have seemed possible at any time since the end of the Vietnam War. Indeed, Congress's opposition formed around the very possibility of "another Vietnam."

Opposition to war in Central America built up gradually in the 1980s. In the Senate there were more loyal Republicans than at any time since the 1950s. The House, controlled by a Democratic majority, was less easily tamed. Those in Congress who changed their mind about supporting the president apparently were not influenced by presidential threats to make them the scapegoats for "losing" Central America.[20]

"Success," President John Kennedy once observed in a rueful moment, "has a thousand fathers. Failure is an orphan." Congress was hardly prepared to challenge a president who could show "success" with a quick "victory" at low apparent cost. If Reagan's success in the Caribbean could not be shared as a cooperative decision, it still could be toasted with a great chorus of congressional cheers.

Grenada

In the June 1983 invasion of the tiny eastern Caribbean island of Grenada the limits to Reagan-era interventions began to take shape. To the degree that Grenada was known at all, it was as an out-of-the-way resort, as a scenic locale for a small American medical college, and for its export of nutmeg. President Reagan, like President Carter, had expressed concern that the Marxist regime on the island would turn it into yet another steppingstone of Soviet influence in the area.[21] When a bloody band of Marxists overthrew the quirky Marxist that had run the islands for some four years, President Reagan, claiming to fear for the lives of the thousand American medical school students, sent some six thousand men to secure the island and install a regime more congenial to American interests.

The chancellor of the medical school refused to urge evacuation of the students and attested to the necessity of an invasion only after some post hoc urging from the State Department. The Grenadan and Cuban governments had assured the State Department that the students were free to leave. The parents of five hundred of the students pled by telegram, just before the invasion, that the United States not take "precipitous action." In the hours preceding the invasion the vice president of the medical school convened a student body meeting in which only 10 percent of the students expressed a desire to leave. As one military observer put it:

Although the major purpose was supposedly to rescue the medical students, the United States forces had almost no idea where the students were. They knew that there were students . . . just yards away [from the initial landing]. . . . But only after reaching them did they learn that there was a second larger group. . . . Apparently United States forces did not learn about a third group until the fourth day, when units conducting routine clearing operations stumbled on them. Yet . . . the island was open to anyone who wanted to visit it right up to the invasion. The telephone system worked so that anybody could have called the medical school to obtain a list of dormitory locations.[22]

The clear implication, of course, is that if there had been real concern about the students' welfare, somebody would have troubled to find out where they were.

Truth seemed at a discount in this affair. Indeed, a well-respected figure of the Washington establishment, Les Janka, deputy press secretary for foreign affairs at the White House, resigned over the management of the "facts." For the occasion 8,663 medals were especially struck. The number of medals continued to grow, with the total number of "combat" decorations approaching 19,600 by 1985.[23]

Legal principles were no less vulnerable to the tide of political expediency. One constitutional scholar lamented that "the discretion . . . to rescue does not include a collateral right . . . to overthrow the existing political structure. . . . That is war, plain and simple. . . . The invasion of Grenada was a constitutionally irresponsible act."[24] A ranking Republican member of the Senate Foreign Relations Committee complained, "Congressional leaders were simply called to the Oval Office and told that troops were underway." This was not consultation in the context of any normal reading of the War Powers Act. As for the issue of prior notice, the prime minister of Great Britain was advised about the invasion before the president told the Speaker of the House or the majority leader of the Senate.[25]

As with the *Mayaguez* incident, the overriding reason for the invasion was the sense that Grenada provided an opportunity to show, as one administration official mused, that the United States was not a "paper tiger."[26] The well-orchestrated homecoming of the grateful "rescued" students, as well as the discovery of a small arms warehouse full of old Soviet bloc arms, deflated congressional critics. It was, after all, the first clear-cut victory of American arms since World War II, and it happened just days after a bombing in Beirut caused the worst U.S. military losses in a war zone since Khe San.

Lebanon

In 1982 a contingent of American, French, and Italian troops was dispatched to Lebanon in the context of a multinational force in order to ease the retreat of Israelis who had earlier invaded Lebanon and to reestablish an independent Lebanese authority. The Christian-dominated Lebanese government's base was narrow. The Christians had been at war with each other and with the Islamic majority factions of Lebanon for ten years. The multinational force had to contend with not only the extremely testy Israelis but also the warring militias within and surrounding Beirut.

In April 1983, the American embassy was bombed and destroyed by terrorists. As the Israelis finally departed, the Lebanese army, made up largely of Christian soldiers, sought to reoccupy the areas evacuated by the Israelis. In turn, the sixteen hundred marines stationed around the airport came in for increasingly hostile fire from Syrian-backed Moslem militias. By the fall of 1983 an impressive flotilla comprising two U.S. aircraft carriers, the battleship *New Jersey,* and thirty other ships assembled off the Lebanese coast and began to shell the hills above the airport in support of the Marines and an ineffective Lebanese army, with which the United States was increasingly identified. Meanwhile the CIA aided a "private" Christian militia headed by President Bashir Gemeyal.[27] "Success" or even a clear definition of U.S. interests in Lebanon proved to be elusive, and public and congressional concern mounted.

In September and October of 1983 Congress passed follow-on legislation to the early 1983 Lebanese Emergency Act, which had prohibited increasing the number of Marines in Lebanon. The follow-on legislation authorized a continued Marine presence in Beirut for 18 months in exchange for executive assurances that the number of Marines and their role would be limited.[28] It was the first time the "clock" in the War Powers Act had been officially set in motion by Congress, albeit not for sixty days but for eighteen months. Nonetheless, Congress did exercise its institutional prerogative in the matter. However, Congress extended the time the troops would be in Lebanon in order to allow the president's policy to prove itself, or unravel, and to push the issue past the next election.[29]

On the night of October 23, twenty days after the war powers "clock" had been set, 241 U.S. Marines were killed while they slept when a lone terrorist raced his truck-bomb into their barracks. As pictures of the carnage came home, so did a kind of macabre déjà vu: another civil war, another ill-defined sense of mission, and the use of too few men to accomplish what could be managed only by protracted conflict and virtual occupation, if at all.

There were angry recriminations from Congress and more than a little hesitation in the Defense Department to persist in the mission. But the Marines stayed, in part because of Secretary of State Shultz's insistence that a withdrawal under fire would yield chaos and discredit American power. The Druse, along with Syrian-backed Shiite Moslems, increased the tempo of fighting in February 1984. The Italians and the British withdrew from the multinational force. The Reagan administration was left no choice: "The marines are being deployed 2½ to 3 miles west" was the laconic announcement on February 7, 1984; that is, the Marines were going back to their ships. As the Marines departed, the guns of the *New Jersey* lobbed huge shells on Syrian positions. But the fire could not cover the obvious fact, stunning to the Lebanese: the Americans were going home.

For the Reagan administration, the Lebanese enterprise was the avatar of a serious institutional handicap. It attested to, in the argot of a miffed high-level Reagan bureaucrat, "the temptation" of Congress "to micromanage diplomatic tactics."[30] The restriction on the number and role of the Marines, one high foreign policy adviser complained, "locked us into a fixed, minimal, and less and less appropriate deployment. . . . The examination of the marine bombing . . . which was regurgitated by the Long Commission led to renewed rumblings . . . this in turn convinced the Syrians that the United States was "short of breath" . . . thus undermining delicate diplomatic efforts . . . that sought a negotiated solution."[31]

Once peaceful Lebanon had become an abattoir, the idea that the United States could negotiate a viable solution to a civil war seemed fanciful. The civil war was remarkable for its random ferocity. The United States had backed sections of the Christian minority in a situation where no side seemed to have any advantage. Neither the executive nor Congress could tolerate heavy casualties any more than the Israelis, who, along with the Syrians, had the most substantive interest in the outcome.

Lebanon also seemed to confirm the administration's worst fears about the role of Congress in the management of force. As Secretary Shultz put it: "If you say the President is the Commander in Chief and then you have a piece of legislation that says . . . he must move forces within some period of days, how could you say he is the Commander in Chief. . . . There has to be a capacity for decisions without being . . . surrounded by so many conditions that you don't have room for maneuver."[32] If it had not been for Congress, Shultz implied, disaster could have been avoided. But retrieving U.S. forces and bringing them to safety was done because no reasonable increase in their number could have changed the course of events in Lebanon. Eventually, the strongest power on the ground and the parties themselves would settle the matter. As one high administration official confessed: "Such an outcome might have occurred even without a war powers resolution . . . the reality is that the President retains the initiative in military deployments and he retains freedom to succeed or fail on his own. Operations that succeed encountered no serious war powers complaints. . . . Success commands support."[33]

That policy is measured by success is a fact of life in the corporate world and the political world as well. That foreign policy is also measured by a criterion allowing ever-diminishing flexibility is probably less a function of the War Powers Act than of limited public tolerance for indeterminacy (and the memory of Vietnam). In the end, many complaints against the War Powers Act are not based on a reverence for any notion of proper presidential and legislative spheres. Rather, most discomforts with the War Powers Act are predicated on certain presumptions regarding the need for speed and expediency in foreign policy.[34]

The War Powers and Iran-Contra

Within three months of taking office, the Reagan administration tripled its military assistance to El Salvador and began to bring economic pressure on the nascent Marxist regime in Nicaragua. The diplomatic rhetoric rang with cries of "going to the source" of terrorism in the Western Hemisphere, that is, Cuba and Nicaragua, both of whom were said to be arming the insurgents in El Salvador and elsewhere. Direct assaults on Cuba and Nicaragua were almost immediately vetoed by a Pentagon reluctant to devote ships, matériel, and men to any protracted invasion or blockade. The military were especially worried about the casualties that might ensue from an invasion. They were also squeamish about engaging allies of the Soviet Union over a period of not just days but months, perhaps years.[35] The military feared, as well, that any effort aimed at direct confrontation would, as in Vietnam, wither the promised fruits of a massive rearmament program.

Congress was no less uneasy with the administration's fixation on Central America.[36] The prospect of a Vietnam-like involvement—an open-ended commitment of U.S. resources in civil wars with no evident U.S. interests and where U.S. allies were morally dubious—was, to say the least, unsettling. As early as 1981, Congress stipulated that military aid to El Salvador be predicated on a presidential certification that the regime was attempting to conduct fair elections, improve its human rights record, and search for a political solution to its civil war. The administration, while complaining that the reporting requirements were "onerous and contrary to United States interest,"[37] managed perfunctorily to submit the required reports.

In May 1981 a group of twenty-nine liberal members of Congress sought, for the first time, to invoke the War Powers Act as the basis for their opposition to U.S. policy in Central America when they filed suit in the U.S. District Court of Columbia to force the president to withdraw advisers from El Salvador. The plaintiffs alleged that troops were, in fact, "introduced into hostilities . . . although there had been no declaration of war by Congress [nor] specific . . . authorization [nor any] national emergency." Furthermore, U.S. advisers "remained, despite the failure to comply with [the] reporting requirements [of the War Powers Act] and beyond the 60 days allotted to the President to send forces in the absence of a declaration of war."[38] Although the case was dismissed, Judge Joyce Green admitted the "standing" of the members, that is, that they had a right to sue. But in this case, Judge Green seemed to say, she simply could not get at the truth. "The Court does not decide that all disputes under the War Powers Resolution would be inappropriate for judicial resolution. . . . But fact finding . . . to determine whether United States forces have been introduced into hostilities or imminent hostilities renders this case, in its current posture, nonjusticiable."[39]

In 1982 Senate Minority Leader Robert Byrd fretted about a process of escalation for U.S. arms in the region. Byrd worried that American forces would be involved in combat. U.S. troops, he noted, were carrying weapons on patrols with Salvadoran regulars. These were not "training exercises," Byrd pointed out. Furthermore, not only were the war powers provisions being skirted but, equally disturbing, the United States had embarked on a dangerous road. Byrd suggested that the remedy might be to strengthen the War Powers Act.[40]

In Nicaragua, troop numbers quickly expanded. By the end of 1985 there were some 18,000 to 20,000 exile "Contras" fighting the Managua regime. If the scope of the effort could be compared with the U.S. effort to overthrow Castro, the Nicaraguans numbered roughly eleven times the number involved in the Bay of Pigs.[41] In April 1982 and again in 1983 an uneasy House passed a prohibition on aid to groups established for the purpose of overthrowing the Nicaraguan government. The White

House argued that the law would not inhibit covert aid to the Contras (or counterrevolutionaries), and the CIA provided the Contras about $90 million throughout 1982 and 1983. The White House asserted that the support of the Contras was designed to put pressure on the Sandinistas to negotiate, and not to help the Contras win, although it was plain that the Contras had more far-reaching ambitions.

Faced with persistent congressional resistance, President Reagan resorted to addressing an extraordinary joint session of Congress. On national television he tried to make it clear that if any of the dire consequences he projected for Central America came true, the blame would fall directly on the shoulders of Congress. Congress relented on overt aid to El Salvador. But covert aid to the Contras was suspended for several months in 1983[42] and was limited to $24 million for fiscal year 1984.

Finally, in early spring 1984 the administration again presented a covert funding measure as a "rider" to an African famine-relief bill. As aid to the Contras was being debated, the press revealed that the CIA had mined Nicaragua's harbors. Ships from over a dozen countries, most of them U.S. allies, had run afoul of the mines.[43] When the Nicaraguans complained of these activities to the World Court, the United States refused to submit to the jurisdiction of that body. This only compounded an image that the administration held U.S. domestic and international legal inhibitions in low regard when it came to issues of war and peace in Central America.[44] Many members of Congress were incensed. The upshot was the passage in October 1984 of the restrictive Boland Amendment, which barred all aid to the Contras by the CIA, the Defense Department, or other agencies of the U.S. government.

In the wake of this defeat of administration policy, the Reagan administration set in motion, through the NSC and under the direction of Lt. Col. Oliver North, its secret aid program to support the Contras.[45] Employing a mix of privately recruited agents and money solicited from foreign governments and wealthy private American contributors, North raised millions of dollars. In late 1985 North funneled a portion of Iran's payments for the U.S. arms into the Contra accounts. Perhaps $30 million had been generated from the arms-for-hostages Iranian arms sales, but much of that money ended up in the accounts of American, Israeli, and Iranian middlemen used by North in the transactions.

By 1984 there were training bases in six states where American volunteers and Contras could train. National Guard units, as well as Air Force planes, were pressed into service by the NSC to transport war-fighting matériel to the Contras from Alabama on a "space available" basis. Once in Central America, logistics officers in Honduras and El Salvador expedited the flow of arms. According to the NSC plan, approved by the president, a retired American general, Maj. Gen. John K. Singlaub, a former commander of U.S. forces in Korea (cashiered in 1978 by President Carter for attempting to undermine Carter's drawdown of U.S. forces there), was authorized to coordinate these efforts.[46]

The Boland Amendment and the War Powers Act prohibited U.S. forces from coordinating combat operations, whether they might be with either the government of El Salvador or the Contras. Title 18, Paragraph 960, of the U.S. Criminal Code makes it a criminal offense to participate in a group that takes armed action against foreign property or nationals. It also prohibits assistance to "armed expeditionaries begin[ning] or set[ting] foot or provid[ing] for or furnish[ing] the money [to] any expedition" with any nation with whom the United States is not in a formal state of war.[47] Notwithstanding the law, CIA hirelings from El Salvador, Honduras, Chile, Argentina, Ecuador, and Bolivia received training in Panama to sabotage ports, bridges, and refineries and make it appear that the Contras were an effective fighting and commando force.[48]

By early 1982 nearly all Contra funds, no matter how they had been raised, were being disbursed directly from the CIA.[49] Meanwhile, the United States put together a number of action teams for special duty inside Nicaragua itself. Some American units organized suppressive fire and provided transport for the Contras. In eighteen months the Contras moved from small-time holdup artists and sneak thieves to a substantial security problem for the Sandinistas.[50]

By 1985, Congress was overtly funding the Contras. Twenty-seven million dollars was authorized for humanitarian aid to the Contras, and more than $3 million was reportedly authorized for "advice" and "information" as well as communications and training. "Real-time" information was gathered from reconnaissance planes and from sophisticated radars on an offshore Honduran island. From Panama, the intelligence was relayed back to U.S. advisers in El Salvador and to advisers with the Contras. One CIA analyst recalled warning that the activity in Honduras could have unhappy and, in the argot of the profession, unintended "blowback," since the Contra operations could "provoke cross border attacks by Nicaragua and possibly call into play the Organization of American States provisions [for self-defense]. . . . the Nicaraguan government would clamp down on civil liberties . . . there would be reaction against United States . . . diplomatic personnel."[51]

But the professional intelligence and military foreboding (especially at the level of the service chiefs) was actually CIA Director William Casey's proximate goal. Casey apparently hoped that Contra incursions and resultant counterattacks would elicit a Sandinista incursion into Honduras or Costa Rica in hot pursuit or as retaliation. If the Sandinistas "could be provoked into doing something stupid," as one intelligence official put it, then direct action aimed at clearing the Sandinista "flea" from the Americas would be possible.[52]

An annual series of maneuvers in Honduras proved a convenient cover for further U.S. participation. Several airfields capable of landing heavy cargos, supply depots, ammunition, roads, and radars were turned over to the exclusive use of the CIA after each of the maneuvers had ended. Funds were not taken from the Defense Department's foreign military-assistance accounts, but from its operations budget, so there were no costs to the CIA. Therefore, no monies were reported as spent on assisting the Contras that had not been authorized.[53] When the Honduran conduit was uncovered in October 1986, the State Department and the CIA denied they had been involved. But the denials were discredited in the subsequent congressional hearings, trials, and investigations of the Iran-Contra affair.

Ronald Reagan needed all of his popularity to survive as the investigations exposed the curious mix of deception and gullibility on the part of his closest advisers and operatives. Furthermore, as the layers of the linked affairs were peeled back, Reagan's own administrative inattention, if not culpability, became undeniable, though he denied both. Nonetheless, Reagan, his popularity diminished, survived.

The investigations tended to remain focused on the men who had been the operatives—McFarlane, North, Poindexter, deceased CIA director Casey, and the others—and not the president. Furthermore, Lieutenant Colonel North, in particular, was a television performer of some power. Therefore, with few exceptions, the public congressional hearings on Iran-Contra never moved beyond personal confrontations. Once the powerfully photogenic and likable North stepped out of the picture, the evidence of intricate supply networks, Swiss bank accounts, and trips in the night to negotiate with shady arms merchants and Iranian "moderates" moved between the comedic and the incomprehensible. Thus, as so often in his tenure, President Reagan was able to maintain some distance between himself and his own administration.

Iran-Contra was also ultimately overtaken by the end of the cold war. The onset of Soviet imperial retrenchment and a parade of summit meetings assumed center stage during the last two years of the Reagan administration. Reagan may not have played the starring role in all of these spectacles, but at least the spotlight was not on his role in Iran-Contra. The televised congressional hearings petered out. Once that show was off television, the affair became veiled behind a series of prolonged criminal proceedings.

In explaining the inconclusive end of the Iran-Contra scandal—a series of events that could well have ended in the same dreary way the Nixon administration did—it is important to recall that the scandals broke within a context of success in dealing with America's adversaries. By early 1986 press reports of Oliver North's activities were regular news fare, but at about the same time the Reagan administration deployed a massive U.S. Navy task force in the Gulf of Sidra off Libya, successfully baiting the Libyans into an attack on U.S. naval forces. U.S. carrier-based planes responded with air strikes against Libyan planes, vessels, and shore targets. Only after the attacks were launched were congressional leaders informed—although, in an effort to minimize the likelihood of international escalation, the Soviet chargé d'affaires was called to the State Department and warned to remove Soviet advisers from probable bombing targets before the operation was launched.[54] As Michael Rubner notes, "It thus appears that in the administration's curious judgment, the Kremlin could, and Congress could not be entrusted with highly sensitive details about American military moves against Libya."[55]

On April 14, 1986, the administration launched another air strike against Libya in response to a terrorist attack in West Berlin. Using naval aircraft in the Mediterranean and F-111s launched from the United Kingdom, the attack was targeted in part on Qaddafi's personal compound. Members of Congress were called to the White House, where the congressional leaders were briefed for almost ninety minutes; but the briefings occurred four hours *after* the F-111s had left England for their seven-hour flight to Libya. Forty minutes before the bombings were to begin, Poindexter informed them that "'this is consultation' and assured them at that point that the aerial bombardment mission . . . could still be canceled if the congressmen objected 'unanimously and strongly.'" Senator Robert Byrd, who was among those present, argued that the briefing was inadequate to the spirit of the War Powers Act, since "it was obvious it [the raid] would not have been called off" if they had, in fact, voiced any objection, and House Minority Leader Robert Michel (R.-Ill.) mused, "If I had some serious objection, how could I make it now?"

However problematical in terms of the War Powers Act, these attacks were extremely popular with the American public. Reagan's handling of foreign affairs had been sliding toward the 50 percent mark before the attacks, but afterwards more than 70 percent of Americans felt that Reagan was doing a good job. Sixty percent said that the raids "made me feel proud to be an American," and both the *New York Times* and the *Washington Post* endorsed the attacks.[56]

More Tin Cups in the Future?

In July 1989 Senator Daniel Patrick Moynihan sought to legislate a prohibition on the solicitation of private funds of the sort used by the White House to support the Contras. Under Moynihan's bill, the evasion of express congressional restrictions on U.S. assistance of the sort prohibited by the Boland Amendment would be treated as a felony. The Bush administration argued that the bill was a violation of presidential prerogatives in the conduct of foreign affairs. Senator Jesse Helms argued in defense of the Bush position: "Congress has no constitutional power to prohibit, let alone criminalize, a foreign policy which any President wishes to pursue. If the policy can be implemented without the expenditure of funds, Congress can have no effect on the outcome in any manner under the Constitution of the United States."[57]

Against this forthright statement of a longstanding executive position, Kate Stith has argued in a manner worthy of Madison:

If the Executive could avoid limitations imposed by Congress in appropriations legislation—by independently financing its activities with private funds, transferring funds among appropriations accounts, or selling government assets and services—this would vitiate the foundational constitutional decision to empower Congress to determine what accounts shall be undertaken in the name of the United States.

Federal agencies may not resort to nonappropriation financing *because their activities are authorized only to the extent of their appropriations.* Accordingly, without legislative permission, a federal agency may not resort to private funds to supplement its appropriations because it has no authority to engage in the additional activity on which it would spend the private funds.[58]

Moynihan's bill was approved by both the Senate and the House. It was vetoed by President Bush on November 21, 1989. Clearly, in Theodore Draper's words, much "unfinished business" regarding the balance of executive-legislative authority was carried over into the 1990s.

"PRESIDENTIALISM" IN THE 1990S

A hallmark of the Bush administration was its clear and insistent claim that it is for the president to decide if, when, and how arms are to be used as an instrument of policy. This new presidentialism debuted at Christmas of 1989, when President Bush launched Operation Just Cause against Manuel Noriega of Panama. In the hours preceding the Panamanian expedition, the president did not consult Congress "in every possible instance" as he was required to do by the War Powers Act. Rather, on the day after the invasion, President Bush dispatched a letter to the Senate allowing that he was "providing [his] report" in order to "inform" Congress so that he might be "consistent with" the War Powers Resolution. The reference to the War Powers Resolution was hardly more than an institutional courtesy to the legislature, since, as Bush explained, he had not decided to commit forces because of any congressional warrant; instead, he had acted "pursuant" to his "constitutional authority with respect to the conduct of foreign relations and as Commander in Chief."

In Operation Desert Shield, begun in August 1990, President Bush dispatched a battle group of more than 230,000 troops to Saudi Arabia while Congress was in summer recess. Despite the requirement of the War Powers Resolution that the president report in writing within forty-eight hours "any commitment" of U.S. forces or any "substantial enlargement" of combat forces, Bush waited for six days to notify Congress. He sent his "report" to congressional leaders only after the first American deployments actually landed. As in the case of Panama, he announced that it was his "desire that Congress be fully informed," while he also claimed that his letter demonstrated that U.S. policy was being conducted in a fashion "consistent with the War Powers Resolution."

The core provision of the War Powers Act, a ninety-day time limit on the deployment if U.S. troops were in danger of seeing "imminent combat," was neatly finessed. Operation Desert Shield did not bode any real danger for U.S. troops, President Bush contended, since no military action was anticipated. "To the contrary," Bush stated, "it is my belief that this deployment will facilitate a peaceful resolution of the crisis." Three months later, even after calling up the reserves in order to deploy over 450,000 troops as the U.N. deadline authorizing war neared, the Justice Department still claimed that President Bush's August 9, 1990, letters to the Speaker of the House and the president *pro tempore* of the Senate were clear evidence of the defensive, peacekeeping purport of U.S. policy.[59]

The executive's insouciant insistence on its war-making prerogatives grew as its commitment increased. Secretary of State James Baker told the Senate Foreign Relations Committee on October 17, 1990, that "the President has the right as a matter of practice and principle to initiate military action." Secretary of Defense Richard Cheney informed the Senate Armed Services Committee on December 3, 1990, that he did "not believe that the President requires any additional authorization from the Congress before committing U.S. forces to the Gulf to achieve our objectives." By January 1991 the president had apparently decided on armed action no matter what Congress's disposition toward the use of force might be.[60] Bush's conclusion that he alone had the "constitutional authority" to send troops to war was backed by the "many attorneys" who had advised him on the matter.[61]

Given the public qualms of former secretaries of defense, national security advisers, and chairmen of the Joint Chiefs of Staff,[62] as well as the misgivings of his commander in the field and the unease of the CIA director,[63] it is hard to understand why President Bush and his national security team surmised that an early war in 1991 was better than letting sanctions run their course. Perhaps the Bush policy team really believed that when it submitted a U.N. Security Council Resolution asking for a certain date for the use of forces if Iraq had not withdrawn from Kuwait, Saddam Hussein would see reason and withdraw. According to some accounts, however, many in the president's small policy-making circle had not realized that the decision to augment U.S. forces dramatically would place the huge land, sea, and air armada in a position where it would have to either fight or redeploy within months.[64] An incomprehension of the consequences of his October 30, 1990, decision to deploy massive forces may explain why President Bush waited until two days after the November election to inform any member of Congress.[65] On November 6, 1990, in a Washington restaurant, an astonished chairman of the Senate Armed Services Committee was told for the first time that a decision to "take an offensive posture" was to be announced— within the hour.[66]

With the dreadful determination of a sleepwalker, Bush went his own way. With only a week left before the expiration of the U.N. deadline for the withdrawal of Iraqi forces from Kuwait, the war option was presented to Congress. Even though Congress authorized the use of arms on January 12, 1991, the vote was hardly a resounding mandate for war. Indeed, the number who favored war in relation to those who did not was the lowest in U.S. history: 52–47 in the Senate and 250–182 in the

House.[67] While the personal dismay and doubts of the members were abundant, Congress's institutional response was tepid. Almost as an afterthought to its authorization for the use of force against Saddam Hussein, Congress appended a curtsy to the War Powers Act.

The executive also argued that in light of the November 29, 1990, U.N. Security Council deadline that authorized armed action in the event that Iraq did not withdraw from Kuwait, Congress had no lawful choice but to opt for war, as it reluctantly did, in fact, in January 1991. Some legal observers concurred, arguing that war was the president's prerogative,[68] since the U.N. Participation Act allowed forces to be sent unilaterally by the president without congressional approval as long as an action had been duly approved by the U.N. Security Council.

It seemed to many, however, that it was impossible that an international body could choose war for the United States when Congress had not yet done any such thing. Indeed, Congress had a plain, even customary, option: it could have chosen silence even beyond the January 15, 1991, U.N. deadline. As Harold Koh reminded the Senate Judiciary Committee on January 8, 1991, "Silence [would have] its own sound, and the sound is no." Moreover, as the former State Department legal adviser Louis Henkin has pointed out, Section 6 of the 1946 U.N. Participation Act stipulates that the president must negotiate agreements with the Security Council under Article 43 of the U.N. Charter spelling out the conditions under which U.S. forces may be employed by the United Nations. Furthermore, the agreements must be submitted to Congress for approval. Inasmuch as those agreements have never been negotiated, the conditions under which a Security Council vote could commit U.S. forces without a congressional declaration cannot be met. Finally, Security Council Resolution 678, of November 29, 1990, was a "request" for military action and, therefore, hortatory rather than a "decision" of the Security Council requiring U.S. compliance under Article 25 of the Charter.[69]

With the passing of the Gulf War, there was another hiatus in the rhythm of intervention and armed combat, and another window for debate. But the time to consider new legislation before events once again closed in passed with the call to send troops to Somalia at the end of 1992. Some thirty thousand U.S. forces were mustered by President Bush to feed the starving in a ravaged piece of Africa's Horn.

Plans for the U.N.-authorized "peacemaking" enterprise surfaced slowly through press leaks and private U.N. negotiations. Congress was not reconvened, and the congressional leadership seemed unconcerned. Senate Majority Leader George Mitchell averred that since the mission was "to assist in the distribution of supplies," he did not believe that it would "involve Americans in a shooting war." The congressional leadership thus finessed their obligations under the War Powers Act, which required that Congress take action when U.S. forces are placed in areas of imminent or actual hostilities.[70] The whole of Somalia had returned to the rawest Hobbesian version of the "state of nature." Even children toted heavy weapons about the countryside. Food and arms became the means of survival and the currency of the moment. Yet neither the Bush administration nor Congress was willing to debate the extent and purposes of the American humanitarian mission. Once again, this time in the waning hours of President Bush's watch, a matter of war and peace was left to a president's judgment and the play of events.

THE WAR POWERS AT THE END OF THE COLD WAR

Our review of the post-Vietnam history of executive-legislative relations under the War Powers Act underscores that it has not proved an effective check on the unilateral use of force by a president. The reasons for this are by no means confined to the propensity for institutional aggrandizement on the part of presidents. Congressional acquiescence has also been evident in some measure in virtually every case examined. Professor Koh's claim notwithstanding, congressional "silence" has seldom meant no.

In part, acquiescence can be traced to the institutional fragmentation built into Congress and exacerbated by the institutional reforms of the mid- and late 1970s. The congressional leadership no longer seems able to alert the rank and file to institutional dangers. Indeed, institutional sentiments have lost much of their hold as Congress has adopted a kind of every-man-for-himself attitude. Congress has become even more reactive and less coherent. Increasingly, the congressional leadership seems like Lear in the storm, walking perilously close to cliffs and crying unheard jeremiads.

But the "leadership" itself has become more and more like Congress itself, fragmented and reflective of the deepening partisanship of the body. During the first half of the 1980s the partisan division paralleled the structure of Congress, with the Senate and House controlled by different parties. During this period an assertive executive was especially effective in initiating military interventions. Only when misadventure became undeniable, as in Lebanon and in the Iran-Contra affair, did the political climate allow Congress to constrain the president. And even in these instances, partisanship contributed to inconclusive institutional engagements.

Finally, the half-life of the cold war resembles the lingering toxicity of the nuclear materials that made up the weaponry of deterrence. The post-Vietnam and, now, the post–cold war international environment remains defined by the president as a kind of permanent emergency: the sources of threat are more diffuse, but in the "new world order" the White House remains very dangerous. For over forty years, in the face of one kind of emergency or another, the appropriate role of Congress has been defined as a bipartisan posture of bowing more or less reverentially before executive portraits of imminent menace. Absent an alternative vision, even the most ethereal threat will probably obtain by default.

It has been argued that even an incomplete fidelity to the War Powers Act is better than nothing. In this respect, the 1973 legislation may have spurred the U.S. exodus from Grenada within the time period established by the War Powers "clock." The Congressional Research Service specialist Ellen Collier has noted: "Congress, in fact, has been served up over a dozen Presidential reports that have, indeed, acknowledged the War Powers Act." These reports, she argues, confirm that the War Powers Act remains in the executive's field of vision. Using the example of the U.S. involvement in the Lebanon peacekeeping force, Collier suggests that no matter how dubious or ill-conceived the mission, but for the War Powers Act, it might have been worse.[71] Indeed, had it not been for the War Powers Act, President Bush might have dispensed with Congress altogether in the Gulf War.

Perhaps the War Powers Act helped force the executive to seek congressional authority for war in December of 1990. But the president's dim awareness of his minimum responsibility to inform the governed, as well as his constitutional partner, reduces constitutionalism to mere ritual. If executive war is waged often enough, Congress will never assume the mature role the founders intended for it. Instead of being the great bulwark against what the founders called the most oppressive of the king's oppressions, Congress's war powers role will remain one of legitimizing the hypocrisies, such as lusty cheers for the "rescue" of the *Mayaguez* or agreement that a "briefing" really constitutes "consultations" (as required under the War Powers Act) even as F-111 weapons officers program their final approach for their bombing runs. Too often, alas, Congress acts like one of those television evangelists who asserts high moral principle on Sunday but by Thursday evening can be found somewhere out on Highway 40 in the "No Tell Motel."

The great generality of the Constitution in the area of the war powers was testimony to the founders' pragmatism and confidence in those who would serve the republic in the future. The founders expected subsequent generations to exercise their own judgment in terms of their experiences. The requirements of containment and the nuclear threat forced the grant of considerable executive discretion. But the claims of Bush, his predecessors, and the praetorian guard of national security intellectuals that has built up around the presidency would flabbergast the founders.[72]

Yet, even though the cold war has passed, old habits die hard. Congress can come to grips with the fact of America's post–cold war exposure to great-power politics, not by amending the Constitution, but by strengthening it with more consistent fidelity to its call for codetermining policy when it comes to the use of force. Perhaps it is not too late to reestablish a discourse based on what is probable instead of summoning the worst goblins of our imagination and memory. The executive could do better than recapitulating routines more appropriate to an age of swagger than the present plight of complex interdependence. Reasoned judgments about our adversaries could be advanced, placing measured estimates of interests and behavior of others against our own interests. To continue along the path of the last twenty years is to put collective faith in a few cloistered individuals, usually with an attention span no less fragmented than that of Congress.

It is a great irony that in the Gulf War debate Congress was again asked to pass a resolution under conditions much like those at the time of the Tonkin Gulf Resolution. In the Gulf War, as in Vietnam, the U.S. was precommitted, by the president and a small group of advisers, to actions with indeterminate consequences. The accompanying din of approaching battle and the pressure to make the best of a bad situation boxed in a clearly reluctant Congress. In legitimizing the president's Gulf War, Congress abdicated almost any attempt to enforce the War Powers Act as it stands. If the evidently reluctant and doubtful Congress could have had more regular procedures in place, and had it managed to pound out meaningful war powers procedures earlier, some clearer specifications of our national ends and means might have emerged before the smell of cordite, burning petroleum, and death fouled the Middle East's winter air.

CHAPTER 9

Public Opinion and Foreign Policy

THROUGHOUT THE cold war, most students of public opinion have viewed the public as too steeped in lethargy and parochial self-interests to offer responsible contributions to the decision-making process. To be sure, analysts also hold that given the democratic framework of American politics, the public cannot be ignored. But public opinion should be leavened by deference to seasoned leadership. As Hans J. Morgenthau's widely read text put it, "The popular mind wants quick results; it will sacrifice tomorrow's real benefit for today's apparent advantage. . . . a government must avoid widening the unavoidable gap between the requirements of good foreign policy and the preferences of public opinion."[1]

Most observers invoke a dismaying recital: the rejection of the Versailles Treaty at the end of World War I; the isolationism of the period between the two great wars; the post–World War II reaction to the division of Europe; the readiness to believe that the State Department "lost" China; the rampage of Senator Joseph McCarthy; the public anger during the Vietnam years. The last, it has been said, contributed to an inability to conclude the war advantageously, on the one hand, and a subsequently incapacitating "Vietnam Syndrome," on the other.

The conventional truth adduced from this litany is that the public cannot be discounted; yet, at the same time, the people cannot be counted an asset in the pursuit of any long-term diplomatic design. Thus throughout the period leading up to the Vietnam War, and for a time afterwards, public opinion analysts and policymakers tended to reflect the 1950s' classic study by Gabriel Almond, who had asserted that "Americans tend to exhaust their emotional and intellectual energies in private pursuits. . . . On questions . . . such as foreign policy, they tend to react in formless and plastic moods which undergo frequent alteration."[2]

One diplomat-turned-historian, Louis Halle, attributed many of the ills of this century to public participation in politics. The price paid for the "shift of political power from a cosmopolitan elite to a nationalistic and often xenophobic" public, Halle wrote, is the "decline in standards of interest and conduct."[3] George Kennan, Halle's old friend and colleague, despaired that the public's attention span was hardly better than that of any large, Paleolithic reptile:

I sometimes wonder whether . . . a democracy is . . . similar to one of those prehistoric monsters with a body as long as this room and the brain the size of a pin: he lies there in his comfortable primeval mud and pays little attention to his environment; he is slow to wrath—in fact you practically have to whack his tail off to make him aware that his interests are being disturbed; but, once he grasps this, he lays about him with such blind determination that he not only destroys his adversary but largely wrecks his native habitat.[4]

The public is, therefore, an unwelcome kibitzer at a most dangerous game.

American leaders have frequently believed the public to be at best a body that must be mobilized to support policy. Thus, they believe that the day-to-day operations of diplomacy are best left to the professional managers of foreign policy.[5] Indeed, "crisis managers" proliferated in the cold war period. The management of force, and not diplomacy, was the coin of the realm of foreign policy. The public could not know the delicate signals and maneuvers of such operations. These were skills that were acquired through lengthy apprenticeship. The craft of foreign policy was, in the words of former State Department official Roger Hilsman, "like blue cheese, . . . an acquired taste."[6]

This traditional skepticism of political elites concerning the foreign affairs capacities of the American people is shared by the contemporary leadership. In an extensive survey of "elites" undertaken in the wake of the Vietnam War, political scientists Ole Holsti and James Rosenau found a widely held view that people "are lacking in two important requisites for a sound foreign policy—patience and an understanding of the role of power in world politics."[7] Further, it has been argued that the public is volatile, its usual contribution to policy being not so much setting the bounds of discourse as a churlish clubbing of those thought responsible for unsuccessful policy.

Only as the effects of the Vietnam War began to manifest themselves more clearly did analysts begin a systematic and somewhat more reassuring reappraisal of public attitudes.[8] Nonetheless, the uncharitable view of American public opinion persists, and it encourages attempts to ensure that information is structured so as to minimize damage to ongoing policy. If the public is deemed incapable of real understanding of the ambiguities of complex negotiations, almost any serious agreement will be at risk once the details became public. It follows, therefore, that secret accords are justified. Indeed, the perception among policymakers that the public is both ignorant and dangerous is the rationale and the fillip to the practice of resorting to executive agreements, the withholding of information about the external world, and various efforts to "spin" public interpretations of events.

Even if the public mood were thought stable, albeit sluggish, as some recent evidence suggests,[9] the argument persists that the public cannot make judgments, since events overtake the sum of public perceptions. In "the quicksilver world of international politics," as political scientist Thomas Halper put it, "the public is concerned about situations which have ceased to exist. . . . Information, once accurate, becomes obsolete, and consequently, erroneous . . . the results . . . may be even more deleterious than . . . no information at all."[10]

Common "elite" cold war views of the capacities of the American people have serious implications. Although the United States is by no means a direct or "pure" democracy, a founding premise of the republic was that people are capable of understanding their interests and of forming reasoned judgments.[11] In any democratic system, those officials engaged in the conduct of foreign policy are obliged to represent the people's interests. There is, as well, an equivalent obligation for policymakers to be accountable to the people and their elected representatives. But if the people are incapable of making informed judgments concerning their interests and prone to irrational and unpredictable behavior, then strict adherence to democratic norms of accountability by public officials may no longer be prudent, nor, in the end, may they serve the people's real interests.

Assessment of this dilemma requires, therefore, attention to several issues. Are the American people benighted and bellicose when it comes to grasping the nature of international affairs? Can they formulate coherent views of American interests? Does the American public hold identifiable notions of the means appropriate to pursuing those interests? Are there significant differences between the views held by the public and the U.S. policy elites concerning the international system and American interests?

THE AMERICAN PUBLIC AND THE WORLD

The evidence concerning public knowledge is not always conclusive. Contributing to the confusion about public opinion is the fact that responses by the public have varied with the wording of a question or the placement of a question relative to other questions in an interview schedule. Thus, respondents have favored increases in defense spending when asked about the issue in isolation from other programs, but when the issue is placed in the context of competing programs, such as education, a clear sentiment for cutting defense emerges.[12]

Furthermore, in any analysis of public opinion and foreign policy it is useful to distinguish between the knowledge of specific events and issues and more general attitudes toward American involvement in world politics. Although particular knowledge requires regular attention to a daunting tide of information, general sentiments form over time. Daniel Yankelovich and his associates have long maintained, in this regard, that it is important to distinguish between "mass opinion," on the one hand, and what might be termed "public judgement," on the other.[13]

"Mass opinion" refers to the volatile, confused, ill-informed, and emotionally clouded public responses to an issue when underlying value conflicts remain unresolved. "Public judgement" refers to the public's viewpoint once people have had an opportunity to confront an issue for a time and arrive at a settled conviction. A "public judgement" is the sum of people's second thoughts after they have pondered an issue deeply enough to resolve conflicts and tradeoffs and to accept responsibility for the consequences of their beliefs. Converting mass opinion into public judgment is no easy task. It can take months or years or even decades to accomplish.[14]

This distinction between mass opinion and public judgments is useful in understanding not only apparently contradictory findings concerning the volatility of public opinion but clear evidence of relative stability of public opinion concerning the broader objectives of U.S. foreign policy. This distinction is also useful in understanding the relationship between the public and policy elites.

The Structure and Content of Public Opinion

There is agreement among public opinion analysts that it is not very useful to view the public as a monolithic, undifferentiated mass. Rather, it can be broken down into clusters based on levels of knowledge and kinds of attitudes. Several classifications have been developed over the years since World War II, but all of them distinguish between the "public" and "elites."[15] Some observers group those who hold government positions with individuals outside government in constructing a definition of the elites, while others distinguish between governmental and nongovernmental elites.[16] There is agreement that elites possess high levels of knowledge, more consistent views, and quite intensely held attitudes. There is also some agreement that the levels of knowledge and attitudes held by the "public" are more varied.

Most analysts distinguish among the broader public in terms of levels of knowledge, coherence of views, and the intensity with which they hold their views. Eugene Wittkopf delineates the existence of essentially three groups within the public at large that are distinct from the rather small policy elite (a group that Wittkopf estimates would probably number well under 100,000 individuals).[17] For Wittkopf, the "attentives" constitute less than 10 percent of the public and display levels of knowledge and attitudes quite similar to those of the "elite." The "inattentives," in contrast, constitute less than 10 percent of the population, have very low levels of information, and demonstrate poorly formed views of foreign affairs. The remainder of the population—more than 80 percent—Wittkopf classifies as the "mass public." The mass public possess a general knowledge and evince reasonably coherent attitudes, even though they do not always display a detailed factual knowledge of foreign policy.[18] Wittkopf's breakdown of the public into subgroups based on general levels of information does little to disabuse the conventional wisdom concerning the levels of factual knowledge about foreign policy: the factual base of most public information is at best uneven and not as good as practitioners might hope.

Any inference one should draw from presumed or real public factual ignorance is not, however, self-evident. In 1964, for example, a cross section of American people were asked, "Do you happen to know if there is a Communist government in China now?" Twenty-eight percent confessed that they did not know.[19] But whether this is cause for despair is not certain. After all, about 70 percent gave the correct answer. Earlier, in an American Institute of Public Opinion (AIPO) poll in May 1950 that asked, "Will you tell me offhand what the Marshall Plan is?" 63 percent of respondents answered "reasonably correctly." Yet only 5 percent could give meaningful answers to a related question about the term "Point 4."[20] Similarly, items presented in an important study by Free and Cantril to demonstrate public ignorance about foreign affairs show that an "astounding" 28 percent of the public could not identify the acronym NATO in 1964.[21] Yet the researchers might have noted that, on the other hand, an equally astounding 72 percent of the population could. It would seem, then, that drastic conclusions based on any single item would be hasty.

Nonetheless, failure to recognize obscure information or perform esoteric operations is sometimes used as proof of the public's incapacity to judge foreign affairs. At this point we would ask whether our readers can spell the name of the late Swedish secretary-general of the United Nations. If our readers cannot correctly spell Dag Hammarskjold, they should not despair, for they are in the company of 99 percent of the adult population who were asked to perform the same task in an effort to demonstrate the public's ignorance about foreign affairs. On the other hand, in the 1960s nearly 60 percent of the public could correctly identify Mao Zedong as the leader of Communist China; all but 2 of 557 respondents in a 1960 Detroit study could correctly say that Russia had in fact developed and tested its own atomic weapons; and again in 1960, 96 percent of the public had heard of the U-2 incident.[22] In contrast, in 1979 only 23 percent of the American people could name the countries involved in the SALT negotiations; and in 1985 fewer than two-thirds of the American people knew which side the United States had supported in Vietnam a decade earlier.[23]

One systematic study of youth attitudes and information about national and international politics in the late 1960s and early 1970s detected no significant differences from their predecessors in the range, richness, or intensity of their views.[24] At the same time, nobody has doubted in recent years that among people under thirty years of age political consciousness has slipped from its peak in the Vietnam era.[25] For example, perhaps 90 percent of college students have an "inadequate" grasp of world affairs. Fewer than a third of the three thousand students who took national tests understood recent global population trends, patterns of world energy consumption, world cultures and religions, or global politics. Explanations include the pervasiveness of television, the breakdown of families, poor school instruction, and a composite malaise brewed from mixing marijuana and narcissism with permissiveness. On the other hand, questions have been raised about the validity of the test itself, in that many of the areas tested are devoid of consensus among experts.[26]

The meaning of any assessment of youthful attitudes is questionable, when, in terms of voting and political participation, most political activity occurs after age thirty. Indeed, electoral participation seems to be increasingly confined to those in the upper reaches of the more attentive sector of the public, more than two-thirds of whom are fifty years or older. The percentage between the ages of eighteen and twenty-four who claim to have voted has declined from levels near 50 percent in 1972 to about 33 percent in 1988. Americans between the ages of twenty-five and forty-four seem to be voting at rates above 50 percent, down from the 60 percent and more who voted in 1972. But people between the ages of forty-five and sixty-four seem to be voting at a rate approaching 70 percent throughout the last several decades.[27]

That perhaps 40 percent or more of the population does not exercise the most basic form of participation, namely, informing oneself about the issues of the day, is no comfort for the partisan of democracy. But among adults, with some years of care about families, incomes, and taxes, public events do seem well heeded.[28] If the 50 percent or more of the population that does participate possesses more than minimal levels of knowledge and has reasonably consistent belief systems, then is not the picture more hopeful than bleak?

A Belligerent Beast?

But even if the public is granted some capacity for attention, analysis, and retention of information, are people really volatile, fickle, and churlish? Perhaps if belligerence were an indelible feature of the American psyche, news and information would have to be managed, lest the consequences be an orgy of rage ending in catastrophe. It was certainly a fear that Americans were too pacifist in peace and too belligerent in war that drove much of American foreign policy during Vietnam.[29] Dean Rusk told James Nathan in the spring of 1976 that it was the proudest achievement of his years in public office that the policy-making establishment did not "make the eagle scream." Robert McNamara echoed this sentiment: "The greatest contribution Vietnam is making—right or wrong beside the point—is . . . an ability . . . to go to war without the necessity of arousing public ire. In that sense, Vietnam is almost a necessity of our history, because it is the kind of war we'll most likely be facing for the next fifty years."[30]

Yet when American involvement in Vietnam finally ended, the popular reaction was not the upheaval feared by Johnson and every administration from the beginning of America's engagement with Vietnam.[31] The recriminations were largely confined to President Ford's efforts to shift blame for the final collapse onto Congress. But the attention of the American people was focused on the inflationary results of presidential mismanagement of the wartime economy by Presidents Johnson and Nixon.

It is not evident that the public's volatility is dramatically greater than the mood changes manifested by opinion leaders such as presidents, pundits, and politicians. By and large, during the course of the cold war the public reacted cautiously to some rather pronounced swings between optimism and despair about the future of Great Power relations on the part of public officials.[32] Poll data collected between 1949 and 1969 by William Caspary and John Mueller show that 60–80 percent of the American people consistently voiced support or at least acceptance of the necessity for active American involvement in world affairs.[33] But even when the public mood has shifted, as it undeniably did after Vietnam, it has rarely been with the suddenness with which Jimmy Carter's opinion of the Soviets changed following the Soviet invasion of Afghanistan: Carter confessed to an interviewer that his opinion "of the Russians has changed [more] drastically in the last week than even [in] the previous two and a half years before that."[34]

In the postwar period, Americans have usually rejected belligerency, rash solutions, and quick fixes. In May 1953, when asked about sending help to the French, then besieged in Vietnam by the forces of Ho Chi Minh, who was generally thought by Americans to be an "Asian Stalin," 56 percent were against sending any American troops. On the eve of the Cuban missile crisis, when CIA operations against Castro were at their height and anti-Castro sentiment was a major issue of the upcoming congressional campaign, a clear majority (65 percent) opposed an invasion of Cuba to rid the United States of the bearded nuisance.[35] With five hundred thousand troops suffering heavy casualties in Vietnam, when Americans were asked in 1967 and 1968 to agree or disagree with the statement, "Some people say we should go all out to win a military victory in Vietnam, using atom bombs or other atomic weapons," 65 percent disagreed.[36] All through the 1979–81 hostage crisis in Iran, diplomatic solutions were preferred by margins of 20 percent or more. And when an accord was signed with the Iranians for release of the hostages in exchange for remitting frozen Iranian bank accounts, less than 10 percent of the public favored a vengeful military retort. The American public's moderation toward Iran persisted despite a profound sense of humiliation over the crisis, despite public antipathy to Iran, and despite the ill-treatment accorded American hostages.[37]

The American public throughout much of the cold war might be considered pliant rather than bellicose. Opinion is generally supportive of international involvement. The great constant most Americans take to gauge international affairs is the standard of success.[38] As Mueller noted in his analysis of public opinion, during America's two least popular wars—in Korea and Vietnam—opposition was largely a function of casualties. Americans generally support what works. If escalation means a success that is identifiable, and American losses remain low, the public acquiesces. If withdrawal can be called a success, then this too receives support.[39] Broader analysis of public opinion suggests that this pragmatism is not confined to limited "hot" wars that go sour; it is characteristic—indeed, it is the essential characteristic—of American public opinion.

The Public and the Cold War

A deep and persistent strain of pragmatism is also evident with respect to attitudes formed concerning the cold war strategic balance.[40] Thus when the strategic balance immediately after World War II was clearly on the side of the United States, the public was more inclined to view the use of nuclear weapons as acceptable in the event of war. Yet, even during the most intense periods of the cold war and during the most difficult days of the Korean War only about half of the population could be found to favor the use of nuclear weapons in response to a Soviet attack on Western Europe; and a majority never favored the first use of nuclear weapons in Korea itself or against China.[41] As the Soviet Union acquired a credible nuclear capability, the sense of American vulnerability and ambivalence concerning nuclear weapons grew. The willingness to defend America's allies, especially in Western Europe, remained even into the Vietnam War itself, but by the 1980s public uncertainty concerning nuclear weapons had deepened.

Bruce Russett found that by the onset of the 1980s a majority of the American public understood the "reality of mutual nuclear deterrence, plus perhaps the articulation of deterrence theory." Moreover, "high-income, high-education groups do not differ notably from the public in general." By 1983, at the height of the Reagan administration's surging military buildup, a substantial majority of the American people wanted "a balance of power, not advantage or dominance." "Overall," Russett concluded, "we see a rather sophisticated and coherent understanding of the basic principles which many mainstream nuclear strategists have been trying to convey. Americans are eager neither to surrender vital global positions nor to nuke their major adversaries."[42]

In their independent assessment of public opinion during the cold war period, Yankelovich and Harman discerned the operation of two "primal fears" driving public opinion. First, there was a profound fear that human survival was threatened by nuclear war. The threat was deemed controllable, and the people were willing to spend enormous amounts of money to meet the Soviet nuclear challenge. Simultaneously, however, there operated throughout the cold war a "cultural" fear of Soviet expansion.

Part of Ronald Reagan's appeal, no doubt, was that his seemingly contradictory policies spoke to both these fears. His calls for a military buildup and excoriation of the "evil empire" and for a strategic defense "rendering . . . nuclear weapons impotent and obsolete" linked deep public concerns. Reagan's subsequent arms control efforts, based on formulas designed to bring about massive reductions, were predicated on the same fears as the Reagan-era buildup. Yankelovich and Harman maintain, however, that the American people weighted their concerns differently than did the councils of the Reagan administration: "Where the majority of the American people part company with the Reagan Doctrine is over the priority assigned to the two threats. In the public mind the threat of Soviet expansion is not more dangerous than the threat of nuclear war. The electorate is pragmatic, more eager to negotiate constraints on our competition with the Soviets than to flirt with confrontation."[43]

Although the public urge to oppose communism was a constant in post–World War II public opinion, there was, as well, an intense desire to experiment with any formula that might bring about a peaceful resolution of disputes with the Soviets. All the peace moves of the cold war found public acceptance. Rita Simon has called attention to a January 1948 poll that indicated that "78 percent thought the United States ought to halt its production of atomic bombs even before an international control agency was established." Even though fear of public retribution stymied overtures to Communist powers, poll results show that the American people invariably favored summit meetings with Soviet leaders.[44]

During the cold war, 75 percent of the public approved the Korean armistice, and over 65 percent supported both the limited test-ban treaty and the nuclear non-proliferation treaty.[45] At the onset of the 1970s, albeit a time of officially proclaimed détente, large majorities favored cooperation with the Soviet Union concerning limiting antimissile systems, exploring outer space and the oceans, educational and cultural exchange, expanded trade, and even combined efforts to control the spread of nuclear weapons and the outbreak of war in Europe and Asia.[46] In 1982, at the height of the Reagan administration's advertisement of an American "vulnerability" to Soviet weapons (as well as Soviet perfidy when it came to keeping agreements), a majority of the American people responded positively to the idea of a nuclear weapons freeze between the United States and the Soviet Union. Public support of negotiations did not extend to unilateral concessions or "disarmament"; there was, however, always support for negotiated mutual agreements that looked to extensive reductions and concessions.

Throughout the 1970s and early 1980s, majorities believed President Reagan's assertion that the Soviets "lie and cheat." But by the late 1980s clear majorities were prepared to run the risk of Soviet cheating. More than 80 percent of the public felt that the Soviets had cheated on prior arms control agreements, but a majority maintained that the United States had also cheated, and almost three-fourths agreed that "both the U.S. and the Soviets cheat on treaties to some extent; it's just part of the game."[47]

The American public had reached what the analysts term a "public judgment" concerning Soviet-American relations. This judgment, which embraced "boundaries of political acceptability," can be seen as having four elements:

1. Nuclear war would be suicidal. The danger of such a war is real. Therefore, *the United States should act so as to reduce its vulnerability to nuclear war.*
2. The Soviet Union is a dangerous adversary, but coexistence is possible. Therefore, *the United States should negotiate with the Soviet Union in good faith.*
3. The American people "like and admire the Russian people," but they are deeply suspicious of the Soviet government. Therefore, *the United States must not be dependent on Soviet goodwill.*
4. The United States cannot win an arms race, but it can lose if it is perceived as weak. Since the Soviet Union "responds only to military strength," *the United States must maintain military strength.*[48]

Although agreements with the Soviets found constant favor during the cold war, presidential initiatives in the direction of belligerence reap sizable support, at least in the short run. Presidential popularity and approval ratings consistently rise in moments of crisis. Truman at the onset of Korea, Eisenhower during the Quemoy and Matsu crises and when he sent Marines to Lebanon, Kennedy during the Bay of Pigs invasion and the Cuban missile crisis, Johnson and Nixon at various crisis points during the Vietnam period, Ford during the *Mayaguez* crisis, Carter when hostages were seized in Iran, Reagan in response to the Grenada invasion and the bombing in Beirut, Bush at the time of the Persian Gulf War, and Clinton's reprisal raid on Iraq in June 1993—all benefited from a surge in public support. But popular support has receded in every case.[49]

No analyst of American public opinion disagrees that fear can usually move large segments of the public in the direction of presidential rhetoric over the short run. But this is mass opinion, with all of its volatility. The longer view of the last forty years suggests that the public judgment is more centered and stable than these crisis-driven surges suggest. The operational implications of this more considered public judgment reflect what Russett has termed a "fundamental centrism of most American opinion on security issues."[50]

INTERNATIONALISM AT THE END OF THE COLD WAR

By the mid-1970s, public opinion analysis began to reveal that the American people, after a brief, quasi-isolationist interlude at the end of the Vietnam War, had resumed an internationalist posture, though at lower levels than at the peak, prior to Vietnam.[51] The internationalism of the late 1970s, however, was fragmented and divided between a liberal, "nonmilitary" (or "cooperative") internationalism (perhaps a quarter of the population) and a more conservative, or "military" (or "competitive") internationalism (perhaps a third of the population).[52] The remainder of the population was identified as noninternationalist. But even the "noninternationalist" segment was not so much isolationist as it was simply indifferent toward most foreign policy most of the time. This usually indifferent noninternationalist group, however, held attitudes that made it a more likely ally of the conservative internationalists. Thus, when events forced some attention to world affairs, conservative "competitive internationalism" commanded a slim majority that was the bedrock of President Reagan's support for reinvigorating U.S. military power.

The liberal internationalists tended to support cooperative forms of international engagement: economic aid, development assistance, arms control, and strengthening of the United Nations. Conservative internationalists were no less supportive of world involvement but emphasized the enduring character of Soviet-American competition, the salience of military instruments, and U.S. self-interest. Noninternationalists, when pressed, also revealed a preoccupation with power akin to conservative internationalism; however, unlike conservative internationalists, they had little enthusiasm for entanglement with the world. As Michael Mandelbaum and William Schneider put it, "Noninternationalists want the United States to be strong and independent—not interdependent."[53]

In his 1976 campaign, Jimmy Carter succeeded in appealing to ideals common to most Americans. Such a position was sufficiently abstract to appeal to all segments of a split public. Once in office, however, Carter found his administration splayed across contradictory rhetoric and policies designed, in part, to sustain his appeal to a cleaved internationalist body politic. The Carter administration's often contradictory initiatives were also, however, a reflection of a no less fractured elite view of international reality. Holsti and Rosenau's survey of American elite opinion on foreign affairs, conducted as the Carter administration entered office, revealed an elite opinion that corresponded to that of the general public. According to Holsti, American elites represented a kind of three-headed eagle on foreign policy, one head being the cold war internationalists, who looked back to the axioms of the cold war for their bearings; the second, the post–cold war internationalists, concerned with such issues as North-South politics, international economics, and strategic arms control; and the third, the isolationists, who looked inward to the problems of American society.[54]

Internationalists agreed on the necessity of sustaining American international involvement; however, the post–cold war internationalists were ambivalent about active containment of communism, especially if it entailed intervention of the sort undertaken during the runup to the Vietnam War. Internationalists were convinced of the operation of some kind of domino theory, in which American difficulties could encourage instability. But the post–cold war internationalists were not persuaded that instability inevitably worked against the interests of the United States; in their view, serious threats to American security stemmed from new issues that emerged during the 1970s: political economics, energy, and the environment. The post–cold war internationalist locus of activism, then, tended to be in the context of multilateral cooperation. The cold war internationalist, in contrast, envisioned and welcomed a much more self-centered and assertive pursuit of American interests.

Holsti and Rosenau concluded that the third of their sample that was isolationist held little stock in the notion that the Soviet Union was bent on expansion and the provocation of nuclear war. Isolationists viewed the Third World, with its poverty and anti-Western resentment, as inevitably unstable but essentially beyond the influence of the West. From this perspective, it followed that the United States could export neither democracy nor development. In any event, the elite isolationists argued, the real threats to American security were domestic and must be attended to first if American influence was to be extended later.

A New Defense-Oriented Internationalism?

Essential to many liberal students of American foreign policy in post-Vietnam America was the construction and, what was more important, maintenance of a new kind of consensus that left behind cold war verities.[55] Yet, poll data[56] also showed what appeared to be precisely the opposite: a crystallizing of public opinion around "a much more assertive, or hawkish, posture in world affairs, . . . a widespread determination to rebuild American military capabilities and to reaffirm a readiness to use those capabilities in defense of perceived interests abroad."[57]

Late 1979 marked the recoalescence of concern about America's defense posture. Confronted with Afghanistan, the hostage seizure in Tehran, and public nail-biting in policy circles regarding the Soviet threat, many concluded that the cold war had returned. The Gallup organization asked in February 1980, "Ten years from now, do you think the United States should be playing a more important and powerful role as a world leader, a less important role, or about the same as it plays today?" Fifty-five percent of the 1,111 registered voters preferred a more assertive role. A similar response was given by 47 percent of the sample polled by the Chicago Council on Foreign Relations (CCFR) in 1978: 60 percent supported an increase in defense spending before the Iranian crisis in the fall of 1979, with support increasing to 76 percent in March of 1980.[58]

It was a time of reevaluation. Especially after Watergate and Vietnam, there was potential to choose a direction away from a militarized version of containment.[59] By 1980, military force again commanded support (however fragile), conceived, as it was, as the linchpin of U.S. interests. Support for the use of American troops in Europe to defend vital interests increased from a low of 30 percent in 1973–75 to an average of 65 percent by the spring of 1980. By 1978, 42 percent of the business community was willing to use troops in the Middle East in case of an oil cutoff. Other opinion leaders were only 5–7 percentage points behind on this issue of using force to secure economic ends. In contrast, in 1974 the overall percentage of the elite willing to use force in such contingencies stood at only 22 percent. When the Soviets were introduced into the oil–U.S. security equation, an overwhelming percentage of the Harris poll respondents of January and February 1980—some 75 percent—agreed with the "Carter Doctrine," according to which force should be used, if necessary, to protect the oil fields.[60] As Lloyd Free and William Watts put it, a "defense-oriented internationalism had come of age."[61]

To conservative internationalists the new mood was welcome. But to George Kennan, who thirty years before had decried mass hysteria in America's dealings with the Russians, the war atmosphere in Washington at the beginning of 1980 was clearly the responsibility of the policy-making establishment. He despaired: "Never since World War II has there been so far-reaching a militarization of thought and discourse in the capital. An unsuspecting stranger, plunged into its midst, could only conclude that the last hope of peaceful, nonmilitary solutions had been exhausted—that from now on only weapons, however used, could count. We are now in the danger zone."[62]

The majority of the American people now supported getting tougher with the Soviets, as well as increased defense spending, unleashing the CIA, and defending traditional allies. But ambiguities remained. Thus, as the Soviet invasion of Afghanistan and the shock of the hostage seizure receded, public support for using force in the region subsided. Within six weeks fewer than 20 percent of the public were reported willing to use military force in either Afghanistan or Iran. Only in the immediate wake of Carter's advocacy of using force in the Persian Gulf could bare majorities (52 percent) be found supporting such a move. Here again, within weeks a majority could be found advocating economic and other approaches rather than a resort to force. Simultaneously, domestic issues began to assume more importance than foreign affairs in polls testing issue salience among the American people.[63] Moreover, in the midst of increasing defense budgets and deteriorating relations with the Soviet Union during the early Reagan administration, the American public, in large numbers and with an intensity that surprised most observers, seemed to support the idea of a nuclear freeze.

The new internationalism did not, therefore, flow from a wellspring of animus and bellicosity stored in the American collective mind. Instead, it emerged from a congruence of events that seemed to confirm the projections of cold war Cassandras mobilized during the Carter years. The new internationalism was also encouraged by the administration's own scrambling to match the hard-line Reagan challenge to Carter's presidency.

The reembrace of military means reflected a public reaction that had moved from a yearning for respite to bewilderment, frustration, and then angry determination to reassert American credibility. Perhaps the last straw did not involve the Soviet Union at all but was propelled instead by the ongoing humiliation involving the seizure of American embassy personnel in Tehran. Ayatollah Khomeini's unusual challenge to U.S. credibility and the renascent centrality of Soviet power moved President Carter, in a stunning turn, to call for a trillion-dollar military buildup by the mid-1980s. The new assertiveness in the 1980 election campaign fed on itself as candidates Carter and Reagan sought to outdo one another in their assessments of the security challenge before the United States in the 1980s.

Moreover, the new assertiveness proved to be potent electoral politics for Ronald Reagan. It allowed him to form a coalition of conservative internationalists and noninternationalists, since both were attracted to the prospect of reestablishing American strength. But in the new preparedness consensus there was little support for a return to the 1960s' activism and confrontation. Indeed, by the end of 1981 three out of four Americans supported George Kennan's proposed 50 percent mutual reduction in nuclear weapons. The plan to cut by half the number of nuclear weapons, reported George Gallup, received solid support in all regions and classes and in both parties.[64]

By the mid-1980s the new defense consensus had evaporated. Six years into the Reagan administration, slightly less than $2 trillion had been committed to defense, almost as much as had been spent in all the years following World War II. In light of the conditions in much of rural America and in American cities, the revelations regarding $600 toilet seats and $2,000 coffeepots in military aircraft supported a perception that President Reagan was lavish to the military while neglecting other needs. The Reagan administration repeated an arguable "fact" that the Soviets were outspending the United States, but this seemed incongruous, even baffling, in light of the Soviet defeat in Afghanistan. Moreover, by 1986 Mikhail Gorbachev was ensconced in the Kremlin advancing *perestroika,* détente, and his own standing in Western public opinion polls. Even before the Iran-Contra scandal broke over the Reagan administration in early 1986, 50–60 percent of the people polled supported decreases in defense spending.[65] The percentage of the public supporting an increase in defense spending continued to plunge from the peak of 60 percent in 1980 to 21 percent in 1982 and only 12 percent by 1990.[66]

TABLE 9.1
Support for a U.S. Global Role, 1948–1990 (in percent)

Group	1948	1952	1956	1973	1974	1978	1982	1986	1990
Elite	—	—	—	—	—	97	98	98	97
Mass	70	68	71	66	66	59	54	63	62

Source: John A. Reilly, ed., *American Public Opinion and U.S. Foreign Policy, 1991* (Chicago: Chicago Council on Foreign Relations, 1991), p. 12.

The Persistence of Fragmented Internationalism

If the claims of a new "defense"-oriented internationalism asserted at the dawn of the 1980s proved as insubstantial as a summer's ground fog, it would be wrong to conclude that internationalism itself would dissipate as readily. In fact, analysis of public and elite opinion confirms that declining support for an active U.S. role in the world bottomed out in the early 1980s. Table 9.1 traces percentage support for an active U.S. role in world affairs from the end of World War II to the end of the cold war. Though it has by no means returned to the levels reached in the 1950s, public support in the early 1990s for an active role is slightly above the midpoint between its Vietnam high of 66 percent and its post-Vietnam low of 54 percent. Elite opinion between the mid-1970s and 1990 has been consistently in the 97–98 percent range.[67] Recent probes of public and elite opinion data confirm the essential correctness of many early post-Vietnam readings of a divided internationalist structure of attitudes on foreign affairs, inclined either toward "cooperative" internationalism, on the one side, or toward "militant" internationalism, on the other.[68]

Wittkopf finds that with respect to attitudes toward the utility of force, the threat of communism, relations with the Soviet Union, defense spending, foreign aid, covert intervention, terrorism, interdependence, nuclear weapons, and the lessons of Vietnam, the public and the elites cluster into four distinct groups: (1) *hardliners,* internationalists of a "militant" type who support the use of force and are skeptical of cooperative forms of international engagement; (2) *accommodationists,* a form of "cooperative" internationalists whose inclinations are the reverse of the hardliners'; (3) *internationalists,* who are midway between the hardliners and the accommodationists; and (4) *isolationists,* who seek to minimize all international entanglements (see table 9.2).[69]

The character and consistency of the distribution among these positions is striking. Table 9.3 arrays Wittkopf's percentage distributions for

TABLE 9.2
Foreign Policy Orientation in the Mid-1980s

	Group (%)	
Orientation	Elites	Masses
Accommodationist	25	22
Internationalist	58	25
Hardliner	14	27
Isolationist	3	26

Source: Eugene R. Wittkopf, *Faces of Internationalism:
Public Opinion and American Foreign Policy* (Durham,
N.C.: Duke University Press, 1990), fig. 5.1, p. 140.

elites and the mass public across the four belief systems from the end of
the Vietnam War through the middle of the Reagan administration.
Clearly, the isolationist group, both elites and the mass public, remained
small throughout the post-Vietnam period. The overwhelming majority
of both elites and masses are committed to some measure of international
involvement, but internationalist divisions preclude a consensus about
means, however committed the majorities are to activism.[70]

The elites have been markedly more internationalist and accommodationist than the masses throughout the post-Vietnam period. Not only
are the masses much more likely to harbor isolationist beliefs—a quarter
of the masses throughout the period—but their "internationalism" is
more likely to be hard-line than the cooperative "internationalist" positions held by the majority of the elites.

Finally, Wittkopf's analysis suggests another distinction between elite
and mass belief systems. Throughout the post-Vietnam period, elite opinion has shown the greatest tendency to shift. Although it has remained
firmly anchored within an overall perspective committed to global activism and involvement, elite opinion has shifted dramatically. The progres-
sion of the shift can be traced from a predominately "accommodationist"
internationalism (54 percent in 1974) in the immediate post-Vietnam period to a more eclectic "internationalist" position (59 percent in 1986)
and thence, in some cases, to "hard-line" internationalism (from 4 percent in 1974 to 14 percent in 1986) as the cold war began to break up in
the mid-1980s. Mass belief systems, in contrast, show none of this volatility. The distribution of the mass public across the spectrum of foreign
belief systems has remained virtually unchanged from 1974 to 1986.[71]

TABLE 9.3
Distribution of Elite and Mass Belief Systems, 1974–1986 (in percent)

Belief System	1974		1978		1982		1986	
	Elites	Masses	Elites	Masses	Elites	Masses	Elites	Masses
Accommodationist	54	22	46	25	38	22	25	22
Internationalist	38	25	36	25	45	22	59	22
Hardliner	5	28	14	25	11	27	14	27
Isolationist	4	26	6	25	6	26	4	26

Source: Interpolated from Wittkopf, *Faces of Internationalism,* fig. 5.1, p. 140.

Public Opinion at the End of the Cold War

In the broadest structural sense American public opinion seems to remain centered within a broadly internationalist outlook. There has been movement within the elite from an accommodationist and cooperative perspective immediately after the Vietnam War to a much more centrist posture in the late 1980s, which remains, on balance, more cooperative than any kind of militant unilateralism. Analysts of public opinion during the 1980s sensed that the revolutionary global changes of 1989–90 constituted "the kind of dramatic development that transforms durable foreign policy beliefs into new forms."[72] (However, conclusive evidence of such a transformation is not yet available.) And, at least one analyst examining the 1990 CCFR data concluded that the public was equivocal in that at that time, at least, the changes in the Soviet Union were not viewed as irreversible.[73] Unfortunately, the 1990 CCFR surveys were conducted before the collapse of the Soviet Union in late 1991 and early 1992. However, there are indications in the 1990 survey, as well as in some of the findings from the earlier analyses, that although a radical break from broad internationalism of the past may not be in prospect, the fragmentation within elite opinion and differences between the mass public and elite opinion are likely to sharpen.[74]

The military capability mounted by the Soviet Union—and now Russia—is deemed no more than a peripheral threat to U.S. vital interests. In the 1990 CCFR survey, the public saw the economic power of Japan (60 percent of the public sample) and China's development as a world power (40 percent) as more of a threat to U.S. interests than Soviet military power (33 percent). The elite portion of the survey also saw the economic power of Japan as the primary threat (63 percent) but ranked European economic power as a greater threat (41 percent) than Soviet military

TABLE 9.4
National Problems, 1982–1990 (in percent)

Problems	1982 Leaders	1982 Public	1986 Leaders	1986 Public	1990 Leaders	1990 Public
Foreign	29	15	42	26	23	17
Economy	51	55	16	25	25	22
Government	8	8	24	9	25	20
Social	11	22	18	39	28	41
Don't know	0	1	0	1	0	1

Source: Reilly, *American Public Opinion and U.S. Foreign Policy, 1991,* fig. I-2, p. 10.

power (20 percent); Chinese power was viewed as a threat by only 16 percent of the elite sample.[75] Only 3 percent of the public and 21 percent of the elites saw U.S. relations with the Soviets as one of the top three U.S. foreign policy problems.[76] Insofar as U.S.-Soviet relations, the spread of communism, and the efficacy of force were so fundamental to the structuring of belief systems in the late 1970s and throughout the 1980s,[77] these findings imply that the most fundamental dimensions of these belief systems are now undergoing reassessment.

A new anchor for American belief systems may well prove to be economic policy and the primacy of domestic versus foreign concerns. As the 1990 CCFR data make clear, the *economic* power of Japan and Europe now constitutes the most important threat(s) to American vital interests in the view of both the mass public and the elites. "Sometime during the late 1980s," William Schneider observes, "people started to consider nonmilitary issues a more serious threat to our national security than military issues."[78] In 1982, 1986, and 1990, elites and the mass public were asked, "What do you feel are the two or three biggest problems facing the country today?" Their responses are detailed in table 9.4.

In 1989, when poll respondents were asked which was more important in the world, securing democracy or promoting American economic interests, they chose the latter over the former by a margin of two to one (62 percent to 31 percent).[79] An even more explicit indicator of mass public priorities is to be found in a 1990 query concerning federal programs for which the public would be willing to increase spending. In 1990 the public was willing to support increases for aid to education, combating illegal drugs, social security, and welfare and relief programs. Arguably, combating illegal drugs has a foreign policy component. Otherwise, no foreign or national security program received support for increases. Indeed, defense, economic aid to other nations, and military aid were all targets for cuts, as they had been since 1982.[80]

In summary, even as the Reagan defense buildup was gathering momentum, the priorities of the American public and elites began to shift. While "internationalism" had not necessarily declined, the space made for international concerns diminished. Within the domain of international concerns, economic threats and security assumed greater salience. As the cold war began to break up, international economic issues became dominant. For elites, however, more traditional security issues, namely, nuclear proliferation and international arms control, remained very important as well—94 percent and 80 percent, respectively.[81] Security issues were still regarded as "very important" by a majority of the mass public; however, economic concerns were acknowledged as very important by larger numbers in the mass poll data.

Moreover, the approach that was advocated to deal with economic concerns favored by elites and mass publics began to diverge markedly. From 1972 through the late 1980s, substantial majorities—63–70 percent of the public—consistently registered support for protectionism to advance U.S. international economic interests.[82] In the 1990 CCFR poll, the highest-ranked U.S. foreign policy goals for the mass public were "protecting the jobs of American workers" (65 percent) and "protecting the interests of American business abroad" (63 percent). In contrast, these goals were ranked as "very important" by only 39 percent and 27 percent, respectively, of elites.[83]

All analyses of mass and elite opinion throughout the post-Vietnam period underscore that the elite approach to reducing trade deficits (62 percent of elites regard "reducing our trade deficit with foreign countries" as very important) is the application of liberal, free-trade principles emphasizing negotiated tariff reduction. This generally "cooperative internationalism" is the preferred elite modality for virtually all of the "interdependence" issues—trade, energy, the environment—of the post-Vietnam period. Among the mass public (of whom only a slightly lesser percentage, 56 percent, believe the trade deficit is "very important"), even those who otherwise tend toward the "cooperative" cluster of internationalist beliefs find protectionism a preferred means for gaining economic security.[84]

The fact that otherwise internationalist mass opinion supports tariffs[85] has attracted the attention of analysts and professional politicians. Some analysts are contemptuous of mass public opinion concerning protectionism, arguing that there is no "respectable body of opinion" endorsing protectionism even while acknowledging that substantial majorities of mass public opinion support the option. (Does this mean that only elites hold "respectable" opinions?) Mass opinion on the issue is dismissed as a reflection of mere "self-interest" (i.e., "their" jobs are at risk). Elites are seen as more "globalist" in their views and reflecting "world order" positions.[86] Insofar as the elites in these surveys comprise "leaders" whose livelihoods and careers have been shaped by and have benefited from the free-trade, internationalist "theology" of the post–World War II era—e.g., senior executives, academics, and members of the foreign-policy-making establishment—there would seem to be a considerable measure of "self-interest" operating among the elite as well.

Even if some public opinion analysts can dismiss mass public opinion as mere "self-interest," professional politicians seem to understand that the public's perception of self-interest can have major political consequences. In any event, a fault line runs through "internationalist" public opinion on these economic issues. Thus, while 61 percent of some 490 executives polled in early 1992 agreed with the statement that "free trade must be allowed, even if domestic industries are hurt by foreign competition," one-third were supportive of protectionism.[87] This finding is consistent with a long-term trend in which support of free trade is declining among opinion leaders as a group[88] (see table 9.5). Simultaneously, observers of the 1992 campaign were impressed with the extent to which politicians at all levels were playing to what they understood to be a protectionist mood in the public.[89]

Eugene Wittkopf summarizes the situation as a "gulf between leaders and masses on this topic . . . [which] is very wide." Others have argued that however wide the gap may appear, mass public opinion has not yet reached a clear judgment on the issue. Yankelovich and Harman have noted, for example, that mass publics are in fact cross-pressured on the issue of protectionism. On the one hand, "all things being equal," 94 percent would "buy American." On the other, when pressed to specify the most important factors in their decisions to purchase goods and services, people list as their priority concerns, first, quality (78 percent); second, price (58 percent); and only third, "made in the USA" (37 percent). Public opinion on the issues of competitiveness and protectionism can be seen, therefore, as "compartmentalized" and representing "mass opinion rather than public judgement. Protectionism conforms to some public values, but it seriously violates others. Voters have not yet worked through the clash of values underlying protectionism."[90]

At present it cannot be known whether this combination of differ-

TABLE 9.5
Attitudes toward Tariffs, 1976–1992 (in percent)

Q. It has been argued that if all countries would eliminate tariffs and restrictions on imported goods, the costs of goods would go down for everyone. Others have said that such tariffs and restrictions are necessary to protect certain manufacturing jobs in certain industries from the competition of less expensive imports. Generally, would you say you sympathize more with those who want to eliminate tariffs or with those who think such tariffs are necessary?

Response	1976	1978	1982	1986	1990	1992
			Elites			
Eliminate	—	75	67	66	64	61
Necessary	—	23	28	29	33	33
Don't know	—	2	5	5	3	6
			Masses			
Eliminate	23	22	22	28	25	—
Necessary	55	57	57	53	53	—
Don't know	22	21	21	19	21	—

Sources: William Schneider, "The Old Politics and the New World Order" in *Eagle in a New World: American Grand Strategy in the Post–Cold War Era*, ed. Kenneth Oye, Robert J. Lieber, and Donald Rothchild (New York: Harper Collins, 1992), pp. 58–59; Steve Lohr, "In Poll, Executives Back Free Trade," *New York Times*, Apr. 7, 1992.

ences within and between mass and elite opinion on the issue of trade—in the absence of the "cement" provided by the cold war—heralds the crackup of the long-held overarching internationalist consensus. The more optimistic view is that an internationalist "public judgment" will ultimately take shape on the trade issue so that "cooperative and militant internationalism will continue to characterize the orientation of the American people toward the nation's world role, even though the precise elements giving rise to the two faces of internationalism may change."[91] But even if a fragmented internationalist majority can still be found, the divisions may well widen so much between elites and masses that no concrete policy or trade treaty can muster effective support—especially if job growth and a sense of domestic well-being seem problematic.

CHAPTER 10

Presidents, the Media, and Foreign Policy

AMERICAN PUBLIC OPINION seems to be centered on a pragmatic internationalism that generally eschews military intervention in favor of political and economic engagement. Public judgments on specific issues are often ad hoc and may therefore be somewhat "inconsistent and unstable, particularly on issues that the public has not completely thought through."[1] The cleavages of opinions across the conservative-liberal spectrum notwithstanding, there remains general public support for internationalism.

Close observers of public opinion have been impressed with the opportunity that this situation presents to national leadership: "Such a situation is made to order for leaders who are gifted in their ability to communicate with the public."[2] But those who would lead must also listen. A distinguishing characteristic of a democratic society is a responsible accountability on the part of both the leaders and the led. In a democratic society, therefore, leadership opportunities are the companion of great responsibilities. The principles of foreign policy presumably emerge from a kind of dialogue between the public and their representatives. In the American system, the opportunity for initiating this conversation, and much of the responsibility for preserving the quality of debate, falls to the president.

THE PRESIDENCY AND THE POLICY PROCESS

For most of the cold war, the institutions responsible for the political socialization, that is, the political learning, of Americans—family, schools, and peer groups—have tended to reinforce the image of the president as the figure best able to lead the American people in a complex and dangerous world. As a consequence of Vietnam and Watergate, the previously positive image of the president suffered.[3] Nonetheless, in a fragmented political structure the president remains the focus of popular expectations and retains significant capacity, perhaps more than any other figure in the American system, to propose policy and structure the terms of national debate. But this position also means that a president readily becomes a target of popular frustrations. Presidential visibility, inevitable frustrations, and the relatively brief time available to a president all work to constrain presidential leadership.

Leadership and Media Management

Especially during the cold war years, presidents, in trying to respond to contradictory pressures, have often found it difficult to maintain a distinction between leadership and manipulation of public opinion. From the earliest appeal to Congress to help a prostrate Europe, when Truman, his senior advisers, and the leaders of the Senate agreed that the president had to "scare the hell out of the American people,"[4] there has evolved a process of selling, indeed overselling, "the threat." Given that the public is generally supportive of international engagements, there is an irony in the urge to manipulate those who either already concur or would readily concur if the facts as the president saw them were simply relayed. But the ledge from which great danger has sounded has generally been so high that climb-downs and qualifications appear undignified and overly difficult. The policy product has usually been retained, at times proving nearly ineradicable, subsequent facts notwithstanding. The process of overstatement—in Vietnam, in many overstatements of Soviet threat, and, in retrospect, in the Persian Gulf in 1990—has tended to wrap the presidents and the public in a cloak of self-fulfilling dread, from which convincing relief could seldom be found.

In America there is aggressive competition for the public's attention—by media, interest groups, and other forms of private power. Gaining and holding public attention has therefore become the great presidential preoccupation. Some observers regard pervasive telecommunications technologies as complicating the problem of controlling information.[5] If anything, however, the more complex media environment heightens the executive branch's desire for greater control and management of information.

In some instances this preoccupation has become pernicious. In the heyday of the Vietnam War, for instance, presidents resorted to dubious and extralegal mechanisms for managing information. The press was taken to court in an attempt to restrain the publications of embarrassing documents. Reporters were wiretapped; some were beset by Internal Revenue Service auditors. In the Reagan years, the press was cultivated by presidential advisers with an unmatched sensitivity to the media. Speeches were chosen for their backdrop. "Messages of the day" for the six o'clock news were manufactured with mechanical and elegant precision. In the early Clinton administration, the Washington press, to its consternation, was evaded by the White House, and regional markets were targeted instead.[6] The result was a virtual revolt that prompted Clinton to fire his press secretary and take on, instead, one of the more moderate "spinmeisters" from the Reagan years, David Gergen.

Depending on their respective skills and the available technology, presidents from Roosevelt on have used (or avoided) radio broadcasts, televised press conferences, or television addresses to the American people. Ronald Reagan, a professional actor by trade, employed a spate of effective radio and television speeches—more than any other first-term president by some estimates. Reagan's use of broadcasts minimized the potential damage that could result from frequent probing by newspeople of what often emerged from his infrequent press conferences as a limited grasp of major issues. His communication skills abetted his electoral popularity, despite low performance ratings for his administration overall. People blamed Reagan's policies, Congress, his aides, but not the "Great Communicator" himself.[7]

The president's information policies can condition the context of debate. As Dick Cheney, the secretary of defense in the Bush years, put it: "You don't let the press control the agenda. They like to decide what's important. But if you let them do that, they're going to trash your presidency."[8] Public information can be controlled by classification, planting stories with favored reporters, and using a large public relations apparatus to keep the public informed about what the executive wants known and ignorant about things the public would not likely support. In 1965 the executive, judging that the public needed to be convinced that it was fighting a just war, released a self-serving white paper explaining that violence in South Vietnam was largely carried out by invading North Vietnamese forces against a South Vietnam that was an integral part of the Western system of alliances. It was a misrepresentation,[9] but only the most careful scholarly and legal exegesis of the record could rebut it. When Johnson ordered the sustained bombing of North Vietnam, it was said to be in retaliation for the attack on American forces at Pleiku in

February 1965. But Pleiku was but a much-desired pretext for the initiation of a previously decided course of action.[10]

Not every effort to exploit events succeeds, of course. During his reelection campaign in 1980 President Carter attempted to exploit the seizure of over fifty American embassy personnel in Tehran by young zealots loyal to the Ayatollah Khomeini. In late April 1980, with no prospect in sight for the hostages' release, the White House declared an end to the state of emergency. The hostage issue was deemed "under control." To some degree, the hostage crisis stopped being news until just before the election, when it looked as if the Carter team might at long last have secured their release. Thus even a "weakened" president seemed able to "set the context" of public debate.[11]

Yet, it is now clear that the issue did not die. "Nightline" and other programs continued to focus on the hostages and the larger implications of the hostage crisis for the American position in the world. News exposure may have dwindled as the long incarceration of U.S. embassy employees in Tehran wore on. However, fading media interest may have been less the result of the administration's effort to distance itself from the issues than a function of the appetites of broadcast and print journalists to come up with something else to capture the public's mind and, not coincidentally, augment their own "market share," "ratings," and reputations.

The regulation and shaping of the flow of information by the executive requires an enormous public relations apparatus and effort. Gerald Rafshoon, whose public relations and advertising firm was responsible for packaging the 1976 Carter presidential campaign, occupied a central role in the Carter administration, including a massive effort to sell the Panama Canal and SALT II treaties to the American people. Earlier, Kennedy and Nixon had similarly packaged and sold their agreements with the Soviets.

During 1981 the Reagan administration sought to illustrate the threat to American national security posed by insurgents in El Salvador. At the White House's request, the State Department released captured documents tracing arms transfers into El Salvador from the Marxist government in Nicaragua and its Communist allies in Cuba. It worked: notwithstanding testimony that elements of the Salvadoran military were "psychopathic killers," aid to the Salvadoran military continued.[12]

Later, as administration rhetoric against Libya escalated, news of a secret Libyan "hit squad" detailed to attack American leaders was fed to the press and media. The assassination team did not materialize, and administration officials conceded that they never had firm information concerning its composition or plans. Although the story vanished from the front pages and evening news broadcasts, its very appearance was an important indication of the capacity of administration-inspired news to command media coverage.[13]

No less impressive were administrations' attempts to extend their informational reach abroad. During 1981 the administration prepared a slick report on Soviet military strength that was destined, Defense Department officials hoped, "for every coffee table in America." It is doubtful that the document became a conversation piece at American coffee klatches or dinner tables, but foreign observers noted that the book appeared throughout Western Europe, which at that moment was engaged in a continentwide debate over the deployment of a new generation of American nuclear missiles. Simultaneously, the United States Information Agency (USIA), under the direction of Reagan's close Hollywood friend Charles Zwick, mobilized to ensure maximum European exposure for the president's reply to Soviet arms-control proposals for Europe. USIA purchased time on European television, and a Reagan speech was timed to be broadcast live at dinnertime in Europe.

Finally, in early 1982, USIA mounted a star-studded spectacular including Hollywood luminaries such as Charlton Heston and Frank Sinatra designed to dramatize American backing of the Polish people in the face of the imposition of martial law during the winter of 1981–82. The show was not only beamed to Western and Eastern Europe; it was also made available for broadcast in the United States. While USIA operations abroad were not in themselves unusual, the fact that the show was also shown within the United States was extraordinary. In the history of the American propaganda agency only one other USIA effort—a film on the assassination of President John F. Kennedy—had been broadcast in the United States.

The Media: A Countervailing Force?

The vigorous attempts by a succession of administrations to control the flow of information on foreign policy may have had unintended effects. In the immediate post-Vietnam period there was evidence of a more aggressive and skeptical media than at any time since the end of World War II. Not only did the revelations of the "Pentagon Papers" and Watergate produce more suspicion of information promoted by the government, but the scandals of the Vietnam era contributed to a more adversarial relationship with the government. Throughout the Carter administration the press maintained a merciless accounting of the administration's meandering and at times contradictory policies.

Some of the residue of this media skepticism carried into the Reagan years. The Reagan administration's El Salvador white paper received immediate, critical scrutiny. Although the rhetoric of the Reagan administration escalated, mail to the State Department and White House increased, and public sentiment turned against U.S. policy by margins between ten to one and twenty to one.[14]

As the Reagan administration's economic and foreign policies emerged from the postelection honeymoon period, press commentary became more pointed. Early references to the president's easy amiability were replaced by speculation that he lacked a grasp of the substance of policy. By early 1982, reporters and columnists gleefully displayed and corrected Reagan's frequent misstatements of fact and history. Cabinet officers, especially Secretary of State Haig, were also burlesqued for malapropisms, misstatements, and fulminations. Rather than interviewing the secretary of state at year's end, journalists published the notes of participants in staff meetings with the secretary to reveal the secretary's unpolished understanding of issues.[15]

Some observers maintain, however, that the Reagan years were marked by extraordinarily successful management of the press by the White House.[16] Although Reagan's intellectual lapses and gaffes became the vehicle for comedic careers during the 1980s, much critical scrutiny of the Reagan administration was successfully deflected from Reagan onto the members of his administration. As David Gergen, Reagan's former White House communications director, put it, "You only have one four-star general in battle, but you've got a lot of lieutenants who can give blood. And if the going is getting hot and heavy, it is far better to have your lieutenants take the wounds than your general."[17]

An important element of the management strategy, according to Les Janka, a Reagan deputy press secretary, was "manipulation by inundation . . . the media will take what we feed them. As long as you come in here every day, hand them a well-packaged, premasticated story in the format they want, they'll go away." Reagan's chief of staff, Michael Deaver, concurred: "The only day I worried about was Friday, because it's a slow news day. That was the day that bothered me most, because if you didn't have anything, they'd go find something!" The press was therefore fed a steady stream of stories and often grand photo opportunities both at home and abroad, and it did not hurt that in the president his handlers had what Reagan's press secretary described as "the ultimate presidential commodity . . . the right product."[18]

Some observers conclude that Reagan was also the beneficiary of a public backlash against what the public perceived to be an overly aggressive media in the 1970s. Poll results concerning coverage of military affairs confirmed this view; but more broadly, as Ben Bradlee, the executive editor of the *Washington Post,* and the editor who supported the aggressive Watergate reporting of Woodward and Bernstein in the 1970s, noted: "The return to deference was part of the subconscious feeling we had. . . . After Watergate the public was saying about the press, 'Okay, guys, now that's enough, that's enough.' . . . I think we were sensitive to that criticism much more than we should have been, and that we did ease off."[19]

The upshot was that the media either watered down critical commentary or missed major stories. CBS reporter Leslie Stahl's reporting on Reagan was heavily edited to make the stories more upbeat and positive. *New York Times* reporter Raymond Bonner's reporting on human rights violations in Central America—confirmed a decade later by the discovery of the grisly remains of scores of massacred children and others—was foreshortened when he was removed from the Central American bureau and reassigned to New York's metropolitan beat. No less important, however, was that much of the story of the extralegal sale of arms to Iran and the Reagan obsession with the handful of U.S. hostages in Lebanon were missed by the American press.[20]

The questions whether the balance between presidential power and the press is appropriate and whether the media use their power responsibly are probably beyond definitive resolution. There is support for both sides of these arguments. The media have oscillated between the aggressiveness of the Watergate period and the more passive role of the 1980s. Journalists, outside observers, and, of course, presidents have periodically attacked the media for an antigovernment bias. In the Reagan years the media were accused of bias in their coverage of events in Third World conflicts. Conservatives charged that the press tended to romanticize insurgents and discount information provided by government authorities.[21]

During the 1992 campaign the Bush administration regularly blasted the press coverage of the administration's record in both foreign and domestic affairs.[22] Conservative media critics supported the president's position, arguing that media personnel at all levels are overwhelmingly "liberal" in their politics.[23] In the heat of the 1992 campaign other analysts maintained that there was indeed a bias in news coverage but that bias tends to be directed against front-runners. In other words, there is a kind of "tall poppy syndrome," as they say in Australia; that is, the largest flower tends to get cut down. Thus, there is "compensatory reporting" during campaigns, and perhaps, for that matter, in coverage overall.[24]

There is evidence that media coverage of foreign affairs can and does influence public opinion against official policy. Thus, during the Vietnam era, those with greatest exposure to mass media were most likely to turn against government policy. Media coverage of the North Vietnamese–Viet Cong offensive in February 1968 was portrayed as a defeat for the United States. Resulting coverage of the Tet offensive had "a massive psychological effect on the American public," for a putative disaster soon "became conventional wisdom . . . magnified in media commentary and recycled on the hustings in New Hampshire, in campus protest, and in discussions on Capitol Hill. The press 'rebroadcast' it all uncritically, even enthusiastically, although many . . . should have known better."[25]

As with institutional power, judgments are frequently more a reflection of policy preferences than of a calculation of proper institutional weight. When an administration pursues policies that an observer supports, media aggressiveness is held complicitous in any difficulties the program and policy may run into in Congress, with allies, or in finding acceptance among the voters. When a presidential initiative that one opposes appears, an aggressive and critical media confirms that the relationship between media and officialdom is in responsible balance.

It is not an easy task to lay out the continuum of options on complex questions such as a new strategic missile system, the consequences of alternative trade policies, or the implications of international monetary policy. Moreover, these kinds of issues tend to find explication primarily in media of a comparatively narrow reach. Elite print media such as the *New York Times,* the *Washington Post,* and the *Wall Street Journal,* television network special reports, and public radio and television news programming try to shoulder the burden. But it is debatable whether these often brilliant efforts reach mass publics.[26]

In the 1988 presidential debates, NBC anchorman Tom Brokaw's first question was, "Look, we know that there are a lot of issues in the campaigns but voters really want to know what kind of people you are. What is it that made you want to be a president?"[27] In this instance, it is hard to argue that the media are performing as the necessary interlocutor between people and policymakers. If the image of public affairs communicated to mass publics is but sound and fury, a mere clash of ego and ambition, a dramatic swirl of personalities, events, and spectacle, can it be surprising that the public's substantive grasp seems weak and under-developed? Television's instantaneous, uncontrolled, and often incoher-ent "flow" of "transborder imagery" creates and compounds a sense of cascading events with no history or context. Life becomes an eternal present. As analyst David Webster has put it, "Television news just hops through, and the viewer is its prisoner. . . . television insists on telling us things that we did not ask about, and for which we have no response. We can all have opinions, but no power. Continually being informed of problems that one feels impotent to affect must leave its scars. Our attitude becomes either anguished frustrations or more likely, defensive insulation."[28] If the policymaker's cynicism concerning the public's ca-pacity for self-government is thereby confirmed,[29] can it not be said that the messenger who brings the bad news is, in this instance at least, partially to blame?

The president, then, retains significant advantages. Because the execu-tive is the source of much foreign affairs information, one usually needs to go to the source itself to test the information's validity. Since four out of five news stories, media critic Leon V. Sigal once discovered, involve "official sources," journalists become reliant on their relationship with power.[30] Besides the difficulty of asking the executive to present infor-mation that would undercut its own case, there is usually a presumption that what is presented is true, if not always complete. To catch mendacity from a sea of usually true information takes a skilled angler indeed.

The Pulitzer prize–winning editor and writer Philip Geyelin, viewing the relationship between the president and the press from a perspective that spans the entire cold war, has concluded, therefore, that even with the technological revolutions and "news explosion" of the last several years, "there is no reasonable basis for the conclusion that, as a conse-quence, the balance of power between the media and the government has been fundamentally altered. . . . to the extent that first impressions mat-ter, the government controls the first impressions."[31]

Lessons of Vietnam and Government-Media Relations

If there is uncertainty about the effectiveness of the balancing role of the media, there is little doubt about the impact of the Vietnam War on government-media relations. Vietnam was different in this respect from subsequent wars in which the U.S. became engaged. Although the Penta-gon sought to manipulate the information passed on through official channels, restrict access to bases, and insisted that military escorts accompany reporters, the prolonged Vietnam War allowed reporters to develop a network of unofficial sources in both Southeast Asia and Washington. The media had the time to develop an alternative perspective and image of the war and to communicate it to the American people.[32]

In the final analysis, however, most students of the media in Vietnam, including William Hammond, the author of the official history of the military's public relations,[33] agree that the deeper causes of the public's turning against the war were the growing number of casualties and the government's inability to establish a clear policy rationale for the war. Col. Harry Summers, the author of an authoritative strategic study of the Vietnam War, concluded that "blaming the media for the loss of the Vietnam War was wrong. The media, and television in particular, is good at showing the cost of the war. But [the] cost of anything only has meaning in relation to value. . . . It was not the news media, which reported the price, that lost the war. It was the government which, especially in the case of President Lyndon B. Johnson, deliberately failed to establish its value."[34]

In the case of the media coverage of Vietnam, as in the case of the media coverage of the growing American involvement in Central America in the 1980s, attacks can be understood as attempts to discredit the source of information that cast doubt on the official rationale for U.S. policy.[35] Military analysts such as Colonel Summers argued that the central lesson to be drawn from the war was the necessity of establishing clear political goals and pursuing them within a context of public support.[36] This view, widely shared in the U.S. strategic community, constrained the use of military force in the post-Vietnam period.[37]

Despite the careful work of military historians, a widespread notion persists that public support for the Vietnam War was decisively undercut by negative reporting. This understanding of the potential of news reporters to disrupt military operations prompted the Reagan and Bush administrations to exercise precensorship by controlling access to the theater of operations in Grenada, in Panama, and in the Gulf War. After reporters made their way to the combat zone, security reviews of stories and images, concealment of information, and misleading information were common. In addition, discussion of casualties was minimized. Instead, the destruction of enemy weapons, the use of artful euphemisms to sanitize the image of the conflicts, and the controlled release of government images were common.[38]

In the case of Grenada, the press was at first misled concerning the onset of the operation and then refused entry into the theater of operations until the Defense Department was confident that major fighting had ended.[39] In those few instances where the press was already on the island or managed to penetrate the military's restrictions, they were picked up by the military, flown to a Navy ship, and held incommunicado. Protests were voiced by the major press and media organizations, but in the end, networks and newspapers resorted to using information and photographs provided by DOD to fill their stories and television programs.

The furor over the handling of the press in Grenada led to the establishment of a Defense Department review of their procedures, which resulted in the Sidle Panel Report.[40] The report called for concurrent military and public affairs planning for all military operations and the use of press pools but urged that "full coverage" be allowed as soon as practicable. Moreover, the Pentagon was admonished to provide communications and transportation equipment to facilitate coverage of a conflict. In addition, the report called for regular meetings between the Pentagon's public affairs staffs and the media so that mutual problems could be discussed and worked out.

The invasion of Panama in December 1989 revealed that the Bush administration had no intention of facilitating media coverage of the conflict. Indeed, a postinvasion report by Fred Hoffman underscores the failure of the civilian leadership of the Pentagon to heed and implement the most basic recommendations of the Sidle Report.[41] Once again, misleading information was initially fed to the press. When the invasion was launched, Secretary of Defense Dick Cheney and Assistant Secretary of Defense for Public Affairs Pete Williams decided to use a press pool made up of Washington-based reporters rather than a pool gathered from reporters already stationed in Panama. Thus, the reporters in the press pool arrived after the invasion was under way and found their access to the conflict tightly controlled by the military. Moreover, once they were allowed into the field, communications equipment made available to them was inadequate to handle the volume of reports. "The result of all this," Hoffman reported, "was that the 16-member pool produced stories and pictures of essentially secondary value."[42] Pool rules were in fact relaxed for reporters with a reputation for cooperation; meanwhile, the Army actually arrested some reporters who strayed from the pool "pack."[43]

The deployment of U.S. troops to the Persian Gulf on August 7, 1990, for Operation Desert Shield, followed by Operation Desert Storm in January 1991, constituted the largest U.S. military operations since Vietnam. The Defense Department's management of the press in the Gulf capitalized on their successful control of the media in Grenada and Panama. As in Grenada and Panama, the initial deployment of U.S. troops to Saudi Arabia in August 1990 proceeded with no press coverage. The first U.S. troops departed on August 7, but it was not until five days later that the initial seventeen-member press pool was cleared to enter Saudi Arabia. Within two weeks, more than three hundred additional reporters had arrived. The military's insistence on controlled and accompanied access to units quickly overburdened communications and transportation equipment and led to a situation familiar to media veterans of the Panama invasion. In order to arrange transport or access, most network and major print reporters joined "pool packs." At the same time, the Pentagon was prepared to expedite the work of small and medium-sized media interested in doing local-interest, "Hi, Mom" stories. Media events were arranged for hometown reporters even as the hundreds of combat journalists in Dahrain were told that shortages of equipment and personnel made their visits to various units impossible.

Meanwhile, the Kuwaiti government mobilized a massive public relations campaign in the United States to build support for the operation. The public relations firm Hill and Knowlton, whose chief operating officer of public affairs worldwide was Craig Fuller, formerly chief of staff to then vice president Bush, was retained for $10 million. Hill and Knowlton undertook an intensive public relations effort that included providing more than seven hundred video releases to media around the world. In many instances, pictures provided to Hill and Knowlton by the Kuwaiti government were used as straight news. But the firm also helped prepare dramatic testimony of a young Kuwaiti girl who recounted Iraqi soldiers' disconnecting incubators in Kuwaiti hospitals, leaving babies to die, and moving the equipment back to Iraq. Only later was it revealed that the girl was the Kuwaiti ambassador's daughter and that although similar events had happened, the testimony was a composite, and not at all her own tale.

As hostilities in the Gulf drew closer, the Pentagon announced that the press would be denied access to Dover Air Force Base, the receiving point for the bodies of American casualties. In Saudi Arabia, DOD completed its arrangements for a small number of combat pools that restricted access to operations. Since the initial phase of the war was a prolonged air war, much of the initial coverage was confined to pictures of aircraft taking off, landing, and being loaded for missions. CNN's reporters in Baghdad were an exception in that they provided dramatic eyewitness reports of the initial air attacks on the Iraqi capital. Subsequently, however, all but Peter Arnett were withdrawn. Although Arnett and CNN clearly stated that Arnett's reports were censored, Arnett's reports on bomb damage became the focus of savage attacks in the United States.

Senator Alan Simpson (R.-Wyo.) asserted that Arnett was a "sympathizer" of the Iraqis and charged that his reporting from Vietnam decades earlier had been biased and that his Vietnamese brother-in-law had been employed by the Communists. But then the Iraqis released tapes of Simpson's April 1990 visit to Baghdad, a part of the Bush administration's attempts to support the Iraqi dictator. At one point in the recordings, a clear Wyoming twang could be heard telling Saddam that the press was "haughty and pampered. . . . They are very cynical."[44] As Simpson's own fawning over Saddam came to light, the senator withdrew his charges. But the incident revealed that the administration and its supporters hoped to establish an expectation that the press was to buttress U.S. policy as much as it was to serve as an instrument of public information.

The limited press pool arrangements in the Gulf made independent reporting difficult. As the hundred-hour ground war began on February 23, 1991, a news blackout was imposed, and briefings were suspended. Pool reporters found endless obstacles to delivering their stories and pictures for transmission. In many instances, the stories did not get out until long after the war had ended. The result was an image of a Gulf war in which American precision-guided weapons unerringly flew down ventilator shafts into buildings and onto bridges destroying their targets with perfect accuracy. U.S. weapons such as the Tomahawk cruise missiles and the Patriot air defense system were said to have worked to near perfection. The Pentagon noted proudly that 282 of 288 cruise missiles had "successfully transitioned to a cruise profile for a 98 percent launch success rate." Forty-one of 42 Iraqi Scud missiles were said to have been intercepted by Patriot. Casualty figures were not issued by the Pentagon, although hundreds of Iraqi tanks, aircraft, vehicles, and other weapons were meticulously counted as "killed." Civilian casualties were reported only by Peter Arnett via his censored reporting from Baghdad.[45]

Reality seems to have been more complex. While the image of the weaponry used by the United States was that of high-tech precision that seemed never to miss, the reality was that these weapons constituted less than 9 percent of the 84,200 tons of bombs dropped by the United States. The remainder were "dumb bombs," the accuracy of which remained unaccounted for. In this regard, one military analyst noted that Gen. Norman Schwarzkopf's report that some 790 sorties had been flown against 33 bridges in Iraq meant that each bridge was attacked an average of 24 times. Assuming that each attack involved dropping more than one bomb, the result is a success rate of less than 10 percent.[46] The Navy's claim of a 98 percent *launch* success rate for the Tomahawks had nothing to do with how many *hit* their targets; it simply meant that 98 percent of the Tomahawks emerged from their launch canisters. Subsequent analysis of the Patriot's success rate placed it between 50 percent and as low as 10 percent, television shots of spectacular intercepts over Israeli and Saudi Arabian cities notwithstanding.[47]

Battlefield restrictions and the ordinary "fog of war" conspired to lead many professionals to guess at far higher casualties than seem to have been the actual case. Early estimates were that the bloody reality of Saddam's defeat could have been as many as three hundred thousand dead or wounded at or near the front and a like number of civilian deaths due to disease and malnutrition. In fact, it took months to discover that the real figure was much lower: perhaps fewer than ten thousand battlefield casualties and even fewer losses among civilians than had been reported.[48] Nonetheless, the Pentagon feared, with good reason, that real-time pictures of carnage from the front would have disturbed the great welling of support the coalition enjoyed for most of the campaign. Thus, coverage of the intense damage inflicted on fleeing Iraqi forces came after the war was halted by President Bush. But as a $6 million report makes clear, the president and the commander in the field were influenced by the prospect of what would happen once there was wider coverage of the destruction along the road running out of Kuwait City to Basra.[49]

The Bush administration effectively controlled the initial image of the war as well as its gory conclusion. Lt. Gen. Thomas Kelly, director of operations for the Joint Staff, handled most of the press briefings from the Pentagon. In an interview after the war and his retirement, Kelly reflected great pride in managing the media through the briefings:

For the first time ever, the administration—the Department of Defense—was talking directly to the American people, using the vehicle of a press briefing, whereas in Vietnam, everything was filtered through the press. I think that was a major advantage for the government. The press, wittingly or unwittingly, between Riyadh and Washington, was giving us an hour-and-a-half a day to tell our story to the American people. . . . the American people were getting their information from the government—not from the press. . . . I think the lesson for the future is, that we should endeavor to do that more.[50]

Throughout the buildup and conflict, the news of the Gulf War focused on how well the operation was going. The media told the story of the buildup of forces, but they failed to provide the public with the larger historical and geostrategic dimensions of the crisis. The upshot was generally uncritical reporting of the official policy line. The media were used as an adjunct of allied arms. Briefers drew the media's attention to the possibility of an amphibious assault on Kuwait City in order to mask the allied sweep around the western flank of the Iraqi forces.[51] And in order to build support for and confidence in U.S. weapons as engines of pristine battle, U.S. precision-guided weapons were given a prominence that was somewhat misleading with regard to their actual battlefield use and effectiveness.[52] To the extent that the media became the instrument of political and military strategy, there was a reversal in the balance of the government-media relationship that had existed since Vietnam. As Stephen Rosenfeld, a veteran foreign affairs reporter writes, "If Vietnam was in a sense the media's war, Iraq was the military's."[53]

AN UNCERTAIN BALANCE

The purported imperatives of policy making have led some administrations to take vigorous efforts, both legal and extralegal, to control the media. During the 1970s the media aggressively countered these attempts, but as the relationship traversed the 1980s, the balance between the needs of the executive and the rights of the press oscillated indeterminately.

The Imperial Presidency in Court

The Nixon administration went farther than its predecessors or successors in attempting to control the press. In addition to seeking legal justification for prepublication review and censorship of materials deemed harmful to ongoing diplomacy, the Nixon administration tapped the phones of prominent journalists, burglarized their files, and conceived plans to burglarize and even firebomb presumed repositories of information and documents leaked to the press. The administration also sought to intimidate the media by pressing what they knew to be false charges against reporters and pressuring corporate media leadership.[54] These were extraordinary, even bizarre acts. However, they were conceived and justified within a framework of presidential need with which virtually every president during the post–World War II era could associate himself.

This legal rationalization of presidential control of information emerged in litigation. The precipitating event in this chain of court cases was the leak by former DOD official Daniel Ellsberg to the *New York Times* and the *Washington Post* of the DOD secret history of the Vietnam War prepared during the late 1960s. Although these "Pentagon Papers," as they came to be known, revealed little that was not already known, the Nixon administration obtained a temporary restraining order blocking their further publication. When appeal to the espionage laws was rejected by the courts, the administration argued to the Supreme Court that it possessed an inherent power to exercise prior restraint over the release of material that might threaten the national security.

In the 1971 case of *New York Times Co. v. U.S.,* the Supreme Court denied the constitutionality of the sweeping claim lodged by the administration. It recognized that if an explicit congressional mandate was provided and/or the executive could demonstrate to the Court that the release of information would, in Justice Brennan's words, "inevitably, directly and immediately" cause harm equivalent to that of wartime disclosure, then prior restraint might be imposed.[55]

In 1972 the government successfully enjoined a former CIA employee, Victor Marchetti, from publishing a book on the agency that contained materials that the CIA claimed would damage the agency and the national security. The government's restraint on Marchetti was the contractual arrangement between government employees and the government that provides the government with the authority to review and censor any material subsequently published by the employee even if the individual has left government service. Although such an arrangement constitutes a waiver of the employee's First Amendment rights, lower federal courts found the requirement of the waiver to be a reasonable exercise of the president's powers.[56]

In 1977 the government sued another former CIA employee, Frank Snepp, using the *Marchetti* precedent. Snepp's book, *A Decent Interval,* chronicled what Snepp believed was the unconscionable failure of Ambassador Graham Martin and Henry Kissinger to prepare for the debacle that accompanied the U.S. withdrawal from Vietnam.[57] On appeal, the Supreme Court confirmed the *Marchetti* ruling.[58]

During the same years that Snepp gained access to the public through the sacrifice of what he had earned from his book, sympathetic government alumni were *not* asked to submit their works for review. Confirmation of fears that the government would use its preemployment pledges to inhibit critics but not supporters could be found in the unimpeded publication of Henry Kissinger's memoirs, *The White House Years.* Kissinger worked from materials that he removed on his departure from government. He asserted that arrangements had been "worked out" with the office of his successor, Zbigniew Brzezinski, concerning the use of classified materials and that these materials had then been donated to the Library of Congress under a twenty-year secrecy stipulation.[59] However, in litigation instituted by a group of scholars and journalists to gain access to Kissinger's papers under the Freedom of Information Act, Brzezinski's office revealed that Kissinger's assertion concerning clearance of the classified materials "vastly overstates at least by implication, the degree of classification review to which the book was subjected by Brzezinski's office."[60]

Nobody alleged, although it was vaguely hinted, that government secrets had been divulged by Snepp. On the other hand, Kissinger's memoirs are widely considered the most revealing and intimate portraits of individuals and events ever published by a living statesman so recently retired from office. Yet only a fraction of the material was reviewed by current government officers.[61] Like CIA officers such as Snepp, all State Department officers are requested upon retirement to sign an affirmation that they no longer possess "classified or administratively controlled information furnished to [them] during the course of such employment."[62] But the government did not press any breach of contract even though the national archivist concluded that about 90 percent of Kissinger's transcripts had the character of official records and should be returned to government control instead of remaining subject to Kissinger's stipulations. Although the Supreme Court ruled that Kissinger's papers were indeed "official records," it held that once the papers were in the custody of the Library of Congress, only another government agency could initiate a suit for access to the documents. Thus the scholars and journalists had pressed their suit too late, notwithstanding the fact that they could not have known of the transfer!

A recent survey of the control and use of documents and other materials generated by officials during their service concludes that these practices continued at least through the Reagan administration. Most memoirists of the 1980s—Alexander Haig, Donald Regan, Oliver North, Larry Speakes, Michael Deaver, Martin Anderson, David Stockman, Reagan himself—are silent concerning their access to and use of classified materials.[63]

In the 1974 case of *U.S. v. Nixon,* the Supreme Court granted the need for some measure of "protection of communications between high government officials and those who advise and assist them in the performance of their manifold duties." However, the Court rejected Nixon's claim that with respect to his taped conversations concerning the Watergate scandal this privilege was absolute and constitutionally grounded under the doctrine of separation of powers. At least with respect to a criminal trial, "the generalized interest in confidentiality . . . cannot prevail over the fundamental demands of due process of law in the fair administration of criminal justice. The generalized assertion of privilege must yield to the demonstrated, specific need for evidence in a pending criminal trial."[64]

The standing of the doctrine of executive privilege in other domains remains unclear, however. In cases involving the 1967 Freedom of Information Act, designed to establish a right of citizen access to information held by the executive, the courts have proved extremely reluctant to challenge the executive's classification prerogatives. Moreover, as post-Vietnam concern about excessive secrecy waned, both Congress and the president moved to close off even more of the limited access provided under the Freedom of Information Act.

Whereas the Carter administration had taken some steps toward limiting the authority of government officials to classify materials, Ronald Reagan brought with him a far more restrictive view. In the spring of 1981, Reagan's attorney general announced that instead of looking for reasons to release information—the inclination of the Carter administration—warrant would be found to keep information under government control. In September 1981, CIA Director William Casey successfully argued that the CIA should be exempted entirely from the Freedom of Information Act. In October 1981 a new draft freedom of information act was introduced that denied requests for documents showing illegal government activity. The draft act deleted previous stipulations that the public's interest in fullest access be a consideration in the release of information. Indeed, it would allow officials to classify documents even after they had been previously declassified. In other words, if an individual identified a document that he or she wanted access to, the document could be classified secret retroactively.

In June 1981 the administration sought to make it a crime to identify in print a current or former CIA officer even if the name had been gleaned from a previously printed source and was already in the public domain. In 1981 President Reagan signed an executive order restricting the attorney general's oversight of CIA domestic activities and allowing CIA monitoring of CIA job applicants, past or present employees, and firms working for the agency. Any organization not "composed primarily of United States citizens" could be placed under surveillance. Finally, the CIA could engage in covert activities in the United States, including legal infiltration of universities and media groups, if the CIA's intent was not to influence public opinion and the media.[65] In 1982 the administration sought, unsuccessfully, to introduce controls on the university teaching and publication of sensitive research and to restrict the activities of foreign graduate students studying in the United States.

After Reagan's first term, the Washington editor of the *New York Times* summed up press sentiment: "There is no area of government that is not harder to get at now than it was when I was here in the Nixon and Ford years. Their whole attitude is government information belongs to the Government." Media access to the midlevel bureaucrat with a working knowledge of an issue was restricted systematically in the Reagan years. Clearly, many in the Reagan administration saw the press as a negative force in American politics. As a White House science adviser put it in a February 1985 interview, the press "is drawn from a relatively narrow fringe on the far left . . . [that is] trying to tear America down."[66] And in 1986 Secretary of Defense Caspar Weinberger described the press in words that were compatible with a legal definition of treason.[67]

The Reagan administration's attitude toward the press was given legal cover by the courts. Samuel Loring Morison, a Navy civilian analyst, was arrested in October 1984 and charged under the espionage statutes with selling three pictures of a new Soviet aircraft to *Jane's Defense Weekly*, a hawkish English publication.[68] Unlike Daniel Ellsberg, however, Morison became the first person convicted under the Espionage Act of 1917. But Morison's crime was not selling secrets to an enemy but leaking classified information. The two contentions in the trial were that, first, the publication disclosed harmful material and, second, that the information was "willfully disclose[d]" to persons "not entitled to receive . . . information relating to the national defense which . . . [the government] . . . has reason to believe could be used to the injury of the United States or the advantage of any foreign nation." There was little question that the three photos had not damaged U.S. security; the crime, it was clear by the trial's conclusion, was "leaking."[69]

Thus, the mere act of leaking any classified information, whether it ought to be classified or whether it was already part of the public record, had now become a prosecutable offense. The massive effort of the U.S.

government to claim prepublication review sent the actual number of documents skyrocketing. In 1983, over 10,000 books and articles were reviewed by the Pentagon alone, up from fewer than 3,000 in 1981.[70] By the end of the decade the numbers were down somewhat but still substantial: 163 books and 2,915 articles were submitted for Pentagon prepublication review between October 1989 and April 1990.[71] The whole process is wasteful; and to those who think that a well-informed electorate is a part of good public policy it is disturbing.[72]

In 1985 William Casey, in an attempt to buttress the administration's victory in the Morison trial, suggested that the espionage statutes could also be used to prosecute any journalist who "knowingly receives classified documents or information." The draft proposal for punishing those who disclose secrets was itself apparently secret.[73] Two years earlier, in March 1983, President Reagan had claimed that he had had it up to his "keister" with leaks. A new directive to remedy the president's discomfort came in the form of National Security Decision Directive 84. The directive imposed an obligation for employees with access to highly classified information to enter perpetual agreements like the one the CIA required, obliging employees to clear anything they might write in or out of government employment that had a bearing on anything of a classified nature. The directive also obliged employees to keep a log of their contacts with media representatives and to submit to polygraphs in case of unauthorized disclosures. The "voluntary waiver" of rights has been pushed by Defense, State, Agriculture, Commerce, Justice, Treasury, and even the Transportation Department.

Not only American journalists and government employees fueled the administration's sensitivities about exposure to ideas that "could tear America down."[74] Gabriel Garcia Marquez, the Nobel prize–winning author, a retired but antinuclear Italian general, and Hortensa Allende, the widow of the socialist former president of Chile, were all denied visas to travel to the United States to give speeches. Three prize-winning Canadian film documentaries were declared "political propaganda," and their distribution was restricted. The dimensions of the problems of classification began to have elements of farce. When congressional analyst Bruce Blair did an impressive classified study on the vulnerabilities of U.S. communications systems, the Pentagon hired him away from the Congressional Research Service so that he could advise how to upgrade U.S. command and control systems. After some months the study he had done at the Congressional Research Service came to the attention of Army Chief of Staff General Vessey. Vessey was concerned that this material was too sensitive and had it reclassified at such a high level that the author could neither continue his research nor even look at the original document. Because Blair had done a study that the Pentagon now considered too dangerous for him to have done, he was denied a clearance for the job for which he was hired. Congress never did get to see the manuscript it had commissioned: it was seized before it could be delivered.[75]

Finally, the Supreme Court seemed more than ready to assist the executive in the control and management of information. In 1985, in *Sims v. Central Intelligence Agency,* the Court held that even information from such open sources might be classified.[76] The case arose over an attempt to sue the CIA for information regarding a project that lasted from 1953 to 1966 involving "brain washing" research and the use of LSD on unsuspecting individuals. Two people are known to have died as a result of this experiment. When a public interest firm requested the release of the names of the reported eighty or so universities and other institutions involved in this research, the CIA claimed that to release the names would oblige them to reveal sources and methods relating to intelligence collection. The Supreme Court upheld the CIA. Chief Justice Burger argued that Congress "simply and pointedly protected all sources" when it passed the National Security Act of 1947. Congress, Burger argued, gave "sweeping power" in "plain statutory language."

But Thomas Troy, a historian and former CIA official who published a highly respected newsletter on the intelligence community, took issue with the argument in *Sims.* Troy argued that neither Chief Justice Burger "nor anyone else produced one scintilla of any evidence that any congressmen . . . or anybody anywhere ever said anything about" sources and methods. In short, Troy argued, history had been generously stretched both to produce one of the most expansive arguments for the sweeping prerogatives of the CIA and to establish an impressively elastic interpretation of the degree to which national security can serve as a justification for any unusual restrictions.[77]

In the final analysis, then, the courts will sometimes strike down the most egregious and extreme claims and practices. But since Vietnam, the courts have been prepared to grant the executive the benefit of the doubt with respect to most administrative practices and discretionary claims in national security affairs. This has meant, of course, that the relationship between executive authority and the people's right to know is ambiguous and has been decided on a case-by-case basis.

Cutting Their Innards

Perhaps the most troubling challenges to a democratic society have been the instances where policymakers have come to regard the opponents of policy as no longer protected by the rules of the democratic game. On occasion, officials, including presidents, have resorted to harassment of their political opponents. This activity does not stem from any formal, constitutional grant of power, to be sure, but such power has been used. Throughout the cold war period, but especially during the Vietnam War, the FBI and other elements of the domestic and foreign intelligence establishment systematically undertook operations to discredit and disrupt the activities and personal lives of those actively engaged in dissent from American policy. The Kennedy administration, for example, by denying Dr. Linus Pauling a passport in the early 1960s because of his stance against nuclear weapons testing, severely limited his professional as well as his political activities. But once again, these tactics reached their peak during the Johnson and Nixon administrations.

The executive had only to tie up the antiwar activists of the late 1960s in lengthy legal wrangles to stifle dissent. Legal actions were taken so that protesters would become inactive or discouraged and so that their following might be left without leaders and made wary by the example of their leaders' plight. Even if such government action was ultimately thrown out of court, it was successful in the sense that it crippled the momentum of protest and drained financial and organizational resources. In fact, every conspiracy charge pressed by the Nixon administration against foreign policy dissidents failed in court. But the ability to levy and prosecute such charges was a powerful and familiar means of the Nixon administration to harass its critics.[78]

Daniel Ellsberg's trial ended because of government actions that "offended justice," in the words of the judge. Efforts were made by the Nixon White House to bribe the judge with an offer to head the FBI. Further, Ellsberg's psychiatrist's office was burglarized by White House staffers to secure possibly damaging pretrial information on him. Ellsberg was even beaten by thugs dispatched by the White House as he was speaking on the Capitol steps. Charles Colson, former White House special counsel, testified that Nixon's principal motive in all of this was to "get out" damaging information on Ellsberg's character in order "to counter his public views."[79] Or as presidential aide Patrick Buchanan wrote to John Ehrlichman, "Project Ellsberg" was to demonstrate a "conspiracy" of "ex-NSC types" and "leftist writers" such as Neil Sheehan of the *New York Times.*[80] Presumably, then, if Ellsberg could, in the words of Buchanan, have his "innards cut," Ellsberg's disgrace would be shared by those with whom he was associated. One former NSC member assigned to the task, Egil Krogh, wrote to his associate David Young that "there was no apparent damage" as the result of the Ellsberg disclosure; yet it was, Colson realized, an "opportunity" to "arouse the heartland . . . with a natural villain."[81]

Echoes

As the first post–cold war president was being elected in 1992, there were echoes of the abuses of twenty years earlier. As the Bush reelection campaign floundered, one of the only tactics that seemed to elicit a flicker of popular response was to attack Democratic presidential candidate Bill Clinton's "character." The Bush campaign focused on Clinton's avoidance of the draft during the Vietnam War and his antiwar activities while a Rhodes Scholar at Oxford University in 1969 and 1970. The president, conceding that he had no evidence, sought to portray a Clinton trip to the Soviet Union and Eastern Europe as having some sort of sinister intent. But the lack of evidence, it turned out, was not the result of any lack of effort on the part of members of his administration to find it.

Subsequently, after first denying any wrongdoing, the State Department conceded that Bush political appointee Elizabeth Tamposi, the assistant secretary of state for consular affairs, had ordered a search of not only Clinton's passport records but also those of Clinton's mother and of Bush's other challenger, Ross Perot.[82] The State Department insisted that the search had been carried out in response to a Freedom of Information Act request from the press but acknowledged that the request was given priority over more than four thousand unrelated requests, notwithstanding Department procedures requiring that such requests be handled on a first-come basis.

State Department Inspector General Sherman Funk confirmed after the election that Tamposi had been in contact with close aides of former secretary of state James Baker,[83] who was then running the Bush campaign from the White House, and that he and his aides certainly knew the search was under way but did not intervene to stop it. Although Funk noted that "there were people in Washington who were salivating . . . for information detrimental to Clinton," he "found no evidence that the White House—or any other external source—orchestrated an 'attack' on the Clinton files." But "in a broader sense, . . . what we did find was more disturbing[:] . . . an attempt to use the records and employees of . . . the U.S. Department of State, to influence the outcome of a Presidential election."[84] Acting Secretary of State Lawrence Eagleburger accepted full responsibility for the "mess" and the evident politicization of the State Department. Nonetheless, to the chagrin of the professional Foreign Service, he did not emphasize that political appointees, and not members of the professional Foreign Service, were responsible for the file search.[85]

In late November 1992 another echo of Watergate could be heard when it was revealed that two days after the election, C. Boyden Gray, President Bush's counsel, had authorized White House personnel to destroy "'non-record' materials like scratch pads, unimportant notes to one's secretary, phone and visitor logs or informal notes (of meetings, etc.) used only by the staff member." The telephone logs of Baker and his staff had not been requested during the State Department investigation.[86]

THE PUBLIC AND POLICY MAKING

Ironically, Richard Nixon himself cogently identified the dangers to democracy inherent in manipulating information in a speech on March 7, 1972: "When information which properly belongs to the public is systematically withheld by those in power, the people soon become ignorant of their own affairs, distrustful of those who manage them, and—eventually— incapable of determining their own destinies."[87] No one argues that all information in American society is systematically controlled by those in power. Obviously, this is not so, or Richard Nixon would have served out his term in office and books such as this one could not be written. Few would argue that the day-to-day details of negotiations should be routinely revealed. Previously undisclosed sources and methods of intelligence gathering should be shielded, though some measure of congressional oversight is in order. Similarly, military secrets about defense technologies, contingency planning, and military movements are legitimate secrets in the view of most observers. But in a democratic society, the blanket restriction of information by those with a purported "need to know," the assertion of a vague right of prior censorship of information, and the ambiguous doctrine of executive privilege contribute to a caste system, a government priesthood weighted against accountability.

Ultimately there is the danger that spillover from foreign policy will touch other sectors of domestic life. During the 1960s and 1970s a series of presidents rationalized the employment of the personnel and technical assets of the foreign intelligence establishment against U.S. citizens who disagreed with the policies of the government. It has been argued, however, that these cold war efforts to silence and harass opposition were ultimately unsuccessful and have actually resulted in the extension of civil liberties. Thus, as courts rule against these measures, the areas protected explicitly by case law become wider.[88] Perhaps. Perhaps it is true in politics, as in health, that some diseases can be survived and the body develops an immunity that limits the contraction of the disease in the future. Surely, however, it is better not to have experienced the disease in the first place.

In sum, the ambiguous and inherently tense relationship between authority and accountability has become more uncertain as the United States has assumed world leadership. At its best, that relationship rests on mutual confidence. But if there is an imbalance in the control and dissemination of information, power can go unchecked. In any case, given the reluctance of the courts unequivocally to restrain the executive, there is a danger that a climate of either excessive suspicion or unwarranted trust can emerge, leaving leadership isolated from necessary reality testing.

Public censure may be harsh and sometimes unfair; public education may be burdensome. But to the extent that criticism is denied or information withheld, future opportunities to deal with the public forthrightly are exchanged for today's administrative, personal, or policy convenience. The people should be exposed to as much information as possible about the fundamental policies that affect what is, in the end, their destiny. As Edward Cahn once explained, "The people's right to obtain information does not, of course, depend on any assumed ability to understand its significance or use it wisely. Facts belong to the people simply because they relate to interests that are theirs [and a] government that is theirs."[89] Furthermore, it is not evident that people are incapable of coming to grips with fundamental international realities. It may be convenient to believe that the people are benighted in foreign affairs, but even if it were so, the presumption should not carry the day if democratic institutions are to survive.

CHAPTER 11

Interest Groups, Lobbying, and American Foreign Policy Making

THE AMERICAN POLITICAL system has always encouraged the exercise of private power in public affairs. The First Amendment guarantee that the people possess the "right . . . peaceably to assemble, and to petition the Government for a redress of grievances" is the formal enabling grant for private demands on the U.S. government. American constitutionalism emphasizes the necessity of preserving a sizable domain that stands apart from government. Moreover, it is now held that corporations are, for all intents and purposes, "individuals," with their attendant rights under the Constitution. The central role of private associations and interest groups in American society also forms the core argument of one of the most important behavioral (as opposed to institutional) analyses of the American political system by a political scientist since World War II.[1] The development of large concentrations of private economic power, such as labor unions and corporations, and the activities of multinational corporations (MNCs) and international financial institutions abroad are all testament to the reality and dynamism of private power. And the sheer volume of interest-group activity (lobbying of Congress, the president, the courts, and the bureaucracy) compels attention and study.

Some writers have expressed concern about the ultimate effect of private power. In the mid-1960s Grant McConnell asked whether private associations of various sorts might not be assuming many of the functions of government in American society. Because of their protected and privileged constitutional status, McConnell suggested, private associations might escape accountability for their actions.[2] A decade later Samuel Huntington submitted that interest groups can place so many claims on public resources and institutions that they might sap government energy and reduce the governability of the American system.[3]

In this chapter and the next we will address both of these issues raised by the prominence of private power—governance and accountability—as they relate to American foreign and national security policy. Because private power takes so many forms, we will establish a more precise characterization of the nature of private power and American foreign policy. Then we will offer a framework for distinguishing the forms of private power. Finally, we will draw some conclusions concerning private power and its impact on American foreign policy making.

THE CHARACTER OF PRIVATE POWER

A much analyzed relationship between private power and government involves lobbying, the activity of private groups as they try to influence the decisions taken by public officials. This effort may take many forms. Influence is commonly sought by providing information to public officials about a group's position on a particular issue, mobilizing political support for or opposition to an issue, or providing inducements (data, favors, campaign contributions, in some cases bribes) to public officials.[4] Lobbying concerns the representation of interests and demands in the policy-making process. In most instances, members of the interest groups do not actually participate in the act of making policy. Occasionally, however, representatives of private power do enter into public policy making; in some cases, they have actually produced draft legislation.[5]

The private-public nexus is perhaps tightest between the corporations that produce the military hardware purchased by the Department of Defense and the DOD. Although these corporations produce goods and services for buyers other than the U.S. government, the volume of sales to DOD makes for a more intimate relationship between government and industry than textbook capitalism might otherwise suggest. In instances where there is total dependence on a small number of industries with a nearly exclusive call on defense expertise and industrial capability, the DOD-industrial ligature has virtually no slack at all.

Some MNCs and private international financial institutions act in the international domain with virtual autonomy. MNCs may engage in lobbying where legislation or government regulations are likely to affect their interests and operations. The most common example of MNCs working with governments are the attempts to coordinate efforts between international organizations, governments, and commercial banks in stabilizing currencies, promoting economic growth, and, not coincidentally, creating opportunities for MNC investment.

The characteristic that sets MNCs apart from other forms of private power, however, is their capacity for international action independent of government. In an interdependent international system, few if any actors are in fact completely independent. However, the largest MNCs command communications and financial resources and in some cases their own intelligence and security services[6] comparable to those of many nation-states. Moreover, MNC decisions are often based on a calculus of interest distinct from those of national actors. To the degree that MNCs have autonomy and lack accountability, they tend to perform as private governments. Indeed, much of the recent analysis of MNCs implicitly views their behavior as at least approximating "foreign policy."

In summary, private power can seek to influence foreign policy making, enter into a symbiotic partnership with makers of public policy, or exercise power independent of the framework of the state. Private actors can have several kinds of relationships with the policy-making process; for example, MNCs might act as independently of U.S. laws as they are able to, while lobbying for particular trade legislation or regulation.

INTEREST REPRESENTATION AND LOBBYING

Foreign policy lobbying involves a mix of groups, institutions, individuals, and foreign governments. At times, various departments, agencies, and even the White House engage in lobbying Congress. Among the more important categories of foreign policy lobbying are: ethnic groups; economic groups, including associations of senior executives of American industry, broadly based trade and professional associations, single-industry groups, and organized labor; public interest groups; single-issue groups; foreign interests; and foreign governments.

Ethnic Groups

The ethnic and racial diversity of the United States, combined with its global involvement, ensures that many ethnically based interest groups are active at one time or another. Associations of Italian-, Polish-, Irish-, Chinese-, and African-Americans, to name a few, seek to influence American foreign policy. Polish-American and other Eastern European groups were highly visible and active during the years immediately after World

War II. During the cold war, when the division of Europe seemed a permanent feature of the international terrain, this activity was less visible. With the end of the cold war, however, Cuban-American[7] and Eastern European interest groups reemerged, and Latinos emerged for the first time.[8] But of all the ethnic political activity, the so-called Jewish lobby is widely regarded as the most important throughout the post–World War II period.[9]

Israel, established at the onset of the cold war, has served as an emotionally charged and singular focus for the mobilization of the American Jewish community. The number of Jews in the United States is not great compared with other prominent ethnic groups: there are fewer than 6 million Jews, while there are more than 20 million African-Americans and more than 10 million Latinos. On the other hand, Jewish voting participation is high. Moreover, Jewish voters tend to be largely urban and concentrated in states with large electoral votes, thereby magnifying their political importance.[10]

Of the several Jewish-American organizations involved in lobbying on issues affecting Israel, the American Israel Public Affairs Committee (AIPAC) is the most active and is widely regarded as the most effective. AIPAC's resources are considerable, including fifty-five thousand members throughout the United States and an extensive and sensitive network of sources within the U.S. government. AIPAC's leadership is frequently informed of issues before they break into the public domain. For instance, prospective arms sales by the U.S. government are sometimes vetted by AIPAC officials before they are announced. The outcome of controversies surrounding these arms sales does not confirm that the AIPAC position invariably wins, but the degree to which AIPAC is consulted is a marker of the respect held for its influence.[11]

In the case of a proposed missile sale to Arab states in the late 1970s, for example, AIPAC leadership was alerted to the deal by sources within the Defense Department even before the sale was announced to Congress. Later, AIPAC was provided with a top-secret JCS report that raised questions about the sale. Armed with this information, AIPAC was able to prepare congressional opposition to the arrangement. Hundreds of local Jewish communities were mobilized to besiege Congress and the Department of State with calls, letters, and inquiries expressing opposition to the sale. Other interest groups, such as Americans for Democratic Action, the labor movement, and other Jewish groups were encouraged to oppose the deal. Although AIPAC could not block the 1978 multination arms sale, it did succeed in modifying the conditions of the sale to make the arms transfer less threatening to Israel.[12] Similarly, in 1981 the administration went ahead with a sale of surveillance aircraft over the opposition of AIPAC, but according to one official: "They learned about AIPAC. We blew three fuses with those guys, and we don't want to go to the mat with them again."[13] And in 1985, on the eve of a Saudi Arabian state visit, sixty-four senators signed a letter declaring their "deep concern" and "serious reservations" over arms sales to Saudi Arabia. The letter was signed by eleven out of seventeen members of the Senate Foreign Relations Committee. For the National Association of Arab Americans (NAAA) it was an exasperating confirmation of AIPAC's clout. "They could have been expected to at least wait for the announcement of a sale before opposing it," complained one NAAA spokesperson.[14]

Measured in terms of their ability to generate revenue for electoral support, spending by Jewish groups is proportionally no greater than their numbers in the U.S. population; however, no other ethnic groups or political action committees have been as consistently successful in mobilizing large blocks of money for campaign purposes.[15] In the 1985–86 campaign, for example, monies raised and delivered to congressional campaigns amounted to $3.8 million. The next largest single contributor, realtors' PACs, gave some $2.7 million. Jewish PACs constituted less than 3 percent of total PAC contributions. But, taken together, the AIPAC affiliates, each limited by law to $10,000 per candidate, organized funding efforts into a tightly focused and coordinated pattern. In 1984, of the $1.82 million that was devoted to Senate races, 44 percent was devoted to defeating the five senators who voted for the 1981 sale of AWACS to Saudi Arabia.[16] "Like the Indian elephant," Thomas Dine, the director of AIPAC, said, "we don't forget." Yet, even with AIPAC's impressive organizational skills, of the top ten recipients of Jewish PAC money, six were failures.

During the 1980s, counter lobbies organized to oppose AIPAC. Emerging in the mid-1980s, the NAAA gained representation in both parties and in Congress.[17] By the mid-1980s, Arab-Americans could be found at all levels of American political life. Members of the NAAA formed a disproportionate part of the volunteer effort for President Reagan in both his campaigns. In 1984 the NAAA formed its own PAC and claimed credit for defeating the chair of the Subcommittee on Foreign Operations of the House Appropriations Committee. With an increase in Arab-American numbers and organizational skills, and a population concentrated in states heavily weighted in the electoral college (California, New Jersey, New York, Pennsylvania, Illinois, and Texas), the NAAA planned to make a difference in individual congressional campaigns. But Arab-American groups remain less well organized and less well funded than AIPAC, and they have not yet commanded the numbers that AIPAC has.[18]

In recent years groups such as the National Council on U.S.-Arab Relations have begun to send relatively large numbers of high-school and university teachers to the Middle East for seminars and travel in the hope that they would return with a more favorable impression of the Arab position. The council also began to distribute newsletters and to provide speakers to schools and civic groups. As the Persian Gulf crisis escalated in late 1990 and early 1991, Kuwaiti exiles, with White House approval, mobilized more than $5 million to pay Hill and Knowlton Public Affairs Worldwide to stimulate support for Kuwait and the Arab coalition that opposed Iraq.[19] It seemed unlikely, however, that the effort and the related organizations spawned by the war would survive.[20] And as the memory of the Gulf War faded, the public relations problem of Arab-Americans remained acute.

The NAAA has been little helped by the prominence of terrorist acts that have a Moslem connection. More frequently than not, terrorism is prefaced in the news media by the appellation *Arab*. There are of course many terrorist organizations that are not Arab, for example, the Irish Republican Army, the Basque separatists, and the Peruvian Shining Path. But in terms of media exposure, from newspaper cartoons to Hollywood escape films, *Arab* and *terrorists* seemed to be linked. Not a few Arab-Americans asked their fellow Americans how they would feel if Irish-Americans or Hispanic-Americans had been tagged as terrorists. Arab-Americans feel vulnerable to nativist and racist antipathies because their numbers are small, their culture and history are unfamiliar, and their religion is substantially different from mainstream American faiths.

AIPAC, on the other hand, represents a community that has been prominent since the Pilgrims and also has an impressive organization and technically well-informed staff. AIPAC's coherent focus on a single country within a single geostrategically critical area—the Middle East—is yet another ingredient in its ability to organize and use effectively the relationships it has cultivated and sustained in Congress and the executive branch. Additionally, one cannot dismiss the strong emotional commitment—and in some Christian churches, it is a religious commitment—to the survival of Israel. Equally, there is a hundred-year-old sensitivity of many Americans to the persecuted Jews of Europe, the Middle East, and Africa that was heightened by the slaughter of six million Jews in Hitler's "Final Solution."

Israel also occupied a special place in U.S. strategic thinking during the cold war. This position, and the leverage that has flowed from it, peaked during the 1980s. Indeed, in 1981 Israel was officially denominated a "strategic ally" of the United States. The relationship was formalized through a memorandum of understanding between the two governments recognizing what Richard Armitage, the assistant secretary of defense at the time, called "the unique relationship that exists between the U.S. and Israel." In 1986, Thomas Dine, AIPAC's executive director, went further and characterized the developments of the 1980s as a "revolution in the area of strategic cooperation." Dine predicted that "[t]his President and this Secretary of State are going to leave a legacy that will be important to Israel's security for decades to come."[21]

Yet within five years the U.S.-Israeli relationship was operating in a post–cold war context within which the strategic relationship was of ambiguous value. In the Bush administration's prosecution of the Persian Gulf War against Iraq, Israel was as much a problem as an ally as the president sought to hold together an Arab alliance against Saddam Hussein. Moreover, the Likud government's handling of the *intifada,* the uprising against Israeli occupation of the West Bank, and the Israeli refusal to compromise on the issues growing out of Israeli occupation of the area undercut Israel's image. In addition, American public opinion, though supportive of Israel, was nonetheless deeply skeptical of all foreign aid. Israel, as the largest recipient of U.S. aid, could not escape a more critical public judgment.[22]

In this changed international and American domestic context, President Bush and Secretary of State James Baker sought to exploit the enhanced American position in the wake of the Gulf War to promote negotiations leading to a settlement of the outstanding issues in the Arab-Israeli conflict. As part of a strategy of showing U.S. evenhandedness, in September 1991 Bush refused to support $10 billion in loan guarantees that the Shamir government needed to continue housing construction.[23] A crucial element of the Bush administration's effort was its credibility with the Arabs. Portraying himself as "one lonely little guy" standing up to a pro-Israel lobbying juggernaut, Bush threatened to veto legislation calling for the loan guarantees. The ensuing test of political will between the administration, Shamir, and Israel's supporters in Congress and the United States quickly became perhaps the worst crisis in U.S.-Israeli relations since the 1956 Suez crisis, when the Eisenhower administration used its financial muscle to force the Israelis to withdraw from the Sinai.[24]

Ultimately, however, Bush and Baker were successful in moving the

Israelis and the Arabs into a negotiating process. But the personal relationship between the president and Shamir had frayed to the point where the deterioration of U.S.-Israeli relations became a factor in Israeli elections that saw the Likud defeated by a new center-left Israeli government that was more inclined toward compromise and toward reconstructing the U.S.-Israeli relationship.

Throughout the entire episode, it was evident that AIPAC and other Jewish groups, their past influence and effectiveness notwithstanding, were unable to affect decisively the course of events. Organization, expertise, and resources had not overcome a disjuncture of real interests between Israel and the United States. A serious crisis in U.S.-Israeli relations was resolved only when both the U.S. and Israeli administrations changed, and when Israeli leadership acceded to the American position.

Even with a new government in Israel, and even with overwhelming Jewish support for Clinton in the 1992 campaign, Israel was not able to reestablish its old hold on policy. Indeed, in congressional testimony in early 1993, Secretary of State Warren Christopher said that he would do everything he could to ensure that the United States maintained a neutral position between Israel and her Arab neighbors in any future regional peace talks.[25] In the final analysis, then, the much vaunted power of this remarkable ethnic lobby was revealed to be as contextually bounded as any other.

Other Ethnic Lobbies

There were other significant ethnic lobbies. The Greek-American community, for instance, is represented by the American Hellenic Progressive Association (AHEPA), a group with some fifty thousand members. AHEPA helped mobilize a community that numbers perhaps seven hundred thousand to support an American arms embargo of Turkey when the Turks invaded Cyprus in 1974. AHEPA successfully employed many of the grassroots techniques used by AIPAC to get Congress to impose the embargo over White House opposition. But counter-lobbying by Turkish-Americans and others in time forced a retreat on Turkish aid.[26]

In recent years AHEPA has concentrated on getting the annual aid package for Turkey maintained at seven dollars to Turkey for every ten dollars to Greece. The task was made more difficult in 1981 by the appearance of a strongly anti-American government in Greece. In the end, however, the Greek aid package went forward with its traditional ratio intact, with a concessional financial package included as well. A lobby pushing hard for a single issue had managed to get Congress to satisfy a tiny but determined constituency. One administration official lamented that the whole process signaled the belief that "no matter how much you provoke us, Congress will roll over."[27]

Notwithstanding the fact that they are the largest minority community, African-Americans' foreign policy efforts have not been consistently successful. U.S. aid to Africa remains concentrated on Egypt rather than on the larger and poorer sub-Saharan portion of the continent.[28] On the other hand, unprecedented violence against blacks televised nightly from South Africa moved the administration to retreat from its policy of "constructive engagement" and to preempt congressional action with a presidential order in September 1985 that restricted American loans to South Africa. It was an action that commanded wide support, and that support was mobilized in part by TransAfrica, the major African-American foreign policy lobbying group.

The overall foreign policy presence of African-Americans on foreign policy issues and in the policy-making process was not a strong one through the mid-1980s.[29] By the end of the decade, however, the situation began to change. Lt. Gen. Colin Powell became the deputy director of the NSC in 1987 and then became the national security adviser before being appointed chairman of the Joint Chiefs of Staff. Condoleezza Rice, a professor at Stanford, joined the NSC as the senior adviser on Soviet affairs in 1989. An African-American, Edward Perkins, was U.S. ambassador to the United Nations at the end of 1992. In 1993 Cliff Wharton, the African-American head of the largest pension fund in America, assumed the number-two position in the State Department.

The African-American position on African and Caribbean issues seems to have become a part of normal political discourse. The increasing migration of blacks from the Caribbean is also being felt. But the substantial Haitian community located in New York and Florida was notably unsuccessful in making Washington sympathetic to the plight of the many refugees coming to the United States in makeshift boats in the 1980s.[30] As so many in the African-American community at home are still so distant from realizing the American dream, it is uncertain how much attention black Americans can or will devote to their ancestral lands in Africa or still larger issues of human rights. It is noteworthy, therefore, that in mid-1993 TransAfrica established a formal "think tank," for as Executive Director Randall Robinson put it, "This town produces policy as a result of a competition of policy ideas. We have never competed evenly institutionally in the arena of foreign affairs. That's why we wanted a fully fleshed out think tank to grind out the analysis that represents the interest of our community."[31]

Economic Groups

It is estimated that more than five hundred corporations maintain legislative liaison offices in Washington. In addition, influential groups of senior executives have ready access to the foreign-economic-policy establishment.[32] The Chamber of Commerce and the National Association of Manufacturers are perhaps the best-known business associations, with the former widely regarded as the most professional and influential of the business groups. The Chamber of Commerce represents tens of thousands of firms and individuals throughout the country, and its extensive network of local chapters and offices provides it with political access to virtually every congressional district in the country. Its large Washington operation ensures considerable impact within Congress and the executive bureaucracy.

A second important group of economic or business lobbyists is the various single-industry groups. Four have been especially prominent. The fisheries and associated industries have lobbied both Congress and the executive concerning the lengthy negotiations over the legal regime of the oceans. Of particular importance to these groups has been the status of international law relating to the coastal zone and the establishment of a two-hundred-mile-wide exclusive fisheries zone. Despite Department of State fears that establishment of such a zone by the United States would disrupt negotiations in the ongoing Law of the Sea Conference, Congress relented to the pressures of those seeking such a zone and legislatively established it in 1975. It is important to note in passing that other segments of the American fisheries industry, such as tuna and shrimp interests who fish off the coasts of other countries, were opposed to the legislation.

Another industry group concerned with the Law of the Sea negotiations is the mining companies and companies involved in the manufacture of equipment for deep-seabed mining. The pressure from these groups has been for legislation to allow them to begin seabed exploration and exploitation of mineral resources notwithstanding the fact that international control of such activity has not yet been worked out. Here again the Department of State initially opposed such a legislative mandate, fearing that it would disrupt difficult international negotiations. By the end of the 1970s, however, the question of international control of deep-seabed mining had deadlocked, and State Department representatives began to support seabed exploration laws, possibly as a prod to Third World countries, who were demanding tight restrictions on exploitation of the seabed by the industrialized world. With the arrival of the Reagan administration, industry pressures reportedly peaked as Reagan moved in early 1981 to reopen the entire treaty to renegotiation (and thereby ended American accession to the treaty, effectively killing it).[33]

A third industry group of major significance is the oil industry. Whether lobbying as individual corporations or under their umbrella organization, the American Petroleum Institute, representing more than three hundred oil industry corporations, has sought to advance the interests of oil-producing states in the Middle East as well as pro-Arab groups in the United States. Obviously, this stance means that the petroleum interests are frequently found in opposition to Jewish groups; in the view of some analysts, the American Petroleum Institute provides an important counterweight to the influence of these groups.[34] On the other hand, its political voice is sometimes muted, for petroleum interests mobilize money better than they could command public sympathy.

Finally, the arms industry comprises one of the most consequential industrial lobbying forces in Washington. The scope of the American defense industry includes most congressional districts in the United States, thereby guaranteeing it a hearing in Washington. Moreover, this industry group employs literally hundreds of former Department of Defense officials and former members of Congress, most of whom are therefore well acquainted with the multiple access points to Congress and the bureaucracy. On the other hand, there is some evidence that as a lobbying force the industry's efforts exhibit a significant degree of incoherence. As one member of Congress has noted, "Nobody orchestrates because all of its members are fighting for their own piece of turf."[35] As will be apparent in the next chapter, the end of the cold war has exacerbated this situation significantly.

Another major economic group engaged in lobbying is organized labor. Some fifty labor organizations operate in Washington, with the American Federation of Labor and Congress of Industrial Organizations (AFL-CIO) long regarded as the most important. With the sometimes disruptive effects of increased interdependence on domestic economics, the American labor movement began to shift from its traditional internationalist position during the 1970s.

For much of the period after World War II, most of labor could be counted on to take fairly liberal and internationalist positions on questions of trade and tariff restrictions. Intense competition and market penetration from abroad, especially in the automobile, textile, steel, and some light manufacturing industries, however, have led labor to take a far more protectionist posture. On virtually all legislation for trade reform and expansion during the 1970s and 1980s, labor adopted a "fair trade" rather than a "free trade" position. As the portion of unionized labor in the work force diminished, labor found itself at an increasing distance from traditional liberal allies in Congress and instead frequently allied with industrial lobbyists seeking relief from foreign competition.

Similarly, the traditional liberal, globalist posture of the labor movement fragmented as the strategic superiority of the United States diminished during the 1970s and then as the cold war ended. Initially, labor allied itself with those who favored expanding defense budgets and were opposed to the SALT II agreements. By the mid-1980s the unavoidable tradeoffs between social programs and defense expenditures pushed some away from new defense programs. Likewise, the drain of the public resources under the "Reagan revolution" encouraged labor to be more supportive of negotiations with the Soviets in the hope that arms control might free up some monies for social welfare programs.

Public Interest and Single-Issue Groups

Many environmental groups, or "good government" lobbies, such as Common Cause or the many groups spawned by consumer activist Ralph Nader, in the past have concerned themselves primarily with domestic legislation affecting their interests. In recent years, however, Nader has produced a *Multinational Monitor,* a bulletin that basically mirrors the interests of American labor. Environmental groups have become much more intensely engaged with foreign policy as the result of the emerging salience of such issues as deforestation, global warming, and ozone depletion. Thus, early in the summer of 1993 environmental groups successfully sued in federal court to demand that the executive prepare an environmental-impact statement to accompany the North American Free Trade Agreement (NAFTA). The action would delay for months a vote on NAFTA. Other, more general public affairs groups, such as the League of Women Voters, and some church groups and associations frequently lobby Congress and executive agencies on issues of foreign policy or foreign economic policy. Similarly, groups such as the Foreign Policy Association and the Arms Control Association consistently seek to influence foreign policy decisions.

In contrast to groups that promote "good government" and social activism, there are single-issue groups that focus on domestic issues almost exclusively. Even some of these groups have had a significant foreign policy impact, however. Thus, those groups that opposed abortion were successful in killing U.S. assistance via the United Nations in family planning programs for much of the 1980s because they feared that the monies might help programs that promote abortion.

For much of the cold war, foreign policy served as a catalyst for the formation of single-issue pressure groups. Throughout the Vietnam War years, for example, campus-based groups worked in opposition to the war. Antiwar groups organized to take their message directly to Washington by means of conventional lobbying and, more dramatically, by means of massive demonstrations.

The rise of protectionist sentiment in the early 1970s spawned several coalitions that lobbied for free trade, such as the business-led Emergency Committee for American Trade. In the Carter years, the debate over ratification of the Panama Canal treaties stimulated the formation of an Emergency Coalition to Save the Panama Canal, which coordinated the antiratification efforts of conservative groups such as the American Legion, the Veterans of Foreign Wars, the American Conservative Union, the Young Americans for Freedom, and the Committee for the Survival of a Free Congress.[36]

In each of these cases, as the stimulus was removed, single-issue "emergency committees" tended to vanish. On the other hand, many single-issue coalitions consist of established interest groups. Thus the raw material for alliances is always at hand for "new" groups that spring up to contest the issues of the day. Close attention to the composition of the Emergency Coalition to Save the Panama Canal, for example, reveals a collection of conservative groups that can be found in coalition on virtually any subsequent major political, social, or economic issue. There is considerable sharing and pooling of resources, especially the use of mailing lists of contributors to various causes. A grass-roots campaign can therefore be mounted almost instantaneously on any issue that taps these intensely ideological segments of the American polity.[37]

Governments as Lobbyists

Many foreign governments with extensive trade and financial relations with the United States maintain contacts with Congress both thorough their embassies and through special offices as well.[38] Many countries also support trade councils designed to mobilize members of the American business community with an interest in a specific aspect of foreign trade. Foreign governments have also contributed to American universities and research institutes in an effort to develop a sympathetic hearing within the foreign policy establishment.[39]

There are now more than six hundred registered representatives of foreign governments. In many instances, the most prominent members of the Washington establishment, including former senators such as J. William Fulbright and former high-ranking members of the executive branch, act on behalf of overseas interests. Henry Kissinger and his Kissinger Associates are perhaps the most well-known operators of the Washington "revolving door," through which well-connected individuals move readily between the "private sector," where they serve as brokers, consultants, and deal makers, and the highest levels of public policy making.[40] Kissinger, of course, served as national security adviser and secretary of state during the Nixon and Ford administrations.

When Kissinger left government service in the mid-1970s, he took with him men who would continue to play prominent roles in foreign and national security policy making throughout the 1980s and early 1990s. Thus, Brent Scowcroft and Lawrence Eagleburger alternated between careers in which they consulted with foreign governments, defense contractors, and multinational corporations for Kissinger Associates, on the one hand, and served variously as top-ranking policymakers, on the other.[41] General Scowcroft served on the Tower Commission investigating Iran-Contra and on Reagan's Commission on Strategic Forces even as he was serving as a consultant to Lockheed, the manager of the Navy's D-5 Trident missile program and a subject of the commission's recommendations. Scowcroft was also, of course, national security adviser, for President Ford and then for President Bush. Lawrence Eagleburger served as under secretary and then secretary of state in the Bush administration. For his part, Kissinger served during the late 1980s on the sensitive Foreign Intelligence Advisory Board, on which he was charged with responsibility to give independent advice on intelligence activities, even as he continued to run his unique consulting enterprise. These men did not recuse themselves from many of the decisions in which conflicts were possible. In some cases, they entered ambiguous and convoluted disclosure statements, using limited recusal arrangements upon reentering public service.[42]

The Reagan years were marred by an especially large number of ethical ambiguities and outright improprieties. For example, Ronald Reagan's first national security adviser, Richard Allen, proved to be a major embarrassment when it was revealed that he had served as a lobbyist for foreign automobile interests. Later, Allen was forced from office when it was revealed that he had accepted gifts in return for arranging interviews for Japanese journalists with Nancy Reagan. Similarly, Vice President George Bush's chief of staff received $250,000 for representing the Japanese government for one month. Clearly, influence and lobbying commanded a tariff of a different order of magnitude in the Reagan years.[43] It was more of a disappointment than a surprise, therefore, that shortly after President Reagan retired, he left for Japan, where he received a fee reportedly in excess of $2 million for two twenty-minute speeches.

Michael Deaver, the Reagan administration's director of public relations and a longtime Reagan associate, opened a public relations firm in Washington that began with a contract from South Korean government sources paying $2 million a year, exclusive of expenses. Deaver was said to offer "access" to the White House, where he retained a pass and remained on intimate terms with the first family. Three other advertising men who ran the 1984 Reagan campaign took a contract from the government of the Philippines for $1 million a year, but it was rescinded by the firm two days before President Marcos was forced to flee his dictatorship for Hawaii in order to try to enjoy the billions with which he had absconded. Access could do many things, but even some of the crassest lobbying since Ulysses Grant could not stem a popular Philippine uprising against twenty years of misrule.

Foreign governments occasionally resort to extraordinary and even illegal means in attempts to gain a favorable hearing for their interests. Throughout the 1970s the Korean CIA, working through South Korean businessman Tongsun Park, placed agents on the staffs of key members of Congress, including the Speaker of the House, and dispensed thousands of dollars in campaign contributions, occasional bribes, and entertainment. Trips were arranged to South Korea, where members of Congress and other dignitaries would receive honorary degrees and lavish entertainment, including, as one member of Congress put it, "an attractive Korean woman who would be pleased to meet with the congressman on matters of mutual interest."[44] Investigation of the Korean activity revealed that over the years some thirty-one members of Congress had received money; in only a handful of cases were indictments brought and convictions obtained.

Of all the foreign lobbying efforts—some 161 different countries have secured officially registered lobbyists[45]—by far the most controversial efforts have been on behalf of Japanese concerns. In recent years a spate of books have argued that Japanese firms feel, in the words of Michael Crichton's fictional bestseller *Rising Sun,* that "business is war." As one political economist, Pat Choate, argues in his widely read *Agents of Influence,* Japan "launched a global political and propaganda offensive . . . to strengthen Japanese power." But "the only way that Japan can achieve" that power, warns Choate, "is by attaining effective political domination of the United States."[46]

To Choate, it is important not only that Japanese firms spend a great deal of money in order to influence American lawmakers and regulators but that they operate in a fashion that, though legal, is veiled and marginally ethical. Japan, Choate contends, suborns former officials and lawmakers with high fees, while operating highly efficient commercial intelligence and public relations campaigns. Japanese intelligence efforts, claims Choate, employ "thousands of Americans . . . many of whom have direct access to the most intimate political information of virtually every important organization or network in this country." This effort, says Choate, "rivals the information gathering efforts of the Soviet KGB." By way of explaining why the Japanese behave in this way, Choate asserts that it is part of Japan's national political culture: the Japanese are obsessed with secret intelligence. "Secrecy, deceit, camouflage, and betrayal are . . . an integral part of Japanese politics and business."[47]

There is a legitimate concern that if defense industries rely on critical overseas suppliers or are owned outright by overseas investors, then when an emergency arises, if allied governments disagree, supplies might be denied. Also, there is the case of the Ohio-based machine tool company Matrix Churchill, which seems to have transferred to Iraq before the Gulf War components useful in manufacturing atomic bombs. During the Vietnam War, two Japanese firms, Kyocera and Sony, refused to sell parts that only they could readily supply. Similarly, some Japanese firms have delayed selling computer chips and other supplies to restrain foreign competition in consumer electronics.[48] According to Congressman Dan Glickman (D.-Kans.), the chair of the House Intelligence Oversight Committee, U.S. intelligence discovered that American Telephone and Telegraph (AT&T) was about to lose a $100 million contract with Indonesia to Japan's NEC because the Japanese government threatened to cut off Indonesian aid. Before the deal was completed, however, President Bush wrote a letter to the Indonesian government that pointedly emphasized the value of U.S. trade agreements with Indonesia. The result was that AT&T and NEC split the value of the contract between them.[49]

Because of the new awareness of the significance of overseas competition and the apparent lack of inhibition on the part of some of America's allies in pursuing "commercial intelligence" (according to one estimate, up to 80 percent of the Japanese intelligence budget is directed to economic concerns), both the Bush and Clinton administrations began to consider redirecting CIA assets toward similar efforts or at least engaging more actively in countermeasures.[50] But many criticisms of overseas investment in the United States are overdrawn and overwrought; and indeed, when applied only to Japan, they are not unlike the racist, anti-Jewish charges contained in the notorious Czarist police forgery entitled *The Protocols of the Elders of Zion,* which detailed a worldwide Jewish financial and political conspiracy.[51] Moreover, the French, for instance, have been more flagrant, and for a longer time, in the raiding of American commercial secrets. Thus in 1964, for example, they used a countess to burglarize the Paris hotel room of George Ball, then under secretary of state for economic affairs, in order to lift from his briefcase the U.S. position on trade negotiations.[52]

The truth is that Japanese influence and money, like the more substantial influence of British investment, are a part of the history of America's larger international relationships. Britain, after all, was a major investor in the United States in the nineteenth century and remains the largest investor at the end of the twentieth century as well. For a hundred years, British influence has not been controlling, notwithstanding shared language, similar institutions, and the mixed benefits of a former colonial association. Japan's relationship with the United States similarly fluctuates as a function of the growth of Japanese economic prowess and, equally, important shared strategic goals. As American strategic goals undergo post–cold war revision and as the Japanese—like the British—begin to suffer the normal consequences of domestic and international business cycles, Japanese influence will wax and wane accordingly.

In fact, much of the perceived menace of the Japanese commercial challenge declined with the collapse of the Tokyo stock market after 1990. With the bursting of the Japanese "bubble economy," Japanese firms in the United States began to shut down production, investment slowed, and Japanese institutional investors retreated from the low-yielding U.S. bond market. Huge Japanese investments in American real estate took an especially brutal hit, losing 30 percent or more of appraised value. As a consequence of the depressed real estate market and stock market at home and abroad, Japanese banks suffered an enormous contraction of their capital base, leaving many emerging markets largely to their American competitors.[53]

Moreover, the worry that critical U.S. industry is susceptible to commercial hijacking is somewhat misplaced. After all, the capacity of the U.S. government to audit critical technologies is largely a matter of executive will. Legislation to foster such monitoring was passed in 1988 despite the best efforts of many well-placed lobbyists, led by the redoubtable Elliot Richardson (attorney general in the Nixon administration and secretary of defense in the Ford administration). But enforcement of the act, which would have scrutinized the sale of critical industries to foreigners on defense, environmental, antitrust, and other grounds, was not a high priority of the Bush administration. As President Bush's chairman of the Council of Economic Advisers, Michael Boskin, reportedly put it, "There is no difference between computer chips and potato chips in this White House."[54]

Foreign lobbies are hardly trivial or irrelevant, but they are rarely determinate without ideological sympathy to their position in the highest counsels of state. Foreign lobbyists in the form of registered political action groups contributed over $2 million to the congressional campaigns of 1990.[55] But that figure pales beside the more than $678 million collected from domestic PACs for the campaigns of 1992.[56] And notwithstanding the conventional wisdom that Republicans always extract more money than Democrats, the fact is that Democrats, if they have a ticket that seems likely to garner some success, frequently do better than Republicans.[57]

Reform?

The Clinton administration campaigned against the "political action committee industry," which tries to "buy access to Congress and the White House," and pledged in his first State of the Union address to reform the campaign process. Clinton forbade his administration's appointees from lobbying their respective agencies for five years after the date they ended their service in his administration. Notwithstanding administration rhetoric, however, Clinton reform efforts could hardly be seen as a radical departure. Rather, they were of a piece with a succession of executive, congressional, and private undertakings that have sought to define and redefine the bounds of personal material interest in the context of public service.

Men and women of talent need to be attracted to government service, but it is a dubious endeavor if they face the prospect of demonstrating that they either never associated with power and wealth before they entertained the challenge of public service or if they will have to agree to a vow of postservice penury. Indeed, even as President Clinton reiterated his concerns about the revolving door, it was clear that top-level members of his transition team—Vernon Jordan; his commerce secretary, Ron Brown; his secretary of state, Warren Christopher; and his deputy national security adviser, Sandy Berger—had received substantial fees to represent foreign governments' interests in Washington.[58] Hence, it remained to be seen whether the new rules established early in the Clinton administration would succeed in keeping the efforts of lobbyists a seemly distance from power, on the one hand, while attracting the best talent to government service, on the other.

LOBBYING AND INFLUENCE

It should come as no surprise that individuals and interest groups with the prospect of economic gain or loss are accorded ongoing access, a high degree of legitimacy, and a respectful hearing. One would expect groups that command and can mobilize resources relevant to the electoral process to be influential. But circumstances, such as a dramatically failing foreign policy, can open opportunities for groups and coalitions not normally active or influential. Similarly, the transformation of the international context can undercut the position of even such powerful groups as AIPAC. In addition, in an era of massive deficits and little remaining money for new program initiatives, special-interest groups of all kinds will go into high gear, waging a defensive war "designed to protect advantages gained in the past." But as one observer has noted, they will often be forced to "settle for less."[59]

The sheer magnitude, prestige, and intensity of the activity and the resources committed by private power do not translate in any simple way into "influence." The character of the issue being lobbied, the perceived legitimacy of those lobbying, the existence of counterpressure, timing, and, especially in the foreign policy area, the context of international events can impinge on the process. No less important is the president. In 1947 virtually all of President Truman's advisers and the great oil companies were against recognizing Israel as an independent state. Truman, however, thought it was the right thing to do, and it was done.[60]

Private Power and American Foreign Policy: The Military-Industrial Complex and Multinational Corporations

INTEREST GROUPS constitute an important and constitutionally protected form of private power in the American political system. Although there are important exceptions, interest groups exercise their private power primarily through lobbying, interest representation, attempts to influence electoral outcomes, and public relations. Multinational corporations and the companies that have made up the industrial portion of the military-industrial complex may also engage in lobbying and interest representation. However, these companies stand and interact with government in ways that are distinct both from interest groups and from each other.

THE MILITARY-INDUSTRIAL COMPLEX

As President Eisenhower left office in 1960 he warned the nation:

We have been compelled to create a permanent armaments industry of vast proportions. . . . This conjunction of an immense military establishment and a large arms industry is new in the American experience. The total influence—economic, political, even spiritual—is felt in every city, every statehouse, every office of the federal government. We recognize the imperative need for this development. Yet we must not fail to comprehend its grave implications. Our toil, resources, and livelihood are all involved; so is the very structure of our society.

In the councils of government we must guard against the acquisition of unwarranted influence, whether sought or unsought, by the military-industrial complex. The potential for the disastrous use of misplaced power exists and will persist.[1]

As American foreign policy came to rely on military capability, the "imperative need for . . . development" of the military-industrial complex became more exacting.[2] Unlike some other developed nations, the United States has never met its military needs with extensive, publicly owned arsenals. Instead, the Defense Department has relied upon corporations in the private sector. As corporations came to depend on government contracts, Eisenhower's foreboding of a "conjunction of an immense military establishment and a large arms industry" seemed realized. As this prototypical symbiosis of public and private power matured, defense spending ebbed and flowed.

Major spikes in defense outlays came at the time of Korea, during the first two years of the Kennedy administration, in the late 1960s at the height of the Vietnam War, and in the first half of the 1980s.[3] The latest buildup peaked between 1985 and 1987. A decline in defense contracts and employment set in. For a while, it was possible to believe that the latest dip in spending was the normal course of the cycle. By 1989–90, however, it was evident that the Soviet-American relationship was undergoing fundamental change and that the defense industry would be faced with a no less fundamental transformation.[4] By 1992, with Soviet power dismantled in Central Europe and the Soviet Union itself sundered, the cold war no longer served as the defining assumption of U.S. defense policy. But drawing down the industrial–Defense Department base—an economy move that few gainsaid—proved to be one of the more painful parts of the cold war's demise.

The Structure and Dynamics of the Military-Industrial Complex

The military-industrial complex is rooted in the process whereby weapons have been developed, tested, evaluated, and eventually purchased.[5] In the initial phase of research and development DOD identified a need for a weapon, and then it undertook design, engineering, and budget development. Contractors then submitted specific proposals, and then one or more contractors were selected to undertake development of the weapons system. DOD tested and evaluated prototypes and then selected one of the prototypes for production.

There was interaction between the military and the contractors at every step in the process. Even the identification of a security need was frequently influenced by the arms industry; and many of the largest companies maintained foreign and national security policy "think tanks" that evaluated, either on their own or under contract from the government, the security needs of the United States. The presence of thousands of former Defense Department officials in the defense industry and the years of close working relationships between DOD and the technical experts in private companies ensured that throughout the weapons acquisition process there were ongoing exchanges of information and ideas. Thus, there have not been many surprises when prototypes have been produced and testing has begun.

In addition, close interaction is virtually required by the complexity of weapons systems. Weapons technologies build upon previous technologies. Because of the escalating performance demands DOD places on modern weapons systems, the technologies become ever more complex. Aircraft, for example, involve hundreds of thousands of parts, hundreds of thousands of feet of wire, thousands of resistors, capacitors, relays, and related electronic devices. All these parts must operate at extremely high levels of reliability for long periods of time and under the most extreme conditions. Technical manuals involve tens of thousands of pages; the coordination and management of the entire process of research, design, testing, evaluation, and procurement involves thousands of people.

The immense costs and complexity associated with modern weapons have the effect of reducing the number of companies capable of mobilizing the necessary skills and capital. In the case, for instance, of the billion-dollar Aegis cruiser made at Maine's Bath Iron Works, each bolt must be milled by hand to tolerances far beyond the requirements of commercial ships. Thousands more front-office personnel are needed to wade through the contracting intricacies of the Navy. Far less ordinary steel but far more expensive and highly specialized alloys are used in the ship's hull than would be used in the case of commercial building.

In sum, the making of most defense products is a unique enterprise, with no exact civilian analogue.[6] Moreover, many companies engaged in both commercial and defense work found their dependency upon DOD growing when consumer product sales languished. For instance, after the United States abandoned subsidies to commercial transoceanic "bottoms" in the 1980s, U.S. commercial ship sales fell to zero. As a result, some companies with defense business became "hooked" on DOD orders.[7]

Defense contracts were enormously profitable for the companies that pursued them. During the Reagan years, according to one Navy study,

TABLE 12.1
The U.S. Government as a Source of Revenues, 1990
(in billions of dollars)

Company	Government Revenues	Total Revenues	% from Government
Martin Marietta	5.6	6.1	91.8
Lockheed	9.0	10.0	90.0
Grumman	3.5	4.0	87.5
General Dynamics	8.9	10.2	87.3
Hughes Aircraft	6.5	7.7	85.0
McDonnell Douglas	10.8	16.3	66.3
Raytheon	4.1	9.3	44.1
Boeing	5.8	28.0	20.7

Source: *New York Times,* May 2, 1991.

defense contractors had profits between two and ten times those of their civilian counterparts, measured in terms of return on assets or return on investment.[8] Table 12.1 provides examples of this dependency as of 1990 and the onset of dramatic post–cold war changes in the structure of the relationship between industry and DOD.

Finally, the dependency of the national security establishment on the industry was intensified by the imperative of getting systems produced and in the hands of American forces as soon as possible. Urgency compelled the military to ignore cost, antitrust, and other management considerations that otherwise might work to hold down costs and place some distance between private and public sectors.[9]

What developed during the cold war was what defense industry analysts Merton Peck and Frederick Scherer have called a "bilateral monopoly" between the seller (the defense industry) and the buyer (the government) that bore little or no resemblance to conventional conceptions of the marketplace.[10] In this market there was no real interaction of supply and demand. Congress set demand through defense appropriations. The amount and type of appropriations were determined by international events, the political needs of the members of Congress making the decisions, and the lobbying of the military-industrial complex. Prices and profit were determined through negotiations between the industry and the government. Because costs associated with research, development, testing, and evaluation were beyond the resources of the supplying companies, the government—the buyer—"underwrites a sizable share of the contractor's financial investment . . . provides industrial facilities, makes advance and progress payments, and assists in strategic material acquisition."[11] This peculiar relationship was described during the Vietnam years with piquant self-awareness by one defense contractor: "We need a different gender for our industry. At present, we are neither fish nor fowl; neither private industry nor government."[12]

The Conjunction of Public and Private Power

The concentrated and stable composition of the arms industry was an outstanding characteristic of the cold war era.[13] By the mid-1950s the largest hundred defense contractors held contracts whose dollar value was more than 73 percent of the dollar value of all the major contracts awarded by the U.S. government, with the top twenty-five contractors holding contracts valued at more than 55 percent of the dollar value of all the major contracts. In the mid-1960s the top hundred contractors held contracts valued at about 70 percent of the dollar value of all the major contracts, with the top twenty-five holding contracts valued at 46 percent of the dollar value of the major contracts. By the mid-1970s, a time of falling defense spending relative to the gross national product of the country, the hundred largest contractors still received contracts valued at 70 percent of the dollar value of the major contracts (about $42 billion), with the top twenty-five accounting for 47 percent. Moreover, the composition of the group comprising the top twenty-five to fifty companies was steady.[14] There were changes in the relative positions of the top companies but only a few changes in the composition of the group as a whole. Moreover, most of these top companies, which received contracts valued at about 60 percent of the dollar value of the major contracts granted in the late 1950s, were in the same category at the end of the 1970s.

During the 1970s, as the size of the defense budget began to contract somewhat, the concentration of contract awards to the largest companies was noticeable. For example, at mid-decade almost 70 percent of the dollar amount for all contracts was going to one hundred companies, but the top five received over 19 percent of the amount for all contracts (about $8 billion), while the bottom seventy-five companies received just over 20 percent (about $8.4 billion). By the end of the 1980s the concentration of defense companies handling most of the prime contracts had become especially tight (see table 12.1). Twelve companies were awarded contracts worth between $50 billion and $60 billion.[15]

The Reagan administration's emphasis on research and development, as well as certain "high-tech" aspects of space research, saw an uneven concentration of the benefits of Pentagon monies throughout the United States. A study of 435 congressional districts indicated that 225 congressional districts actually had a net loss in terms of the ratio of taxes paid to Pentagon dollars invested in the local economy. However, Virginia and California benefited the most from the distribution of defense spending in the mid-1980s.[16] By the end of the decade, Pentagon spending was still concentrated in California ($90 billion), but there was also heavy spending in New York ($40.7 billion), Texas ($34.8 billion), Virginia ($25 billion), Florida ($22.9 billion), and Pennsylvania ($20.2 billion). Ohio, Massachusetts, Illinois, and New Jersey followed with between $19.7 billion and $15.5 billion in defense purchases.[17]

Even though some states might receive more defense revenue than others, prime contractors dispersed lucrative subcontracts to as many strategic locales, in terms of congressional votes, as possible. For instance, visitors to the headquarters of the Rockwell Corporation, makers of the controversial B-1 bomber, recall a map on the wall with lines radiating to virtually every congressional district in the country. The map of Rockwell subcontractors was distributed to the appropriations committees during the critical debates in 1977.[18]

Thus, an "iron triangle" was constituted of the arms contractors, the Pentagon, and Congress, who were linked by profit and patriotism with a constituency of engineers, consultants, industrialists, workers, and members of Congress who pushed for weapons and the money to buy, develop, build, and rationalize them. Clearly, the delegations from congressional districts in which the arms industry was heavily represented were careful patrons of defense spending, with little incentive to question the overall mix of spending or the kind of defense programs funded if they were of benefit locally.

Defense companies would help generate support for systems by directly entering the wider political process. A typical PAC of a defense contractor might "request" that each employee contribute "voluntarily" about .5 percent to 1 percent of their annual salary. At a minimum, the money would buy a hearing for a position; and the airing of a weapons system's virtues can make a difference on key votes. On a controversial vote for extra funds for the MX missile in 1985, for example, 85 percent of the House members whose districts received more than fifteen thousand dollars from defense industry PACs voted for the new missile. In the Senate, 93 percent of members whose states received more than thirty thousand dollars from military contractors voted for the MX. It is not surprising that the country's largest defense contractors doubled their political donations as their own profits boomed in the Reagan years.[19]

The End of the Cold War: The End of Symbiosis?

The Reagan administration did not purchase a different military force than that envisaged by President Carter, but the defense sector was funded more lavishly. The scale of the U.S. military enterprise, with 37,000 prime contractors, 100,000 subcontractors, 3 million persons employed in industry, 1 million civilian employees in the Defense Department, and 2 million in the uniformed services, made it the world's largest enterprise under one "management." By the mid-1980s, for every hundred dollars of civilian capital formation created, more than thirty-three dollars was dedicated to military plant and equipment. The overall ratio of military use of capital to civilian use was 87 to 100.[20] A year after the collapse of the Soviet Union, in late 1992, military research still consumed more than 70 percent of total U.S. outlays for research and development (including private and university-based research).[21]

The Reagan defense spending boom peaked between 1985 and 1987. New defense outlays for procurement climbed to over $125 billion in 1985 and then began to drop off to $100 billion in 1987. Defense outlays continued to decline after 1987, although pipeline monies tended to slow the downturn. By 1992, however, total spending for procurement had dropped from $200 billion in 1987 to just over $160 billion, with projections of no more than $133 billion in 1997.[22]

Defense industry employment paralleled the rise and decline in procurement, reaching a peak of 1.44 million in 1987 and dropping slowly thereafter to about 1.4 million in 1990. By mid-1990 a seeming free-fall in defense industry employment set in. Over the next eighteen months, employment dropped to 1.19 million—a rate of more than 100,000 a year. Defense sector displacement accounted for some 15 percent of the 1.47 million jobs lost during the national recession that began in 1990. General Dynamics, consistently one of the top five defense contractors, cut its work force by 17,000, or nearly 20 percent, during the drop. Simultaneously, the armed forces cut 160,000 people during the 1990–92 period.[23] Similar cuts were announced at Boeing, General Electric, IBM, McDonnell Douglas, and other defense-related firms. Paralleling the cuts in procurement, military installations began to be scheduled for shutdowns.[24]

The causes of the dramatic decline in the defense industry's fortunes are not difficult to discern. The cold war ended. The death of the Warsaw Pact, followed by treaties calling for huge reductions in the size of strategic forces, drained the rationale for the military buildup initiated by the Reagan administration. George Bush's Defense Department fought a rearguard action against even more dramatic cuts, but the evaporation of the cold war left accounting shortfalls exposed for the reduced, post–cold war "base force" of 1.6 million. In fact, the $260 billion budgeted for the 1993 base force each year to 1997 was nearly $200 billion light according to CBO and DOD estimates. There were three alternatives for the Clinton administration: it could add $50 billion annually to the budget deficit, already known to run around $300 billion a year; it could raise taxes; or it could reduce the defense structure by more than the Cheney-Bush-Powell base force. And indeed it was likely, as politics works in incremental ways in any case, that all three options would be combined in some way.[25]

In addition to dwindling monies for defense, the contractual arrangements in force during the buildup now redounded against the defense contractors. In the past, defense companies operated on contracts that allowed them to recoup whatever cost overruns they might encounter during the development phase. In an attempt to control costs during the booming 1980s, DOD obligated contractors to produce new weapons systems at a predetermined price. Many contractors, however, regarded the fixed-price approach as unrealistic in that it assumed accurate forecasts of costs as well as evolving, new, and/or untested technologies.

The operating assumption in much of the weapons acquisition process held that the needs for weapons would override cost concerns. Further, some contractors seemed to assume that unrealistically low bids would ultimately be redeemed at a higher price and that DOD would eventually bail them out when the inevitable development difficulties—and escalating costs—emerged. By the early 1990s, however, the expectation of perpetual DOD support brutally met the new fiscal and international reality.

In January 1991, for instance, Secretary of Defense Dick Cheney announced that the Pentagon was canceling its contract with General Dynamics and McDonnell Douglas for a new Navy stealth aircraft, the A-12, heralded as the new attack aircraft of the 1990s and beyond. In 1988 contractors had won a $4.8 billion contract for the aircraft. The Navy had planned to purchase 620 of the radar-evading planes to replace the three-decade-old A-6. McDonnell Douglas and General Dynamics expected to make at least $57 billion off the contract. By late 1990, however, the project was already overbudget, and the first aircraft had not yet been produced.[26]

Nonetheless, most in the military and the defense industry assumed that the old, unwritten rules were still in effect. If the military and the industry did not fully appreciate the new realities, the A-12 cancellation tended to concentrate collective minds. As one Wall Street analyst observed, "The mentality ingrained over the last 30 years where you could sign up to do things at prices you knew were unrealistic . . . is over."[27] The new realities began to sink in. A senior vice president at General Dynamics observed, "We don't see the traditional rebound, and we are preparing ourselves on that basis."[28] Defense analyst Gordon Adams, watching the shocks pulsing through the industry, noted, "The downsizing is not cyclical. You're looking at an industry whose size and shape is fundamentally changing."[29]

The case of a new transport aircraft, McDonnell Douglas's C-17, suggested that the old politics of defense procurement retained some clout. The Boston-based Defense Alternative Project charged that the Pentagon's studies of global mobility requirements inflated the need for the aircraft.[30] The C-17 had been beset by problems with its landing gear, flaps, and wings and was hundreds of millions of dollars over-budget. Defense Secretary Les Aspin defended the need for the program but confessed, "We can't seem to get the plane to work."[31] But McDonnell Douglas derived over 20 percent of its revenue from the C-17 project, and the plane employed over seven thousand people in Long Beach, California, a community already reeling under defense cutbacks. McDonnell Douglas had not found success in head-to-head competition in the civilian market with Boeing and the European "Airbus" consortia, but the company was a critical supplier of such systems as the Navy's F-18. Pentagon Inspector General Derek Vander charged that DOD, in order to keep McDonnell Douglas afloat, had funneled $500 million over and above the $4 billion the government had already paid to the company.[32] Nonetheless, the C-17 will retain its funding at least through 1994. It was an indication that even when few would deny the needs for further defense economies, each decision was tough, and some were too hard to take in one swallow.

Nonetheless, some defense contractors clearly faced extinction, or at best descent from the ranks of major defense contractors to the status of subcontractor.[33] Other defense contractors pursued some combination of four strategies for dealing with the post–cold war world, namely, lobbying, conversion, enhanced exports, and corporate resizing.

In the first instance, some contractors turned to an aggressive lobbying of Congress to try and sustain whatever pieces of government business they might have.[34] Thus, during 1991 and 1992 congressional delegations were subjected to enormous pressure to preserve vestiges of the C-17, the B-2 bomber program, and the Navy's Seawolf submarine program and thereby preserve some piece of the rapidly declining Electric Boat Company labor force in Connecticut. Similarly, the New York congressional delegation, along with Grumman, promoted upgrades of the F-14 and the A-6 in the wake of the A-12 cancellation.[35] This approach was, however, clearly a short-term response.

The path of converting defense industries to civilian production was a second course widely discussed during the early months of the post–cold war period. Hughes Aircraft Company, a subsidiary of General Motors, attempted to move into civilian lines of business by contributing to GM's attempt to develop a car powered by electricity. Its success was limited,[36] and previous attempts by other companies to enter civilian markets had not been promising either. During the 1970s, for example, Grumman had lost $300 million in an attempt to diversify into bus production, and Rockwell had failed in an effort to produce television sets.[37]

The reasons for the limited success of conversion efforts seemed to lie in the peculiar context in which defense companies operate. First, defense contractors, because they do not operate in a truly competitive environment, have never had to concern themselves seriously with costs. Pentagon demand for weapons technology is intense. As a consequence, much defense engineering never develops the cost controls that are essential in a normal world of commercial competition. Second, defense engineering requirements are quite different from requirements in commercial engineering. Part of the reason a coffeepot might cost the Air Force six hundred dollars is that it is required to withstand stresses discounted in the commercial market.

Third, the specifications for government procurement and engineering are more detailed than most industry would require or tolerate. An otherwise ordinary screw might be described in a fourteen-page procurement document. The detail is required partly because government procurement is more administratively layered than procurement in most other industries is and partly because overspecification is the perverse consequence of otherwise reasonable efforts to protect the taxpayers. Fourth, because the consumption surges that weapons and matériel undergo in combat vary significantly from the demand for products in peacetime, stockpiles accrue in anticipation of need but are sometimes rarely used.

Finally, notwithstanding the pyrotechnic technological displays during the Gulf War of antimissile systems and precision-guided cruise missiles, much of the technology developed by defense contractors is in fact less sophisticated than commercial technology. Most of the weapons in the Defense Department's current high-tech arsenal, such as the Patriot and the Tomahawk, are a decade or more old. Garden-variety personal computer technology is often more advanced than that developed and still produced by the defense industry. In fact, the Pentagon continues to support a computer chip manufacturer to produce chips no longer used by the industry simply because they are essential to both the Patriot and the Tomahawk, as well as a number of other systems used in the Gulf War. The chief of the Pentagon's procurement during the Reagan administration noted in 1991: "Defense is not a leader. In many cases it's not even a consumer of the latest technology."[38]

Under these circumstances, most of the defense contractors find themselves pursuing two other strategies in their effort to cope with the post–cold war world: foreign sales and "asset realignment."

The competition for foreign sales, with increased U.S. government support, intensified during the early 1990s.[39] In the years 1982–90, only in 1982 did foreign sales by U.S. arms manufacturers exceed $15 billion. From 1982 to 1987, the peak years of the Reagan buildup, overseas sales declined to just over $5 billion. During 1991, however, sales shot up to almost $25 billion, and in 1992 they exceeded $30 billion. Not surprisingly, the most active companies in these overseas sales were those that were most dramatically affected by the cuts of the early 1990s, McDonnell Douglas and General Dynamics, with almost $16.3 billion and $12.9 billion, respectively, during 1991 and 1992. Raytheon, the prime contractor on the Patriot, had sales of more than $6.1 billion in the same period. McDonnell Douglas estimated that 33 percent of all its sales in 1993 would be foreign, compared with 20 percent in 1992; and General Dynamics estimated that between 1992 and 1997 it would sell seven times as many tanks to Saudi Arabia as to the U.S. Army.[40] As the Clinton administration began to face the increasing tempo of disemployment in the defense sector, there was increased pressure to transfer the promised $20 billion scheduled for defense conversion to the guarantee of overseas sales for ailing defense contractors and frightened defense workers.[41]

By the end of the Bush administration, however, it seemed that the most likely long-term strategy for dealing with the end of the cold war would be a major restructuring of the defense industry by means of internal consolidation, acquisition, and the selling off of significant portions of businesses by major contractors. During 1992 McDonnell Douglas, previously one of the most internally diverse of the defense companies, underwent a major restructuring of its operations. In November 1992 General Electric sold its Aerospace and Government Services divisions to Martin Marietta for $3 billion in the largest deal of its kind. In December 1992 FMC and Harsco, both manufacturers of military vehicles, announced that they had reached tentative agreement to enter into a joint venture under FMC direction with possible sales of more than $1.2 billion in 1993. Also in December 1992 a possibly even more far-reaching deal was announced: General Dynamics was selling its entire aircraft division to Lockheed for $1.53 billion. Earlier, General Dynamics had sold another $1.3 billion of its business, including its missile division, to Cessna, prompting some speculation that General Dynamics was contemplating leaving the defense business altogether.[42]

A Wall Street consulting firm, Booz, Allen and Hamilton, speculated in early 1993 that 75–80 percent of the existing weapons contractors could be gone by the end of the 1990s.[43] One analyst concluded that "defense contractors have three options: becoming the very best in a specific area through acquisitions, selling off their overcapacity or simply shutting down. . . . This will not pass. It is a permanent resizing and reshaping of the industry."[44] Ironically, therefore, much of the defense industry finds itself in a situation not unlike that of the cold war foe it helped vanquish. Soviet industry, operating in a command economy, found itself uncompetitive because of its obsolete technology and unfamiliarity with the rigors of the market. A General Dynamics vice president issued the grim but prescient forecast that "for military contractors, it will be rag tag, rough and tumble, and dog-eat-dog. It's going to be a bloodletting and the guy with the most blood will win."[45]

"PRIVATE GOVERNMENTS" AND U.S. FOREIGN POLICY: THE MULTINATIONAL CORPORATIONS

In the last few decades, students of international relations have focused much attention on a third category of private power, namely, American multinational corporations (MNCs). MNCs are not a new phenomenon; large corporations' operating and owning assets in several countries is very nearly as old as the republic.[46] But during the later cold war period their numbers and size increased, and their presence provoked an often heated debate.

The size and resources commanded by the largest MNCs outstrip the wealth of all but the largest nation-states. The annual sales for the largest MNC in 1990, General Motors, exceeded the 1989 gross national product of all but twenty-one countries. Ten American MNCs—GM, Exxon, Ford, IBM, Mobil, GE, Philip Morris, Texaco, Du Pont, and Chevron— had sales larger than the GNP of any sub-Saharan African state except South Africa. Indeed, among the hundred largest nation-states and MNCs, ranked according to their GNP and gross economic product, there are fourteen American MNCs and thirty European and Japanese MNCs.[47] Raymond Vernon, a pathbreaking student of the MNC, has observed that "they sprawl across national boundaries, linking the assets and activities of different national jurisdictions with an intimacy that seems to threaten the concept of the nation as an integral unit. Accordingly, they stir uneasy questions."[48] Do MNCs undercut the ability of nation-states to meet the needs of their citizens? Are American MNCs extensions of U.S. power? Do MNCs represent independent and near autonomous forces?[49] Or are MNCs ultimately vulnerable entities with little overall effect on the policies of either the host state or the foreign nation in which they do business?

MNCs and the Liberal World Order

Most recent empirical analyses support the view that American MNCs exercise a measure of autonomy but are nonetheless constrained by U.S. policy interests, prevailing international conditions, and, increasingly, the host countries in which they operate.[50] In other words, the MNCs are not unlike other actors in contemporary politics. MNCs possess interests and a demonstrable capacity to act in pursuit of those interests. But like even the largest of nations, MNCs are constrained by the environment in which they operate.

American MNCs are different from national units, of course, since their corporate officers and administrators remain overwhelmingly American and reflect prevailing American attitudes toward international relations.[51] Even so, the loyalties of American-held MNCs often are mixed. Their interests sometimes run parallel to those of their national origins; in other instances, the interests of the state where MNCs are headquartered and the interests of the MNC itself are at odds.

The nature of many American MNCs' dependence on the United States is not obscure. U.S. foreign policy after World War II centered on the creation and then maintenance of a world political and economic order that would be compatible with the kinds of international economic interests pursued by MNCs. The Bretton Woods system of financial institutions and the Marshall Plan were conceived as means of fostering an open political economy in which free trade, direct foreign investment, and economic development would flourish. Indeed, the entire postwar economic structure was conceived as an integral part of the broader concept of containment of Soviet power. The prosperity assumed to result from such an international economy would, it was hoped, remove the chaotic social and economic conditions upon which Communist subversion fed. When the economic policies seemed inadequate to the Soviet threat, they were relegated to the realm of "low politics." But the assumptions and institutions of an open world economy remain largely in place to this day.[52]

By the 1960s both the strategic and the economic order were sufficiently well established that American-held MNCs could prosper. The establishment of a more open monetary system in Europe after 1958, combined with the prospect of higher tariff barriers imposed by the European Common Market, made direct investment in Europe both necessary (to vault the tariff wall) and easier (full convertibility of European currencies and the emergence of a transnational banking establishment made business operations within Europe more attractive). But once in place, the American-held MNCs pursued their respective interests with mixed effects on U.S. foreign policy.

An important instance of American-held MNCs pursuing their own interests occurred during the chaotic monetary crises of the early 1970s. Predictably, corporate financial managers sought to protect the financial positions of their corporations during the period of most intense monetary instability, late 1972 and especially early 1973. Thus, MNCs sought to increase their holdings of the strongest currencies—German marks, Swiss francs, Dutch guilders, and Japanese yen—and unload the weakest currencies, such as the dollar. The effect of aggregate action of MNC currency traders, who only wished to protect the value of their currencies on hand and the worth of the future of sales if they were denominated in a stronger currency, was to drive the value of the dollar down vis-à-vis other currencies.

The hedging of MNCs' financial position, encouraged by some elements in the Nixon administration, contributed to a short-term strengthening of the trade position of the United States (U.S. goods grew cheaper overseas as the dollar fell), but the overall stresses introduced into the international monetary system eventually became unbearable. The Nixon administration's Treasury Department was given the excuse it had been seeking to abandon the Bretton Woods guarantee to always redeem dollars for a fixed amount of gold if dollars were presented to the Treasury by foreigners. The short-term effect of this was a period of instability and inflation. Traders abandoned all paper currencies for commodities; trades were denominated in rising prices of lettuce, oil, and minerals. Eventually, however, the inflation of the 1970s and early 1980s worked its way out of the world economy, and a more flexible, more responsive international monetary system was established.[53]

This shift to a more flexible international monetary system is now widely regarded as a good thing. The MNCs' pursuit of self-interest, it can be argued, worked to the benefit of all, including the United States. Moreover, there is little evidence that the MNCs engaged in excessive speculation or profiteering during the early 1970s. Indeed, in late 1971 U.S.-based MNCs added their weight to the pressure applied by the Europeans to resolve the crisis in order to save the North Atlantic alliance.[54]

The attempt by the Reagan administration to halt the sale of gas pipeline equipment to the Soviet Union by American and European MNCs in the summer of 1982 underscored yet again the complex relationship between MNCs and American foreign policy. In this case, the Reagan administration ordered the French subsidiary of Dresser Industries, an American oil and gas technology firm, as well as foreign companies in England, Germany, and Italy that had either purchased equipment from or had constructed equipment under franchise from another American firm (General Electric), not to sell pipeline technology to the Soviet Union under the terms of contracts already negotiated by several European governments and signed with the Soviets. The French government, however, ordered the Dresser subsidiary in France—a company incorporated under the laws of France—to sell the equipment or risk nationalization by the French government. The American parent firm ordered its French subsidiary to honor its contract with the Soviet Union and follow the French government's orders. Meanwhile, in U.S. federal court, Dresser challenged the legality of the U.S. government's attempt to extend American law to MNC subsidiaries operating abroad. The United States, in turn, imposed sanctions on Dresser, ordering it not to sell any technology or information to their French subsidiary. The United States threatened similar sanctions against the other European firms, leading to angry denunciations from European leaders. The legality of the American government's actions is uncertain, since the threatened sanctions never got to court in either England, France, or the United States.

It is hard to see what profit there would have been for the Reagan administration to press the case. For the balance of precedent favored Dresser's and the Europeans' argument that the reach of American law and commercial control does not extend into the legal and commercial domain of another state. Indeed, when the shoe was on the other foot, the United States Supreme Court held (in *Avaligno v. Sumitomo Shoji America,* in an affirmative-action case) that U.S. subsidiaries of foreign firms must abide by American law and cannot defer to the law of the place where they are headquartered or owned.

The French, British, German, and Italian governments regarded Reagan's actions on pipeline contracts as an intrusion into their commercial and national interests. The European allies ordered their own companies and American subsidiaries to ignore Reagan's demands. By the late summer of 1982 the Reagan administration seemed to grasp that the cohesion of the NATO alliance was at stake and began to seek a diplomatic resolution of the impasse. By the end of 1982 the administration bowed to European pressure and dropped the matter. Although the political issues faded, the legal questions concerning the status of the MNCs and American control remained unresolved.[55]

MNC Activities in the Third World

The presence of American MNCs engaged in extractive industries and the export of agricultural commodities throughout the Third World has long been a symbol of what many would characterize as the exploitative essence of the American world order. Especially in the 1970s, it was a common view that the MNCs operated as agents of American interests, imposing a political and economic order that was insensitive to the host countries' aspirations. The image was seemingly confirmed by the revelations of the machinations of the International Telephone and Telegraph Company in Chile in the early 1970s, either independently or in concert with the United States, to bring down a constitutionally elected government of that country.[56]

American MNCs proved unable to serve American interests during the oil crisis of 1973 and 1974 and subsequent OPEC price increases. In fact, even before the 1973 crisis the oil companies offered only limited resistance to OPEC's insistence that they join the producing companies on the price escalator. Since the prices charged by the producing countries to the oil companies could be passed on to consumers in the industrialized and developing countries, the oil companies apparently could not lose. In time, of course, the companies would have their controlling interests in the production of the oil taken over by the producing countries. Nonetheless, to the extent they have maintained their distribution and marketing systems, as well as their refining capacity, high profit levels have still attended high prices.

The MNC-OPEC relationship, rather than the conventional neoimperialist relationship, is likely to be the model for future MNC operations in the Third World.[57] As Third World countries become more sophisticated in their response to the MNC presence, and as MNCs seek to protect their base of operations, more often than not they seem accommodating to host-country demands. There need not be, for example, any inherent incompatibility between host-country desires to export goods and services to the rest of the world, on the one hand, and the MNC desire to take advantage of lower labor costs and weaker regulatory regimes abroad (e.g., environmental-impact regulation), on the other. The negative effects of such an arrangement are likely to show up in industrialized countries that become the object of these lower-cost imports and suffer the political and economic disruptions from any labor displacement. In the longer run, of course, environmental degradation hurts everyone. And precisely these concerns became one of the complaints against the North American Free Trade Agreement negotiated by the Bush administration in the late 1980s and early 1990s.

Mixed Allegiances?

In the broadest sense, the MNC can act as a private government, with interests of its own and the resources to pursue them. On the other hand, its very existence and its ability to operate flexibly depends upon an order largely created and sustained by a clear and largely unchallenged American economic and military hegemony. As the cold war recedes, the interests the MNCs pursue may diverge more frequently from those of the United States.[58]

Mixed MNC allegiances sometimes produce ironic situations. Thus, during the early days of the Clinton administration the Commerce Department ruled that an American company—Smith Corona—was unfairly dumping underpriced electric typewriters manufactured by its Singapore subsidiary on the American market. Ironically, the charges were brought against Smith Corona by Brother USA, a Japanese company producing typewriters in the United States. Compounding the complexity of the case was the fact that a British Company, Hanson PLC, owned more than 47 percent of Smith Corona, and Smith Corona was in the process of closing its one remaining production facility in the United States and moving it to Mexico, as a result of which 775 Americans would lose their jobs.[59] President Clinton's labor secretary, Robert Reich, writing in the *Harvard Business Review,* summarized the situation aptly: "In the global enterprise the bonds between company and country . . . are rapidly eroding. Today corporate decisions about production and location are driven by the dictates of global competition, not by national allegiance."[60]

PRIVATE POWER AND THE POLICY PROCESS

A phenomenon with as many dimensions as private power has does not lend itself to simple conclusions. As with much else in the American policy-making system, judgments concerning the relationships between private and public power are frequently colored by judgments concerning the policy outcomes. Thus, MNCs could become a cause for alarm when they pursued their interests in conjunction with OPEC in 1973–74 or when they close American manufacturing facilities in pursuit of lower labor costs and a less demanding regulatory environment in the Third World. But some MNCs, in this case multinational financial institutions, have been applauded for their capacity and willingness to manage the massive financial consequences of the oil crisis. In some cases, MNCs are the leading corporate citizens. MNCs in many underdeveloped countries pay higher wages, pay taxes with more regularity than domestic firms, and heed higher environmental standards.

Where one stands on special interests frequently depends on with whom one sits. Not infrequently policy activists roundly condemn special-interest groups when they block comprehensive energy legislation or pursue higher defense spending, but the same behavior is acceptable when one's own interests are represented by groups that, for example, favor the Panama Canal treaties or the Vietnam War or support tough international environmental regulation.[61]

Nonetheless, those who have ventured an assessment of the effects of the exercise of private power during the last decade have tended to draw essentially negative conclusions. The most serious problem resulting from private power is related not so much to the policy outcomes as to the effect that the upsurge in private activity has had on democracy, governance, and, therefore, American foreign policy.

The exercise of private power has been seen as exacerbating the inherent fragmentation of the American policy-making process as well as increasing the claims on finite resources.[62] First, the already fragmented process of constitutionally decreed shared power takes on an added complexity when it contends with well-funded private interests. Second, the existence of private concentrations of power constrains policy making. Third, large-scale private power recalls the problems of accountability within government. Institutional complexity and shared power among the three branches were designed into the policy-making process to ensure a measure of accountability within government. After all, multiple centers of public policy making provide multiple points of access for interest groups. But when the process moves into a gray netherworld between, for example, Congress, the Pentagon, and the industrial centers that provide the material wherewithal to meet security needs, accountability becomes diffuse and uncertain. Similarly, when MNCs move beyond the control of national authorities, democratic policy making itself seems more problematic.[63]

Private power and special access, if abused, call into question the basic functions of representational institutions. But one should not be surprised when concentrations of power are brought to bear on public policy making. Indeed, the American constitutional design and political culture encourage private economic power. The tension between the right of groups to find their own voice and the smooth functioning of a democracy based, ultimately, on popular sovereignty was compounded by the cold war. The military-industrial complex provided a strong defense, but as President Eisenhower warned, this conjunction of industry and government posed serious questions.

The international system has been transformed with the end of the cold war. A smaller U.S. military establishment is now widely assumed. But since considerable uncertainty remains about the stability of the international system,[64] few deny the necessity of maintaining some form of arms production and acquisition process. Well before the collapse of the Soviet power, it was suggested that the ostensibly private defense sector simply be nationalized in recognition of the fact that defense suppliers can no longer conform to traditional conceptions of private enterprise.[65]

Such a step would not be without precedent. In the United States, much of the railroad system is nationalized; and overseas, in a great many countries the entire defense sector is configured solely or mostly as national corporations. It is hard to imagine that a nationalized defense sector would necessarily be less efficient or more dependent on public financing than is currently the case, but proposals for nationalization have little popular support. Indeed, as the Pentagon tries to shore up more ailing companies, an increasing amount of defense work that was done "in house" is now being contracted to private firms starved for business and in danger of extinction. The operant Washington objective is a husbanding of the defense-industrial base.[66] It is more than a little likely, therefore, that short of an across-the-board crisis even more severe than the retrenchments of the early 1990s, the remaining defense contractors will remain privately owned.

In the early years of the cold war, an expanding network of private economic transactions was regarded as an essential element of international order. Since this network of transactions was managed by privately held multinational firms, they naturally developed interests and capabilities of their own. In this respect, some MNCs perform as if they were "private governments" with their own interests. On the other hand, MNCs have relied on an advantageous political and economic order established by American power. Now that these private interests possess a kind of autonomy, they can constrain American foreign policy. And now that American power is not what it was, the autonomy of MNCs may well expand.

CHAPTER 13

Foreign Policy Making
and American Democracy

ASSESSMENTS OF THE American approach to international affairs frequently echo Tocqueville's conclusion that "it is especially in the conduct of their foreign relations that democracies appear to me decidedly inferior to other governments." He continued:

Foreign politics demand scarcely any of those qualities which are peculiar to a democracy; they require, on the contrary, the perfect use of almost all those in which it is deficient. . . . a democracy can only with great difficulty regulate the details of an important undertaking, persevere in a fixed design, and work out its execution in spite of serious obstacles. It cannot combine its measures with secrecy or await their consequences with patience.[1]

There is ample evidence that policymakers have been as much troubled by these domestic limits as by foreign conditions.

In this book we have surveyed the many elements of this domestic framework. Here we shall review the main themes and offer some closing observations concerning the foreign policy process at the end of the cold war era.[2]

CONSTRAINTS AND LIMITS

No matter what the concerns of the day, the limits imposed by the Constitution and the sheer size and complexity of the U.S. government have caused policymakers to yearn for an easier row to hoe. The fragmented policy processes and the unpredictable character of a democratic society have been considered liabilities in the conduct of foreign policy. The implication has been that the American system is inefficient, even dangerous, for a policy-making system of fragmented and diffused power frustrates a policy that has sought to impose order upon the international system. Accordingly, American institutions and processes need "protection" from the "excesses of democracy." Over the course of the cold war the executive strove to centralize and "rationalize" policy-making institutions and processes to enhance flexibility and responsiveness in dealing with a dangerous and complex international environment.

Constitutional Constraints

Not the least of the obstacles to a transformation is the American constitutional framework. The Constitution militates against coherence and efficiency. From the very outset, an unresolved tension has resided at the nexus of the constitutionally prescribed foreign- and national-security-policy-making authority.

On the one hand, there is Alexander Hamilton's assertion that

the authorities essential to the common defense . . . ought to exist without limitation, *because it is impossible to foresee or to define the extent and variety of national exigencies, and the correspondent extent and variety of the means which may be necessary to satisfy them.* The circumstances that endanger the safety of nations are infinite, and for this reason no constitutional shackles can wisely be imposed on the power to which the care of it is committed. The power ought to be coextensive with all the possible combinations of such circumstances; and ought to be under the direction of the same councils which are appointed to preside over the common defense.[3]

In contrast, however, there was the statement of James Madison:

In time of *actual* war, great discretionary powers are constantly given to the Executive magistrate. Constant apprehension of war, has the same tendency to render the head too large for the body. A standing military force, with an overgrown Executive will not long be safe companions to liberty. The means of defense against foreign danger, have been always the instruments of tyranny at home.[4]

Madison's fear of tyranny proved the stronger force in the construction of the constitutional design. While Hamilton's concern that the exigencies of the common defense demanded centralization of authority in the national government was accepted, that authority was itself subject to the now familiar Madisonian approach of "checks and balances."[5]

Thus decisional power was fragmented, and processes were established that would, it was hoped, at least minimize the possibility of preeminent power accruing to any single individual or institution, though Madison, perhaps the most influential drafter of the Constitution, believed that the legislature would be somewhat stronger than the executive.[6] But Hamilton's arguments were not without force. A single commander in chief was given treaty-making and other diplomatic functions and operational command of the military function, but the power to declare war, to raise and maintain armies and navies, and to ratify treaties was vested in Congress.

The pattern of overlapping, shared, and even conflicting powers was deemed a necessary price to pay to protect transcendent republican values. This position was reaffirmed by the twentieth-century jurist Justice Louis Brandeis: "The doctrine of separation of powers was adopted by the Convention of 1787, not to promote efficiency but to preclude the exercise of arbitrary power. The purpose was, not to avoid friction, but, by means of the inevitable friction incident to the distribution of the governmental powers among three departments, to save the people from autocracy."[7]

But if the problems presented by the original constitutional design could be justified in terms of transcendent principles of political liberty, subsequent developments seemed to demand structural modifications. A commitment to the course of global activism (and the ever-present specter of nuclear war) led to a modification of constitutional interpretation. By the 1960s there was a transformed executive-legislative relationship.

Cold War Permutations and Pathologies

Under the original constitutional design, substantial foreign policy power was given to Congress, with the expectation that legislators would provide judgments that would include considerations larger than an individual member's political survival. Unfortunately, critics assert, the reality has frequently contradicted constitutional theory. Congress, it is argued, is preoccupied with the press of reelection and hampered by a cumbersome internal structure. Nowhere, therefore, was Tocqueville's critique of democracy more appropriate than with respect to Congress. It seemed that the need for a global policy required an energetic executive. Thus, throughout the 1950s and 1960s Congress granted authority to a succession of presidents. As the cold war developed, Hamiltonian "axioms as simple as they are universal" were called to mind: "the *means* ought to be proportioned to the *end;* the persons from whose agency the attainment of any *end* is expected ought to possess the *means* by which it is attained."[8]

But the circumstances of the late 1960s and early 1970s underscored the wisdom of the Constitution's constraints. Presidents Johnson and Nixon resorted to increasingly bald assertions of presidential prerogative. By the 1970s it had become commonplace to speak of an "imperial presidency," with powers greater than those of history's great autocrats. As the excesses of the Nixon presidency became more manifest and culminated in the Watergate scandal, more attention was concentrated on the swollen institution and powers of the office. The resort to secrecy, control of information, and interference with the legitimate exercise of American rights was seen as a function of a national security bureaucracy that was out of control. By the mid- and late 1970s many had begun openly to ask whether the kind of presidency seemingly demanded by American foreign policy was compatible with traditional American freedoms.

As the dangers and even pathologies of the cold war presidency became manifest, Madisonian fears seemed more compelling. There was a renascence of congressional vigor as a consequence of widespread opposition to the Vietnam War. Congress's revivification was also a response to the claims of presidential power advanced by the Johnson and especially the Nixon administrations. Accordingly, interest in "congressional government" surged. Congressional reaction to the war and the Nixon administration contributed to significant reforms within Congress and the assertion of new powers, such as the legislative veto.

But Congress remained an essentially reactive participant. Policy initiative could be exercised by Congress only episodically. Thus, by the end of the Reagan-Bush presidencies in the early 1990s, the dominant concern was persistent deadlock in the executive-legislative relationship. To the extent that Congress had become more effective as a check on presidential power, the system bogged down. It was an ironic denouement to the victorious close of the cold war: two-hundred-year-old constitutional constants retained their force. Institutions forged in the heat of a forty-five-year struggle never achieved the desired flexibility, and once the threat was gone, the resultant policy process evinced little dexterity in coming to grips with radically new challenges.

After the Cold War

For the small isolated nation that fretted more about freedom than about external attack, some of the chafe of institutional deadlock was tolerable. A world role was explicitly abjured by President Washington in his farewell address, in part out of a fear of what such a role would do to the constitutional design and the values it was to protect.[9] For the framers, structural tension and policy-making complexity were necessary, even elegant, accoutrements of a republican government. But for nearly the entire course of the cold war, the makers of American foreign policy found fractured authority to be a nearly intractable impediment to effective policy.

Does the end of the cold war relieve the pressure of foreign involvement on American constitutionalism? If we have lived in an era of unremitting crisis leading to an imperial presidency, does the new world order promise surcease, thereby allowing a "normal" foreign policy process? Part of the answer depends on one's conception of the kind of world we are moving into.

There has been too much speculation concerning the future of the international system to review in any detail here.[10] But let us note some of the broad lines of argument concerning the American system. One line of analysis suggests that the post–cold war world will be one in which strategic military forces can be reduced significantly because of the diminished threat of nuclear war. But what does this imply in terms of policy processes? Clearly, if true, this projection of a vastly diminished military requirement undercuts one of the strongest rationales for the imperial presidency and the national security state. No longer, it would seem, is there much prospect that the United States could be at war "within thirty minutes." The argument that the president must be given extraordinary latitude in the making of national security policy at least to some extent dwindles in proportion to the threat of nuclear Armageddon.

Nonetheless, after the cold war, first President Bush and then spokespersons of the Clinton administration continued to argue that "the world remains a very dangerous place" and therefore presidential national security prerogatives must be preserved. In this regard, one should recall that perhaps the most extraordinary of claims made for absolute presidential prerogatives concerning the commitment of U.S. forces to combat was made during the debate on the Persian Gulf War, a conflict that had nothing to do with the cold war. Moreover, the argument has been made that the Gulf War may be archetypical of the kinds of conflicts in which the United States will find itself engaged in the future. Therefore, it is contended, U.S. military forces must be sized and deployed so as to preserve and maximize flexibility. One suspects that "flexibility" also extends to command and control of the forces; and clearly, the president and the executive branch are by definition the pinnacle of that command and control system. Insofar as this claim is credible, then the persistent debate concerning presidential versus congressional prerogatives in questions of war and peace will not diminish in the post–cold war international system.

But there is another projection of what the future might hold with respect to the use of military force. The horrific Balkan conflict of the early 1990s, rather than the Gulf War, may prove to be the more likely model of future conflict, that is, civil conflicts or internationalized civil conflicts leading to some form of external military intervention.[11] Under these circumstances, the use of U.S. forces will be more likely as part of international or regional peacekeeping and peacemaking forces. Such a future may not carry with it the threat of instantaneous incineration, the end of history, or the draining demands of extended deterrence of the Soviet Union, but it exerts its own, more subtle but no less demanding pressure on American policy-making institutions.

If the United States organizes and sponsors coalitional military intervention, it retains much of the initiative, but questions such as those raised by the Gulf War concerning the necessity of congressional approval for intervention remain. If the United States participates as a member of an international force under international instead of U.S. command, other questions emerge: How does Congress or the president "control" the commitment of U.S. forces serving as a standing contingent to an international military arrangement? What kind of "control" do these international institutions retain once forces are committed and casualties are taken? Who pays what share when the financial-support bills exceed initial estimates?

The security dimensions of the post–cold war world imply, in short, continued problems for American foreign policy making whether one conceives of this new world as involving a continuation of U.S. unilateralism in lower-intensity conflict or one conceives of the United States as becoming more deeply involved in truly internationalized uses of force.

Yet another vision of the "new world order" suggests that the resort to military force will recede and international and foreign affairs will become more concerned with political-economic, trade, environmental, and even social issues, for example, immigration. Whatever the issue domain, the quality of these external relations will run the gamut from conflict to cooperation. In any case, there will be problems for American foreign policy making both with respect to executive-legislative relations and with respect to fragmented governance.

Bureaucratic Constraints

Constitutional constraints have been seen as onerous because the constitutional machinery has been called to serve interests beyond anything imagined in the eighteenth century. But there are other institutional bottlenecks present in the American system. The implementation of containment eventually required tens of thousands of people organized around programs designed to mobilize the money, people, information, and technology necessary for the establishment and maintenance of world order. A large national security establishment's very size and diversity have come to be viewed as constraints as important as the constitutional structure itself.

The fragmentation of a now enormous foreign policy establishment is therefore a legitimate source of concern, for it pushes the constitutionally mandated fragmentation of the American government to a point where it is fair to ask whether such a complex bureaucratic milieu may not undermine the very national interests these bureaucracies purportedly serve. Might the ponderous coordination of these many departments, agencies, and bureaus produce an ultimately inadequate compromise of many departments' interests rather than a foreign policy that serves American interests? Or failing such compromise and coordination, might not so many actors promote such conflicting interests that a result is but a chaotic congeries of foreign policies?

The National Security Act of 1947 anticipated this problem of a growing national security bureaucracy to a certain extent. The NSC was to be a means for coordinating the activities of the various departments and agencies, but by the late 1960s, the NSC and especially the national security adviser had become a power and "a player" in policy. Critics contended that the national security adviser and the NSC staff had become the center of an inordinate and dangerous concentration of power within the White House. Thus, even as the growth of the bureaucracy constituted an excessive and dangerous caricature of the Madisonian fragmentation of power, the attempt to counter administrative disarray produced an excessive and dangerous centralization of power.

Yet, with all the tug and pull of fissiparous institutions and bureaucratic organization, it would still be conceivable to steer events by now customary repertories, even in a new international environment, if the

United States were governed by elite consensus such as that which under-
pinned the early cold war. Elite consensus on the wisdom of containment
and an activist presidency helped amend and meliorate the inherent limitations of "a government of separated institutions sharing power."[12] But
in the wake of Vietnam and Watergate, the elite consensus fractured, and
there were many who questioned, as Samuel Huntington explained it,
"the legitimacy of hierarchy, coercion, discipline, secrecy and deception—
all of which are, in some measure, inescapable attributes of the process of
government."[13] And they all, Huntington might also have concluded,
logically proceed from executive power.

The late 1970s, however, saw a great volte-face in domestic opinion
and in policy circles on the issue of Soviet power and the need for greater
preparedness. By 1980 the new strategic consensus was well formed; and
as Zbigniew Brzezinski pridefully told reporters on the eve of the Reagan
transition, even the cold war was once again "fashionable." The global
vision that was the hallmark of the cold war was always subject to
bureaucratic fragmentation, hence the need for executive control. As
Brzezinski explained it,

Ultimately, the president does need some sort of a coordinating framework or
organ within which a broader vision is generated. This is one reason why, over the
years, a presidential office for national security affairs emerged.

It is not because of the personal talents or peculiarities of individuals who have
held that position. . . . [Rather, the office emerged because of] the logic of
America's engagement in the world and the president's need for a perspective that
integrates the different institutional divisions.[14]

The Reagan administration flirted briefly with reducing the stature
of the security adviser. Even so, the administrative hierarchy that remained was centered in the personal staff of the president, ostensibly
under his direct control. In 1982, after a year of foreign affairs disarray
and bickering rivaling that which developed during the Carter administration, the position of security adviser was once again elevated to
primacy in the coordination of the national security bureaucracy; and it
remained there notwithstanding the disastrous Iran-Contra affair covertly operated out of the office of the national security adviser. The
subsequent bureaucratic harmony of the Bush years differed markedly
from the pattern of the preceding decades. But only the most optimistic
of observers left off wondering whether bureaucratic fragmentation and
struggle were not inevitable and irremediable concomitants of an activ-

ist foreign policy, especially as the end of the cold war removed the one element that served to hold the system together: a clear and self-evident external threat.

The Post–Cold War World: Political Economy and Policy Making

The "new agenda" of international relations will, by the very diversity of elements that it spans, increase the problems of coordination within the U.S. government and congressional-executive relations. Whereas for most of the cold war the NSC and DOD shared de facto primacy, it is less likely that this situation will now obtain. Whether one speaks of trade, the environment, or immigration, multiple-agency involvement is inevitable. Moreover, the U.S. is no better organized to coordinate policy in regard to this new situation now than it was at the end of World War II.

Executive-legislative relations could be, if anything, *more* conflictual than when policy was dominated by political-military affairs. In the cold war period, even in the case of Korea and Vietnam, the president initiated American involvement and escalation, with a consensus concerning the necessity for involvement. A self-evident consensus is not likely with respect to international economic policy. Economic policy strikes different segments of the population with very different consequences and thereby exacerbates domestic conflict. This conflict, in turn, compounds the problems of coherent congressional policy and, therefore, executive-legislative relations.

The financial consequences of budget deficits also seems likely to contribute to both bureaucratic and executive-legislative conflict. In the early months of the post–cold war era, U.S. resource constraints enfeebled the American response to the collapse of Soviet power. Thus, between 1989 and the close of 1992, for example, German assistance to the former Soviet Union was in excess of $50 billion, whereas American assistance from mid-1990 through 1993 was programmed at just under $10 billion.[15] Similarly, the German share of humanitarian support for the former state of Yugoslavia in 1991–92 exceeded that of the United States by $28 million.[16]

What was more important domestically, there was little support for an increased U.S. assistance role. Foreign aid receives less public support than almost any other possible line of U.S. initiative in foreign affairs. During the cold war, this deep resistance to foreign assistance expenditures could be overcome by advertising the Soviet challenge. In a post–cold war world preemptive foreign claims on resources are unlikely to withstand even superficial scrutiny and political attack.

Another line of executive-legislative tension is likely to form around international environmental, social, medical, and immigration problems. The resolution and management of new issues will likely depend on technical agreements and ultimately international regulatory arrangements administered by international bureaucracies in some measure beyond unilateral U.S. control.[17] In sum, there might be a radical redefinition of security and security management.[18]

Obviously, Congress has dealt with analogous problems in domestic politics before, but the approach generally has been for Congress to cede responsibility to the federal bureaucracy in which expertise and resources are lodged. But since the bureaucracies charged with negotiating, managing, and regulating a new post–cold war agenda will be increasingly "internationalized," Congress will find its oversight role even more attenuated. And to the extent that international or transnational bureaucracies assume "control" over policy administration and regulation, the "people" and their elected representatives will be moved yet one step farther away.

Democracy as a Constraint

The American system has developed into a far more democratic system than the original designers of the Constitution foresaw. The electorate has expanded, and so, too, have the number, range, and access of organized interest groups. The complex mass constituency to which policymakers answer is frequently cited as the essence of the problem. As one student of the American political system concluded, "The masses are incompetent in the tasks of government. They have neither the time, intelligence, information, skills, nor knowledge to direct the course of a nation."[19] Furthermore, some claim that Americans are the most ill-informed and unconcerned in foreign policy matters: "Public opinion polls reveal a startling lack of knowledge. . . . it is a near-impossibility for individuals to make intelligent decisions—or even any decisions at all."[20] This combination of an uneven public awareness of foreign affairs and the frequently disruptive nature of the American electoral process contributes to an uneasiness concerning the democratic processes. George Kennan reflected this ambivalence when he lamented that "it is sometimes easier for a strong and authoritative government to shape its external conduct in an enlightened manner . . . than it is for a democratic government locked in the throes of domestic political conflict."[21]

In addition, by the late 1960s there was a veritable boom in the exercise of private power as various groups sought to emulate the success of the labor and civil rights movements. By the 1970s the collapse of the cold war consensus created an even larger space within which small, well-organized groups operated. A highly professional and organized policy-analysis establishment developed outside of, but in intimate contact with, the official policy-making establishment. Moreover, the articulation of demands became increasingly direct and intensely focused on Congress and the presidency. As a result, the traditional intermediary role played by the political parties was in some measure short-circuited by political, economic, social, and environmental activists.

More subtle but nonetheless real is public exposure to numerous alternative views of international reality. The ubiquity of contemporary electronic and print media has effects beyond serving as a ready means for highly mobilized activists to gain a hearing. Moreover, the aggressiveness of the media now makes it more difficult for the government to maintain a consistent public posture. Leaking to the media is virtually pandemic, and the government has reluctantly but ineluctably lost its hold on information. Hence, if a predicate of a policy is stealth, a ubiquitous media can be counted on to subvert support. Under such circumstances, the legitimacy of governmental policy is easily challenged, and with each challenge, authority and policy coherence are placed at risk.

The consequences of this combination of augmented public mobilization and media impact became apparent during the late 1960s and most of the 1970s. First, with respect to Vietnam, government yielded. The government also proved susceptible to similar but smaller tightly focused mobilizations around a host of single issues. But as Huntington argued, leadership's response was ultimately inadequate: "Polarization over issues generated distrust about government, as those who had strong positions on issues became dissatisfied with the ambivalent, compromising policies of government. Political leaders, in effect, alienated more and more people by attempting to please them through time-honored traditional politics of compromise."[22]

By the end of the cold war, therefore, some observers felt that the democratic character of the American system held deep and diverse dangers. A democratic "excess," as Huntington put it, unfurled, and in the process the American political system became a slatternly arena in which contending demands jostled and elbowed in an uninhibited search for advantage. The common purpose necessary to successful foreign policy could not emerge in these circumstances. The failure of Vietnam, the spectacles of Watergate, Iran-Contra, and the seeming inability of government to cushion people from foreign competition undermined the legitimacy and authority of the policy establishment. The upshot was a "zero-sum society" in which no one willingly paid the price of adjustment to America's international position. Furthermore, the fragmented character of the American governmental system and the fractious nature of American society made it extraordinarily difficult to apportion the costs of the burdens that new international circumstances seemed to demand.[23] There was, in short, a "democratic distemper"[24]—the fulfillment of Tocqueville's gloomy prognosis.

A DECIDEDLY INFERIOR FORM?

To the extent that the United States remained at the time of Tocqueville's visit in the early nineteenth century an essentially agrarian nation on the periphery of the world and international relations, his concerns about the prospects for democracy in America were largely theoretical. Now, however, the global entanglements and aspirations of the United States far exceed those of even the greatest of powers of the previous century. At the same time, American democracy is, if anything, more extensive. Thus, Tocqueville's concerns about the ultimate viability of American democracy have an immediacy and relevance far beyond his speculation on the future of a young republic.

Fragmentation and Coherence

In the United States, sovereignty is constitutionally defined as "popular." It "belongs" to the people and is institutionally embedded in three branches of government. When foreigners deal with the American system, there is always perplexity regarding the decisional processes. Even the strongest of presidents is constrained by the formal and informal routines of bureaucrats, legislators, and the courts, not to speak of the press, lobbyists, and special-interest groups. The peculiar "defects" of the American Constitution, which institutionalizes pluralism, have always seemed to mean that the United States would be at a disadvantage in diplomatic and military enterprises. In the nineteenth century other states had a single sovereign. When the old states of Europe dealt with one another, they could be reasonably sure who spoke authoritatively and who did not. Today, even U.S. analysts are sometimes unsure how much weight to assign to the public statements of officials and private interests. Foreigners might find this process at least as baffling when they try to tune themselves to the cacophony of voices in the American system.

No one wonders why there is an urge to clarify it all. Moreover, to many observers, the political and institutional fragmentation at home not only begets policy incoherence, it also betokens a larger disorder: a lingering species of political immaturity. Whereas other democratic nations were seen as having resolved the "dangers . . . inherent in the democratic conduct of foreign policy" through the mechanisms of parliamentary government,[25] the United States remained wedded to the anachronistic Madisonian construction. It is hard, however, to demonstrate empirically that other significant actors in international politics— the British, the French, or the Germans, for instance—have much of an advantage abroad in terms of their success over the years, save perhaps in their capacity to dissimulate with more ease.

Moreover, the great totalitarian adversary of the United States in the late twentieth century, the Soviet Union, was certainly no less beset by institutional, social, racial, and ethnic tensions than the United States. The Soviet state was anything but a monolithic entity lacking in interest groups and complex (and for Soviet authorities frustratingly unresponsive) bureaucratic politics.[26] Resource constraints were as prevalent and more limiting within the Soviet economic context.[27] In the end, of course, the Soviet system proved unable to respond to its leadership's efforts at reform. *Perestroika, glasnost,* and democratization—seen by Gorbachev as the necessary steps to preserve the Soviet Union's position as a superpower—were insufficient, the Soviet Union's empire dissolved, and the Soviet state itself collapsed.

Authoritarian and totalitarian systems may have about them an air of coherence and stability stemming from concentration of power in the hands of an individual or small group of individuals, but the transfer of power and societal transformation have proved tumultuous for them. Thus, in the wake of Stalin's death literally years passed—virtually two-thirds of the Eisenhower administration—before Khrushchev consolidated his position. And if, after finally consolidating control, a totalitarian regime is long-lived (an uncertain prospect in itself), its policy, though perhaps consistent, is nonetheless bounded by the creativity and virtuosity of those in control.

It would seem, therefore, to be an error to equate institutional homogeneity with diplomatic success or even greater prospect of success. During the 1970s and much of the 1980s veritable choruses bewailed the imminent seizure of the global initiative by the Soviets. But Soviet foreign policy proved anything but coherent or consistently successful. It was no guarantee of success in Egypt in the late 1960s and early 1970s. To be sure, there was a kind of unity in the obsessive Soviet pursuit of strategic parity with the United States. But the single-minded characteristics of their policy did not serve the Soviets especially well in Southeast Asia or in the Middle East throughout the eighties; nor did policy coherence guarantee wisdom in dealing with indigenous instability within their empire in Eastern Europe or offer an escape from the difficulties ensuing from the momentous rupture of their relations with Communist China.

Institutional fragmentation need not lead to an incoherent foreign policy. On the contrary, the post–World War II course of American policy suggests that once the American system is mobilized, it is quite capable of pursuing a consistent foreign policy. From 1947 until the end of the 1960s American policy pursued objectives first defined by Harry Truman. Debates were largely confined to the question of the appropriate means to construct and then maintain containment. The process of fashioning consensus was not without difficulty. The period between Truman's speech to Congress in March 1947 and the end of the Korean War was by no means placid. But once institutionalized in the early Eisenhower administration, the policy of containment remained remarkably stable for the next twenty years. Indeed, policy consistency, built on the smothering of the inherently conflictual institutional relationships, contributed to the collapse of policy consensus in the seventies. A twenty-year bipartisan slumber also led to an atrophy of Congress's ability to define or reconstruct the national agenda in the wake of Vietnam and Watergate.

American policy suffered ultimate disaster in Southeast Asia in part because Congress forswore an active role in the 1950s. The subsequent confusion and even occasional wrongheadedness attendant to the reassertion of the congressional role in the seventies is not in itself proof of a paralyzed system; rather, it suggests the necessity of consistent attention within Congress to its constitutionally mandated role in the policy-making process. To be sure, the Constitution does not extend the congressional role far, if at all, into the realm of the *conduct* of foreign policy. And attempts by Congress to develop mechanisms that facilitate congressional involvement in the conduct of policy are potentially mischievous; in fact, they detract from the task of institutionalizing a role in the process of shaping policy objectives. The means necessary for Congress to fashion policy are at hand. It was, after all, no coincidence that the men who framed the Constitution placed in the hands of Congress the budgetary process (and thus the means for oversight), the power to declare war, important treaty powers, and the power to give advice and consent concerning the most important foreign policy officers.

Bureaucracy and Diplomacy

The modern bureaucratic state represents an advance from the rule of the shaman, the mystic, the animist, or the messiah. As the great turn-of-the-century sociologist Max Weber pointed out, bureaucracy has its virtues.[28] Not long ago, for example, Americans cursed the "irrationality" and "anarchy" of an Iran gripped by Islamic fundamentalist fanaticism and an ayatollah who counseled chiefly with God. Here, if ever, was consistency and coherence in the form of one man; but where, it was indignantly demanded throughout 1980, was the Iranian government?

It is, of course, heretical to suggest that bureaucracies are anything less than the source of evil in the modern nation-state. For decades, presidential candidates of both parties have been promising "to get Washington off the people's back." To argue against oppressive and overadministered government is one thing; to argue against governmental services rationally apportioned is another. Not the least of the advances that come with bureaucratic procedures are public rules and a generally public, knowable agenda. Hence, bureaucracy can be sued, contained, opposed, even expanded, on rational or legal grounds. The political world of the bureaucracy is permeable, the personal office of the president less so. The door to the Oval Office is open or shut largely at the discretion of the individual who resides therein.

A bureaucracy stores extant knowledge; however, it tends to create new knowledge with great hesitation. This is a handicap, it is sometimes argued. After all, the world changes with great rapidity, and new answers to old challenges are needed; hence, typical bureaucratic reactions will surely be inappropriate and stale. Still, established policies have passed a certain test. To be sure, a collective memory may mistake the future for the past, but often as not, the past and the future do resemble one another. If there is no public agency for recalling which official policies have succeeded and which have failed, then innovation may be inept. Or what would be worse, new tactics might be predictably inept and avoidable, especially if old responses are forgotten or discarded too readily.

It is true, of course, that bureaucracy tends to routinize responses and to view what others see as crises as mere exaggerations of the usual. Here, too, however, bureaucracy performs a service. It does slow down reactions, but most novel events are not nearly as revolutionary as they are usually portrayed to be. The usual, by definition, predominates over the catastrophic. By moving with caution, bureaucracies tend to let events run a natural course. We get used to them. They seem less menacing, in part because they prove to be, in part because they become defined as "normal," and in part because usual routines can be brought into play. Like individuals, events defined as normal subsequently tend to become normal, conforming to expectation.

Diplomacy is the adjustment of interests between sovereign states. Classic diplomacy views conflicts of interest as usual. To the diplomat, international conflicts are viewed not as a concatenation of crises but as problems that are solvable with patience and by compromise. To those who view international relations as unpredictable, crisis-ridden, and wholly different from normal politics, the inability of bureaucracies to create is a great debility. Thus Henry Kissinger was wont to contrast the statesman, who creates policy, with a disdainful caricature of a bureaucratized diplomat. As Kissinger wrote, "The diplomat's quest for 'objectivity'—while desirable theoretically—involves the danger . . . that an average standard of performance is established . . . attention tends to be diverted from the act of choice. . . . Decisions can be avoided until crisis brooks no further delay."[29]

If, however, foreign politics are becoming more intertwined with domestic politics—indeed, if international society and domestic society have come to resemble each other[30]—then the necessity for viewing statecraft as an act of creation and a series of choices at critical junctures is as hypothetical and unlikely as the precise management of any contemporary domestic policy. From this point of view, the essential task of the foreign policy apparatus is not crisis management but rather the storage of routines and information regarding divergent post–cold war interests. Finally, even if one conceives of foreign policy as the management of a succession of crises or the employment of tactical virtuosity to construct a new world order, the effort is for naught if the results cannot be institutionalized. Short of a perpetually employed Metternich, Bismarck, or Kissinger, the task of curating their achievements must fall to a foreign ministry. And if the achievements prove so ephemeral that they cannot be transmitted to a foreign ministry and institutionalized through some "average standard of performance," their standing as diplomatic achievements is at least arguable.

Democratic Constraints and Opportunities and the New World Order

In the final analysis, of course, a high degree of public support is the foundation of a successful foreign policy in a democracy. But on perhaps no other aspect of the American policy-making context is there greater ambivalence among policy elites. Leadership, we have noted, commonly views the public as narrow, ignorant, and ominous. The upshot is that makers of foreign policy feel compelled to "sell" their policy departures. Commonly, they fear that unless policy is stated in the strongest and starkest terms, they—the policymakers themselves—will be misunderstood and ultimately destroyed by a distracted or uncaring public. But the results of overselling are sometimes paradoxical.

The Truman administration, in its call to cold war, portrayed the Soviet Union as embodying all that was evil and antithetical to Western civilization. Inasmuch as the public responded as the Truman administration had hoped, the president should not have been surprised that three years later the public was purblind to the rationale of a limited war in Korea against this universal menace. Fear of an aroused and ignorant public haunted subsequent presidents. Eisenhower was unwilling to confront McCarthyism; Kennedy was reportedly unwilling, until after he would be reelected, to draw back from a war that he knew was beyond winning; and Johnson apparently feared that the American people would misunderstand any effort to exit Vietnam with anything less than victory. Nixon, when he sought to construct a new and fairly limited strategic relationship with the Soviet Union, tried to reverse this portrayal of the Soviet Union. Accordingly, détente was advanced as a new relationship with a transformed Soviet state. When the deep underlying conflicts in interest between the United States and the Soviet Union emerged, persistent public skepticism about détente frustrated Jimmy Carter's effort to conclude the SALT process. Indeed, Carter found himself shrilly scolding the Soviets for a military presence in Cuba that was almost two decades old in a vain attempt to save the SALT treaty by countering a public image that he was not tough enough on the Soviets.

But this historical litany of constraints imposed by the public may mislead. Daniel Yankelovich, after some twenty-five years of polling the American people on their public policy attitudes, suggests policy-makers get the public opinion and, therefore, the constraints that they deserve:

> In its statements to the American public, the U.S. leadership blows hot and cold. The tone is rarely balanced, ambiguities are played down, subtlety is sacrificed to overstatement. Some (perhaps all) . . . government statements harbor the assumption that the public is simpleminded, capable of holding only one extreme alternative in mind at a time—black *or* white, for *or* against, friend *or* foe. As policy needs dictate, the appropriate switch is thrown in an attempt to elicit the appropriate single-dimensioned response.[31]

It need not be that policymakers have to confabulate and exaggerate in order to make foreign policy fly if, as we have suggested, the view of a dark, sullen public is overdrawn. The meaning of poll data is always controversial, but Yankelovich and others have concluded that Americans, *in the presence of a full debate* on complex issues, are quite capable of forming and articulating informed judgments about their interests and the national interest. It would be fatuous to argue that more than some small fraction of the public is fully informed and consistent in its foreign policy opinions. But as Yankelovich argues, "this should not be interpreted as meaning that the public has no rational means of arriving at judgments on pressing issues in the foreign policy field. There is a definite 'public mind' at work—a special way in which the American people view the role of the United States in the foreign policy field."[32]

In the wake of the Vietnam War there was reason to believe that the public was "balancing the moral and the practical, calibrating the appropriate degree of involvement." As the public attempted to come to grips with the implications of U.S. activism in the 1980s, they retained the memory of the Vietnam experience.[33] It was not coincidental that these poll findings were drawn at a time when foreign-policy makers and opinion leaders were compelled by public skepticism to articulate and debate questions about the use of force more openly than at perhaps any other time since the end of World War II. But if full debate of foreign policy assumptions, objectives, or alternative means (as distinct from the technical parameters of warheads, for example) is the exception rather than the rule, is it not reasonable to expect the public to hold overly simple and sometimes unstable or inconsistent opinions?

The collapse of the Soviet Union exacerbates the problem confronting a leadership still committed to internationalism. The public opinion data of the early 1990s reveal a skeptical public, but the public is not averse to a reasoned, restrained, and focused internationalism. The popular indifference to George Bush's vague call to build a "new world order" in favor of Clinton's appeal for a renewed concern for domestic priorities underscores the task: presidents, legislators, and opinion leaders will have to explain rather than declaim global engagements. They will also have to listen to those they would lead.

The post–cold war world order will place enormous demands on any public, but especially, one suspects, the American public. To the extent that the world is tending toward mutual vulnerabilities and limited resources, the ability to respond cooperatively becomes the essence of leadership. Quick-fix sophistry and ad-agency or homespun one-liners, like popcorn, can fill empty time and space for a while, but they will hardly substitute for the meat and potatoes of real argument. The foundation of successful policy is fashioned from the kind of sustained debate that the founders knew and relished. The "new world order" will offer new opportunities. Realizing opportunities and avoiding disasters will demand great flexibility, sensitivity, and patience.

The demands on American foreign policy making will prove no less great than those of the cold war era, now mercifully closed. The demands will probably require a response that is framed in terms of tolerance. Ultimately, nationalism and racism will prove crippling in that a public opinion characterized by these pathologies will find itself unable to deal cooperatively and creatively with the real international agenda of global growth, welfare, and environmental security. Any country afflicted by chauvinistic insularity will soon find itself at a moral and economic competitive disadvantage. The real test of the American institutional structure will be its capacity to evolve, develop, adapt, and cooperate in multilateral ventures rather than unilaterally producing a priori blueprints. The adequacy of the response should not be defined and evaluated in terms of perfection. Such a demand would likely be frustrated, and those who demanded it would find despair their partner.

In any event, perhaps the most important issue is the quality of the leadership provided in the debate concerning the new directions of foreign affairs. If the policy elite presents an analysis of the new situation and the alternatives available for dealing with it in oversimplistic terms (e.g., "Japan-bashing"), then they can expect a no more informed public debate and response than they have provided for.

THE AMERICAN SYSTEM AND THE NEW WORLD ORDER

Does the American system in fact have the capacity to respond to the challenges posed by the "new world order"? The answer comes in two parts. First, there is the question of the institutional capacity of the American system to respond. In approaching this question, it is useful to recall that when the cold war "national security state" was being constructed, there was no "pattern" or "model." The NSC system evolved as the cold war developed and took shape. The demands of the post–cold war world are likely to be even more variegated in character, and response time will likely be foreshortened, but this does not preclude institutional adaptation.

Second, there is the question of the adequacy of the American people and American political culture to rise to the challenge of the "new world order." Certainly a case can be made that elites have been found wanting if measured in terms of their prescience, prudence, and responsibility. Similarly, a review of the measures of the information level of the mass public concerning foreign affairs provides warrant for concern. But the data on the public's capacity to deal with complexity and reach pragmatic public judgments suggest a more substantial capacity than is usually acknowledged. Predictably, there is a considerable degree of frustration in the face of new categories of intrusions and disruption, but aversion to the unpleasant consequences of global competition, immigration, and so on, is by no means a uniquely American characteristic. It is the capacity for a more reasoned and stable public judgment that is crucial. Once again, the historical record is hardly synonymous with Tocquevillian gloom.

In the final analysis, therefore, the assertion that democracy in America is a decidedly inferior form of government for undertaking foreign policy may be as much a comment on the foreign policy as a comment on the democratic form of government. In Tocqueville's day, the regnant European foreign policies were predicated on military and mercantile prowess and proper position within the balance of power. Much of the state's resources were devoted to overseas expansion and war. A contemporary foreign policy analogue would require the permanent mobilization of the American political economy and the efficient global application of force. The threat of force, including the resort to nuclear war, or xenophobic international economic warfare may indeed be beyond the capacity of American democracy and government traditionally defined. More to the point, there is every reason to believe that a militant nationalist policy is both inappropriate to the world politics of the late twentieth century and incapable of commanding the sustained support of the American people.

An interdependent world of many nuclear powers, persistent ethnic conflict, environmental fragility, crushing poverty for most of humanity, and uncertain economic prospects for its most developed countries may require a considerable measure of mutual responsiveness. A framework of legitimate international institutional structures and imaginative ad hoc arrangements to manage conflict will have to be constructed if the United States is to survive and prosper.

NOTES

CHAPTER 1 INTRODUCTION

1. See, e.g., Lawrence R. Houston's memorandum to the director of central intelligence, Jan. 15, 1962, CC-0083, cited in John Ranelagh, *The Agency: The Rise and Decline of the CIA* (New York: Simon & Schuster, 1987), p. 536.

2. Alexis de Tocqueville, *Democracy in America,* vol. 1 (New York: Vintage, 1945), p. 243.

3. See, e.g., W. Ebenstein et al., *American Democracy in World Perspective* (New York: Harper & Row, 1967), pp. 645–46.

4. Alexander Hamilton, Federalist No. 6, "Concerning Dangers from War between the States," in *The Federalist Papers Reader,* ed. Frederick Quinn (Washington, D.C.: Seven Locks, 1993), p. 52.

5. John Jay, Federalist Nos. 2 and 3, "Concerning Dangers from Foreign Force and Influence," ibid., pp. 48 ff.

6. This power can be inferred from the authority the Constitution gives Congress to "grant letters of Marque and Reprisal" (see Art. 1, Sec. 8; see also Arthur Schlesinger, Jr., *The Imperial Presidency* [Boston: Houghton Mifflin, 1973], p. 3).

7. James Madison, Federalist Nos. 48 and 51, in *The Federalist Papers,* ed. Clinton Rossiter (New York: Mentor, 1961), pp. 308, 321–22.

8. See *Boston Globe,* Nov. 12, 1985.

9. Washington is legendary for such rivalries as those between Shultz and Weinberger and between Cyrus Vance and Zbigniew Brzezinski, secretary of state and national security adviser, respectively, during the Carter years. Others, such as those between Richard Nixon's first secretary of state, William Rogers, and his national security adviser, Henry Kissinger, have been the stuff of countless treatises. For a good summary see Gerry Argyris Andrianopoulos, *Kissinger and Brzezinski: The NSC and the Struggle for Control of U.S. National Security Policy* (New York: St. Martin's, 1991).

10. The literature on bureaucratic politics has grown enormously in the last few years. Perhaps the most important works are Graham T. Allison, *Essence of Decision: Explaining the Cuban Missile Crisis* (Boston: Little, Brown, 1971); Morton H. Halperin, *Bureaucratic Politics and Foreign Policy* (Washington, D.C.: Brookings Institution, 1974); Allison and Halperin, "Bureaucratic Politics: A Paradigm and Some Policy Implications," *World Politics* 24 (suppl., Spring 1972): 40–79; Halperin and Arnold Kanter, eds., *Readings in American Foreign*

Policy: A Bureaucratic Perspective (Boston: Little, Brown, 1973), esp. the intro-
duction, pp. 1–42; and Richard Neustadt, *Alliance Politics* (New York: Columbia
University Press, 1970). See also the critiques of the perspective by Stephen D.
Krasner, "Are Bureaucracies Important? (Or Allison Wonderland)," *Foreign Policy*, no. 7 (Summer 1971): 159–79; Robert Art, "Bureaucratic Politics and American Foreign Policy: A Critique," *Policy Sciences* 40 (1973): 467–90; and James A.
Nathan and James K. Oliver, "Bureaucratic Politics: Academic Windfalls and
Intellectual Pitfalls," *Journal of Political and Military Sociology* 6, no. 1 (Spring
1978): 81–91.

11. For development of this concept of administration see Richard E. Neustadt, *Presidential Power and the Modern Presidents: The Politics of Leadership
from Roosevelt to Reagan* (New York: Free Press / Macmillan, 1990).

12. George Kennan has perhaps expressed these concerns most straightfor-
wardly. See his *American Diplomacy, 1900–1950* (New York: New American
World Library, 1959), esp. p. 59. See also Leslie H. Gelb, "The Essential Domino:
American Politics and Vietnam," *Foreign Affairs* 50, no. 3 (1972): 459–75.

13. For a statement of this view see Daniel Yankelovich, "Farewell to 'President Knows Best,'" *Foreign Affairs* 57, no. 3 (1979): 687 ff. See also John Immer-
wahr, Jean Johnson, and John Doble, *The Speaker and the Listener: A Public
Perspective on Freedom of Expression* (New York: Public Agenda Foundation,
1980). For a reconsideration of the public and its "raw" opinion versus its considered "public judgment" see Yankelovich, "Foreign Policy after the Election,"
Foreign Affairs 71, no. 4 (1992): 6.

14. See Yankelovich, "Farewell to 'President Knows Best,'" esp. pp. 687–88,
for a discussion of these possibilities.

15. See Samuel P. Huntington's contribution to *The Crisis of Democracy:
Report on the Governability of Democracies to the Trilateral Commission*, by
Michael J. Crozier, Samuel P. Huntington, and Joji Watanuki (New York: New
York University Press, 1975). See also Lester Thurow, *The Zero-Sum Society*
(New York: Basic, 1980).

16. For a historical overview of this process see Schlesinger, *Imperial Presidency*. Schlesinger's book is also an invaluable source on the history of the
executive-legislative relationship up to the Vietnam War.

17. We have explored the external dimensions of U.S. policy making else-
where, chronologically and thematically. See James A. Nathan and James K.
Oliver, *United States Foreign Policy and World Order*, 4th ed. (Glenview, Ill.:
Scott, Foresman, 1989).

CHAPTER 2   THE FOREIGN POLICY PRESIDENCY

1. Harry Truman, quoted in Clinton Rossiter, *The American Presidency*, 2d
ed. (New York: Harcourt Brace Jovanovich, 1960), p. 30.

2. On the "imperial presidency" see Arthur M. Schlesinger, Jr., *The Imperial*

Presidency (Boston: Houghton Mifflin, 1973). For a view of the presidency as "imperiled" see Thomas E. Cronin, "An Imperiled Presidency?" *Society,* Nov.–Dec. 1978, and his *State of the Presidency,* 2d ed. (Boston: Little, Brown, 1980).

3. See R. W. Apple's analysis in *New York Times,* Jan. 9, 1985.

4. Mark Hertsgaard, *On Bended Knee: The Press and the Reagan Presidency* (New York: Farrar, Straus & Giroux, 1988), p. 4.

5. See Theodore Draper, *A Very Thin Line: The Iran-Contra Affairs* (New York: Hill & Wang, 1991).

6. Cronin, *State of the Presidency,* p. 22.

7. For an official assessment of the very low probability of any military threat to the United States see the testimony of CIA director Robert Gates and Lt. Gen. James R. Clapper, director of the Defense Intelligence Agency, in Elaine Sciolino, "C.I.A. Chief Says Threat by Ex-Soviets Is Small," *New York Times,* Jan. 23, 1992.

8. Barry Rubin, *Affairs of State: The State Department and the Struggle over U.S. Foreign Policy* (New York: Oxford University Press, 1985), p. 53.

9. The number of intelligence operations increased by a factor of five over the number in the Carter administration, and the operations directorate of the CIA more than doubled in size and budget in the Reagan years (see Jeffery Richelson, *The U.S. Intelligence Community* [Cambridge, Mass.: Ballinger, 1985]; and for the 1990s budget figure see Ruth Sinai, "Gates Says CIA to Focus on Economic Espionage," *Philadelphia Inquirer,* Apr. 14, 1992).

10. The National Security Agency employs more than 60,000 people (see Michael Wines, "Security Agency Debates New Role: Economic Spying," *New York Times,* June 18, 1990).

11. The Pentagon account, Tactical Intelligence and Related Activities (TIRA), accounts for around 60 percent of the current budget (*Washington Post,* Mar. 31, 1986). The management of the TIRA budget is under the Defense Department. The Defense Department's "intelligence czar" is the assistant secretary for command, communications, and intelligence (See Patrick Taylor, "How the United States Cloaks a 24 Billion Dollar Budget," ibid., Mar. 26, 1986).

12. Paul Y. Hammond, *Organizing for Defense: The American Military Establishment in the Twentieth Century* (Princeton: Princeton University Press, 1961), pp. 288–353.

13. Ellis Briggs, quoted in John Franklin Campbell, *The Foreign Affairs Fudge Factory* (New York: Basic, 1971), pp. 206–7.

14. Secretary of State's Public Committee on Personnel, *Toward a Stronger Foreign Service* (Washington, D.C.: U.S. Government Printing Office, 1954).

15. Burton M. Sapin, *The Making of United States Foreign Policy* (New York: Praeger, for the Brookings Institution, 1966), pp. 104–6 and esp. 126–28.

16. *Washington Post,* Mar. 28, 1986.

17. There also was not an inconsiderable amount of pressure from various affirmative-action suits (see *Allison Palmer v. Baker,* Civil Action 76–1439 [AER]

and *Cooper v. Baker,* Civil Action 77–2006 [AER]. See also "Grievance Actions," *State,* no. 322 [May 1989]: 21).

18. Joseph McCarthy, quoted in Eric F. Goldman, *The Crucial Decade—and After: America, 1945–1960* (New York: Vintage, 1960), p. 142. For accounts of the McCarthy era see pp. 212–14, 250–57, 270–79.

19. Dwight D. Eisenhower, quoted in Emmet John Hughes, *The Ordeal of Power* (New York: Dell, 1962), p. 81.

20. Ibid., p. 82.

21. Goldman, *Crucial Decade,* p. 258.

22. For the institutional evolution of the Defense Department see Hammond, *Organizing for Defense.*

23. Ibid., pp. 329–53.

24. Ibid.

25. On McNamara's personal philosophy of administration see Charles J. Hitch, *Decision-Making for Defense* (Berkeley and Los Angeles: University of California Press, 1970), p. 27.

26. Samuel P. Huntington, "Organization and Strategy," in *Reorganizing America's Defense: Leadership in War and Peace,* by Robert J. Art, Vincent Davis, and Samuel P. Huntington (Washington, D.C.: Pergamon-Brassey, 1985), p. 231.

27. Deborah Shapley, *Promise and Power* (Boston: Little, Brown, 1993).

28. Kenneth Campbell, "The U.S. Military's 'Vietnam Syndrome' and the Persian Gulf War" (Paper presented at the annual meeting of the Northeastern Political Science Association, Philadelphia, Nov. 14–16, 1991), pp. 2, 5. See also his "The Crucial Constraint: Containment and the American Military's Post-Vietnam Reluctance to Use Force" (Ph.D. diss., Temple University, 1989) and "The Roots of the Military's 'Vietnam Syndrome' in the Gulf War" (Paper presented at the annual meeting of the Society for Historians of American Foreign Relations, Washington, D.C., June 22, 1991); and David H. Petraeus, "Military Influence and the Post-Vietnam Use of Force," *Armed Forces and Society* 15, no. 4 (1989): 489–505. For the definitive and extended professional military expression of this view see Col. Harry G. Summers, Jr., *On Strategy: A Critical Analysis of the Vietnam War* (New York: Dell, 1984).

29. Caspar Weinberger, "The Uses of Military Power," *Defense,* Jan. 1985, pp. 2–11.

30. See Campbell, "U.S. Military's 'Vietnam Syndrome' and the Gulf War"; and Bob Woodward, *The Commanders* (New York: Simon & Schuster, 1991).

31. Campbell, "U.S. Military's 'Vietnam Syndrome' and the Gulf War," p. 2; Woodward, quoting Chairman of the Joint Chiefs of Staff Colin Powell, in *The Commanders,* p. 117. Powell makes special note of Secretary of State George Shultz's propensity for military solutions and, therefore, frequent collisions with Weinberger.

32. Woodward, *The Commanders,* pp. 230 ff.

33. George Bush, quoted in R. W. Apple, Jr., "Done. A Short, Persuasive Lesson in Warfare," *New York Times,* Mar. 3, 1991.

34. See John F. Burns, "In Sarajevo, the Cavalry Seems Far Away," ibid., Aug. 9, 1992.

35. See Campbell, "The Roots of the Military's 'Vietnam Syndrome' in the Gulf War."

36. The predicate for this carrier and hundreds more combat ships was a series of internal studies designed to demonstrate the need for a expanded global role for seapower. The authors had a reluctant, albeit peripheral, role in one of these studies, "Sea Plan 2000"; for an elaboration see James Nathan, "The Maritime Strategy: Prospects and Foreboding," *International Relations* 9 (Nov. 1987), and "U.S. Naval Policy in the 1990's," *Journal of Strategic Studies,* Feb. 1989.

37. Huntington, "Organization and Strategy."

38. "Pentagon Reorganization," in Congressional Quarterly, *Congress and the Nation, 1985–1988* (Washington, D.C., 1989), pp. 299–300; Art, Davis, and Huntington, *Reorganizing America's Defense,* pp. 207–428.

39. See the hearings before Congressman Nichols's subcommittee in U.S. Congress, House, Committee on Armed Services, *Reorganization Proposals for the Joint Chiefs of Staff: Hearings before the Investigations Subcommittee,* 98th Cong., 1st sess., 1983.

40. See "Pentagon Reorganization," pp. 300–301.

41. Woodward, *The Commanders,* p. 82.

42. For overviews of the intelligence function, its organization within the U.S. government, and the development of the CIA see Philip Agee, *Inside the Company: CIA Diary* (New York: Bantam, 1984); Ray Cline, *The CIA under Reagan, Bush, and Casey: The Evolution of the Agency from Roosevelt to Reagan* (Washington, D.C.: Acropolis, 1981); William Colby, *Honorable Men: My Life in the CIA* (New York: Simon & Schuster, 1978); Lyman Kirkpatrick, *The U.S. Intelligence Community* (New York: Hill & Wang, 1973); and Victor Marchetti and John D. Marks, *The CIA and the Cult of Intelligence* (New York: Dell, 1974).

43. See Bob Woodward, *Veil: The Secret Wars of the CIA, 1981–1987* (New York: Pocket Books, 1987); and Joseph E. Persico, *Casey: From the OSS to the CIA* (New York: Viking, 1990).

44. Keith Schneider, "Bush Aid Assails U.S. Preparations for Earth Summit," *New York Times,* Aug. 1, 1992.

CHAPTER 3   THE DEVELOPMENT OF THE NATIONAL SECURITY COUNCIL SYSTEM

1. Ernest May, "The US Government, A Legacy of the Cold War," *Diplomatic History* 16, no. 2 (1992): 271; Anna K. Nelson, "President Truman and the Evolution of the National Security Council," *Journal of American History* 72 (Sept. 1985): 360–78.

2. Harry S. Truman, *Memoirs: Years of Trial and Hope* (Garden City, N.Y.: Doubleday, 1956), p. 60.

3. Nelson, "President Truman," p. 360.

4. Still the best sources on foreign and national security policy making during the 1950s are Senator Henry Jackson's subcommittee hearings and reports, U.S. Congress, Senate, Committee on Government Operations, *Organizing for National Security: Hearings and Reports before the Subcommittee on National Policy Machinery,* 86th Cong., 2d sess., 1960. On Eisenhower's administration see Fred I. Greenstein, *The Hidden-Hand Presidency* (New York: Basic, 1982).

5. Greenstein, *Hidden-Hand Presidency,* pp. 578–79.

6. Ibid., pp. 582–83, 601–2.

7. Sherman Adams, *First Hand Report: The Story of the Eisenhower Administration* (New York: Harper & Row, 1961), p. 110. Emmet John Hughes, *The Ordeal of Power* (New York: Dell, 1962), p. 243; see also 218.

8. See James A. Nathan and James K. Oliver, *United States Foreign Policy and World Order,* 3d ed. (Boston: Little, Brown, 1985), chap. 5.

9. Theodore C. Sorensen, *Kennedy* (New York: Bantam, 1965), pp. 315–16.

10. This criticism runs throughout the Jackson Subcommittee hearings and reports of 1960.

11. Sorensen, p. 315; Arthur Schlesinger, Jr., *A Thousand Days: John F. Kennedy in the White House* (Boston: Houghton Mifflin, 1965), pp. 209–10.

12. See Sorensen, *Kennedy,* pp. 319–20.

13. Schlesinger, *A Thousand Days,* pp. 406–37, esp. 407.

14. U.S. Congress, Senate, Committee on Government Operations, *The Ambassador and the Problem of Coordination: A Study Submitted to the Subcommittee on National Security Staffing and Operations,* 88th Cong., 1st sess., 1963, p. 155.

15. Richard Neustadt, in U.S. Congress, Senate, Committee on Government Operations, *Administration of National Security: Inquiry of the Subcommittee on National Security Operations,* 88th Cong., 1st sess., 1965, p. 77.

16. Dean Rusk, "The President," *Foreign Affairs* 38, no. 2 (1960): 353–69.

17. Schlesinger, *A Thousand Days,* pp. 432–34.

18. See James Nathan, "The Heyday of the New Strategy," *Diplomacy and Statecraft* 3, no. 2 (1992): 303–42.

19. Lyndon B. Johnson, "White House Announcement of New Procedures for Overseas Interdepartmental Matters, March 4, 1966," *Weekly Compilation of Presidential Documents,* vol. 2 (Washington, D.C.: U.S. Government Printing Office, Mar. 7, 1966), p. 506.

20. *Department of State Foreign Affairs Manual,* circular no. 385 (Washington, D.C.: U.S. Government Printing Office, 1966).

21. See U.S. Congress, Senate, Committee on Government Operations, *Planning–Programming–Budgeting: Hearings and Studies Prepared for the Subcommittee on National Security and International Operations,* 90th Cong., 1st sess., 1968; and Frederick C. Mosher and John E. Harr, *Programming Systems and*

Foreign Affairs Leadership: An Attempted Innovation (New York: Oxford University Press, 1970).

22. See John Franklin Campbell, *The Foreign Affairs Fudge Factory* (New York: Basic, 1971), pp. 88–90.

23. Nicholas D. Katzenbach, "Administration of Foreign Policy," *Department of State Newsletter,* Nov. 1967, p. 2; William B. Macomber, Jr., "Management Strategy: A Program for the 1970's," ibid., Jan. 1970, p. 2.

24. David Halberstam, *The Best and the Brightest* (New York: Random House, 1969); Townsend Hoopes, *The Limits of Intervention* (New York: David McKay, 1969).

25. See Richard M. Nixon, *U.S. Foreign Policy for the 1970s: A New Strategy for Peace* (Washington, D.C.: U.S. Government Printing Office, 1970), esp. pp. 17–23; quote from p. 17.

26. U.S. Congress, Senate, Committee on Government Operations, "Letter to Senator Henry M. Jackson concerning the National Security Council from Henry A. Kissinger, Assistant to the President for National Security Affairs, 3 March 1970," in *The National Security Council: Comment by Henry A. Kissinger,* submitted to the Subcommittee on National Security and International Operations, 91st Cong., 2d sess., 1970, p. 2.

27. *New York Times,* Oct. 25, 1968, quoted in Gerry Argyris Andrianopoulos, *Kissinger and Brzezinski: The NSC and The Struggle for Control of U.S. National Security Policy* (New York: St. Martin's, 1991), p. 127.

28. *New York Times,* Dec. 3, 1968, quoted in Andrianopoulos, *Kissinger and Brzezinski,* p. 126.

29. Andrianopoulos, *Kissinger and Brzezinski,* p. 126.

30. But even here the policy initiative lay not with the Department of State but with the Treasury Department and with specialists on the president's staff.

31. News release, Department of State Bureau of Public Affairs, Department of State Office of Media Services press conference, Secretary of State Kissinger, Oct. 12, 1973.

32. Henry Kissinger, cited in *Newsweek,* Sept. 3, 1973, p. 28.

33. Roger Morris, *Uncertain Greatness* (New York: Harper & Row, 1977), p. 114.

34. Ibid., p. 156.

35. See I. M. Destler, "Can One Man Do?" *Foreign Policy,* no. 5 (Winter 1971–72): 3–27.

36. Walter Isaacson, *Kissinger* (New York: Simon & Schuster, 1992), p. 502.

37. Tad Szulc, *The Illusion of Peace* (New York: Viking, 1978), p. 478.

38. See John Ranelagh, *The Agency: The Rise and Decline of the CIA* (New York: Simon & Schuster, 1987), pp. 545–46; U.S. Congress, Senate, Select Committee on Intelligence, *Final Report of the Select Committee to Study Government Operations with Respect to Intelligence Activities* (Washington, D.C.: U.S. Government Printing Office, 1976); and Szulc, *Illusion of Peace,* p. 480.

39. Henry Kissinger, interview by Oriana Fallaci, *New Republic,* Dec. 16, 1972, p. 21.

40. *New York Times,* Dec. 24, 1973.

41. Ibid., Mar. 5, 1974.

42. *Washington Post,* Sept. 16, 1974.

43. Henry Kissinger, "Revolutionary Reflections on Bismarck," *Daedalus* 97, no. 3 (1968): 889–90.

44. Jimmy Carter, in a debate sponsored by the Chicago Council on Foreign Relations, 1976, *The Presidential Campaign, 1976* (Chicago: Foreign Policy Association, 1976), vol. 1, pt. 1, pp. 97, 105, cited in Andrianopoulos, *Kissinger and Brzezinski,* p. 136 n. 31.

45. *Washington Post,* Jan. 24, 1977.

46. Robert E. Hunter, *Presidential Control of Foreign Policy: Management or Mishap* (New York: Praeger, 1982), pp. 105–8.

47. *Time,* Aug. 8, 1977, p. 11.

48. James Wooten, "Here Comes Zbig," *Esquire,* Nov. 1979.

49. Victor Zorza, "A Man to Out-Kissinger," *Washington Post,* Jan. 19, 1977.

50. NSC-2, Jan. 20, 1977, released Apr. 22, 1977. The text may be found in U.S. Congress, Senate, *The National Security Adviser: Role and Accountability: Hearing before the Committee on Foreign Relations,* 96th Cong., 2d sess., 1980, p. 48 (hereafter cited as *NSC Hearing*).

51. Executive Order No. 12036, Jan. 24, 1978, secs. 1–302 through 1–304.

52. *NSC Hearing,* p. 50.

53. U.S. Congress, House, Committee on Foreign Affairs, *United States Policy and United States–Soviet Relations, 1979: Hearing before the Subcommittee on Europe and the Middle East,* 96th Cong., 1st sess., Committee Print, Oct. 16, 1979, p. 37. See also Leslie Gelb, in a speech at the Twenty-third National Security Seminar, Army War College, Carlisle, Pa., June 8, 1977, cited in *Parameters,* no. 3 (July 1977).

54. Philip Odeen, "National Security Policy Integration," President's Reorganization Project (Washington, D.C.: Office of Management and Budget, Sept. 1979, mimeographed), p. 12.

55. Dick Kirschten, "Beyond the Vance-Brzezinski Clash Lurks an NSC under Fire," *National Journal,* May 17, 1980, p. 816.

56. Anthony Lake, "Managing Complexity in U.S. Foreign Policy" (Speech delivered to the San Francisco World Affairs Council, San Francisco, Mar. 14, 1978).

57. See James A. Nathan and James K. Oliver, *United States Foreign Policy and World Order,* 4th ed. (Glenview, Ill.: Scott, Foresman, 1989).

58. Brzezinski spoke on this theme on "Bill Moyers' Journal," Public Broadcasting Service, Nov. 16, 1980.

59. David C. Martin, "Inside the Rescue Mission," *Newsweek,* July 12, 1982, pp. 16–22.

60. *New York Times,* Aug. 10, 1980.

61. Bernard Gwertzman, "It's a Tough Company for On-the-Job Training," ibid., Aug. 17, 1980.

62. Leslie Gelb, interview, "All Things Considered," National Public Radio, Tape no. 80081304, Aug. 13, 1980.

63. *Washington Post,* Jan. 28, 1980.

64. "Remarks of President Jimmy Carter at the United States Naval Academy," Annapolis, Maryland, June 7, 1978, *Weekly Compilation of Presidential Documents* (Washington, D.C.: U.S. Government Printing Office, June 12, 1978), pp. 1052–57, is a good example of the way virtually every bureaucratic actor was served in what must have been to the Soviets an utterly befuddling address (see Murray Marder, "Behind Carter's Annapolis Speech," *Washington Post,* June 11, 1980).

CHAPTER 4   THE NATIONAL SECURITY COUNCIL SYSTEM
AT THE END OF THE COLD WAR

1. This is an ironic supposition in view of the veiled anti-Semitic innuendos Haig was want to levy against Kissinger when they served together on the NSC (see Walter Isaacson, *Kissinger* [New York: Simon & Schuster, 1992], p. 389).

2. See Hedrick Smith, "Reagan Picks a Mediator," *New York Times,* Jan. 5, 1982.

3. See, e.g., John M. Goshko, "A Veteran of Order and Precision Unholsters His Troubleshooter," *Washington Post,* Jan. 6, 1982.

4. Tad Szulc, "The Vicar Vanquished," *Foreign Policy,* no. 43 (Summer 1981): 173–87.

5. *Newsweek,* Apr. 12, 1982.

6. Morton Kondracke, "The Sinister Force Returns," *New Republic,* Nov. 25, 1981, pp. 10–12.

7. "Briefing," *New York Times,* Nov. 21, 1981.

8. *Newsweek,* Nov. 16, 1981, p. 31.

9. This description and analysis is based on two excellent reports by Leslie Gelb, "Foreign Policy System Criticized by Aides," *New York Times,* Oct. 19, 1981, and "Two Laws concerning the National Security Adviser," ibid., Jan. 7, 1982.

10. Edwin Meese, quoted in Leslie Gelb, "Is Washington Big Enough for Two State Departments?" ibid., Feb. 21, 1982.

11. Similarly, the president was unaware that most missiles could not be recalled or destroyed after launch (see Lou Cannon, *President Reagan: The Role of a Lifetime* [New York: Simon & Schuster, 1991], p. 305).

12. Report by Brian Nailor, "All Things Considered," National Public Radio, May 3, 1988; Owen Ullmann, "Reagan Based Decisions on Astrology, Insiders Say," *Philadelphia Inquirer,* May 3, 1988. But see Paul Houston, "Reagan Denies Using Astrology in Decisions," *Wilmington News Journal,* May 4, 1988.

13. The best summary, although a bit overwrought, is Andrew Lang, "The

Politics of Armageddon: Reagan Links Bible Prophecy with Nuclear War," *Convergence* (Washington, D.C.: Christic Institute, 1985), pp. 3, 12.

14. For an academic analysis questioning Reagan's mental acuity see Louis Gottschalk et al., "Presidential Candidates and Cognitive Impairment Measured from Behavior in Campaign Debates," *Public Administration Review*, Mar.–Apr. 1988, pp. 613–19.

15. Both Lou Cannon and Fred Barnes, of the *New Republic*, claim that the president's memory was astoundingly clear (Oct. 2, 1987). Other's have said, however, that Reagan forgot names, nodded off to sleep during important meetings, and even confused countries when talking to heads of state.

16. Cannon, *President Reagan*.

17. Edwin Meese, quoted in Gelb, "Is Washington Big Enough for Two State Departments?"

18. This is W. W. Kaufmann's summary of Weinberger's discussion in Weinberger's *Department of Defense Annual Report, Fiscal Year 1987* (Washington, D.C.: U.S. Government Printing Office, 1987), pp. 13–25. Kaufmann's summary is found in "A Defense Agenda for Fiscal Years 1990–1994," in *Restructuring American Foreign Policy*, ed. John Steinbrunner (Washington, D.C.: Brookings Institution, 1989), pp. 58–59. A formal Defense Guidance would be developed, but only in mid-1982, long after the funds had been committed. See Thomas C. Reed, "Details of National Security Strategy: Prevailing with Pride," *Vital Speeches of the Day*, vol. 47 (Aug. 15, 1982); and Richard Halloran, *To Arm a Nation* (New York: Macmillan, 1986), pp. 216–22, 282–93.

19. For Stockman's description of how the Reagan defense budget was put together see David Stockman, *The Triumph of Politics: Why the Reagan Revolution Failed* (New York: Harper & Row, 1986), esp. pp. 108 ff., whence the following quotations are taken.

20. William Clark, quoted in Gelb, "Two Laws concerning the National Security Adviser."

21. Equally important in Haig's dismissal were differences over the Middle East and Nancy Reagan's perception that Haig had made a fool of himself over protocol questions and that it was starting to reflect badly on her husband (see Cannon, *President Reagan*, pp. 202–5).

22. James McCartney, "Making of a Foreign Policy," *Philadelphia Inquirer*, Feb. 7, 1982.

23. Goshko, "Veteran of Order and Precision."

24. See, e.g., Caspar Weinberger, *Fighting for Peace: Seven Critical Years in the Pentagon* (New York: Warner, 1990), pp. 135–74, where Weinberger presents his account of his role in the Lebanon intervention.

25. See *Washington Post*, Aug. 29, 1981, including George Will, "Solid Shultz."

26. The panel idea collapsed after the first year or so. As with so many long-range planning exercises since World War II, the secretary began to neglect it under the pressure of time.

27. *Washington Post*, Dec. 17, 20, 1984.

28. *New York Times*, Apr. 20, 1984; author interviews conducted in January 1986.

29. Adm. William Crowe, quoted in Don Oberdorfer, *The Turn: From the Cold War to a New Era: The United States and the Soviet Union, 1983–1990* (New York: Poseidon, 1991), p. 100.

30. John Newhouse, "The Abolitionist—I," *New Yorker*, Jan. 2, 1989, p. 44.

31. Strobe Talbott, *Deadly Gambits: The Reagan Administration and the Stalemate in Nuclear Arms Control* (New York: Knopf, 1984), pp. 13 ff.

32. Oberdorfer, *The Turn*, p. 99.

33. *Wall Street Journal*, Dec. 6, 1985.

34. A presidential "finding" is required by law to authorize covert operations. The president is also required to notify the appropriate congressional committees in a timely fashion. In these instances there was no congressional notification.

35. There is some question whether the president understood fully the very first broaching of the subject to him by Robert MacFarlane, in July 1985, since he was coming out of surgery at the time. In Reagan's memoirs he notes his approval and the linkage in his mind to opening up a "process" of contacts that might lead to the release of hostages.

36. Theodore Draper, *A Very Thin Line: The Iran-Contra Affairs* (New York: Hill & Wang, 1991), p. 263. Each time, the president gave specific clearances to pursue contacts with the Iranians. Indeed, in the January 1986 meeting Reagan, with the support of Vice President Bush, Casey, and Admiral Poindexter, explicitly rejected Shultz and Weinberger's opposition.

37. Ibid., pp. 162, 372.

38. John M. Poindexter, *Testimony at Joint Hearings before the House Select Committee to Investigate Covert Arms Transactions with Iran and the Senate Select Committee on Secret Military Assistance to Iran and the Nicaraguan Opposition*, 100th Cong., 1st sess., 1987, vol. 100–8, p. 168.

39. Oliver North, testimony in ibid., vol. 100–7, p. 48, and quoted in Draper, *A Very Thin Line*, p. 220.

40. Draper summarizes the attitude of Poindexter and North as follows: "They were not ordinary officeholders or bureaucrats, and they gloried in their deviation from the norm. They were, in their own eyes, a breed apart" (Draper, *A Very Thin Line*, p. 220).

41. Ibid., pp. 75–78. Baker denies having referred specifically to impeachment, but he did testify that he was doubtful about the legality of the funding schemes.

42. Ibid., pp. 98–105. See also U.S. Congress, Senate, *Drugs, Law Enforcement and Foreign Policy: A Report of the Subcommittee on Narcotics, Terrorism, and International Operations*, 101st Cong., 1st sess., vol. 1, p. 89; Bob Woodward, *Veil: The Secret Wars of the CIA, 1981–1987* (New York: Pocket Books, 1987), pp. 328–29; Steven Emerson, "The Secrets of North's Notebooks," *New*

York Times, June 17, 1988; and Joel Brinkley and Stephen Engelberg, *Report of the Congressional Committees Investigating the Iran-Contra Affair,* abr. ed. (New York: Random House, 1988), pp. 48–49. Shultz, who regularly handled relations with Saudi Arabia, was not told about these monies until eighteen months later; Macfarlane called this an "oversight" (see John Prados, *Presidents' Secret Wars* (New York: Quill and William Morrow, 1986), p. 409; see also the transcript of "Guns, Drugs, and the CIA," broadcast on "Frontline" on May 18, 1988, produced and written by Andrew Cockburn with Leslie Cockburn, and "Guns for Drugs?" *Newsweek,* May 22, 1988.

43. Cannon, *President Reagan,* pp. 709–11.

44. U.S. Congress, House, Select Committee to Investigate Covert Arms Transactions with Iran, *Iran-Contra Affair,* 100th Cong., 1st sess., Nov. 1987, p. 298.

45. Louis Fisher, *Constitutional Conflicts between Congress and the President,* 3d ed. (Lawrence: University of Kansas Press, 1989), pp. 212–14.

46. See House Select Committee to Investigate Covert Arms Transactions with Iran, *Iran-Contra Affair,* p. 261.

47. "Face the Nation," Nov. 16, 1986. See also ibid., p. 262.

48. For a scathing review on this point see Theodore Draper, "An Autopsy," *New York Review of Books,* Dec. 17, 1987, pp. 67–77; see also "Iran-Contra Prosecutor Reports of High-Level Cover-up in Case," *New York Times,* Oct. 16, 1993.

49. John Tower, Edmund Muskie, and Brent Scowcroft, *The Tower Commission Report* (New York: Bantam, 1987), pp. 81, 79–80.

50. Cannon, *President Reagan,* p. 725.

51. Frank Carlucci, quoted in ibid., p. 732.

52. Ibid., p. 733.

53. Oberdorfer, *The Turn,* pp. 263 ff.

54. Gerald M. Boyd, "The Bush Style of Management: After Reagan, It's Back to Details," *New York Times,* Mar. 19, 1989.

55. On Baker's State Department see John M. Goshko, "Foreign Policy in Turmoil—or Transition?" *Washington Post,* National Weekly Edition, Mar. 13–19, 1989.

56. See I. M. Destler, "National Security Management: What Presidents Have Wrought," *Political Science Quarterly,* Winter 1980–81, pp. 573–88.

57. Woodward, *Veil,* pp. 50–51.

58. The Deputies Committee was made up of the second-ranking officers from State, Defense, the CIA, and the JCS. There were also "policy coordination committees" comprising senior officials of the relevant agencies whose job was to ensure that policy implementation was carried out (see Bernard Weinraub, "Bush Backs Plan to Enhance Role of Security Staff," *New York Times,* Feb. 2, 1989).

59. Woodward, *Veil,* p. 50.

60. Personal interviews with James A. Nathan, summer and fall of 1992.

61. Marjorie Williams, "Bush's Top Gun," *Washington Post,* National Weekly Edition, Feb. 6–12, 1989.

62. Henry Allen, "The Quintessential Establishmentarian," ibid., Jan. 9–15, 1989.

63. See James A. Nathan, "A New World Order: Policy or Platitude?" *Virginia Quarterly Review,* July 1992, pp. 16 ff.

64. Harold Nicholson, *Diplomacy* (New York: Oxford University Press, 1964), pp. 4–5 (emphasis added).

65. Perhaps the best summary analysis is Destler, "National Security Management."

66. Henry Kissinger, quoted in the *National Journal,* May 17, 1980, p. 817.

CHAPTER 5   CONGRESS AND FOREIGN POLICY

1. Thomas M. Frank and Edward Weisband called it "an entirely new framework of rules for power sharing among the branches of government" (*Foreign Policy by Congress* [New York: Oxford University Press, 1979], p. 61).

2. Dean Acheson, *Present at the Creation: My Years at the State Department* (New York: Norton, 1969), p. 415.

3. David McCullough, *Truman* (New York: Simon & Schuster, 1992), pp. 531 ff.

4. See, e.g., Merlo J. Pusey, *The Way We Go to War* (Boston: Houghton Mifflin, 1969), pp. 79–95.

5. *The Private Papers of Senator Arthur Vandenberg,* ed. Arthur H. Vandenberg, Jr. (Boston: Houghton Mifflin, 1982), p. 342, cited in Walter LaFeber, *America, Russia, and the Cold War, 1945–1971,* 2d ed. (New York: Wiley, 1972), p. 60.

6. William Fulbright, "Meet the Press," June 7, 1959, quoted in James Robinson, *Congress and Foreign Policy-Making,* rev. ed. (Homewood, Ill.: Dorsey, 1967), pp. 185–86.

7. Senator J. William Fulbright, testimony before the Senate Subcommittee on Separation of Powers of the Judiciary Committee, *Separation of Powers,* 90th Cong., 1st sess., 1967, p. 42.

8. Public Law 88–408, approved Aug. 10, 1964. The Tonkin Gulf Resolution passed 88–2 in the Senate and 414–0 in the House. There is a great deal of controversy surrounding this event. It seems, as Anthony Austin makes clear, that the administration did not want to take a second reading (see Anthony Austin, *The President's War* [Philadelphia: J. B. Lippincott, 1971]). On the other hand, some reviews of the incidents have the initial sonar readings of the *Maddox* and the *Turner Joy* as accurate (see Douglas Pike, "What Really Happened in the Gulf of Tonkin," *Washington Post Book World,* May 3, 1987). The best summary of this dreary period is found in Stanley Karnow's *Vietnam: A History* (New York: Penguin, 1983), pp. 445 ff.

9. At least two senators, Wayne Morse (D.-Wash.) and Ernest Gruening (R.-Ala.), were skeptical. See Morse's highly censored colloquy with Secretary of Defense McNamara in U.S. Congress, Senate, *Southeast Asia Resolution: Joint Hearings before the Senate Committees on Foreign Relations and Armed Services,* 88th Cong., 2d sess., 1964, released Nov. 24, 1966, pp. 13–15, 32–33. The Tonkin Gulf Resolution read, in part: "The Congress approves and supports the determination of the President, as Commander in Chief, to take all necessary means to repel armed attack against the forces of the United States and to prevent further aggression. . . . The United States regards as vital to its national interest and to world peace the maintenance of international peace and security in southeast Asia. . . . the United States is therefore, prepared, as the President determines, to take all necessary steps, including the use of armed force, to assist any member or protocol state of the Southeast Asia Collective Defense Treaty requesting assistance in defense of its freedom."

10. *New Republic,* May 1961, quoted in Henry Fairlie, "We Knew What We Were Doing When We Went into Vietnam," *Washington Monthly* 5, no. 3 (1973): 14.

11. Ibid., p. 7.

12. *Congressional Record,* 88th Cong., 2d sess., 1964, vol. 110, pt. 14, pp. 18409–10.

13. Ibid., pp. 18407–9.

14. "Secretary-Designate Kissinger Meets the Press at San Clemente," *Department of State Newsletter,* Aug.–Sept. 1973, p. 7.

15. Adlai Stevenson, "Party of the Second Part," *Harper's,* Feb. 1956, p. 32.

16. See, e.g., McGeorge Bundy's testimony in U.S. Congress, House, Committee on Foreign Affairs, *Congress, the President, and the War Powers,* 91st Cong., 2d sess., 1970.

17. Henry Kissinger, opening statement before the Senate Foreign Relations Committee, Sept. 7, 1973, quoted in *Department of State Newsletter,* Aug.–Sept. 1973, p. 4.

18. U.S. Congress, Senate, Committee on Appropriations, *Report, Second Supplemental Appropriations Bill, 1973, H.R. 7447, and Additional Views,* no. 93–160, 93d Cong., 1st sess., 1973.

19. Most legislators were greatly moved by the idea of the human disaster that was sure to follow what all perceived would be the inevitable fall of the Lon Nol government, but there was simply no consensus in Washington or in the field on how to cut the inevitable loss. Congress simply chose the classic Washington strategy, namely, that when in doubt, do nothing (William Shawcross, *Sideshow: Kissinger, Nixon, and the Destruction of Cambodia* [New York: Simon & Schuster Pocket Books, 1979], pp. 345–70 passim). As we write these lines, we cannot help but note the parallel paralysis—much like the paralysis that took Washington during the slow-motion fall of Saigon and Phnom Penh—that seems to have gripped the executive, Congress, NATO, and the United Nations in 1992 while

Serbian and Croatian forces, official and unofficial, rampaged and "cleansed" great chunks of the former Yugoslavia of their former inhabitants.

20. War-powers-legislation framer Jacob Javits (R.-N.Y.) called this provision (section 5) the War Powers Act's "structural heart." See his testimony, Mar. 7, 1973, in U.S. Congress, House, Committee on Foreign Affairs, *War Powers: Hearings,* 93d Cong., 1st sess., 1973.

21. We will extend this analysis in chapter 8.

22. The hearings were issued as a report, *The War Powers after 200 Years: Congress and the President at a Constitutional Impasse: Hearings before the Special Subcommittee on War Powers of the Committee on Foreign Relations,* 100th Cong., 2d sess., 1989.

23. *I.N.S. v. Chadha,* 1983. It can be argued that the *Chadha* case was unique, as Justice Powell noted in his concurring opinion: "The legislative veto had been included in a wide variety of statutes, ranging from bills to reorganize the Executive to the War Powers Resolution. . . . Whether the veto complies with the Presentment clause may well turn on the particular context in which it is exercised, and I would be hesitant to conclude that every veto is unconstitutional on the basis of the unusual example presented by this legislation." This is the argument in G. Sidney Buchanan, "In Defense of the War Powers Resolution: Chadha Does Not Apply," *Houston Law Review* 22 (1985): 1180; and James Nathan, "Salvaging the War Powers Resolution," *Presidential Studies Quarterly* 23, no. 2 (1993): 235–368.

24. The Turkish invasion had upset the delicately poised Greek-Turkish balance on Cyprus, and Congress was strongly pushed by a powerful lobby of pro-Greek members of Congress.

25. Henry Kissinger, quoted in *New York Times,* Jan. 25, 1975.

26. The United States was willing to negotiate unequal aggregates without the Soviets at the time because of the U.S. edge in accuracies, an asset of diminishing utility as the Russians improved their accuracies and increased the numbers of warheads they could place on targets.

27. John Kerry, quoted in David Shipler, "The Vietnam Experience and the Congressman of the 1980s," *New York Times,* May 28, 1987.

28. John McCain, quoted in ibid.

29. Richard Haass, *Congressional Power: Implications for American Security Policy,* Adelphi Papers, no. 153 (London: International Institute for Strategic Studies, 1979), esp. p. 31.

30. Lawrence J. Haas, "As Partisan as Ever," *National Journal,* June 15, 1991, p. 1493.

31. Lawrence J. Haas, "Living with Less Clout," ibid., pp. 1419–20.

32. Lawrence J. Haas, "Appropriations Still Rules!" ibid., June 1, 1991, pp. 1293–94.

33. Only the CIA was exempt from GAO's investigations.

34. Robert Pear, "When He Speaks, Washington Jumps," *New York Times,* July 30, 1990.

35. Congress established an Office of Technology Assessment, which, among other things, provides expertise on foreign and national security matters in areas such as arms control and the dissemination of critical technology to commercial competitors or hostile powers.

36. David Price, *The Congressional Experience: A View from the Hill* (New York: Westview, 1992), p. 79.

37. For a review of the increases in staff assistance in Congress see Frank and Weisband, *Foreign Policy by Congress*, pp. 227–45, esp. 228–33.

38. Henry Hyde, quoted in Clifford Krauss, "House Reformers of '74 Have Woes in '92," *New York Times*, Apr. 18, 1992.

39. William S. Broomfield, quoted in Kenneth J. Cooper and Eric Pianin, "Retirements from House Reach 50," *Washington Post*, Apr. 22, 1992.

40. Timothy Wirth, "Diary of a Dropout," *New York Times Magazine*, Aug. 9, 1992; John E. Yang, "Chairmen Toppled, Presidential Power Reigned In," *Washington Post*, June 15, 1992.

41. Adam Clymer, "Foley in a Harsher Light," *New York Times*, Mar. 14, 1992.

42. Frank and Weisband, *Foreign Policy by Congress*, pp. 215–16.

43. Ibid., p. 213.

44. Price, *The Congressional Experience*, p. 48.

45. Helen Dewar, "Senate Foreign Relations Panel Founders," *Washington Post*, Oct. 10, 1990.

46. On the House side, Congressmen Stephen Solarz and Thomas Downey were visited with electoral rejection for allegedly similar sins of inattention to domestic business (see below). Indeed, President Bush himself was susceptible to the criticism that though he was alert to the external world, he neither attended to nor cared very much about domestic affairs.

47. Indeed, in part because of increasing disinterest on the part of both the media and the members, public hearings such as the avowedly educative efforts by Senator Fulbright in the 1960s nearly disappeared.

48. *Washington Post*, Nov. 3, 1985.

49. Pell delegated responsibility for major foreign affairs legislation, such as arms control, foreign aid, and State Department authorizations, to subcommittees chaired by vigorous (and post-Vietnam-era) legislators such as Joseph Biden, Christopher Dodd, John Kerry, and Paul Sarbanes (D.-Md.) (see Christopher Madison, "A New Look for Sen. Pell's Committee," *National Journal*, Feb. 2, 1991, p. 279, and idem, "Rescue Mission," ibid., June 15, 1991, pp. 1513–14).

50. Christopher Madison, "Paper Tiger," ibid., June 15, 1991, p. 1435.

51. Larry Rohter, "Florida Congressman Quits after His District Is Changed," *New York Times*, May 28, 1992.

52. Madison, "Paper Tiger," p. 1435.

53. Lois Komano and Tom Kenworthy, "The Past and Paradox of Steve Solarz," *Washington Post*, May 29, 1991.

54. See, James M. McCormick, "The Changing Role of the House Foreign Affairs Committee," *Congress and the Presidency* 12, no. 1 (1986): 17 ff.

55. This assessment is based largely on the annual assessments of congressional voting undertaken by the *National Journal,* specifically Richard E. Cohen, "Rating Congress—A Guide to Separating the Liberals from the Conservatives," May 8, 1982, pp. 800–810; William Schneider, "Party Unity on Tax, Spending Issues—Less in House, More in Senate in 1982," May 7, 1983, pp. 936–52; idem, "Democrats, Republicans Move Further Apart on Most Issues in 1983 Session," May 12, 1984, pp. 904–20; idem, "Politics of the '80s Widen the Gap between the Two Parties in Congress," June 1, 1985, pp. 1268–82; idem, "A Year of Continuity," May 17, 1986, pp. 1162–91; Cohen and Schneider, "Moving to the Center," Mar. 21, 1987, pp. 672–701; idem, "Shift to the Left," Apr. 2, 1988, pp. 873–99; and idem, "The More Things Change . . . ," Jan. 27, 1990, pp. 195–221.

56. See the *National Journal* assessments in n. 55; and Richard E. Cohen and William Schneider, "Partisan Patterns," ibid., Jan. 19, 1991, pp. 134–61.

57. Lawrence C. Dodd and Bruce L. Oppenheim, *Congress Reconsidered* (Washington, D.C.: Congressional Quarterly Press, 1985), p. 10.

58. Cohen and Schneider, "Partisan Patterns," p. 134; idem, "Partisan Polarization," *National Journal,* Jan. 18, 1992, pp. 132–55. Cohen and Schneider report some narrowing of differences on social policy during the 1991 session, but overall the move toward greater partisanship was confirmed (see ibid., p. 132).

59. See Richard E. Cohen, "Lame-Duck Congress," *National Journal,* Jan. 19, 1991, pp. 122–27; and Adam Clymer, "Citing Rise in Frustration, Dozens of Lawmakers Quit," *New York Times,* Apr. 5, 1992.

60. Kenneth J. Cooper, "Rep. Dante Fascell Won't Seek Reelection," *Washington Post,* May 28, 1992.

CHAPTER 6   THE CONSTITUTIONAL FRAMEWORK OF
EXECUTIVE-LEGISLATIVE RELATIONS

1. See, e.g., the extended essay by Louis Henkin, *Constitutionalism, Democracy, and Foreign Affairs* (New York: Columbia University Press, 1990), esp. pp. 17–44. Other important and extensive explorations of this constitutional terrain that reach the conclusion that the prevailing reading of the constitutional balance is improperly tilted toward the presidency are Michael J. Glennon, *Constitutional Diplomacy* (Princeton: Princeton University Press, 1990); and Harold Hongju Koh, *The National Security Constitution: Sharing Power after the Iran-Contra Affair* (New Haven: Yale University Press, 1990). For commentary that reaches a different view see Jean Smith, *The Constitution and American Foreign Policy* (St. Paul: West, 1989).

2. Constitutional commentary on foreign affairs is not, however, as substantial as that relating to domestic affairs. For a synopsis of most of the relevant

cases see Smith, *The Constitution and American Foreign Policy*; and for what is widely viewed as an authoritative commentary see Louis Henkin, *Foreign Affairs and the Constitution* (New York: Norton, 1975).

3. 299 U.S. 304 (1936) and 343 U.S. 579 (1952), respectively.

4. See Koh, *National Security Constitution*, esp. pp. 93–113, and Glennon, *Constitutional Diplomacy*, esp. pp. 3–34, for their exposition of the *Curtiss-Wright* versus a *Youngstown* "vision" of the Constitution.

5. Indeed, Koh, who served as a clerk for Associate Justice Harry Blackmun and served two years as an attorney and adviser in the Department of Justice, has noted that the opinion is so frequently cited by government attorneys in defending presidents' primacy that it is referred to as the "'Curtiss-Wright, so I'm right,' cite" (Koh, *National Security Constitution*, p. 94). That Sutherland wrote the opinion is ironic in that in all other areas he was one of the most conservative of justices and consistently supported the most narrow interpretation of presidential power. Here, however, his nationalism was dominant, and he wrote the cornerstone opinion for the development of the imperial presidency (see Smith's discussion of Sutherland in *The Constitution and American Foreign Policy*, pp. 5–6).

6. *United States v. Curtiss-Wright*, 299 U.S. 304 (1936).

7. Charles F. Merriam, *History of the Theory of Sovereignty since Rousseau* (New York: Columbia University Press, 1900), pp. 161 ff. Naturally, this was a popular argument with post–World War II realists (see the section "Is Sovereignty Divisible?" in Hans J. Morgenthau's classic first edition *Politics among Nations* [New York: Knopf, 1948], pp. 258 ff.).

8. Smith, *The Constitution and American Foreign Policy*, p. 3.

9. Glennon, *Constitutional Diplomacy*, pp. 23 ff.

10. Henkin, *Constitutionalism*, p. 7.

11. Glennon, *Constitutional Diplomacy*, p. 21.

12. 299 U.S. 304 (1936) (emphasis added).

13. Associate Justice Hugo Black in his statement of the arguments in his majority opinion in the *Youngstown* case, 343 U.S. 579 (1952). The quotations of justices in the next several paragraphs are from this same source.

14. See, e.g., Smith, *The Constitution and American Foreign Policy*.

15. Koh, *National Security Constitution*, p. 108.

16. The whole argument is related to a curious debate about "original intent" (see Louis Fisher, "Methods of Interpreting the Constitution: The Limits of Original Intent," *Cumberland Law Review* 42 [1987]: 18).

17. See James Nathan, "Salvaging the War Powers Resolution," *Presidential Studies Quarterly* 23, no. 2 (1993): 235–368, nn. 122 ff., for some relevant case law concerning the issue of "political questions."

18. President Carter made no Supreme Court appointments during his term in office.

19. Koh, *National Security Constitution*, p. 137.

20. Justice Jackson concurring in 343 U.S. 579 (1952).

21. John M. Berry, "Foreign Policy Making and the Congress," *Editorial Research Reprints* 1, no. 15 (1967): 282.

22. See Joseph E. Kallenbach, *The American Chief Executive: The Presidency and Governorship* (New York: Harper & Row, 1966), p. 506; and Loch Johnson and James McCormick, "Foreign Policy by Executive Fiat," *Foreign Policy,* no. 28 (Fall 1977): 117–38.

23. Arthur M. Schlesinger, Jr., *The Imperial Presidency* (Boston: Houghton Mifflin, 1973), pp. 85–86. For the data in the following paragraphs see Schlesinger and Louis Fisher, *President and Congress: Power and Policy* (New York: Free Press, 1973), p. 45.

24. Allison Lippa, "The Legality, Efficacy, and Future Use of International Executive Agreements: An Analysis of Agreements in Criminal Matters," *American Criminal Law Review* 29 (Summer 1992): 1306.

25. See Raoul Berger, testimony, in U.S. Congress, House, Committee on International Relations, *Congressional Review of International Agreements: Hearings before the Subcommittee on International Security and Scientific Affairs,* 94th Cong., 2d sess., 1976, pp. 69–70. See also *United States v. Curtiss-Wright.*

26. U.S. Congress, Senate, Committee on Foreign Relations, *Treaties and Other International Agreements: The Role of the United States Senate,* 98th Cong., 2d sess., 1984, Committee Print 98–205; Lippa, "Legality, Efficacy, and Future Use of International Executive Agreements," p. 1309 n. 53.

27. *B. Altman Co. v. United States,* 224 U.S. 601 (1912).

28. E.g., S. 4556, 91st Cong., 2d sess., Dec. 2, 1970.

29. Henkin, *Foreign Affairs and the Constitution,* p. 426 n. 16.

30. Lippa, "Legality, Efficacy, and Future Use of International Executive Agreements," p. 1316 nn. 102–5.

31. For a presentation of this argument see Berger, testimony, pp. 69–70. In Berger's view, only the "housekeeping" aspects of foreign affairs, e.g., receiving the credentials of ambassadors, were to be left to the president to carry out without consultation.

32. *New York Times,* June 6, 1972.

33. Strobe Talbot, *Endgame: The Inside Story of SALT II* (New York: Harper & Row, 1979), pp. 215–16. The survey of executive-legislative relations regarding SALT II in this chapter is drawn largely from Talbot's account.

34. Ibid., p. 207.

35. See the letter of Gerald C. Smith, chief negotiator of the SALT I ABM Treaty, in *New York Times,* Oct. 23, 1985. See also Thomas Longstretch, John Pike, and John Rhinelander, "The Impact of U.S. and Soviet Missile Defense Programs on the ABM Treaty," *Report of the National Campaign to Save the ABM Treaty* (Washington, D.C., Mar. 1985), pp. 26–27. For problems with the September 1986 test see R. Jeffrey Smith, "SDI and Compliance," *Washington Post,* Sept. 15, 1986.

36. Louis Fisher, *Constitutional Conflicts between Congress and the President,* 3d ed. (Lawrence: University Press of Kansas, 1989), p. 236.

37. Ibid., p. 233.

38. See Harold Hongju Koh, "The Treaty Power," *University of Miami Law Review* 43 (Sept. 1988): 110–11.

39. See the dissent of Justice Harry A. Blackmun in *Sale v. Haitian, Center Council,* reprinted in *New York Times,* June 23, 1993.

40. See H. Wriston, "The Special Envoy," *Foreign Affairs* 38, no. 2 (1960): 219–57. In this century, for example, Wilson's friend Colonel House had vastly more influence on the president than did his secretaries of state, William Jennings Bryan and Robert Lansing. Similarly, Cordell Hull, the secretary of state in much of Franklin Roosevelt's presidency, was largely relegated to diplomatic trivia, while Roosevelt's friend Harry Hopkins became a presidential envoy to Churchill and Stalin. Hopkins never passed through a congressional chamber, and his salary was paid out of "contingency funds" that did not have to be accounted for.

41. See U.S. Congress, Senate, Committee on Foreign Relations, *Background Information on the Foreign Relations Committee,* 90th Cong., 2d sess., 1968, pp. 27–32.

42. Charles E. Bohlen, *Witness to History, 1929–1969* (New York: Norton, 1973), pp. 309–36.

43. Helen Dewar, "Senate Confirms Hecht as Envoy to the Bahamas," *Washington Post,* July 12, 1989.

44. Thus, Senator J. William Fulbright once philosophized: "It is ridiculous to send [men and women] with so little preparation to an area where . . . these people are a sensitive and strange people, and I think it will do us no good. However, I am not going to raise Cain. I know it is an old and evil custom that afflicts us" (quoted in Cecil V. Crabb, Jr., *American Foreign Policy in the Nuclear Age,* 2d ed. [New York: Harper & Row, 1960], p. 60).

45. The ambassadors to the Netherlands, Switzerland, Austria, and France paid over $100,000 to the GOP in the years of the Nixon presidency (*New York Times,* Mar. 17, 1974).

46. Irvin Molotosky, "Writer Reports Contents of Secret Nixon Tapes," ibid., Dec. 7, 1992.

47. George Bush's appointees to ambassadorships in Australia and Spain had each contributed more than $140,000 to mostly Republican candidates between 1985 and 1988. Other Bush loyalists received ambassadorships in France, Italy, New Zealand, the United Kingdom, China, Germany, and South Korea (Elaine Sciolino, "True to Custom, Bush Appoints Allies as Envoys," ibid., Feb. 14, 1989). On Reagan's appointments see *New York Times,* Apr. 20, 1984.

48. *New York Times,* Apr. 20, 1984.

49. See, e.g., the remarks by Charles Lichenstein, U.S. ambassador to the United Nations from 1981 to 1984, in "The State Department vs. Ronald Reagan:

Four Ambassadors Speak Out," *Heritage Foundation Lectures,* no. 44 (Washington, D.C., 1985), pp. 13–14.

50. In fact, some observers viewed the opposition block as a rough indicator of how many votes Carter would need for SALT ratification, although the text of the treaty remained to be completed.

51. See Helen Dewar, "Defeat of Tower Reflects Dramatic Changes in Senate," *Washington Post,* Mar. 13, 1989. The subject of sexual harassment, when it was clumsily raised in the 1992 confirmation hearings for Judge Clarence Thomas's nomination to the Supreme Court, seems to vitiate any prima facie assumption that younger members of Congress might be more sensitive to the delicate issue of harassment in the workplace. In the case of Tower, the conclusion seems to be that he was a man little liked, and when an excuse was found for his undoing, it was used with alacrity by old colleagues and adversaries alike.

52. See Robert A. Strong, "Jimmy Carter and the Panama Canal Treaties," *Presidential Studies Quarterly* 21, no. 2 (1991): 269–86.

CHAPTER 7   THE POWER OF THE PURSE AND
CONGRESSIONAL OVERSIGHT

1. On the extent of the franchise and the Jeffersonian ideal of an educated yeomanry see Walter LeFeber, *The American Age* (New York: Norton, 1989), p. 20. LeFeber estimates that white males were over 95 percent literate and that this was the highest rate in the world.

2. On the mind-set of the framers see Leonard W. Levy, *Original Intent and the Framers' Constitution* (New York: Macmillan, 1989). The most impressive exposition of the founders' search for efficiency is Louis Fisher, "The Efficiency Side of the Separated Powers," *Journal of American Studies* 5, no. 2 (1971), esp. pp. 114–15. Louis Fisher is a senior analyst at the Library of Congress and a national asset. Our arguments owe much to his indulgent tutorials. Naturally, Dr. Fisher is responsible for none of the results.

3. See the cases cited in Louis Fisher, *Constitutional Conflicts between Congress and the President,* 3d ed. (Lawrence: University Press of Kansas, 1991), pp. 20, 128–30.

4. See Louis Fisher, *Presidential Spending Power* (Princeton: Princeton University Press, 1975), p. 200. For an account of impoundment legislation, see Congressional Quarterly, *Congress and the Nation, 1973–1976* (Washington, D.C., 1977), pp. 60–61.

5. Louis Fisher, "Dark Corners in the Budget," *Nation,* Jan. 19, 1974, p. 75; Timothy H. Ingram, "Billions in the Basement," *Washington Monthly* 3, no. 11 (1972).

6. For an example of the bizarre lengths to which DOD went in Southeast Asia from 1966 to 1972 see U.S. Congress, Senate, *National Emergency: Hearings*

before the Special Committee on the Termination of the National Emergency in the United States, 93d Cong., 1st sess., July 24, 1973, pt. 2, p. 529.

7. Stephen Alexis Cain, *Analysis of the FY 1992–93 Defense Budget Request, with Historical Defense Budget Tables* (Washington, D.C.: Defense Budget Project, 1991), table 5.

8. *Washington Post,* May 16, 17, 1985. But Senator Dixon should not have been surprised: this same ploy had been used during the last days of U.S. involvement in Vietnam (see "Senate Blocks Pentagon Request for More Vietnam Aid," *Congressional Quarterly Weekly Report,* May 11, 1974, pp. 1234–35; *New York Times,* Apr. 17, 1974; *Philadelphia Inquirer,* Mar. 18, 1975; and Leslie Gelb, "Indochina Deja Vu," *New York Times,* Mar. 23, 1975, Week in Review).

9. Warren Strobel, "Staying Mum on Iraq: Misuse of Funds No Secret to State," *Washington Times,* Oct. 22, 1992.

10. Leslie Gelb, "A Bush Green Light to Iraq: The Message the US Never Sent," *New York Times,* Oct. 22, 1992; Michael R. Gordon, "Pentagon Objected to a Message Bush Sent to Iraq before Its Invasion," ibid., Oct. 25, 1992.

11. Murray Waas and Douglas Frantz, "US Bent Aid Rules to Gain Turkey's Help in Gulf War," *Los Angeles Times,* June 18, 1992, Washington edition.

12. Carlos Brezina, "Treasury Gave Subsidy to Mexico, GAO Says," *Washington Post,* Aug. 15, 1990.

13. Richard H. P. Sia, "U.S. Conceals $100 Billion in Reserve Funds," *Baltimore Sun,* June 7, 1990.

14. Quoted in Richard H. P. Sia, "Despite Furor, 'Slush Fund' Isn't News to Congress," ibid., June 24, 1990.

15. Cain, *Analysis of the FY 1992–93 Defense Budget Request.*

16. Barbara Opall, "Pentagon Rushes to Deplete M Account," *Defense News,* July 19–25, 1993, pp. 6 ff.

17. See Steven Emerson, "The Secrets of North's Notebooks," *New York Times,* June 17, 1988.

18. See U.S. Congress, House Select Committee to Investigate Covert Arms Transfers with Iran and Senate Select Committee on Secret Military Assistance to Iran and the Nicaraguan Opposition, *Report of the Congressional Committees Investigating the Iran-Contra Affair* (Washington, D.C.: U.S. Government Printing Office, 1987), pp. 38–48 ff.

19. See the transcript of "Guns, Drugs and the CIA," broadcast on "Frontline," May 18, 1988, produced and written by Andrew Cockburn with Leslie Cockburn; and "Guns for Drugs?" *Newsweek,* May 22, 1988.

20. This point is amplified considerably in U.S. Congress, Senate, *A Report of the Subcommittee on Narcotics, Terrorism, and International Operations,* 101st Cong., 1st sess., 1989, vol. 1, pp. 97–99 ff., Apr. 13, 1989.

21. See Steven Engleberg with Jeff Garth, "Officials Say Bush Heard '85 Charge against Noriega," *New York Times,* May 8, 1988; and Tom Wicker, "Bush and Noriega," ibid., Apr. 29, 1987. See the sworn testimony of Donald Gregg, a

CIA official who served through 1988 as Bush's national security adviser, in the joint House-Senate Iran-Contra hearings, pp. 502–3, for Bush and the Contra support activities. Noriega was a CIA asset from the time Bush became director of the CIA in 1976 (see Jim McGhee and David Hoffman, "Rivals Hint Bush Understates Knowledge of Noriega's Ties," *Washington Post,* May 8, 1988; Bill McCallister, "Model Citizen Adopted Life of Smuggling Drugs," ibid., Apr. 15, 1987; Stephen Engleberg, "3 Nicaraguan Rebels Tell Senators of Refueling Drug Planes for Cash," *New York Times,* Apr. 8, 1988; and Dan Morgan "Testimony of Bush Aides Points to Big Latin American Role," *Washington Post,* May 1, 1988). Bush was head of the Reagan antidrug task force in this period and claimed that his close attention to the details of that operation were his proudest achievement (see Daniel Schor, "All Things Considered," *National Public Radio,* Weekend edition, May 1, 1988).

22. Alexander Hamilton, quoted in J. Grahm Noyes, "Getting the President off from Tin Cup Diplomacy," *University of California (Davis) Law Review* 24 (Spring 1991): 862 (Noyes's emphasis).

23. Public Law 98–473, 8066, 98 Stat. 1837, 1935 (1984), commonly referred to as "Boland II." The legislation took its name from Edward P. Boland (D.-Mass.), the chairman of the House Intelligence Committee for six years beginning in 1980.

24. For accounts of the funding and funding arrangements see White House press release, Feb. 22, 1991; Carroll J. Doherty, "Who Will Dole Out the Gulf Donations?" *Congressional Quarterly,* Sept. 22, 1990, p. 3030; Linda Miller, "Saudi Contributions Called Generous," *New York Times,* Jan. 11, 1991; idem, "Saudis Importing Fuel to Fight War," ibid., Jan. 23, 1991; Stephen Weisman, "Tokyo Chief, Facing New Debate, Appeals for Support for War Aid," ibid., Jan. 20, 1991; idem, "Japan Counts the Costs of Gulf Action—or Inaction," ibid., Jan. 27, 1991; and David E. Rosenbaum, "U.S. Has Received $50 Billion in Pledges for War," ibid., Feb. 10, 1991. On the German contribution see Stephen Kinzer, "Germans to Give $5.5 Billion More," ibid., Jan. 30, 1991; and "Germany's Contribution to the Gulf Effort" (Fact sheet distributed by the German Information Center, New York, Feb. 21, 1991).

25. The Defense Department wanted the funds placed in its coffers, where they could be spent with no legislative oversight, but at the insistence of Senator Robert Byrd (D.-W.Va.), Appropriations Committee chairman, the monies were deposited with the Treasury Department, where they were expended under normal oversight producers (Louis Fisher, Congressional Research Service, interview with James Nathan, Washington, D.C., June 25, 1993; Doherty, "Who Will Dole Out the Gulf Donations?").

26. This analysis is indebted to Louis Fisher, *President and Congress: Power and Policy* (New York: Free Press, 1972), pp. 92–110, and Richard F. Grimmet, "The Legislative Veto and United States Arms Sales, in United States House Committee on Rules," in *Studies on the Legislative Veto,* report prepared by the

Congressional Research Service for the Subcommittee on Rules of the House, 96th Cong., 2d sess., Feb. 1980, pp. 248–320.

27. See Grimmet, "Legislative Veto and United States Arms Sales," pp. 252–68.

28. See Fisher, *Constitutional Conflicts,* p. 180.

29. See Louis Fisher, *One Year after* INS v. Chadha: *Congressional and Judicial Developments* (Washington, D.C.: Congressional Research Service, Library of Congress, 1984), p. 1.

30. "Legislative Veto Rulings," in Congressional Quarterly, *Congress and the Nation, 1985–1988* (Washington, D.C., 1989), p. 888.

31. Ibid. We are grateful to Norman Ornstein, of the American Enterprise Institute, for his help on this point.

32. See Louis Fisher, "Judicial Misjudgment about the Lawmaking Process: The Legislative Veto Case," *Public Administration Review,* Nov. 1985, pp. 705–7; and idem, *Constitutional Conflicts,* p. 150.

33. See Fisher, "Judicial Misjudgment," p. 709.

34. See ibid., p. 707; and Fisher, *Constitutional Conflicts,* p. 120.

35. U.S. Congress, House, Committee on Foreign Affairs, *Strengthening the Executive Legislative Consultation on Foreign Policy,* 98th Cong., 1st sess., 1983, Committee Print 8.

36. For an excellent overview of the literature on these issues see James Lindsay, "Congress and the Defense Budget: Parochialism or Policy?" in *Arms, Politics, and the Economy: Historical and Contemporary Perspectives,* ed. Robert Higgs (New York: Holmes & Meier, 1990), pp. 174–201.

37. James Lindsay, "Congressional Oversight of the Department of Defense: Reconsidering the Conventional Wisdom," *Armed Forces and Society* 17, no. 1 (1990): 7.

38. Lindsay, "Congress and the Defense Budget," p. 181, citing Steven S. Smith and Christopher Deering, *Committees in Congress* (Washington, D.C.: Congressional Quarterly, 1984).

39. Ibid., pp. 189, 190; Kirk Johnson, "The Winds of Peace Buffet Connecticut," *New York Times,* Feb. 16, 1992.

40. Gwen Ifill, "Plan to Close Bases Is Met with Protests from Affected States," ibid., Apr. 13, 1991.

41. U.S. Congress, Senate, Committee on Armed Services, *Organization, Structure and Decisionmaking Procedures of the Department of Defense, Part 1,* 98th Cong., 1st sess., 1983, p. 9, cited in Lindsay, "Congress and the Defense Budget," p. 181.

42. See Ifill, "Plan to Close Bases Is Met with Protests," for the original Pentagon list; and idem, "More Bases Considered for Closings," *New York Times,* June 1, 1991.

43. See Eric Schmitt, "Panel Takes First Steps, Modestly, in Closing Bases," *New York Times,* June 24, 1993; and idem, "Clinton Proposes to Soften the Blow of Base Closings," ibid., July 4, 1993.

44. Gwen Ifill, "Frenzy in Capital to Save Military Bases," ibid., June 16, 1991.
45. *Wall Street Journal,* Mar. 18, 1986.
46. Johnson, "Winds of Peace Buffet Connecticut."
47. This literature is reviewed by Lindsay in "Congress and the Defense Budget," pp. 183–87.
48. Robert J. Art, "Congress and the Defense Budget," in *Towards a More Effective Defense,* by Barry Blechman et al. (Washington, D.C.: Georgetown University, Center for International and Strategic Studies, 1985), pp. 132, 134; idem, "Congress and the Defense Budget: Enhancing Policy Oversight," *Political Science Quarterly,* Summer 1985, pp. 227–48.
49. Art, "Congress and the Defense Budget: Enhancing Policy Oversight," p. 238. See also Gordon Adams, *The Role of Defense Budgets in Civil-Military Relations* (Washington, D.C.: Defense Budget Project, 1992).
50. See, e.g., Sam Nunn, *Nunn, 1990: A New Military Strategy* (Washington, D.C.: Center for Strategic and International Studies, 1990); and Les Aspin, *An Approach to Sizing American Conventional Forces for the Post-Soviet Era* (Washington, D.C.: House Armed Services Committee, Feb. 25, 1992).
51. Lindsay, "Congressional Oversight," p. 20.
52. For a review of the technical provisions of Gramm-Rudman-Hollings see Congressional Quarterly, *Congress and the Nation, 1985–1988,* pp. 44–47. The legislation was sponsored by Senators Phil Gramm (R.-Tex.), Warren Rudman (R.-N.H.), and Ernest Hollings (D.-S.C.).
53. Ibid; and see pp. 67–70 for a discussion of the Gramm-Rudman "fix."
54. Susan F. Rasky, "Substantial Power on Spending Is Shifted from Congress to Bush," *New York Times,* Oct. 30, 1990.
55. Frank J. Smist, Jr., *Congress Oversees the United States Intelligence Community: 1947–1988* (Knoxville: University Press of Tennessee, 1990), p. 5. Smist's interview with Clifford was in 1983. Staff subcommittees rarely met, at best some two or three times a year, says Smist.
56. See, e.g., the articles by Senator David L. Boren, the chair of the Senate Select Committee on Intelligence, "The Intelligence Community: How Crucial?" and Ernest R. May, "Intelligence: Backing Into the Future," *Foreign Affairs* 71, no. 3 (1992): 52–62 and 63–72, respectively.
57. Harry Howe Ransom, *Can Democracy Survive the Cold War?* (Garden City, N.Y.: Doubleday, 1964), p. 178.
58. *Congressional Record,* 93d Cong., 2d sess., 1974, vol. 120, p. S9606.
59. Victor Marchetti and John D. Marks, *The CIA and the Cult of Intelligence* (New York: Dell, 1974), p. 345.
60. David Rosenbaum, "Intelligence Oversight Is Done with a Blindfold," *New York Times,* Dec. 29, 1974; Fisher, *Presidential Spending Power,* p. 218.
61. U.S. Congress, Senate, *Final Report of the Select Committee to Study Governmental Operations with Respect to Intelligence Activities,* 94th Cong., 2d sess., 1976, S. R. 94–755.

62. Congressional Quarterly, *Congress and the Nation, 1973–1976,* pp. 182–97; see also the useful collection of documents covering the congressional investigation in all of its phases, T. G. Fain, ed., *The Intelligence Community: History, Organization, and Issues* (New York: Bowker, 1977).

63. Smist, *Congress Oversees the United States Intelligence Community,* p. 10.

64. Seymour Hersh, "Huge CIA Operation Reported in the US against Anti-War Forces, Other Dissidents in Nixon Years," *New York Times,* Dec. 22, 1974.

65. Not revealed was the degree to which DOD intelligence resources were employed. Army intelligence was later reported to have been employed against Martin Luther King Jr.'s maternal grandfather, his father, and then against Dr. King himself. The Army, according to one uncontradicted report, used Ku Klux Klan information to keep track of civil rights workers. U-2 spy planes tracked demonstrations, and Green Berets bugged civil rights leaders' conversations. When Martin Luther King, Jr., was killed on April 4, 1968, eight undercover Green Berets were nearby, keeping him under surveillance ("Army Spied on Black Leaders, Report Says," *Sunday Montgomery Advertiser,* Mar. 21, 1993).

66. John Marks, *The Search for "Manchurian Candidate": The Untold Story of CIA's Secret Effort to Control Human Behavior* (London: Allen Lane, 1979), pp. 6–7 ff. and passim; U.S. Congress, Senate, Hearings before the Select Committee on Intelligence, Subcommittee on Health and Scientific Research of the Committee on Human Resources, *Project MKUltra: The CIA's Program of Research in Behavioral Modification,* 95th Cong., 1st sess., 1977, pp. 123 ff.

67. U.S. Congress, Senate, Hearings before the Select Committee on Intelligence, *The Disclosure of Funds for Intelligence Activities,* 95th Cong., 2d sess., 1978; Rosenbaum, "Intelligence Oversight Is Done with a Blindfold."

68. On the development of the Senate proposal see John Felton, "Intelligence Charter Disputes Emerge Again on Key Issues," *Congressional Quarterly Weekly Report,* Feb. 23, 1980, pp. 537–38; Richard Whittle, "Senate Committee Votes Changes in Intelligence Reporting Requirements," ibid., May 31, 1980, pp. 1520–21; and idem, "Senate Passes Compromise Intelligence Oversight Bill," ibid., June 7, 1980, pp. 1588–89.

69. American Bar Association Standing Committee on National Security, *Oversight and Accountability of the U.S. Intelligence Agencies* (Chicago, 1980), pp. 20–21. The act was part of the intelligence authorization bill of 1980 and codified as Title V of the National Security Act of 1947. See ibid., p. 11.

70. Ibid., p. 21.

71. Ibid.

72. Smist, *Congress Oversees the United States Intelligence Community,* p. 223.

73. *New York Times,* Sept. 28, 1984. Casey, for example, was convinced that "Mexico would be the next Iran" and insisted on changing intelligence estimates to conform to his view (see Bob Woodward, *Veil: The Secret Wars of the CIA, 1981–1987* [New York: Pocket Books, 1987], pp. 342–45 ff.).

74. Fox Butterfield, "Casey Said to Have Failed to Follow Arms Rule," *New York Times,* Apr. 3, 1987. See also Woodward, *Veil,* pp. 375–84, 409–10.

75. For a discussion of the finding see Theodore Draper, *A Very Thin Line: The Iran-Contra Affairs* (New York: Hill & Wang, 1991), pp. 203–16; for the history of subsequent findings related to Iran-Contra see pp. 217–63. Also useful are "Special Report: Iran-Contra Affair," in Congressional Quarterly, *Congress and the Nation, 1985–1988,* pp. 253–70; and Woodward, *Veil,* esp. pp. 473 ff. See also above, chapter 4.

76. *Washington Post,* Mar. 9, 1980.

77. See ibid., Feb. 9 and 13, 1986; and *Oversight and Accountability of the U.S. Intelligence Agencies,* p. 53.

78. Interview in David C. Morrison, "New Challenges for CIA," *National Journal,* Dec. 16, 1989, p. 3038. See also idem, "Pulling In Its Horns," ibid., June 10, 1989, p. 1430.

79. Morrison, "New Challenges for CIA," p. 3036.

80. Quoted in David MacMichael, review of *Lost Promise: How CIA Analysis Misleads the Nation—an Intelligence Assessment,* by John A. Gentry, in *Unclassified, The Newspaper of the Association of National Security Alumni* 5, no. 1 (1993): 13.

81. Angelo Codevilla, "CIA, Losing Its Smarts," *New York Times,* Feb. 13, 1993.

82. MacMichael, review of *Lost Promise,* p. 13.

83. Morrison, "New Challenges for CIA," p. 3041.

84. The proposal was advanced as a part of a Republican minority report of the Iran-Contra Special Investigating Committee (see "Recommendation 1: Joint Intelligence Committee," *Report of the Congressional Committees Investigating the Iran-Contra Affair with the Minority View,* abr. ed. [New York: Random House for the New York Times, 1988], p. 455).

85. See David C. Morrison, "An Eye on the CIA," *National Journal,* Apr. 16, 1988, p. 1010.

86. See David Hoffman and David Ottaway, "Panel Drops Covert-Acts Notification," *Washington Post,* Oct. 27, 1989; and Stephen Engleberg, "Bush to Tell Congress of Covert Plans," *New York Times,* Oct. 28, 1989.

87. See "Oversight—the Intelligence Committees Try Again," *Unclassified, The Newspaper of the Association of National Security Alumni* 3, no. 3 (1991): 3.

88. Elaine Sciolino, "C.I.A. Chief Rejects Push for Change," *New York Times,* Apr. 2, 1992.

89. U.S. Congress, House, *Intelligence Authorization Act for Fiscal Year 1993: Report to Accompany H. R. 5095,* 102d Cong., 2d sess., 1992, H. Rept. 102-544, pt. 1, passim.

90. George Lardner, Jr., "Gates Rejects Overhaul of Spy Agencies," *Washington Post,* Apr. 2, 1992.

91. See Gerald Seib and David Rodgers, "Gates Says CIA Faces Deep Cuts

Due to Congress," *Wall Street Journal,* Dec. 8, 1992; and James Nathan's conversations with senior CIA officials and with David MacMichael, president of the Association of National Security Alumni, Nov. 5, 1992. The Clinton budget was higher than expected, even for the CIA, which was said to have been reduced from some $19 billion to $17 billion, but Democratic lawmakers were decidedly cool to administration arguments that satellites needed replacement and that "you have to spend money to save money" (see Douglas Jeht, "Clinton Requesting More Money for Spy Agencies, Officials Say," *New York Times,* Apr. 13, 1993).

92. Steven V. Roberts, "Reagan-Wright Argument Grows on Central America Policy Role," *New York Times,* Nov. 17, 1987; Joel Brinkley, "Wright, His Latin Role Contested, Signs a 'Peace' Pact with Shultz," ibid., Nov. 18, 1987.

93. See Anthony Lewis, "Congress Was Right," ibid., June 26, 1990.

CHAPTER 8   THE WAR POWERS AND EXECUTIVE-
LEGISLATIVE RELATIONS

1. Portions of this chapter are based on James A. Nathan, "'Curbing the Distress of War': An Outline for a War Powers Resolution That Works," *Polity,* Dec. 1991, and idem, "Salvaging the War Powers Resolution," *Presidential Studies Quarterly* 23, no. 2 (1993): 235–368.

2. Rob Brewin and Sydney Shaw, *Vietnam Trial: Westmoreland v. CBS* (New York: Atheneum, 1987), p. 231.

3. Public Law 88–408. This is not to say that most of the implications of the initial deployments under President Kennedy and the subsequent deployments were mysterious. Nor could it be argued that Congress's appreciation of the dim military prospects was defective or that the facts were not there to be known. Congress, like the executive, plainly did not "want to know" (see on this point Henry Fairlie, "We Knew What We Were Doing When We Went into Vietnam," *Washington Monthly* 5, no. 3 [1973]: 7 ff.; and above, chapter 5).

4. Edward P. Haley, *Congress and the Fall of South Vietnam* (Rutherford, N.J.: Farleigh Dickinson Press, 1982); William Gibbons and Allan Farlow, *Congress and the Termination of the Vietnam War* (Washington, D.C.: Congressional Research Service, Foreign Affairs Division, 1973). See also above, chapter 7.

5. Thomas F. Eagleton, *War and Presidential Power: A Chronicle of Congressional Surrender* (New York: Liveright, 1974), p. 11; see also above, chapter 5.

6. Eagleton, *War and Presidential Power,* pp. 207, 218–19.

7. Ibid., pp. 220–21.

8. "The Uses of Military Power," remarks prepared for delivery by the Honorable Caspar W. Weinberger, Secretary of Defense, News Release (Washington, D.C.: Office of the Assistant Secretary of Defense [Public Affairs], Nov. 28, 1984), p. 6. See also Harry G. Summers, Jr., *On Strategy: A Critical Analysis of the Vietnam War* (Novato, Calif.: Dell, 1984); Bruce Palmer, Jr., *The 25 Year War:*

America's Military Role in Vietnam (Lexington: University of Kentucky Press, 1984); and for a comparison, Gary R. Hess, "The Military Perspective on Strategy in Vietnam," *Diplomatic History* 10, no. 1 (1986): 91–106.

9. Michael J. Glennon, *Constitutional Diplomacy* (Princeton: Princeton University Press, 1990); Harold Hongju Koh, *The National Security Constitution: Sharing Power after the Iran-Contra Affair* (New Haven: Yale University Press, 1990).

10. See Allan S. Nanes, "Legislative Vetoes: The War Powers Resolution," in *Studies on the Legislative Veto,* report prepared by the Congressional Research Service for the Subcommittee on Rules of the House, 96th Cong., 2d sess., Feb. 1980, pp. 579–687.

11. U.S. Congress, House, Committee on International Relations, *Congressional Oversight of War Powers Compliance: Zaire Airlift: Hearings before the Subcommittee on International Security and Scientific Affairs,* 95th Cong., 2d sess., Aug. 10, 1978.

12. For a review of the most important provisions of the act see above, chapter 5.

13. The Cambodian air force comprised an assortment of captured and probably inoperable U.S. aircraft (see Roy Rowan, *The Four Days of Mayaguez* [New York: Norton, 1975], p. 210).

14. Jack Anderson, "Washington Merry-Go-Round," *Washington Post,* May 26, 1975.

15. *Washington Post,* May 13, 1975.

16. *New York Times,* May 14, 1975.

17. See *Congressional Quarterly Weekly Report,* Dec. 29, 1973, p. 3435; H. R. 9055–P.L. 93/50, H. J. Res. 636–P.L. 93/52, H. R. 7645–P.L. 92/126, H. R. 9286–P.L. 93/155, and S. 1443–P.L. 93/189; and "Text of Resolution on Warpowers," *New York Times,* Nov. 8, 1973.

18. Raoul Berger, "The *Mayaguez* Incident and the Constitution," *New York Times,* May 23, 1975. See also Anthony Lewis, "A Chorus of Yahoos," ibid., May 26, 1975.

19. This was the avowed impetus for the funding of the Rapid Deployment Force (see James Nathan, "Exploiting American Vulnerabilities," *Naval War College Review,* Aug. 1979).

20. See Phillip Brenner and William LeoGrande, "Congress and the Not So Secret War against Nicaragua: A Preliminary Analysis" (Paper delivered at the American Political Science Association Convention, New Orleans, Sept. 29, 1985), pp. 18 ff.

21. Administration officials were particularly worried that the ten-thousand-foot airport runway some seven hundred Cuban construction workers were building could be used equally for ferrying Soviet bloc troops and arms as well as for attracting tourists to diversify Grenada's economy.

22. Richard A. Gabriel, *Military Incompetence: Why the Military Doesn't*

Win (New York: Hill & Wang, 1985), chap. 6, cited in *Washington Monthly,* Feb. 1986, p. 39.

23. See Richard A. Gabriel, *Military Incompetence,* excerpted in *Washington Monthly,* Feb. 1986, p. 41.

24. Allan Ides, "Congress, Constitutional Responsibility, and the War Powers," *Loyola of Los Angeles Law Review* 17, no. 3 (1984): 637.

25. Jacob K. Javits, "War Powers Reconsidered," *Foreign Affairs* 64, no. 1 (1985): 137. For an extended review of the Grenada invasion in the context of the War Powers Resolution see Michael Rubner, "The Reagan Administration, the 1973 War Powers Resolution, and the Invasion of Grenada," *Political Science Quarterly,* Winter 1985–86.

26. Rubner, "Reagan Administration," p. 21; see also Jonathan Kwitny, *Endless Enemies* (New York: Penguin Books, 1986), pp. 411, 417.

27. Bob Woodward, *Veil: The Secret Wars of the CIA, 1981–1987* (New York: Simon & Schuster, 1987), pp. 204–5.

28. See Ellen Collier, *The War Powers Resolution: A Decade of Experience* (Washington, D.C.: Congressional Research Service, Library of Congress, 1986), p. 32.

29. But see the anxious minority report filed by Senators Claiborne Pell (D.-R.I.), Joseph Biden (D.-Del.), John Glenn (D.-Ohio), Paul Sarbanes (D.-Md.), Ed Zorinsky (D.-Nebr.), Paul Tsongas (D.-Mass.), Alan Cranston (D.-Calif.), and Christopher Dodd (D.-Conn.), cited in Ides, "Congress, Constitutional Responsibility, and the War Powers," p. 649.

30. Peter Rodman, "The Imperial Congress," *National Interest,* Fall 1985, p. 33.

31. Ibid., pp. 31–32.

32. *New York Times,* Mar. 29, 1984.

33. Rodman, "Imperial Congress," pp. 32–33.

34. Ibid., p. 34.

35. Secretary of State Haig backed off from the idea but argued that, in any case, the administration needed a "rollback." President Reagan concurred. He told associates, "I want to win one" (see Woodward, *Veil,* pp. 116–17, 135).

36. Brenner and LeoGrande, "Congress and the Not So Secret War against Nicaragua," p. 3.

37. *New York Times,* July 12, 1985.

38. "The unilateral actions of the president threaten the institutional interests of Congress," argued the plaintiffs. In *Crockett et al. v. Reagan et al.,* heard in the U.S. District Court of Columbia, 1981, Civil Action no. 81–10434, p. 2.

39. As the countersuit, *Crockett v. Reagan,* 720 F.2d 135 (DC Cir 1983), also 558 F. Sup 893 (1982), implied. See also Michael J. Glennon, "The War Powers Ten Years After: More Politics than Law," *American Journal of International Law* 78, no. 3 (1984): 579. The suit was joined by a countersuit by twenty-nine Republicans who argued that the plaintiffs were trying to "vindicate their foreign policy views in a judicial forum having failed . . . in a political forum."

40. Bill S. 1342, Oct. 19, 1983, debate, *Congressional Record,* 98th Cong., 1st sess., vol. 129, pt. 11, pp. S14163–65, 15270. Changed in conference to S. 16869, Nov. 18, 1983. Enacted as P.L. 98–16497, sec. 1013.

41. Brenner and LeoGrande, "Congress and the Not So Secret War against Nicaragua," p. 4.

42. The 1983 law, P.L. 97377, was restrictive. Sec. 793 passed as an amendment to the fiscal year 1983 budget and expired in 1983.

43. It is unclear who placed the actual devices. According to some press accounts, a trained Cuban group managed the operation, while CIA officers themselves stayed in a command ship beyond the twelve-mile limit. Credible private sources have said that CIA involvement was even more intimate (see Brenner and LeoGrande, "Congress and the Not So Secret War against Nicaragua," p. 4).

44. The State Department legal adviser contended that despite a bilateral arbitration treaty with Nicaragua, as well as the legal commitment to submit disputes to the World Court, the United States was not subject to the Nicaraguan legal action or the jurisdiction of the World Court (see U.S. Congress, House, Committee on Foreign Affairs, *U.S. Decisions to Withdraw from the World Court of Justice: Hearings before the Subcommittee on Human Rights and International Organization,* 99th Cong., 1st sess., 1985, H. 381–15). Later, when Iranian speedboats, mines, and missiles attacked tankers off the Persian Gulf, the U.S. fleet appeared on station to uphold freedom of navigation. But the U.S. assertion of freedom of navigation through a war zone had been damaged in the waters off the Nicaraguan coast. The only way to square this legal anomaly was for the United States to assert that it had a special sovereign right to walk its own path and cut its own wake. But it was a policy that reflected the legal philosophy of John Wayne and Dirty Harry.

45. For an extended overview of the operation see Theodore Draper, *A Very Thin Line: The Iran-Contra Affairs* (New York: Hill & Wang, 1991), esp. pp. 27–136; and above, chapter 4.

46. *Washington Post,* Oct. 8, 1985, Sept. 14, 1984; Congressman Jim Leach (R.-Iowa), letter to *Washington Post,* Sept. 29, 1984; *New York Times,* Aug. 15, 1984.

47. See Jules Lobel, "The Rise and Decline of the Neutrality Act: Sovereignty and Congressional War Powers in United States Foreign Policy," *Harvard International Law Journal* 24 (Summer 1983).

48. See Peter Kornbluh, "Test Case for the Reagan Doctrine: The Covert Contra War," *Third World Quarterly* 10, no. 1 (1988): 12.

49. Scott L. Anderson and Jon Lee Anderson, *Inside the League* (New York: Dodd, Mead, 1986), p. 245.

50. See Steven Emerson, *Secret Warriors* (New York: Putnam, 1988), pp. 150, 400.

51. See testimony before the International Court of Justice, Sept. 8, 1985, p. 8,

quoted in Michael Klare and Peter Kornbluh, *Low Intensity Warfare* (New York: Pantheon, 1988), p. 138 n. 4.

52. Woodward, *Veil,* p. 165.

53. *New York Times,* Jan. 11, 1985; *Washington Post,* Feb. 18, 1986, Feb. 15, 1985.

54. This account of the Libyan attacks is drawn from the excellent analysis of these incidents published by Michael Rubner, "Antiterrorism and the Withering of the 1973 War Powers Resolution," *Political Science Quarterly,* Summer 1987, pp. 193–215. Subsequent quotations from Admiral Poindexter, Senator Byrd, and Congressman Michel are from Rubner's article.

55. Ibid., p. 199.

56. Ibid., p. 211.

57. Quoted in Draper, *A Very Thin Line,* p. 594.

58. Kate Stith, "Congress' Power of the Purse," *Yale Law Journal,* June 1988, p. 1356 (emphasis in the original), quoted in Draper, *A Very Thin Line,* pp. 594–95. Draper's discussion of the constitutional implications of the Iran-Contra affair is comprehensive and provocative.

59. The Justice Department claimed that the threat of imminent action was "remote and conjectural" in mid-December 1990 (see Defendant's exhibit 1, letter to the Speaker and to the president *pro tempore,* Aug. 9, 1990, in *Ronald V. Dellums et al. v. George Bush,* U.S. District Court, 1990, civil action no. 90–286).

60. Lally Weymouth, "How Bush Went to War: Even from the Start, the President was the Number 1 Hawk," *Washington Post,* Mar. 31, 1991.

61. Anthony Lewis, "Presidential Power," *New York Times,* Jan. 14, 1991.

62. U.S. Congress, Senate, Committee on Foreign Relations, *Sanctions in the Persian Gulf: Hearings,* 100th Cong., 1st sess., Sept.–Dec. 1990, pts. 1 and 2.

63. See the testimony of William Webster in U.S. Congress, Senate, Committee on Armed Services, ibid., 100th Cong., 1st sess., 1990. Webster's tone changed somewhat in a letter dated Jan. 10, 1991, to Les Aspin and released by the congressman. For the views of Gen. Norman Schwarzkopf, the U.S. Commander of Desert Storm (as cited by Senator Sam Nunn and the *Los Angeles Times*), see *Congressional Record,* 102d Cong., 1st sess., 1991, vol. 137, pt. 7, pp. S193–94.

64. Tom Mathew et al., "The Road to War," *Newsweek,* Jan. 28, 1991, p. 64.

65. See Wemouth, "How Bush Went to War."

66. Gerald Seib and Gerald Rodgers, "Congress Presses Bush for Voice in Any Confrontation with Iraq," *Wall Street Journal,* Nov. 14, 1990. Presidential spokesperson Marlin Fitzwater said that even though Congress was not in session, some congressional leaders were consulted. Senator Nunn responded: "I was informed not consulted. . . . There is a big difference between being informed after a decision has already been made and getting our views before one is made."

67. The vote was also quite partisan: Senate Republicans voted 42–2 in favor

of the president's position; Democrats, 45–10 against. In the House, Republicans were 164–3 in favor; Democrats, 179–86 against.

68. Thomas Frank, "Declare War? Congress Can't," *New York Times,* Dec. 11, 1990; Frank Patel and Faiza Patel, "U.N. Action in Lieu of War: 'The Old Order Changeth,'" in *Foreign Relations and National Security Law,* ed. Thomas Frank and Michael Glennon, 2d ed. (St. Paul, Minn.: West Publishing, 1993), pp. 684–96; John Norton Moore, testimony before the Senate Committee on the Judiciary, *The War Powers of the Congress and the President in the Gulf Crisis,* 102d Cong., 1st sess., 1991.

69. Henkin was legal counselor when the U.N. took action against North Korea in 1950. See his testimony in U.S. Congress, Senate, Committee on the Judiciary, *The War Powers of Congress and the President in the Gulf Crisis,* pp. 5–6. See also Michael Glennon, "The Constitution and Chapter VII of the United Nations Charter," in Frank and Glennon, *Foreign Relations and National Security Law,* pp. 696–708.

70. "Congress Can't Just Let George Do It," *New York Times,* Dec. 4, 1992.

71. Collier, *War Powers Resolution.*

72. See Madison's admonition quoted in Draper, *A Very Thin Line,* p. 583. See also Judge Greene's statement in *Dellums et al. v. Bush* that if the president alone could decide when moving troops was or was not an "offensive action . . . [then] the congressional power to declare war will be at the mercy of a semantic decision by the executive. . . . Such an 'interpretation' would evade the plain language of the Constitution."

CHAPTER 9   PUBLIC OPINION AND FOREIGN POLICY

1. Hans J. Morgenthau, *Politics among Nations,* 4th ed. (New York: Knopf, 1967), p. 142.

2. Gabriel Almond, *The American People and Foreign Policy* (New York: Praeger, 1954), p. 53.

3. Louis Halle, *Dream and Reality: Aspects of American Foreign Policy* (New York: Harper, 1959), p. 155.

4. George Kennan, *American Diplomacy, 1900–1950* (New York: New American World Library, 1959), p. 59.

5. Some parts of the next few pages are from James Nathan, "The Roots of the Imperial Presidency," *Presidential Studies Quarterly* 5, no. 1 (1975), by permission of the publisher.

6. Roger Hilsman, *To Move a Nation* (Garden City, N.Y.: Doubleday, 1967), quoted in John McDermitt, "Crisis Manager," *New York Review of Books,* Sept. 14, 1967, p. 8.

7. Ole Holsti and James Rosenau, "Vietnam, Consensus, and the Belief Systems of American Leaders," *World Politics* 32 (Oct. 1979): 46–47.

8. Analyses of the 1970s include Barry B. Hughes, *The Domestic Context of*

American Foreign Policy (San Francisco: Freeman, 1978), pp. 21–56; Michael Mandelbaum and William Schneider, "The New Internationalisms," in *Eagle Entangled: U.S. Foreign Policy in a Complex World,* ed. Kenneth A. Oye, Donald Rothchild, and Robert J. Lieber (Boston: Little, Brown, 1979); and Daniel Yankelovich and Larry Kagan, "Assertive America," *Foreign Affairs* 57, no. 3 (1981). For summaries of this early analysis see James A. Nathan and James K. Oliver, *Foreign Policy Making and the American Political System* (Boston: Little, Brown, 1981).

The Chicago Council of Foreign Relations conducted polls in 1974, 1978, 1982, 1986, and 1990; the results of the latter were published in *American Public Opinion and U.S. Foreign Policy, 1991,* ed. John A. Reilly (Chicago: Chicago Council on Foreign Relations, 1991). The most comprehensive analysis of these surveys has been undertaken by Eugene R. Wittkopf, *Faces of Internationalism: Public Opinion and American Foreign Policy* (Durham, N.C.: Duke University Press, 1990). Other important recent overviews and assessments of American public opinion and foreign policy are Bruce Russett, *Controlling the Sword: The Democratic Governance of National Security* (Cambridge, Mass.: Harvard University Press, 1990); idem, "Doves, Hawks, and U.S. Public Opinion," *Political Science Quarterly,* Winter 1990–91, pp. 515–38; and William Schneider, "The Old Politics and the New World Order," in *Eagle in a New World: American Grand Strategy in the Post–Cold War Era,* ed. Kenneth Oye, Robert J. Lieber, and Donald Rothchild (New York: Harper Collins, 1992), pp. 35–68. Holsti and Rosenau's work has been published in a series of papers, including: "Vietnam, Consensus, and the Belief Systems of American Leaders"; "Does Where You Stand Depend on When You Were Born? The Impact of Generation on Post-Vietnam Foreign Policy Beliefs," *Public Opinion Quarterly* 44 (Spring 1980): 1–22; *American Leadership in World Affairs* (Boston: Allen & Unwin, 1984); "Consensus Lost, Consensus Regained? Foreign Policy Beliefs of American Leaders, 1976–1980," *International Studies Quarterly* 30, no. 3 (1986): 375–90; "Domestic and Foreign Policy Belief Systems among American Leaders," *Journal of Conflict Resolution* 32, no. 2 (1988): 248–94; and "The Structure of Foreign Policy Attitudes: American Leaders, 1976–1984," *Journal of Politics* 52 (Feb. 1990): 94–125. Holsti and Rosenau's work has elicited considerable comment. See, e.g., Thomas Ferguson, "The Right Consensus? Holsti and Rosenau's New Foreign Policy Belief Surveys," *International Studies Quarterly* 30, no. 4 (1986): 411–23; Eugene R. Wittkopf, "On the Foreign Policy Beliefs of the American People: A Critique and Some Evidence," ibid., pp. 425–45; and idem, "Elites and Masses: Another Look at Attitudes toward America's World Role," ibid., 31, no. 2 (1987): 131–59. For exhaustive bibliographies of the literature, see Wittkopf, *Faces of Internationalism,* pp. 365–77; and Russett, *Controlling the Sword,* pp. 171–89.

9. See the works cited in n. 8; and the earlier William Caspary, "The Mood Theory: A Study in Public Opinion and Foreign Policy," *American Political Science Review* 64 (June 1970): 536–47.

10. Thomas Halper, *Foreign Policy Crises: Appearance and Reality in Decision Making* (Columbus, Ohio: Charles E. Merrill, 1971), p. 19.

11. For a recent elaboration of this view see Daniel Yankelovich and Sidney Harman, *Starting with the People* (Boston: Houghton Mifflin, 1988).

12. See the discussion in Reilly, *American Public Opinion and U.S. Foreign Policy, 1991*, p. 32; and Mandelbaum and Schneider, "New Internationalisms," pp. 87–88.

13. This and other conceptual distinctions used in this analysis have benefited from a number of discussions with John Doble, former senior research associate at the Public Agenda Foundation, in New York. Doble was responsible for most of the public opinion and attitudes research associated with the Public Agenda Foundation's lengthy project on public attitudes on nuclear arms and security. In addition, Yankelovich's distinctions between public "judgements" and "choices" have been explored in discussions with Robert Kingston and Jean Johnson, also of the Public Agenda Foundation. For additional discussion of these distinctions see Public Agenda Foundation and the Center for Foreign Policy Development, Brown University, "The Public and the Nation's Nuclear Arms Policy" (New York: Public Agenda Foundation, July 1985, mimeographed), pp. 2–9.

14. Yankelovich and Harman, *Starting with the People*, pp. 9–10.

15. Among the more typical categorizations see those of Hughes, *Domestic Context of American Foreign Policy*, pp. 23–25; and James Rosenau, *Public Opinion and Foreign Policy* (New York: Random House, 1961). More recently, Wittkopf has developed his own adaptation in *Faces of Internationalism*, pp. 141–46.

16. See, e.g., Holsti and Rosenau's analyses, "Vietnam, Consensus, and the Belief Systems of American Leaders," "Consensus Lost, Consensus Regained?" and "Domestic and Foreign Policy Belief Systems"; and Wittkopf, *Faces of Internationalism*.

17. Wittkopf, *Faces of Internationalism*, pp. 141–46.

18. Wittkopf's "elite" group comprises governmental and nongovernmental groups, although Wittkopf draws distinctions between them in parts of his analysis *(Faces of Internationalism)*.

19. A. T. Steele, *The American People and China* (New York: McGraw-Hill, 1966), p. 257.

20. R. J. Simon, *Public Opinion in America, 1936–1970* (Chicago: Rand McNally, 1974), p. 184. Point Four was one of the first stabs at large economic assistance to Europe, announced by Harry Truman in a speech that preceded by some months General Marshall's June 1947 Harvard address.

21. Lloyd A. Free and Hadley Cantril, *The Political Beliefs of Americans* (New Brunswick, N.J.: Rutgers University Press, 1968), p. 60.

22. Ibid. The U-2 was a U.S. spy plane shot down over Russia just before a Great Power summit conference scheduled in May 1960.

23. Wittkopf, *Faces of Internationalism*, p. 13.

24. James A. Nathan, "International Socialization" (Ph.D. diss., Johns Hopkins University, School of Advanced International Studies, 1972).

25. *Times Mirror* study quoted in Michael Oreskes, "Profiles of Today's Youth: They Couldn't Care Less," *New York Times,* June 28, 1990.

26. See *New York Times,* Apr. 16, 1981; and "Flunking the Global Test," editorial in *Washington Post,* Apr. 16, 1981.

27. Oreskes, "Profiles of Today's Youth." Some research indicates that education, more than age, is related to attitudinal stability (see Jeffrey W. Koch, "Support of the Persian Gulf War and Attitude Change" [Paper delivered at the annual meeting of the American Political Science Association, Chicago, Sept. 3–6, 1992] p. 13).

28. See also Benjamin Page and Robert Shapiro, "Foreign Policy and the Rational Public," *Journal of Conflict Resolution* 32, no. 2 (1988): 211–47; Benjamin Page, Robert Shapiro, and Glen R. Dempsey, "What Moves Public Opinion?" *American Political Science Review* 87 (1987): 23–43; and Joe Ferrara et al., "Public Response to Prewar Events: The Case of Desert Shield" (Paper delivered at the annual meeting of the American Political Science Association, Chicago, Sept. 3–6, 1992), p. 13.

29. See Walter Lippmann's classic statement in *The Public Philosophy* (New York: New American Library, 1955), pp. 24–25.

30. Quoted in Douglas Kiker, "The Education of Robert McNamara," *Atlantic Monthly,* Mar. 1967, p. 53. For a discussion of the role played by the official perception of public opinion see Leslie H. Gelb, "The Essential Domino: American Politics and Vietnam," *Foreign Affairs* 50, no. 3 (1972): 459–75.

31. Lyndon Johnson, *Vantage Point* (New York: Holt, Rinehart & Winston, 1971), p. 15; and Gelb, "Essential Domino."

32. On the overall stability of mass public opinion see Russett, *Controlling the Sword,* pp. 92–95; on the volatility of elite opinion see ibid, p. 117. For a comparison of leading columnists' opinions and the public mood regarding Soviet-American relations in the 1950s see James A. Nathan, "Detente, the Public, and the Pundits" (Johns Hopkins University, Washington Center for Foreign Policy Analysis, Washington, D.C., 1965).

33. Caspary, "The Mood Theory"; John Mueller, *War, Presidents, and Public Opinion* (New York: Wiley, 1973).

34. *New York Times,* Jan. 1, 1980.

35. Ralph B. Levering, *The Public and American Foreign Policy* (New York: Morrow, 1978), pp. 116, 117.

36. Mueller, *War, Presidents, and Public Opinion,* p. 181. It should be noted that the data presented by Mueller were to buttress an argument different from the one we are advancing. Mueller's contention is that the public will essentially concur with almost any presidential initiative. To Mueller, the process comprises two steps, is lasting, and can be dramatic. First, presidents convince the "attentive elite" by dramatic initiative, and then mass opinion inevitably follows. In general,

however, Mueller believes that the Vietnam experience and even wars form less a part of support for an administration than do economic variables, matters of style, and a general tendency of the public to lower their evaluation of presidents as time passes (see pp. 224–41).

37. *New York Times*, Jan. 27, Feb. 3, 1981.

38. On the Gulf War and "success" see Koch, "Support of the Persian Gulf War," p. 10.

39. See also Levering, *The Public and American Foreign Policy*, pp. 102–3.

40. See Russett, "Doves, Hawks, and U.S. Public Opinion," pp. 519–26; and Yankelovich and Harman, *Starting with the People*, pp. 48–50.

41. See Mueller, *War, Presidents, and Public Opinion*, p. 176; and Russett, "Doves, Hawks, and U.S. Public Opinion," p. 519.

42. Russett, "Doves, Hawks, and U.S. Public Opinion," pp. 524–26.

43. Yankelovich and Harman, *Starting with the People*, p. 100.

44. Simon, *Public Opinion in America*, pp. 162, 155.

45. Harris Polls, Sept. 1, 1963, Oct. 10, 1966.

46. Hughes, *Domestic Context of American Foreign Policy*, p. 36.

47. Russett, "Doves, Hawks, and U.S. Public Opinion," p. 527, citing analyses reported by Ronald Hinckley in "American Opinion toward the Soviet Union," *International Journal for Public Opinion Research* 1 (Winter 1989): 242–57; William Schneider, "Rambo and Reality: Having It Both Ways," in *Eagle Resurgent? The Reagan Era in American Foreign Policy*, ed. Kenneth Oye, Robert Lieber, and Donald Rothchild (Boston: Little, Brown, 1987); *Gallup Report*, no. 249 (June 1986); and Public Agenda Foundation, "Americans Talk Security," *Compendium of Poll Findings on the National Security Issue* (New York: Daniel Yankelovich Group, 1987), p. 215.

48. Adapted from Yankelovich and Harman, *Starting with the People*, pp. 64–69 (emphasis added).

49. Michael R. Kagay, "History Suggests Bush's Popularity Will Ebb," *New York Times*, May 22, 1991; Jong R. Lee, "Rallying around the Flag: Foreign Policy Events and Presidential Popularity," *Presidential Studies Quarterly* 7, no. 4 (1977): 254. We shall return to these "rally round the flag" phenomena in the next chapter.

50. Russett, "Doves, Hawks, and U.S. Public Opinion," pp. 528–33, quote from p. 526.

51. See Hughes, *Domestic Context of American Foreign Policy*, p. 31; and John A. Reilly, ed., *American Public Opinion and U.S. Foreign Policy, 1975* (Chicago: Chicago Council on Foreign Relations, 1975).

52. The terms *nonmilitary* and *military* are from Hughes's *Domestic Context of American Foreign Policy*, p. 30. The liberal, conservative, and noninternationalist distinctions were originally drawn by Mandelbaum and Schneider, "New Internationalisms," and are based on Reilly's data.

53. Mandelbaum and Schneider, "New Internationalisms," p. 54.

54. Ole Holsti, "The Three-Headed Eagle: The United States and System

Change," *International Studies Quarterly,* 23, no. 3 (1979): 339–43. The empirical and conceptual elaboration of Holsti's metaphor are to be found in a series of papers published by Holsti and James Rosenau. The most comprehensive of these, and the two upon which the following survey rests, are "Vietnam, Consensus, and the Belief Systems of American Leaders"; and "Cold War Axioms in the Post-Vietnam Era," in *Change in the International System,* ed. O. Holsti, R. Siverson, and A. George (Boulder: Westview, 1980), pp. 263–301.

55. See, e.g., Alexander L. George, "Domestic Constraints on Regime Change in U.S. Foreign Policy: The Need for Policy Legitimacy," in Holsti, Siverson, and George, *Change in the International System,* pp. 233–62.

56. See Holsti and Rosenau, "Cold War Axioms"; Michael Roskin, "From Pearl Harbor to Vietnam: Shifting Generational Paradigms," *Public Opinion Quarterly* 89 (Fall 1974): 563–88; Bruce Russett and Miroslav Nincic, "American Opinion on the Use of Military Force Abroad," ibid., 91 (Fall 1976): 411–32; and James A. Nathan and James K. Oliver, *United States Foreign Policy and World Order,* 3d ed. (Boston: Little, Brown, 1985), pp. 574–80.

57. Bruce Russett and Donald R. Deluca, "'Don't Tread on Me': Public Opinion and Foreign Policy in the Eighties," *Political Science Quarterly,* Fall 1981, p. 382; see also David Gergen, "The Hardening Mood toward Foreign Policy," *Public Opinion,* Feb.–Mar. 1980, pp. 12–13.

58. Earlier data contrast vividly with data polled just a few years later. In 1974, 33 percent approved an assertive role for the United States; in 1970 a majority of the people felt that defense spending was too high (see Gergen, "Hardening Mood toward Foreign Policy," p. 12; and Russett and Deluca, "'Don't Tread on Me,'" table 1, p. 383).

59. Bruce Russett and Betty C. Hanson, "How Corporate Executives See America's Role in the World," *Fortune,* May 1974, p. 165; and Bruce Russett, "The American Retreat from World Power" (New Haven, n.d., mimeographed), pp. 7–9.

60. Louis Harris and Associates, "A Study of American Attitudes towards Its Allies and the World" (Prepared for *Der Sturn,* Apr. 1980, mimeographed), p. 3.

61. Lloyd Free and William Watts, "Internationalism Comes of Age . . . Again," *Public Opinion,* April–May 1980, p. 47.

62. *New York Times,* Feb. 1, 1980.

63. Gergen, "Hardening Mood toward Foreign Policy," p. 13.

64. Gallup Poll, Dec. 13, 1981, p. 2; see also Russett, "Doves, Hawks, and U.S. Public Opinion," p. 524.

65. *Wall Street Journal*/NBC Poll, *Wall Street Journal,* Feb. 11, 1986, p. 29; *Washington Post*/ABC Poll, *Washington Post,* Feb. 14, 1986.

66. Reilly, *American Public Opinion and U.S. Foreign Policy, 1991,* fig. V-3, p. 32.

67. Ibid., fig. II-1, p. 12.

68. This assessment is drawn from Wittkopf, *Faces of Internationalism;* and Russett, *Controlling the Sword.*

69. See Wittkopf, *Faces of Internationalism,* esp. pp. 21–27, for the delineation of the continuum and the clusters for mass beliefs. That analysis is then carried forward to the discussion of elites at pp. 112–17. Russett, in *Controlling the Sword,* provides a highly simplified and schematic presentation of Wittkopf's analysis at pp. 112–15.

70. Wittkopf, *Faces of Internationalism,* p. 136.

71. For a view of the fragmentation of the "establishment" over Vietnam and the international economic issues see John Judis, "Twilight of the Gods," *Wilson Quarterly* 15, no. 4 (1991): 43.

72. Ibid., p. 237.

73. Schneider, "Old Politics and the New World Order," pp. 50–51. See also Reilly, *American Public Opinion and U.S. Foreign Policy, 1991,* pp. 14, 18–22, for public perceptions of the Soviet Union.

74. Judis, "Twilight of the Gods."

75. Reilly, *American Public Opinion and U.S. Foreign Policy, 1991,* fig. III-3, p. 20.

76. Ibid., fig. II-4, p. 14.

77. Wittkopf, *Faces of Internationalism,* pp. 21–33.

78. Schneider, "Old Politics and the New World Order," p. 55.

79. *Washington Post*/ABC Poll, Jan. 1989, cited in Daniel Yankelovich, "Foreign Policy after the Election," *Foreign Affairs* 71, no. 4 (1992): 8.

80. Reilly, *American Public Opinion and U.S. Foreign Policy, 1991,* fig. I-4, p. 11.

81. Ibid., fig. II-5, p. 15.

82. Yankelovich and Harman, *Starting with the People,* p. 186.

83. Reilly, *American Public Opinion and U.S. Foreign Policy, 1991.*

84. Wittkopf, *Faces of Internationalism,* pp. 90–91, 158–59.

85. This is Wittkopf's characterization of the finding; see ibid., pp. 90–91.

86. See Schneider, "Old Politics and the New World Order," pp. 59, 42 ff.

87. Steve Lohr, "In Poll, Executives Back Free Trade," *New York Times,* Apr. 7, 1992.

88. Schneider, "Old Politics and the New World Order," pp. 59–60.

89. David E. Rosenbaum with Keith Bradsher, "Candidates Playing to Mood of Protectionism," *New York Times,* Jan. 26, 1992.

90. Yankelovich and Harmon, pp. 159, 188.

91. Wittkopf, *Faces of Internationalism,* p. 237.

CHAPTER 10 PRESIDENTS, THE MEDIA,
AND FOREIGN POLICY

1. Daniel Yankelovich, "Farewell to 'President Knows Best,'" *Foreign Affairs* 57, no. 3 (1979): 689.

2. Ibid., p. 690. Similar conclusions were reached by Kenneth Waltz in the

1960s; see his "Electoral Punishment and Foreign Policy Crisis," in *Domestic Sources of Foreign Policy*, ed. James Rosenau (New York: Free Press, 1967).

3. For a review of the early literature on political socialization see James Nathan, "International Socialization" (Ph.D. diss., Johns Hopkins University, School of Advanced International Studies, 1972). On the impact of Watergate see F. Christopher Arterton, "The Impact of Watergate on Children's Attitudes toward Political Authority," *Political Science Quarterly*, Summer 1974; and Yankelovich, "Farewell to 'President Knows Best,'" pp. 670–72.

4. Eric F. Goldman, *The Crucial Decade—and After: America, 1945–1960* (New York: Vintage, 1960), p. 59. A review of this intellectual capitalization of the cold War, with its predicate of fear, can be found in James A. Nathan and James K. Oliver, *United States Foreign Policy and World Order*, 4th ed. (Glenview, Ill.: Scott, Foresman, 1989), chap. 2.

5. See the discussion by David Webster, "New Communications Technology and the International Political Process," in *The Media and Foreign Policy*, ed. Simon Serfaty (New York: St. Martin's, 1991), pp. 219–28.

6. Sidney Blumenthal, "Letter from Washington: The Syndicated Presidency," *New Yorker*, Apr. 5, 1993, pp. 42–48 ff.

7. Newton N. Minnow, John Bartlow Martin, and Lee M. Mitchell, *Presidential Television* (New York: Basic, 1973), p. 56; "Decline of Press Conferences," *USA Today Monthly*, Apr. 1982, p. 16.

8. "Spin Control," *Washington Times*, May 26, 1992.

9. See Stanley Karnow, *Vietnam: A History* (New York: Penguin, 1983), pp. 221 ff. and 534 ff.

10. David Halberstam cites McGeorge Bundy's explanation that Pleiku incidents were like streetcars: they came around every five minutes, and one was just like another (David Halberstam, *The Best and the Brightest* [New York: Random House, 1969], pp. 533–34).

11. *New York Times*, May 23, 1980. For a much disputed account of these events see Gary Sick, *October Surprise*, rev. ed. (New York: Random House, 1991).

12. See Doyle McManus, "Dateline Washington," *Foreign Policy*, no. 66 (Spring 1987): 160.

13. See R. Gregory Nokes, "Libya: A Government Story," in Serfaty, *The Media and Foreign Policy*, pp. 33–46.

14. Robert Perry, "Reagan's Mail Shows Strong Anti-Junta Bias," AP dispatch in *Wilmington Evening Journal*, Feb. 19, 1982.

15. See Bob Woodward, "Meetings' Notes Show the Unvarnished Haig," *Washington Post*, Feb. 19, 1982.

16. The most pointed statement of this position is that of Mark Hertsgaard, *On Bended Knee: The Press and the Reagan Presidency* (New York: Farrar, Straus & Giroux, 1988); see also idem, "How Ronald Reagan Turned News Hounds into Lap Dogs," *Washington Post*, National Weekly Edition, Aug. 29–Sept. 4, 1988.

17. Hertsgaard, "How Ronald Reagan Turned News Hounds into Lap Dogs," p. 25.

18. All quotes in this paragraph are from ibid.

19. Ibid., p. 26; see also Times Mirror Center for the People and the Press, *The People, the Press, and the War in the Gulf: Part II—A Special Times Mirror News Interest Index* (Los Angeles, Mar. 25, 1991).

20. Hertsgaard, *On Bended Knee;* Eleanor Randolph, "The Story the Press Didn't See," *Washington Post,* National Weekly Edition, Nov. 30, 1987.

21. See the reflections of the chief of the U.S. military group in El Salvador in John D. Waghelstein, "El Salvador and the Press: A Personal Account," in *Newsmen and the National Defense,* ed. Lloyd J. Matthews (New York: Brassey's, 1991), pp. 31–38.

22. Michael Wines, "Bush Attacks Media, and Crowds Love It," *New York Times,* Oct. 25, 1992.

23. Brent Bozell, "How Can Liberals Deny the Media's Slanted Coverage?" *Philadelphia Inquirer,* Oct. 5, 1992.

24. S. Robert Lichter, "Left-Leaning Antennas?" *Washington Post,* Sept. 6, 1992. Bozell places his own contrary interpretation on Lichter's work, however (Bozell, "How Can Liberals Deny the Media's Slanted Coverage?"). See also Elizabeth Kolbert, "Maybe the Media DID Treat Bush a Bit Harshly," *New York Times,* Nov. 22, 1992.

25. Bruce Russett and Donald R. Deluca, "'Don't Tread on Me': Public Opinion and Foreign Policy in the Eighties," *Political Science Quarterly,* Fall 1981, p. 397, citing Richard Brody and Benjamin Page, "The Impact of Events on Presidential Popularity: The Johnson and Nixon Administrations," in *Perspectives on the Presidency,* ed. Aaron Wildavsky (Boston: Little, Brown, 1975); Peter Braestrup, *Big Story: How the American Press and Television Reported and Interpreted the Crisis of Tet 1968 in Vietnam and Washington* (Boulder: Westview, 1977), p. xxiii.

26. For a discussion of the growing gap between elite media and the provincial press's coverage of foreign affairs see Charles W. Bailey, "Foreign Policy and the Provincial Press," in Serfaty, *The Media and Foreign Policy,* pp. 179–88.

27. David Stebenne, Seth Rachlin, and Martha Fitz Simons, *Coverage of the Media in College Textbooks: A Report by the Freedom Forum Media Studies Center* (New York: Columbia University, 1992), p. 50.

28. Webster, "New Communications Technology and the International Political Process," p. 222.

29. For an example of such conventional wisdom and cynicism see David Gergen, "Diplomacy in a Television Age: The Dangers of a Teledemocracy," in Serfaty, *The Media and Foreign Policy,* pp. 47–65, esp. 52–53.

30. Walter Karp, "All the Congressmen's Men: How Capitol Hill Controls the Press," *Harper's,* July 1989, pp. 56 ff.

31. Philip Geyelin, "The Strategic Defense Initiative: The President's Story," in Serfaty, *The Media and Foreign Policy,* pp. 21, 24.

32. For an overview of the coverage of the Vietnam War see William M. Hammond, *U.S. Army in Vietnam—Public Affairs: The Military and the Media, 1962–1968* (Washington, D.C.: Center of Military History—United States Army, 1988); Peter Braestrup, *Battle Lines—Report of the Twentieth Century Fund Task Force on the Military and the Media* (New York: Priority Press Publications, 1985); and esp. Jacqueline Sharkey, *Under Fire: U.S. Military Restrictions on the Media from Grenada to the Persian Gulf* (Washington, D.C.: Center for Public Integrity, 1991), pp. 39–40.

33. See Hammond, *U.S. Army in Vietnam;* and the comments of Maj. Gen. Winant Sidle in Sharkey, *Under Fire,* p. 57.

34. Col. Harry G. Summers, Jr., testimony before U.S. Senate Governmental Affairs Committee, *Pentagon Rules Governing Press Access to the Persian Gulf War,* 102d Cong., 1st sess., 1991, pp. 1–2, quoted in Sharkey, *Under Fire,* p. 57.

35. See the exchange on this controversy on the "McNeil/Lehrer Report," Public Broadcasting Service, Feb. 19, 1982; and Hertsgaard, *On Bended Knee.*

36. See Col. Harry G. Summers, Jr., *On Strategy: A Critical Analysis of the Vietnam War* (Novato, Calif.: Presidio, 1982), pp. 11–19.

37. See the discussion in chapter 3, above; and the testimony of Secretary of State Warren Christopher before the Senate Foreign Relations Committee on Apr. 27, 1993, 103d Cong., 1st sess.

38. Sharkey, *Under Fire,* pp. 11, 23–33. For reflections of this "lesson" see Maj. Cass D. Howell, "War, Television, and Public Opinion," *Military Review,* Feb. 1987.

39. This account is drawn from Sharkey's comprehensive histories of the Grenada, Panama, and Gulf War events in *Under Fire,* pp. 67–156.

40. The Sidle Report can be found in ibid., app. B.

41. The Hoffman Report is in ibid., app. C. The following analysis is based on Hoffman's report.

42. Ibid., p. 1.

43. Herbert Mitgang, "In the Gulf War, Managing News and the News Media," *New York Times,* June 24, 1992.

44. See Jean Edward Smith, *George Bush's War* (New York: Henry Holt, 1992), p. 48.

45. See Sharkey, *Under Fire,* pp. 145–52, for a review of these claims.

46. Ibid., p. 146, quoting Rear Adm. (ret.) Eugene Caroll.

47. See the correspondence between Robert M. Stein and Theodore A. Postal on the Patriot experience in the Gulf War in *International Security* 17, no. 1 (1992): 199–240. Stein is a systems manger at Raytheon, the manufacturer of the Patriot, and Postal is a scientist at MIT.

48. See the exploration of the casualty controversy in John G. Heidenrich, "The Gulf War: How Many Iraqis Died?" *Foreign Policy,* no. 90 (Spring 1993): 108–25; and Elliot Cohen et al., *The Gulf War Air Power Survey* (Draft of a

summary volume cleared for publication May 5, 1993, by the U.S. Air Force, Washington, D.C.), p. 217 n. 21.

49. Cohen et al., "Gulf War Air Power Survey," pp. 217–18.

50. Lt. Gen. Thomas Kelly, interview with Jacqueline Sharkey, Aug. 16, 1991, quoted in Sharkey, *Under Fire*, p. 129.

51. Sharkey, *Under Fire*, pp. 250–51, 253.

52. Stephen S. Rosenfeld, "In the Gulf: The Wars of the Press," in Serfaty, *The Media and Foreign Policy*, pp. 252–53. As Cohen et al. put it in "Gulf War Air Power Survey," "Few scenes were as vivid on television as the picture of a guided bomb going though a ventilator shaft. . . . In fact, a new age had only partially arrived: laser-guided bombs (LPGMs) achieved dramatic success . . . , in some measure because of the absence of . . . air defenses, but over-all, laser-guided bombs comprised only a small fraction of the munitions expended" (p. 192).

53. Rosenfeld, "In the Gulf."

54. See Jack Anderson and George Clifford, *The Anderson Papers* (New York: Ballantine, 1974), pp. 219–21; Walter Isaacson, *Kissinger* (New York: Simon & Schuster, 1992), pp. 213–31, 330–31, 380–86; and David Wise, *The American Police State* (New York: Random House, 1976), pp. 33–47.

55. *New York Times Co. v. U.S.*, 403 U.S. 713 (1971).

56. *United States v. Marchetti*, 466 F.2d 1309 (1972).

57. Frank Snepp, *A Decent Interval* (New York: Random House, 1977).

58. *Snepp v. United States*, 444 U.S. 507, 508, 100 S Ct 763, 764, 62 L.Ed. 2. 704 (1980). Wilbur E. Eveland, who served as a CIA officer in the Middle East in the 1950s, was warned that he had failed to gain clearance for his book *Ropes of Sand* (New York: Norton, 1980). Eveland tried for four years to obtain a copy of his agreement but was turned down on the grounds that it was "properly classified." Finally, as the book was about to be published, the CIA released signed contracts of uncertain dates under two pseudonyms. But, said a CIA spokesperson, "with or without dates, as far as we're concerned they are valid contracts" (*Washington Post*, Apr. 6, 1980).

59. Henry Kissinger, *The White House Years* (Boston: Little, Brown, 1980), p. xxiii.

60. Letter from Christine Dodson, of the National Security Council, Washington, D.C., to James A. Nathan, May 21, 1980.

61. Anthony Lewis, "The Kissinger Secrets," *New York Times*, June 9, 1980.

62. Cited in *Henry A. Kissinger v. Reporter's Committee for Freedom of the Press et al.*, 445 U.S. 136.

63. Steve Weinberg, *For Their Eyes Only: How Presidential Appointees Treat Public Documents as Personal Property* (Washington, D.C.: Center for Public Integrity, 1992), esp. pp. 57–59. See also Robert Pear, "Bush's Lawyer Says Aides May Destroy Records," *New York Times*, Nov. 21, 1992.

64. *U.S. v. Nixon*, 481 U.S. 683 (1974).

65. The 1985 disclosure that the CIA had paid a Harvard professor over

$100,000 to do a book on Saudi Arabia indicated that universities were not excluded in the restrictions regarding domestic public opinion (see Duncan L. Clarke and Edward L. Nevelett, "Secrecy, Foreign Intelligence, and Civil Liberties: Has the Pendulum Swung Too Far?" *Political Science Quarterly*, Fall 1984, p. 496).

66. *Washington Post*, June 10, 1985.

67. *New York Times*, Jan. 29, 1986.

68. *U.S. v. Morison*, 486 U.S. 1306, 100 L.Ed. 2d 594 and 844 F.2d 1057 (4th Cir. 1988).

69. *New York Times*, Oct. 8, 1984; *U.S. v. Morison*, 844 F.2d 1057 (4th Cir. 1988), pp. 1063, 1065–1067; *New York Times*, Sept. 27, 1985.

70. *Washington Post*, July 12, Nov. 17, 1985.

71. Weinberg, *For Their Eyes Only*, p. 34.

72. See Tom Wicker, "Leak On, O Ship of State," *New York Times*, Jan. 26, 1982.

73. *New York Times*, Mar. 21, 1985, Feb. 23, 1984.

74. *Philadelphia Inquirer*, Sept. 20, 1984.

75. *Wall Street Journal*, Feb. 18, 1986. See also Walter Karp, "Liberty under Siege: The Reagan Administration's Taste for Autocracy," *Harper's*, Nov. 1985, pp. 53–69.

76. *Sims v. Central Intelligence Agency*, 471 U.S. 159.

77. George Lardner, Jr., "High Court Disputed in CIA Secrecy Case," *Washington Post*, Feb. 24, 1986.

78. "CBS Evening News," Aug. 31, 1973. In a conspiracy case against the "Chicago Seven" antiwar leaders the Justice Department picked an especially unsympathetic judge, who was granted a reception in the White House after he issued contempt citations to the defendants' protesting lawyers. Construction workers received a similar audience after brutally breaking up war protests in New York (David Weis, *The Politics of Lying: Government Deception, Secrecy, and Power* [New York: Random House, 1973], p. 196). In other cases, the administration planted agent provocateurs in antiwar groups to disrupt their activities and create suspicion and fear within their ranks (*New York Review of Books*, Apr. 22, 1971).

79. *New York Times*, July 4, 1974.

80. Memorandum, Patrick Buchanan to John Erlichman, dated July 8, 1971, reprinted in *Washington Post*, June 19, 1974.

81. *Washington Post*, July 19, 1974.

82. Andrew Rosenthal, "High State Dept. Official Ordered Search of Clinton's Embassy Files," *New York Times*, Oct. 15, 1992; Eric Schmitt, "Errors Admitted on Clinton Files," ibid., Oct. 16, 1992.

83. Robert Pear, "High Bush Official Is Linked to Search of File on Clinton," ibid., Nov. 14, 1992; Walter Pincus, "Tamposi Alleges the White House Pushed File Search," *Philadelphia Inquirer*, Nov. 16, 1992.

84. Robert Pear, "Political Motives Imputed in Search of Passport Files," *New York Times*, Nov. 19, 1992.

85. Elaine Sciolino, "'Nonpartisan' Is a Virtue at State," ibid., Nov. 19, 1992.

86. Pear, "Bush's Lawyer Says Aides May Destroy Records."

87. *New York Times*, Mar. 8, 1972.

88. Robert W. Tucker, *Nation or Empire? The Debate over American Foreign Policy* (Baltimore: Johns Hopkins Press, 1968), p. 134.

89. Edward Cahn, *The Predicament of Democratic Man* (New York: Delta, 1962), p. 80.

CHAPTER 11   INTEREST GROUPS, LOBBYING, AND
AMERICAN FOREIGN POLICY MAKING

1. David B. Truman, *The Governmental Process: Political Interests and Public Opinion* (New York: Knopf, 1951).

2. Grant McConnell, *Private Power and American Democracy* (New York: Vintage, 1966).

3. Samuel P. Huntington, "The Governability of Democracies: USA," in *The Crisis of Democracy: Report on the Governability of Democracies to the Trilateral Commission*, by Michael J. Crozier, Samuel P. Huntington, and Joji Watanuki (New York: New York University Press, 1975). Huntington's argument was also published as "The Democratic Distemper," in *The American Commonwealth*, ed. Nathan Glazer and Irving Kristol (New York: Basic, 1976).

4. Numerous schemes for categorizing the types of interest groups operating in the American political system have been devised. See, e.g., Norman J. Ornstein and Shirley Elder, *Interest Groups, Lobbying, and Policymaking* (Washington, D.C.: Congressional Quarterly Press, 1978), esp. pp. 35–53; see also Truman, *Governmental Process*, pp. 111–55. For a discussion of the seamy side of defense procurement see Irwin Ross, "Inside the Biggest Pentagon Scam," *Fortune*, Jan. 1993, pp. 88 ff.

5. Qualification and a blurring of the edges of this category are necessary, however, for in some instances the "information" provided by interest groups may include actual language for legislation or regulations affecting the group's interests. Indeed, there have been cases in which lobbyists or representatives of interest groups were taken into the legislation drafting process itself. In the drafting of complex tax and tariff legislation, for example, it is not uncommon for lobbyists for affected industries actually to take part in the deliberations of congressional committees as they develop legislative language (John Manley, *The Politics of Finance* [Boston: Little, Brown, 1970]).

6. James A. Nathan, "The New Feudalism," *Foreign Policy*, no. 42 (Spring 1981): 156–67.

7. Indeed, the Cuban American National Foundation, the most powerful of the Miami-based exile groups, succeeded in blocking the appointment of Mario

Baeza, a Wall Street lawyer and Clinton loyalist, as assistant secretary for Latin American affairs (see Larry Tother, "Cuban Exiles Flex and Falter," *New York Times,* Mar. 7, 1993).

8. See Rochelle L. Stanfield, "Ethnic Politicking," *National Journal,* Dec. 30, 1989, pp. 3096–99; and Dianna Solis, "US Hispanics Flex Political Muscles as Mexico Lobbies for NAFTA Support," *Wall Street Journal,* Mar. 3, 1993.

9. This analysis is based on Thomas M. Frank and Edward Weisband's excellent, extensive survey of lobbying in Congress, *Foreign Policy by Congress* (New York: Oxford University Press, 1979), pp. 165–209.

10. See Congressional Quarterly, *The Washington Lobby* (Washington, D.C., 1979); and Stephen D. Isaacs, *Jews and American Politics* (New York: Doubleday, 1974).

11. David K. Shipler, "On Middle East Policy, a Major Influence," *New York Times,* July, 6, 1987.

12. Frank and Weisband, *Foreign Policy by Congress,* pp. 102–3, 108–9, 186–90.

13. Quoted in Shipler, "On Middle East Policy."

14. See David J. Sadd and G. Neal Lendenman, "Arab American Grievances," *Foreign Policy,* no. 60 (Fall 1985): 28.

15. Robert Pear with Richard L. Berke, "Pro-Israel Group Exerts Quiet Might As It Rallies Supporters in Congress," *New York Times,* July 7, 1987.

16. *Wall Street Journal,* Feb. 26, 1985.

17. See Sadd and Lendenman, "Arab American Grievances," pp. 22 ff.

18. The population base may well be shifting if the number of resident Arabic speakers is any indication. The number of Arabic-speaking residents in the United States increased by just over 57 percent from 1980 to 1990, to around 355,000. On the other hand, the number of Hebrew-speaking residents was 145,000, up 45 percent, and the number of Yiddish-speaking residents was 213,000, down 33 percent (see the Census data reported in *New York Times,* Apr. 28, 1993).

19. Since the Kuwaiti government had a contract with Hill and Knowlton, it is somewhat artificial to separate the efforts of resident Kuwaitis in the United States and the Kuwaiti government, then exiled in Saudi Arabia (see Jean Edward Smith, *George Bush's War* [New York: Henry Holt, 1992], p. 149).

20. Carol Matlack, "The Home Front," *National Journal,* Feb. 16, 1991, pp. 380–83.

21. Armitage and Dine are both quoted in Shipler, "On Middle East Policy."

22. William E. Schmidt, "Americans' Support for Israel: Solid, but Not the Rock It Was," *New York Times,* July 9, 1990.

23. The money was to help absorb thousands of Russian Jewish immigrants pouring into Israel by building housing on the West Bank of the Jordan River. Israeli occupation of the West Bank since 1967 has never been recognized by the United States or any other country.

24. See the summary of the confrontation in "Win a Battle, Lose a War,"

Economist, Sept. 21, 1991, pp. 47–48; and "Bush Gets Tough on Israel Loan," *International Herald Tribune,* Sept. 13, 1991.

25. "Prime News," Cable News Network, Apr. 27, 1993.

26. The U.S. embargo on aid to Turkey continued until 1978 (Frank and Weisband, *Foreign Policy by Congress,* pp. 191–93).

27. By the mid-1980s, however, the radical posture of the Greek government put AHEPA in the position, one member of Congress claimed, of a "lobby without an ally or a sponsor" in Congress, but this was an overstatement (see Christopher Madison, "Effective Lobbying, Ethnic Politics Preserve U.S. Military Aid for Greece," *National Journal,* May 4, 1985, pp. 964, 961).

28. Israel and Egypt are the single largest recipients of U.S. economic assistance (see "The Good, the Mean, and the Stingy," *Economist,* July 10, 1993, p. 35).

29. See Kenneth Longmyer, "Black Americans' Demands," *Foreign Policy,* no. 60 (Fall 1985): 11 ff.

30. However, by the mid-1980s a fairly casual State Department reversal of the position regarding the tyrant "Baby Doc" Duvalier, having apparently nothing to do with the growing Haitian population in the United States, managed to tip the internal balance of power in Haiti. The hated dictator, faced with angry mobs and convinced that the United States would not support repressive violence, decided to flee, with American embassy assistance, into exile.

31. Quoted in Karen De Witt, "Black 'Think Tank' Opens a Foreign Institute," *New York Times,* June 6, 1993.

32. One of the most influential is the Council on Foreign Relations (CFR). Perhaps 35 percent of its 2,900-odd members are senior corporate executives, lawyers, and academics. But the CFR, notwithstanding the contentions of its many critics, does not have a particular policy agenda. Although many of its members have enormous influence as a result of their position, experience, and access, the CFR has always been more a forum and platform for the exchange of ideas than a lobby (see Kempton Dunn, "Membership Report," in *Council on Foreign Relations Annual Report* [New York, 1992], p. 101). The CFR has been the target of the anti-Communist John Birch Society and some left-wing sociologists for years. For a typical argument see James Parlor, *The Shadows of Power* (Appleton, Wis.: Western Islands Press, 1988). For a balanced, critical appraisal of the CFR's influence (or lack of it) see John Judis, "Twilight of the Gods," *Wilson Quarterly* 15, no. 4 (1991): 44–56; see also the bibliography, pp. 56–58.

33. See *New York Times,* Mar. 9, 1981; and Barry Schweid, "Firing of Seariches Mediator Bares Rift," *Wilmington Morning News,* Mar. 10, 1981.

34. Frank and Weisband, *Foreign Policy by Congress,* p. 196. For a general overview of the oil industry and its operation, see John M. Blair, *The Control of Oil* (New York: Vintage, 1976).

35. *New York Times,* Oct. 10, 1977.

36. Countercoalitions often took shape, frequently with considerable White

House encouragement and support. For examples see Frank and Weisband, *Foreign Policy by Congress,* p. 198.

37. For the use of the resources in the Panama Canal treaties case see William Languette, "The Panama Canal Treaties: Playing in Peoria and the Senate," *National Journal,* Oct. 8, 1977, p. 1560. For instance, the following groups formed during the Persian Gulf War: Citizens for a Free Kuwait, the Coalition for America, the Freedom Task Force, the Committee for Peace and Security in the Gulf, and the Coalition for Desert Storm (Matlack, "Home Front").

38. Rochelle L. Stanfield, "So That's How It Works," *National Journal,* June 24, 1989, pp. 1620–24. Stanfield notes that many Central and South American countries have now become enthusiastic players. One could also include state governments. California, with a population of 31 million and a budget of $700 billion, if it were an independent state, would be the eighth largest in the world. State agencies deal with perhaps as many immigration issues as the U.S. government does. Like other states, California has its own trade representatives abroad. The state is large enough, with enough sense of its own autonomy, that many international issues that used to be handled by the federal government—e.g., pollution control, international worker safety, border patrol, international water management—are handled by the state of California. Although the normal way of influencing policy at the national level for any state is through its representatives in Congress, California and other states are acting in a fashion that is in some ways unique to this century (see Kenichi Ohmae, "The Rise of the Regional State," *Foreign Affairs* 72, no. 2 [1993]: 78–87; and James Goldsborough, "California's Foreign Policy," ibid., pp. 89–96).

39. See *New York Times,* Apr. 30, 1978.

40. For a recent overview of Kissinger Associates, on which this discussion relies, see Jeff Gerth with Sarah Bartlett, "Kissinger and Friends and Revolving Doors," ibid., Apr. 30, 1989.

41. In fact, when Scowcroft left government service in 1993, he started his own Washington consulting firm.

42. See the examples provided in Gerth with Bartlett, "Kissinger and Friends."

43. See "American Interests," a WETA Channel 26 broadcast, Mar. 30, 1986; and *New York Times,* Jan. 17, 1986.

44. *Washington Post,* June 8, 1976.

45. "Report of the Attorney General to the Congress on the Administration of the Foreign Agents Registration Act of 1938, as amended for the Calendar Year 1987," 1989, quoted in Pat Choate, *Agents of Influence* (New York: Simon & Schuster, Touchstone, 1990), p. 268 n. 4.

46. Choate, *Agents of Influence,* p. 35.

47. Ibid., pp. 38, 36.

48. Martin Tolchin and Susan J. Tolchin, *Selling Our Security* (New York: Knopf, 1992), pp. 150, 157.

49. Bill Gentz, "Lawmakers Wary of Raising Spending for Spy Programs," *Washington Times,* Apr. 21, 1993.

50. Richard Ryan, "With Spies Like These, Who Needs Enemies," review of *Friendly Spies: How America's Allies Are Using Economic Espionage to Steal Our Secrets,* by Peter Schweizer, *Christian Science Monitor,* Feb. 25, 1993; R. Jeffrey Smith, "Administration to Study Giving Spy Data to Business," *Washington Post,* Feb. 3, 1993.

51. See Ian Burma, "It Can't Happen Here," review of *Rising Sun,* by Michael Crichton, *New York Review of Books,* Apr. 23, 1992, pp. 3–5.

52. Ryan, "With Spies Like These."

53. For a current, measured examination of Japanese economic prospects see Clive Crook, "The Japanese Economy: From Miracle to Mid-Life Crisis," *Economist,* Mar. 6, 1993, pp. 18 ff.; and James A. Nathan, "Can Japan's Commercial Dominance Continue?" *USA Today Monthly,* Jan. 1993, pp. 34–36.

54. Tolchin and Tolchin, *Selling Our Security,* p. 18.

55. Ibid., p. 26.

56. Michael Wines, "Record $678 Million Was Spent by Candidates for Congress in '92," *New York Times,* Mar. 5, 1993.

57. Michael Wines, "Study Finds Many Donations Flowed to Clinton Late in 1992," ibid., Mar. 4, 1993.

58. Choate, *Agents of Influence,* app. A; Tom Bovee, "Clinton's Pick Mainly White Males," *Montgomery Advertiser,* Mar. 8, 1993.

59. Paul E. Peterson, "The Rise and Fall of Special Interest Politics," *Political Science Quarterly,* Winter 1990–91, p. 540.

60. See Dean Acheson, *Present at the Creation: My Years at the State Department* (New York: Norton, 1969), pp. 169–82.

CHAPTER 12   PRIVATE POWER AND AMERICAN FOREIGN POLICY

1. Dwight D. Eisenhower, *Waging Peace* (Garden City, N.Y.: Doubleday, 1965), p. 616.

2. On this point see Richard Barnet, *The Economy of Death* (New York: Athenaeum, 1969), pp. 112 ff. For a careful description and analysis of the operation of the relationship between the defense industry and government procurement see J. Ronald Fox, *Arming America: How the U.S. Buys Weapons* (Boston: Harvard Business School, Division of Research, 1974). For a comparable analysis of the 1950s and 1960s see Merton J. Peck and Frederick M. Scherer, *The Weapons Acquisition Process: An Economic Analysis* (Boston: Harvard Business School, Division of Research, 1962).

3. For an analysis of these cycles see Samuel P. Huntington, "The Defense Policy of the Reagan Administration, 1981–1982," in *The Reagan Presidency: An Early Assessment,* ed. Fred Greenstein (Baltimore: Johns Hopkins University Press, 1983), pp. 82–116.

4. Leslie Wayne, "Arms Makers Gird for Peace," *New York Times,* Dec. 17, 1989.

5. Fox, *Arming America,* pp. 15–24.

6. Broadcast on defense conversion, "All Things Considered," National Public Radio, July 5, 1993.

7. Thus, a main battle tank that could be produced for about $125,000 in the 1940s now costs the United States Army well in excess of $1 million. The first mass-produced jet fighter aircraft, the F-86, cost about $400,000 apiece; the F-15 and F-14 now cost the Air Force and Navy tens of millions of dollars each.

8. The average was close to four times the cost of comparable civilian goods. Navy Secretary John F. Lehman, Jr., described the whole process as one of "vast bloat." Congress, he charged, "wants it that way." Since "regulations often require that the taxpayer pay for the contractors' capital assets," defense contractors' overhead was as much as 100 percent of direct costs because "each new bureaucracy is legislated into the defense establishment . . . and if a few Lear jets or dog kennels get added along the way, well, who's to know?" *Philadelphia Inquirer,* May 27, 1985.

9. For a detailed discussion of these and other considerations see Fox, *Arming America.*

10. Peck and Scherer, *Weapons Acquisition Process,* p. 60.

11. Fox, *Arming America,* p. 38.

12. Jackson R. McGowan, president of the Douglas Aircraft Division of the McDonnell Douglas Corporation, in *Los Angeles Times,* Oct. 1, 1971, as quoted in Fox, *Arming America,* p. 68.

13. For the data presented in these paragraphs see Fox, *Arming America,* p. 43; and Department of Defense, Office of the Assistant Secretary of Defense (Comptroller), *100 Companies Receiving the Largest Dollar Volume of Military Prime Contracts, Fiscal Year 1976* (Washington, D.C.: U.S. Government Printing Office, 1977), p. 1.

14. Department of Defense, Office of the Assistant Secretary of Defense (Comptroller), *100 Companies Receiving the Largest Dollar Volume of Military Prime Contract Awards, Fiscal Year 1959, Fiscal Year 1970, and Fiscal Year 1976,* (Washington, D.C.: U.S. Government Printing Office, 1979).

15. Richard W. Stevenson, "Hard Choices for Arms Makers," *New York Times,* Nov. 29, 1989; Calvin Sims, "For Weapons Makers, a Time to Deal," ibid., Jan. 17, 1993.

16. *New York Times,* Aug. 13, 1984.

17. Louis Uchitelle, "Economy Expected to Absorb Effects of Military Cuts," ibid., Apr. 15, 1990.

18. Nonetheless, the B-1 was canceled for several years (see *New York Times,* Apr. 19, May 17, 1985; see also the graph in *Washington Post,* National Edition, Apr. 29, 1985).

19. *New York Times,* Apr. 9, 1985.

20. See Seymour Melman, "Limits of Military Power: Economic and Other," *International Security* 11, no. 1 (1986): 72–86.

21. See James Nathan, "Post–Cold War Foreign Policy," in *The Democrats Must Lead,* ed. James MacGregor Burns et al. (Boulder: Westview, 1992).

22. Sims, "For Weapons Makers, a Time to Deal."

23. Louis Uchitelle, "Cutback in Military Spending: No Help for Ailing Economy," *New York Times,* Aug. 12, 1992; Richard W. Stevenson, "Dynamics Set to Trim 27,000 Jobs," ibid., May 2, 1991.

24. In the early 1990s seventeen installations in California alone were closed, and another large group was proposed for closure by Defense Secretary Aspin in his first weeks in office (Eric Schmitt, "Aspin Is Preparing a Broad New Plan for Base Closings: 180 Installations Would Be Shut, Reflecting New Era of Scaled-Back Military," ibid., Mar. 7, 1993).

25. For the CBO figures see CBO Staff Memorandum, *Fiscal Implications of the Administration's Proposed Base Force,* Dec. 1991, p. 5. See also the CBO's comments on the Defense Business Operations Fund, which suffered a 1993 shortfall of $50 billion instead of the $20 billion "surplus" in savings that had been projected ("Financial Mess at the Pentagon," *Baltimore Sun,* Apr. 23, 1993; Richard H. P. Sia, "Aspin Orders Review of Pentagon Fund," ibid., Apr. 21, 1993). For an estimate of a $150 billion shortfall, without reference to the shortfalls revealed in the *Baltimore Sun,* see *National Security Issues,* USGAO Transition Series, Dec. 1992, Document GAO/oCG-93-9TR, p. 5.

26. Eric Schmitt, "Pentagon Scraps $57 Billion Order for Attack Plane," *New York Times,* Jan. 8, 1991; Richard W. Stevenson, "Old Ways Are Dead," ibid.

27. Quoted in Stevenson, "Old Ways Are Dead."

28. Quoted in Uchitelle, "Cutback in Military Spending."

29. Quoted in Stevenson, "Dynamics Set to Trim."

30. David Evans, "Cargo Jet Nearly Fell during Tests," *Chicago Tribune,* Apr. 22, 1993.

31. Bill Gertz, "McDonnell Defends C-17, Denies Costs Passed to Taxpayers," *Washington Times,* Apr. 22, 1993.

32. Ralph Vartabedian, "Air Force Denies Improper Aid to McDonnell," *Los Angeles Times,* Apr. 21, 1993.

33. Such a descent was likely for Grumman, formerly a centerpiece of the military-industrial complex, especially for the Navy (see Steven Pearlstein, "Trying to Give Peace a Chance," *Washington Post,* May 24, 1992; see also Richard W. Stevenson, "An Old Jet May Revive Grumman's Fortunes," *New York Times,* Jan. 11, 1991).

34. Eric Schmitt, "U.S. Weapons Makers Intensify Lobbying Efforts as Budgets Fall," *New York Times,* Aug. 6, 1991.

35. Stevenson, "Old Jet."

36. Richard W. Stevenson, "Finding Profits in Peace at Hughes," *New York Times,* Apr. 20, 1992.

37. Andrew Pollack, "In U.S. Technology, a Gap between Arms and VCR's," ibid., Mar. 4, 1991.

38. Quoted in ibid.

39. See Clyde Farnsworth, "White House Seeks to Revive Credits for Arms Exports," *New York Times,* Mar. 18, 1992; and R. Jeffrey Smith, "U.S. Funds Boost Weapons Sales for Defense Industry," *Philadelphia Inquirer,* May 9, 1992.

40. Eric Schmitt, "Arms Makers' Latest Tune: 'Over There, Over There,'" *New York Times,* Oct. 4, 1992.

41. Report on the Bath Iron Works, "All Things Considered," National Public Radio, July 5, 1993.

42. For accounts of this process see Adam Bryant, "G.E. Will Sell Aerospace Unit for $3 Billion," *New York Times,* Nov. 24, 1992; Anthony Gnoffo, Jr., "GE to Sell Off Two Divisions for $3 Billion," *Philadelphia Inquirer,* Nov. 24, 1992; Barnaby J. Feder, "2 Military Vendors in Joint Effort," *New York Times,* Dec. 3, 1992; and Sims, "For Weapons Makers, a Time to Deal."

43. Sims, "For Weapons Makers, a Time to Deal."

44. Ronald W. Stahlschmidt, quoted in ibid.

45. Quoted in Wayne, "Arms Makers Gird for Peace."

46. For a historical analysis of the MNC see Mira Wilkins, *The Emergence of Multinational Enterprise: American Business Abroad from the Colonial Era to 1914* (Cambridge, Mass.: Harvard University Press, 1970); and idem, *The Making of Multinational Enterprise: American Business Abroad from 1914 to 1970* (Cambridge, Mass.: Harvard University Press, 1974).

47. *Fortune,* July 1991, p. 245; *World Bank Atlas, 1991* (Washington, D.C., 1992); Central Intelligence Agency, *Handbook of Economic Statistics, 1991* (Washington, D.C., 1991).

48. Raymond Vernon, *Sovereignty at Bay: The Multinational Spread of U.S. Enterprises* (New York: Basic, 1971), p. 5.

49. For this view see ibid.; and Richard Barnet and Ronald E. Muller, *Global Reach: The Power of Multinational Corporations* (New York: Simon & Schuster, 1974).

50. See C. Fred Bergsten, Thomas Horst, and Theodore H. Moran, *American Multinationals and American Interests* (Washington, D.C.: Brookings Institution, 1978).

51. On the "American" character of American MNCs see Kenneth Simmonds, "Multinational? Well Not Quite," *Columbia Journal of World Business,* Fall 1966; see also Vernon, *Sovereignty at Bay,* p. 146.

52. For a detailed exposition and elaboration of this thesis see James A. Nathan and James K. Oliver, *United States Foreign Policy and World Order,* 3d ed. (Boston: Little, Brown, 1985).

53. For an analysis of the behavior of American MNCs during the monetary crises see *Multinational Corporations in the Dollar-Devaluation Crisis: Report on a Questionnaire,* prepared by the staff of the Subcommittee on Multinational

Corporations of the Senate Foreign Relations Committee, 94th Cong., 1st sess., 1975; see also Sidney M. Robbins and Robert B. Stobaugh, *Money in the Multinational Enterprise: A Study of Financial Management* (New York: Basic, 1973). For a description of U.S. policy see James A. Nathan and James K. Oliver, *United States Foreign Policy and World Order*, 4th ed. (Glenview, Ill.: Scott, Foresman, 1989), pp. 331–39.

54. Bergsten, Horst, and Moran, *American Multinationals and American Interests*, pp. 289–90.

55. For a discussion of the legal dimensions of the pipeline case see Leslie Gelb, "Pipeline: An Impasse with No End in Sight," *New York Times*, Aug. 31, 1982; on the economics of the deal see Steve Mufson, "Anatomy of Continuing Soviet Pipeline Controversy," *Wall Street Journal*, Aug. 31, 1982.

56. See U.S. Congress, Senate, *Covert Action*, vol. 7, 94th Cong., 1st sess., 1975.

57. Bergsten, Horst, and Moran, *American Multinationals and American Interests*, pp. 335–53.

58. A radio announcement of King Faisal's decision to impose an oil embargo on the United States was enough to propel Frank Jungers, chairman and chief executive officer of Aramco, to order a cutback larger than the percentage demanded by Faisal, just for good measure. "The important thing," according to Jungers, "was to give the immediate image of being *with* the government, not trying to fight it" (quoted in ibid., p. 352 n. 74, and drawn from Allan T. Demarree, "Aramco is a Lesson in the Management of Chaos," *Fortune*, Feb. 1974, pp. 58–65).

59. Nick Ludington, "None Can Put Humpty Dumpty Trade World Back Together," *Wilmington News Journal*, Feb. 4, 1993.

60. Quoted in ibid.

61. Janet Welsh Brown, a senior associate of the World Resources Institute, commenting on her role as the representative of a special interest group at the U.N. Conference on the Environment and Development at Rio de Janeiro in 1992, "Environmental Issues in World Politics after the Cold War" (Lecture delivered at the University of Delaware, Newark, Feb. 1, 1993).

62. Huntington, "Defense Policy of the Reagan Administration," p. 21.

63. For a useful discussion of this aspect of interdependence see Karl Kaiser, "Transnational Relations as a Threat to the Democratic Process," *International Organization* 25, no. 3 (1971): 706–20.

64. See, e.g., the opposed projections for the future of the international system in John Mueller, *Retreat from Doomsday: The Obsolescence of Major War* (New York: Basic, 1989), and John Mearsheimer, "Back to the Future: Instability in Europe after the Cold War," *International Security* 14, no. 4 (1990).

65. John Kenneth Galbraith, *How to Control the Military* (Garden City, N.Y.: Doubleday, 1969); see also the proposals by Secretary of Defense Cheney that the future contract with the defense industry extend only as far as support for re-

search, development, testing, evaluation, and production of prototypes, which would then be subjected to competitive selection, but that there be no commitment to procurement (Eric Schmitt, "Military Proposes to End Production of Most New Arms," *New York Times,* Jan. 24, 1992).

66. Thomas E. Ricks, "Navy Sets Course to Save Industrial Base amid Downsizing of Pentagon's Budget," *Wall Street Journal,* June 23, 1993.

CHAPTER 13 FOREIGN POLICY MAKING AND AMERICAN DEMOCRACY

1. Alexis de Tocqueville, *Democracy in America,* vol. 1 (New York: Vintage, 1945), p. 243.

2. For a review of American policy after World War II that emphasizes (though in balance with other factors) the role of domestic forces and constraints see James A. Nathan and James K. Oliver, *United States Foreign Policy and World Order,* 4th ed. (Glenview, Ill.: Scott, Foresman, 1989).

3. Alexander Hamilton, Federalist No. 24, in *The Federalist Papers,* ed. Clinton Rossiter (New York: Mentor, 1961), p. 153 (emphasis in the original).

4. James Madison, *Notes of Debates in the Federal Convention of 1787* (New York: Norton, 1969), p. 214 (emphasis added).

5. James Madison, Federalist No. 51, in Rossiter, *Federalist Papers,* p. 320.

6. Ibid., p. 322.

7. *Meyers v. United States,* 272 U.S. 293 (1926), Justice Brandeis dissenting.

8. Hamilton, Federalist No. 24, p. 153 (emphasis in the original).

9. Felix Gilbert, *The Beginnings of American Foreign Policy: To the Farewell Address* (New York: Harper Torchbooks, 1961), p. 122.

10. See, e.g., Robert J. Art and Seyom Brown, eds., *U.S. Foreign Policy: The Search for a New Role* (New York: Macmillan, 1993); or Sean M. Lynn-Jones and Steven E. Miller, eds., *America's Strategy in a Changing World* (Cambridge, Mass.: MIT Press, 1992). For an overview by a group many of whom found their way into the Clinton administration see Carnegie Endowment National Commission on America and the New World, *Changing Our Ways: America and the New World* (Washington, D.C.: Carnegie Endowment for International Peace, 1992).

11. The U.S. intervention in Somalia at the end of 1992 was another alternative. Bush sent thirty thousand marines in Operation Provide Hope under a warrant from the U.N. Security Council during the break between the election in which Bush was defeated and President Clinton's inauguration. As U.S. troops withdrew, a U.N. force began to assemble to take their place. President Bush, true to his record, neither consulted with Congress nor supplied the prior notification the War Powers Act would indicate would be required in circumstances when U.S. forces might find armed resistance. As a matter of fact, the whole of Somalia was armed, albeit with light arms, and the United States did find some pockets of

minor resistance. Two months after the first Marines waded onto Somalia beaches lit by klieg lights to facilitate television filming, the Senate passed a resolution authorizing the action. As the Somalia intervention wound down, House leaders claimed that they felt "no pressure" to take up the measure (see Walter Pincus, "Senate Authorized Troops in Somalia," *Washington Post,* Feb. 10, 1993).

12. Richard E. Neustadt, *Presidential Power* (New York: Wiley, 1960), p. 33.

13. Michael J. Crozier, Samuel P. Huntington, and Joji Watanuki, *The Crisis of Democracy: Report on the Governability of Democracies to the Trilateral Commission* (New York: New York University Press, 1975), p. 93.

14. *Washington Post,* Nov. 30, 1980.

15. Cf. "Focus on the Emerging Democracies: A Periodic Update," *U.S. Department of State Dispatch* 3, no. 43 (1992): 789–91; and *Focus on German Support for the Transition to Democracy and Market Economy in the Former Soviet Union,* Position paper of the German Embassy, Washington, D.C. (New York: German Information Center, June 1992), pp. 1–3.

16. See "German Humanitarian Aid for the Former Yugoslavia" and "Humanitarian Aid: Selected Countries in Comparison," in *The Week in Germany,* Jan. 29, 1993, p. 1.

17. For an overview of the magnitude of these international demands see Peter H. Sand, *Lessons Learned in Global Environmental Governance* (Washington, D.C.: World Resource Institute, 1990).

18. Jessica Tuchman Matthews, "Redefining Security," *Foreign Affairs* 68, no. 2 (1989): 162–77; Gareth Porter and Janet Welsh Brown, *Global Environmental Politics* (Boulder: Westview, 1991).

19. Thomas R. Dye, "What to Do about the Establishment: Prescription for Elites," in *The Irony of Democracy: An Uncommon Introduction to American Politics,* by Thomas R. Dye and L. Harmon Zeigler, 2d ed. (Belmont, Calif.: Duxbury, 1972), p. 365.

20. Charles O. Lerche, Jr., *Foreign Policy of the American People,* 3d ed. (Englewood Cliffs, N.J.: Prentice-Hall, 1967), p. 120.

21. George F. Kennan, *The Realities of American Foreign Policy* (Princeton: Princeton University Press, 1954), p. 44.

22. Samuel P. Huntington, in Crozier, Huntington, and Watanuki, *Crisis of Democracy,* p. 21.

23. See Lester Thurow's analysis of the economic implications of this situation in *The Zero-Sum Society* (New York: Basic, 1980).

24. Huntington, in Crozier, Huntington, and Watanuki, *Crisis of Democracy.*

25. H. J. Morganthau, "The American Tradition in Foreign Policy," in *Foreign Policy in World Politics,* ed. Ray C. Macridis, 3d ed. (Englewood Cliffs, N.J.: Prentice-Hall, 1967), p. 261.

26. On Soviet ethnic and racial problems see Helene Carrere d'Encausse, *Decline of an Empire: The Soviet Socialist Republics in Revolt* (New York: Newsweek Books, 1980); on the Soviet system see Seweryn Bialer, *Stalin's Successors:*

Leadership, Stability, and Change in the Soviet Union (New York: Cambridge University Press, 1980).

27. U.S. Congress, Joint Economic Committee, *Soviet Economy in a New Perspective: A Compendium of Papers,* 94th Cong., 2d sess., 1976.

28. C. Wright Mills, ed., *Max Weber: Essays in Sociology* (Oxford: Oxford University Press, 1964).

29. Henry A. Kissinger, *American Foreign Policy,* enl. ed. (New York: Norton, 1974), p. 18.

30. For one of the best discussions of the similarities between domestic and international politics see Edward L. Morse, *The Transformation and Modernization of International Politics* (New York: Free Press / Macmillan, 1977). For a denial of this line of analysis see Kenneth Waltz, *Theory of International Politics* (Reading, Mass.: Addison-Wesley, 1979).

31. Daniel Yankelovich, "Farewell to 'President Knows Best,'" *Foreign Affairs* 57, no. 3 (1979): 687–88.

32. Ibid., p. 688.

33. Ibid., p. 689; U.S. Congress, Senate, Committee on Foreign Relations, *Foreign Policy Choices for the Seventies and Eighties: Hearings,* 94th Cong., 1st sess., 1975, and 2d sess., 1976; and Daniel Yankelovich and Sidney Harman, *Starting with the People* (Boston: Houghton Mifflin, 1988).

INDEX

A-12 aircraft, 223–24
ABM. *See* Antiballistic Missile Treaty
Accommodationists, 165–66
ACDA. *See* Arms Control and Disarmament Agency
Acheson, Dean, 16, 30, 38, 73
Adams, Gordon, 224
Adams, Sherman, 30
Adelman, Kenneth, 55
Afghanistan, Soviet invasion of, 46, 101, 156
AFL-CIO. *See* American Federation of Labor and Congress of Industrial Organizations
Africa, U.S. aid to, 205
Agency for International Development (AID), 12
Agriculture Department, 109–10
AHEPA. *See* American Hellenic Progressive Association
AID. *See* Agency for International Development
AIPAC. *See* American Israel Public Affairs Committee
AIPO. *See* American Institute of Public Opinion
Albert, Carl, 84
Allen, Richard, 50–51, 53, 210–11
Allende, Hortensa, 191
Almond, Gabriel, 149
Ambassadorships, 104–5
American Bar Association, 121–22
American Federation of Labor and Congress of Industrial Organizations (AFL-CIO), 207–8
American Foreign Service Association, 15

American Hellenic Progressive Association (AHEPA), 204
American Institute of Public Opinion, 153
American Israel Public Affairs Committee (AIPAC), 200–204
American Petroleum Institute, 207
American Telephone and Telegraph (AT&T), 212
Antiballistic Missile (ABM) Treaty, 100–101, 102
Arab-Americans, 201–2
Armitage, Richard, 203
Arms Control and Disarmament Agency (ACDA), 12, 55
Arms Control Association, 208
Arms Export Control Act of 1976, 112, 113
Arms industry, 207. *See also* Defense contractors; Military-industrial complex
Arnett, Peter, 184
Art, Robert, 116
Aspin, Les, 116, 224
AT&T. *See* American Telephone and Telegraph
Avaligno v. Sumitomo Shoji America, 231

Baker, Howard, 50, 62
Baker, James, 27, 51, 59, 62, 194; and Bush, 63–64; on presidential authority, 144; as secretary of state, 63–64, 66, 67, 110, 112, 203
Ball, George, 213
Base Closure and Realignment Act of 1988, 115

)

Library of Congress Cataloging-in-Publication Data

Nathan, James A.
Foreign policy making and the American political system /
James A. Nathan and James K. Oliver.—3rd ed.
p.   cm.
Includes bibliographical references and index.
ISBN 0-8018-4771-0 (hc : acid-free paper).—ISBN 0-8018-4772-9 (pbk. : acid-free paper)
1. United States—Foreign relations—1945–1989.
2. United States—Foreign relations—1989–
I. Oliver, James K.   II. Title.
JX1417.N295   1994
353.0089—dc20   94-7530